A Hertfordshire Family

1555 - 1923

with links in Bedfordshire, Suffolk, and Essex.

by

Evelyn Wright

For Wendy, who watched the book grow!

With love and best wishes - Evelyn.

Heath Publications, Bedfordshire

Cover photograph by Angela Williams - The tythe barn at
Tewin Bury

Published by Heath Publications, Bedfordshire

Printed by Drakeloe Press, 7 James Way, Bletchley
Milton Keynes

ISBN 0 9529254 1 9

Sources and Acknowledgements

The main sources of information have been the Victoria County Histories, the Heralds' Visitations (various editions) and the historical works of Sir Henry Chauncy, Robert Clutterbuck and John Edwin Cussons. Other books consulted include: G M Trevelyan - English Social History; The Paston Letters ed. John Warrington; Tudor Food and Pastimes - F G Emmison; Wingfield: Its Church Castle and College - S W Aldwell; History of Bedfordshire - Joyce Godber; Bedfordshire - Simon Houfe; The History of Hitchin - Reginald Hine; The Wymondleys - Noel Farris; Copinger's Manors of Suffolk; Austin's History of Luton; A Pilgrimage in Hertfordshire - H M Alderman; The Muster Books of North and East Hertfordshire ed. Ann J King; The Accounts of Thomas Green ed. Gillian Sheldrick; Clode's Early History of the Guild of Merchant Taylors.

I acknowledge with thanks the help and co-operation of the Hertfordshire Record Office and Local Studies Library, and also the Bedfordshire Record Office, and I am grateful for their permission to reproduce various documents and illustrations. I have received help from the Suffolk and Essex Record Offices, and again I am grateful for permission to use illustrations from their collections. I have also received valuable information from the Kent, Surrey, and Sussex Record Offices and from the Guildhall Library in London.

Chapters 17 and 18 are adapted, with permission, from articles written for the Hertfordshire Countryside in 1988 and 1992.

I am grateful to all who have provided photographs or allowed me to photograph their houses. Special thanks to the Vaughan Williams family for the cover photograph of the tythe barn at Tewin Bury.

The various family arms are reproduced from the Victoria County Histories, Hertfordshire and Bedfordshire, Volumes II, III and IV by permission of the General Editor. The Isaac Oliver miniature of the Browne Brothers is reproduced by permission of Mr J Culverhouse, House Manager at Burghley House, Stamford. The Hans Holbein sketch of the More family is reproduced by permission of the Oeffentliche Kunstsammlung Basel, Kupferstichkabinett. The two photocopies from Suffolk Heraldic Brasses are reproduced by kind permission of Mr T M Felgate of Felixstowe.

I should like to express my thanks to the Harmer Family Association and to acknowledge the help received from the late Brian Harmer, who painstakingly drew up many family trees linking 20th century Harmers with their early Hertfordshire roots. Thanks also to Gill Price for her interest and encouragement.

Very special thanks to my fellow researchers (and distant cousins) Cynthia and Sue Cox of Southampton. Over the past five years we have exchanged more than 80 letters, and together we have solved many problems which at first seemed insoluble. I am particularly grateful to Sue for using her amazing skill and patience in deciphering and transcribing the almost illegible 16th and 17th century wills and documents.

Finally I must record my gratitude to my husband John, without whose technical expertise and artistic skill this project would not have been possible. The setting out of the pedigrees in Appendix A has been a particularly complicated and time-consuming task. Thanks also to all my family for their patience and support.

Evelyn Wright, Aspley Heath
September 1997

Contents

Illustrations

There are also line drawings or etchings of: St Leonard's Church Bengeo p.35; the Soame brass p.45; George Chapman p.53; Bletsoe Castle p.72; Gifford's Hall p.80; Little Hadham Hall p.161; Kentwell Hall p.165; Ickworth Hall p.181; Hyde Hall p.183; Hunt/Day Effigy p.184; Knebworth House p.188; Turvey Abbey p.191; Ingatestone Hall p.199; Boxted Hall p.203; The More Family by Holbein p.206.

Illustrations on pages 35, 53, 61, 161, 183 and 188 are reproduced by permission of the Hertfordshire Record Office; on pages 72 and 191 by permission of the Bedfordshire Record Office; on pages 80, 165, 181 and 203 by permission of the Suffolk Record Office, and on page 199 by permission of the Essex Record Office.

The Harmer Central Tree

THOMAS HARMER

b. c1535 m. 1555 d. 1608

ELIZABETH FAIRCLOUGH

THOMAS HARMER

b. 1565 m. 1592 d. 1624

JANE KYMPTON

GEORGE HARMER

b. 1593 m. 1623 d. 1655

REBECKA BULL

JOHN HARMER

b. 1628 m② 1698 d. 1711

ANN WARREN

JOHN HARMER

b. 1701 m. 1733 d. 1787

MARY RALPHS

JOHN HARMER

b. 1752 m. 1776 d. 1817

SARAH FISHER

GEORGE HARMER

b. 1783 m. 1806 d. c1846

ELIZABETH GOLDSMITH

WILLIAM HARMER

b. 1813 m. 1839 d. 1870

MARY HARMER

WILLIAM HARMER

b. 1849 m. 1883 d. 1907

MARY HARE

THOMAS HARMER

b. 1891 m. 1923 d. 1973

MERCY GALBRAITH

Dedicated to the memory of
my father, Thomas Harmer,
and my cousin John Harmer of Redbourn,
whose lives were an inspiration
to all who knew them.

Introduction

Time present and time past
Are both perhaps present in time future
And time future contained in time past.

T.S. Eliot 'Burnt Norton'

From Thomas Harmer who married Elizabeth Fairclough in 1555, to Thomas Harmer who married Mercy Galbraith in 1923, there are ten generations. Tracing a line back through these generations there are a possible five hundred and twelve ancestors, but only ten (twenty counting the wives) will bear the family name. Therefore to say that this is a history of the Harmer family would be somewhat misleading.

Though it does trace the history of the Harmers from the 16th Century to the present day (focusing mainly on the period 1555 - 1711) it also includes many other names. The Kymptons, the Knightons and the Nedhams, the Piggots of Tewin and the Hydes of Throcking, the Bull family of Hertford, the Ralphs, the Warrens and the Faircloughs - all are direct ancestors.

There are also many other families who are cousins and kinsmen. Most are from Hertfordshire, but there are several from across the border in Bedfordshire. These include the Fyshe family of Southill, the Harveys of Thurleigh, the St. Johns of Bletsoe and the Bechers of Howbury Hall in Renhold. There are also links with a group of families on the Suffolk and Essex borders.

Perhaps the most well-known members of the family are George Chapman, the Hitchin poet whose translation of Homer inspired Keats's famous poem, and Lady Kathleen Ferrers, the highway-woman whose highly romanticised exploits have made her even more famous than the illustrious poet.

The history presented here is on two levels. Details of dates, relationships and land transactions have been researched and verified from Parish Registers, Inquisitions Post Mortem, Marriage Settlements, Feet of Fines and many other archives. Information has also been gathered from various published sources, including the works of those three distinguished Hertfordshire historians: Chauncy, Clutterbuck and Cussons, though they do not always agree with each other!

But having established the facts (as far as possible) it is necessary to draw on the social history of the period in order to bring the characters to life. By finding out how people lived, felt and thought, and by looking at the events which influenced their lives, we can build up a picture of our ancestors. We can imagine what they looked like and how they behaved.

In the introduction to his 'English Social History', Trevelyan talks of the importance of getting to know our ancestors:

> There is nothing that more divides civilised from
> semi-savage man than to be conscious of our forefathers
> as they really were, and bit by bit to reconstruct the
> mosaic of the long-forgotten past ...

It is hoped that many readers will find that this really is a history of their own family. There must be few natives of Hertfordshire who are not connected in some way with one or more of the characters described - whether it be the gentle poet, the learned lawyer or the elegant gentleman at the court of Queen Elizabeth.

But whether or not this may be the case, we all have ancestors who lived through this period of history. To find out how they lived and to re-kindle an interest in their personalities, is to ensure that they will live on, not just in our genes, but in our imaginations. They are our past, and we are their future. To them we owe our very existence and it is fitting that we should acknowledge them and honour their memory.

Chapter 1

John of Baldock

Seated at a small table in the 'parlour next the hall' John Harmer was writing his will:

> The 23rd day of October, Anno Domini 1613, I John Harmer of Baldock in the county of Hertford, being of sound and perfect remembrance, praise be given to Almighty God, do make this my last will and testament in manner and form following ...

This is the oldest of the Harmer wills to survive and together with the inventory which accompanies it, gives a fascinating glimpse into the life of a country gentleman in the early seventeenth century. Exactly where John's house was situated we do not know, but it is possible that one of the 16th century houses still standing in Baldock today could be the one where John Harmer lived and died nearly 400 years ago.

It was obviously a house of some importance, for we read of the gatehouse, the hall and the 'parlour next the hall', as well as the kitchen, brewhouse and cellars. All the rooms had 'lofts' above, and if, as seems likely, it was an early Elizabethan hall house, the upper storey would have been added quite recently, probably by John himself. Until it became the custom to build chimneys on an outside wall the fire would be in the centre of the hall, and the smoke would find its way out through a hole in the roof. With the coming of chimneys it was possible to have an upper floor and lots of extra rooms, but they were not necessarily used as bedrooms. It took time to get used to the idea of moving the beds upstairs, and the upper rooms were lofts or store rooms rather than bedchambers. John still had his bed in the parlour downstairs. We know that there were 13 acres of land, gardens and orchards surrounding the house, so it was probably one of the manor houses which was originally part of his father's estate in Weston.

We can try to picture John as he sat in the parlour, quill pen in hand and a pewter ink-stand on the table in front of him. His doublet and hose would have been of woollen cloth, probably spun and woven in the manor house, and round his neck would be the typical Elizabethan ruff, which was worn by both the men and women of this period. He would have had a full beard, not yet grey, for he was a comparatively young man, only 46 years old.

At last the will was finished, and thankfully John signed his name and added his seal. His brother-in-law Thomas Pomford and his cousin John Cawdell signed their names as witnesses, and James Slone made his mark. Did Thomas Pomford know that John had left him his 'best apparel' in his will, and did he find himself looking with interest at the fine woollen cloth of the doublet, with its silver buttons and lace trimmings?

John died just a month later, leaving his wife Agnes (or Annis) and three daughters - Ann aged 20, Joan 14, and Elizabeth, only 10 years old. There had been a son, Thomas, but sadly he must have died in early childhood, for he is not mentioned in his father's will, when he would have been 16 years old. Instead, John names his nephews, Thomas and Joseph, the sons of his older brother Thomas, to be his heirs if it should happen that none of his daughters managed to produce 'an heir of her body lawfully begotten'.

John was the second son of Thomas Harmer and Elizabeth Fairclough and was born and brought up in the manor house known as Dane End in the parish of Weston. Although he was not the eldest son he seems to have been remarkably well provided for. His will refers to lands, houses and tenements in Weston, Willian, Clothall and Munden Magna, as well as the house and land in Baldock.

Ann Pomford (or Pomfret), whom he married in 1592, no doubt brought with her a good dowry - it would have been one of the conditions of the marriage, which at this time had little to do with love, and everything to do with land and property. Thomas Pomfret who is listed as one of the freeholders of the parish of Baldock in 1561 was almost certainly Agnes's father. Another Thomas Pomfret, Rector of Luton from 1660 to 1705, and his son John, Rector of Maulden and a well-known local poet, probably belonged to the same family.

Although he was a comparatively wealthy man John's personal possessions were few by today's standards. Silver was the main symbol of wealth, and the most frequently mentioned items in wills of this period were silver spoons. No silver was mentioned in John's will, but the inventory lists four silver spoons, which were valued at twenty four shillings (six shillings each). The Reverend William Harrison, writing about 1570, records a change in his own lifetime from wooden platters (treens) to pewter, and from wooden spoons to silver or tin. The age of forks was yet to come.

This was a time of many changes. John's inventory includes at least six beds with bolsters, pillows, mattresses, and feather beds. There were also valences, curtains, coverlets and blankets. But two generations earlier most people, even the nobility and gentry, had no such luxuries. Harrison writes:

> If it were so that our fathers, or the good man of the house, had a mattress or a flockbed and thereto a sack of chaff to rest his head upon he thought himself to be as well lodged as the lord of the town, that peradventure lay seldom in a bed of down or whole feathers. Pillows were thought meet only for women in childbed. As for servants, if they had any sheet above them it was well, for seldom had they any under their bodies to keep them from the pricking straws that ran oft through the canvas of the pallet and razed their hardened hides.

In the house at Baldock it seems likely that even the servants had sheets both above and below their bodies, for John seems to have been particularly well equipped in this department. The inventory reads:

> In the loft over the hall. Item - thirty paire of sheetes.

They were valued at £10, a very considerable sum of money at this time, and more than a labourer would earn in a year. There were also 'nine pairs of pillowbeares, fower cloathes and other childbeed lynen.' No doubt Agnes, like most ladies of the manor, looked after the sick and needy in the parish. When any poor woman of Baldock went into labour, Agnes would be there with a supply of bed-linen, and other small luxuries for the mother and baby. The next item reads:

> Item - fyve dossen of table napkins, xi table cloathes and
> three drinking cloathes.

All this sounds like rather a lot of table and bed linen, even for a large household, but perhaps Agnes liked collecting fine linen and looked upon it as an investment. Certainly it would be passed down through many generations.

John's will was typical of its time. It was the custom to leave one's clothes to friends and relatives - also feather beds and mattresses, valences, blankets and pillows. Since very few items were washable, and dry-cleaning was a thing of the future, it is questionable just how welcome some of these bequests might be. It is to Thomas Pomford, whom he describes as 'my welbe loved frende and brothere in lawe' that John leaves his best cloak and all his best apparel.

To his eldest daughter Ann he leaves some of the lands in Munden Magna and also:

> ... the bede and bedsteede standing in the lowe plor(parlour) next the hall with all the furniture thereto belonginge and my best valence ... and curtains and the table and one trunck standinge in my beste lofte and my grateste brasse pott.

Ten-year-old Elizabeth, with her mother, has been named as joint executrix of her father's will, and is to inherit half of his property. But Agnes herself died four years later, and Elizabeth, at the age of fourteen, became the sole owner of the house and land at Baldock and all the other lands, goods and chattels which had not been specifically bequeathed to her sisters.

John seems to have been slightly worried about his middle daughter Joan, fearing perhaps a runaway marriage or an escape to the bright lights of London. This was the great age of the playhouse and the theatre, with Ben Jonson and William Shakespeare delighting their audiences night after night with thrilling dramas and heart-rending tragedies. Life in the quiet town of Baldock must have seemed, by contrast, extremely dull and boring. John states in his will that if, before the age of 18, Joan goes away from home without her mother's consent, then her Uncle Thomas shall collect the income from her property and pay her an allowance as he thinks fit.

But it seems that all was well and by the time Agnes was writing her will in 1617, both Joan and Ann were married into well-known local families. Joan had obviously behaved herself, because she had the special privilege of inheriting her mother's feather bed. Agnes writes:

> I give to my daughter Joan, the wife of James Maple, the feather bede and boulster where on I now lye, and one coverlet and the bede above, and two joined stooles and a little table standing in the lofte and three pewter dishes and one ketle called the soope ketle.

James Maple was almost certainly a kinsman or ancestor of the Maples who became well-known as upholsterers and furniture makers, setting up business in Tottenham Court Road in the 19th century. From the same family came Sir John Blundell Maple, Member of Parliament for Dulwich from 1887, and also renowned as a cricketer, who helped to provide a cricket and recreation ground for St Albans in 1892.

Agnes's will illustrates a trend which appears frequently in later wills - that of borrowing and lending money within the family. A gentleman's income would come almost entirely from his rents, and if payment was delayed, there would be a serious cash flow problem. Sometimes a debt outstanding from one member of the family was bequeathed to another, in payment of money owed to this other person. Thus the burden of recovering and repaying a debt was passed on. The will continues:

> Whereas Richard Welles of Baldock oweth me by bounde (bond) twentie poundes, my will is that tenn poundes thereof be paid to my brothere Thomas Pomford, for the satisfaccon of a debte which he claymeth was the goodes of my mother Pomfords late deceased if the same be due ... and the same debt of XXs I give unto James Maple my son in law for and towards the payment of a certain debt I now owe him ...

Both John and Agnes follow the usual custom of leaving money to the poor. John leaves 'fortie shillings of good englishe money' to be given to 40 poor people on the day of his funeral, and Agnes, four years later, leaves 20 shillings. No doubt the poor people of the parish always looked forward to funerals!

And so we leave John and Agnes and their family. Whether the nephews Thomas and Joseph inherited some of John's wealth, or whether the daughters managed to produce suitable heirs we do not know, for we follow John's descent no further. The direct line comes down through his brother Thomas, the eldest son of Thomas Harmer and Elizabeth Fairclough.

But before we join Thomas and Elizabeth in 1555 we go back even further to search out the early history of the two families. We also take a brief look at the history of Weston which had been the home of the Faircloughs, and probably the Harmers, for many generations past, and was to be the home of their descendants for many generations to come.

Chapter 2.

The Early Harmers and The Faircloughs of Weston.

Before the year 1538 when Parish Registers began, it is difficult to get a detailed history of our ancestors. The Heralds' Visitations give valuable information about those families who were entitled to bear arms, but often they give no dates, and female offspring tend to be ignored. Wills also provide a certain amount of genealogical information, but few of the early ones have survived.

There are other archives, however, which help us to build up the picture. These include Feet of Fines (records of the buying and selling of land), Inquisitions Post Mortem (explained in a later chapter), marriage settlements, and perhaps most important of all, manorial records. It is from this latter source that we discover a certain John Harmer who was living in Bedfordshire around 1280, and who could well be one of our very early ancestors.

John Harmer held the manor of Wroxhill in Marston Moreteyne a few miles to the south of Bedford. He acquired it from Richard de Argentein for one quarter of a knight's fee in the year 1286, together with 'the advowson of the church of Wroxhill'. This was probably a chapel of ease to Marston parish church. There remains in Marston Moreteyne a farm known as Roxhill Manor, but all trace of the chapel (dedicated to St Lawrence the Martyr) has long since disappeared.

So far there is nothing to link John Harmer of Marston Moreteyne with the 16th century Harmers of Weston - but the story does not end here. This same John Harmer also owned the manor of Thurleigh, sometimes known as Whitwick Manor, just to the north of Bedford. About 1278 his daughter Joan married a certain John Harvey from the adjoining parish of Riseley. When John Harmer died, around 1297, his daughter Joan inherited Thurleigh, while his son John inherited Wroxhill. Thus it was Joan Harmer and her husband John Harvey who founded the Harvey family of Thurleigh.

In the 15th century, when George Harvey was leaving all the Thurleigh estate to his illegitimate son Gerard, his uncle Thomas was fortunate enough to marry a Suffolk heiress, Jane Drury of Ickworth near Bury St Edmunds, and they went on to found the Harvey family of Ickworth Hall. The Bedfordshire and Suffolk branches of the Harvey family kept in close touch, and reinforced the family link with frequent marriages between cousins.

The next discovery is the most amazing of all, for it emerges that the Suffolk Harveys were also related to the Hertfordshire Harmers through completely different lines of descent. Here we have the first indication of the network of relationships which becomes more and more intriguing as time goes on. The Harveys of Ickworth were marrying into other local county families, including the Stutevilles, the Barnardistons, the Cloptons of Kentwell Hall, and the Knightons and Underhills of Little Bradley Manor (which was sometimes known, significantly perhaps, as Harveys). All these were linked in various ways with our family, the Knightons and Underhills being direct ancestors.

In the 16th and 17th centuries the Harveys of Thurleigh obviously knew the Harmers and Faircloughs of Weston. In 1602 Mary Harvey of Thurleigh married Thomas Fairclough of Weston, and a few years later one of the Harveys was mentioned in Rebecka Harmer's will. It seems certain, therefore, that the 13th century Harmers of Bedfordshire were either ancestors or kinsmen of the Harmers of Weston.

By the time our story begins in the 16th century, the Harmer family of Marston and Thurleigh seems to have died out, (though their Harvey descendants remained). There were however, several Harmers in the parishes nearer the Hertfordshire borders, including a rather interesting family at Hatley Park near Gamlingay. Here Edmund Harmer, who died in 1544, left a fascinating will, telling us all about his family, and about the new house which his sons must build for their mother, Joan.

It must have at least four bedrooms and must be designed in accordance with her wishes. She was already inheriting two other houses under the will, one at the east end of Gamlingay and another elsewhere in the village. Edmund leaves all the rest of the property to his son John.

This included yet another house, at the south end of Gamlingay, and also orchards, woods and fields, with instructions as to how the fields should be cropped and cultivated. John was also to inherit 4 horses, 2 oxen, some cows, 'all manner of carts and the dung cart' and 21 quarters of malt. To his son William, Edmund leaves property in Tetworth and a cow, or ten shillings to buy a cow. He also leaves a quarter of malt to 'Margery my maiden'.

Edmund's wife Joan also leaves a will, but does not mention the new house. She is much more concerned with her personal belongings which she bequeaths to her daughters Elizabeth and Ursula. Ursula the younger daughter gets most of her treasures, including a feather bed, a bolster, 3 pairs of sheets, a coverlet, some blankets, 2 platters, 2 candlesticks, 2 brass pots and a pan. Poor Elizabeth simply gets either her best gown or her best coverlet - but not both! How these various Harmer families on the Bedfordshire borders were related to the Hertfordshire Harmers we do not know, but it seems likely that there was a connection.

One of the earliest Harmers recorded in Hertfordshire is William, whose name appears in the list of Chantry Certificates for Hertfordshire in 1547. The Chantry Records were compiled as a result of an enquiry set up by Edward VI to assess the income from charities, colleges and guilds, which had now been diverted to the Crown. William Harmer, recently deceased, bequeathed the rent of 4 acres of land in Graveley 'to the fynding of ij lamps by the year' in the church at Little Wymondley. This William was probably the grandfather of a certain John Harmer whose birth is recorded in the very early Parish Registers.

In 1538 Thomas Cromwell decreed that every parish should keep a record of all baptisms, marriages and burials, but the extent to which this was carried out depended very much on the ability and goodwill of the parish priest. For the first 25 years the records were written on paper, and many were destroyed by vermin and insects. So from about 1565 it was required that all records should be written on parchment, and the earlier records, where possible, should be copied up.

The Weston records must be among the earliest, for they begin in 1539 and the first Harmer entry appears in the baptisms of 1541. The baby's name was John and his father was also recorded as John. The mother's name at this time was seldom mentioned. It seems likely that our ancestor Thomas Harmer was also a son of this John, born before parish registers began. His marriage in 1555 indicates a birth date of around 1535 or earlier.

The baby John who was baptised in April 1541 died a few weeks later and was buried on 15th May, but the parents went on to have at least two more children. A baby, Joan, was baptised in 1546, but probably, like her brother, died in infancy. A second Joan, who was baptised two years later, seems to have survived and was married in Weston church in 1579.

Weston at this time consisted of four or possibly five separate manors, and included all of the present parish of Weston together with certain lands which are now in Baldock, Graveley and Clothall.

From the year 1307 the principal manor, known simply as Weston, was held by the Crown, and in 1312 it was granted by Edward II to the Mowbray family, upon whom he also conferred the title of Earls of Norfolk and Marshalls of England. In 1476 it was held by John Duke of Norfolk, who died leaving his four-year-old daughter Anne as his sole heir. Soon afterwards Anne was married to Richard of York, the younger of the little Princes in the Tower, but she died four years later (still only eight years old) and the young prince became Lord of the Manor of Weston. When he died in 1483 at the hands of an unknown murderer (some say it was a member of the Tyrrell family), the manor reverted to King Richard III.

Back in 1437 we find the first reference to the Faircloughs of Weston, when custody of the park, 'with the custody of all the coneys in it' was granted to the King's esquire, Laurence Fairclough. Another Laurence Fairclough, his grandson, was custodian of the park in 1476, when he was described as 'marshall of the King's hall'. The King would have been Edward IV, the father of the Princes in the Tower.

In the 16th century Weston was granted by Henry VIII to Anne Boleyn, and then to Catherine Parr, and in 1572 it was bought by George Burgoyne of Quickswood manor in Clothall, from whom it came to Sir John Puckering and then to Sir John Hale.

One of the subsidiary manors of Weston was Lannock, to the west of the village. It was given to the Knights Templars around 1140 and remained in their possession until the suppression of the Order in 1309 when it was granted to the Knights Hospitallers. In 1353 there was a bitter dispute between the Prior of the Hospitallers and his neighbour Mary, widow of the Earl of Norfolk. One night Mary, with others, came and 'broke his close and house, and drove away 40 horses, 30 oxen, 12 bullocks, 10 cows and 800 sheep of his worth £300'.

After the dissolution of the monasteries - about 1540 - the manor of Lannock came into the King's hands. He sold it to George Burgoyne, who by this time had acquired the main manor of Weston, and with this it went to the Puckerings and later to the Hale and Pryor families.

The manor of Weston Argentein was held from about 1205 by Richard de Argentein who was already Lord of the Manor of Great and Little Wymondley. He was also Sheriff of Hertfordshire in 1223. The manor descended with that of Wymondley until the 16th century, when it was granted to John Puckering who had recently acquired the manor of Weston.

The manor of Newberry, partly in Weston and partly in Graveley, was granted in the 12th century to Hubert de St. Clare of Walkern. It came down through many generations and in the 16th century was sold to Thomas Bedell, soon after which the manor was divided. The part in Graveley went to William Clarke of Benington, and the part in Weston, by inheritance or purchase, came to the Harmer family.

In 1620 Thomas Harmer sold Newberry Manor to Thomas Puckering and it was absorbed into the manor of Weston. Thomas Harmer seems to have kept back the old manor house known as Dane End and some of the land, including Newberry Wood, which was passed down though several generations and was still in the family as late as 1787 when it is mentioned in John Harmer's will. Later the wood was known as Harmer's Wood, the name by which it is still known today.

Finally there was the 'reputed' manor of Howells, which is mentioned in 1543 as being one of the manors of Weston. But as there is no record of its early history it is uncertain whether it was ever a manor in its own right or whether, like Fairclough Hall, it was part of the main manor of Weston. Howells was the home of the Kympton family, and it was from here in 1592 that Jane Kympton married Thomas Harmer of Dane End, which at this time was still part of Newberry Manor.

Fairclough Hall was the home of the Fairclough family from the reign of King Henry VI and probably earlier. The pedigree in the Heralds' Visitations shows that Sir Laurence Fairclough, with his wife Elizabeth, was there in 1468 and that his father Sir Ralph Fairclough was living there before him. This Laurence would have been the 'marshall of the King's hall' mentioned in 1476, and the Laurence who was the King's esquire in 1437 would have been his grandfather. This takes us back to the age of Joan of Arc, and the final years of the Hundred Years War.

Howells, a late medieval manor house, was the home of the Kympton ancestors in the 16th and 17th century. This view from beyond the moat shows the old blending with the new, bearing witness to the many changes during its long history.

Fairclough Hall, home of the Fairclough family from the 15th century. The present house dates from the 17th century, built on or near the site of an earlier house

In the 16th and 17th centuries, as we have seen, there were links between the Harmers and Faircloughs of Weston and the Harveys of Thurleigh, who were descended from the Harmers of Marston Moreteyne and Thurleigh back in the 13th century. In 1593 a William Fairclough was vicar of Thurleigh, having no doubt been presented to the living by one of the Harveys who held the advowson of the church. In 1602 Mary Harvey of Thurleigh married Thomas Fairclough of Weston, and their son Litton Fairclough married Mary's niece (also Mary Harvey). Somehow, during all these generations, the Faircloughs, Harmers and Harveys had kept in touch, renewing their family links from time to time, and well aware that they were part of an even wider network, which included the Knightons, Stutevilles, Barnardistons and many other families in Bedfordshire, Essex and Suffolk.

In 1678 there is an interesting item in the will of Elizabeth Harvey of Thurleigh showing that the links are as strong as ever. She leaves a bequest to 'my sister Fairclough and her children John, Litton, Elizabeth and Mary, £6 each for life'. The 'sister Fairclough' is Elizabeth's sister Mary, who married Litton Fairclough in 1637.

The name Litton was given to several of the Fairclough sons in the 16th and 17th century and would probably have been quite acceptable, but one poor little Fairclough boy in 1582 was baptised 'Affabelle'. The name occurs elsewhere in Hertfordshire about this time - (Affabel Battel and Aphabel Partridge) - and is thought to have been connected with the 'cult of St. Affabel', based at St. Albans. But one Hertfordshire historian comments that 'modern thinking is that St. Affabel never existed.'

The bequest to Mary Fairclough and her children suggests that Elizabeth is concerned about her sister, and we know from other sources that the family is now in serious financial trouble. In the archives there is a document relating to a debt of £1200 owed by John Fairclough to Rowland Hale. This was an enormous sum of money in 1660 and there was no way it could be repaid. A few years later, John was obliged to forfeit the estate which had been the home of his family for at least eight generations. It was sold to William Hale, who already had the manor of Weston, and was acquiring vast estates throughout Hertfordshire and Bedfordshire.

Members of the Fairclough family stayed on as tenants for several more generations. They continued to marry into wealthy families (they were already connected with the Barres, the Spencers and the Lyttons) and some no doubt inherited estates elsewhere. There were several marriages into the Underwood family (connected also with the Harmers many years later), and one daughter married into the Clarke family of Benington. Frances Fairclough married a gentleman from Riseley who was almost certainly connected with the Harveys of Thurleigh, and another daughter married Edward Kent of Astonbury.

But the Fairclough name in Weston was gradually dying out, and by the 19th century even the name of Fairclough Hall had gone - replaced by 'Halls Green Farm'. Fortunately the old name has now been revived, keeping alive the memory of its earliest inhabitants. Only one Fairclough memorial remains in Weston church. It is to John Fairclough who died in 1630 at the age of 86. This John, who was married to Ann Spencer of Cople, would have been the brother-in-law of Thomas Harmer.

There remain in Weston many beautiful old buildings which our ancestors would have known in the 16th and 17th centuries. These include the church itself, parts of which date from the 12th century, Woodvine Cottage, Frays, Rowanbutt Cottage, Dane End farmhouse (built by the Harmer family) the Red Lion public house, Tilekiln farmhouse (once the home of the Humberstone family), Howells, Irongate farmhouse, Lannock farmhouse, and of course Fairclough Hall. The present Fairclough Hall dates from the 16th or 17th century but it was probably on the site of the older house where our ancestors lived 500 years ago. All these are listed buildings and will be preserved for future generations. Looking at these buildings today, we see a little glimpse of the Weston where, in August 1555, when Queen Mary was on the throne of England, two young people were preparing to take the first steps towards the founding of the family.

Irongate Farmhouse, Weston

Chapter 3

Thomas and Elizabeth

Tuesday 5th August 1555 was the wedding day of Elizabeth Fairclough and Thomas Harmer. At Fairclough Hall there would have been great excitement. In the dining hall the maids were putting the finishing touches to the festive table, while in the kitchen the men were bringing in yet more logs to stoke the enormous fire blazing in the open hearth. The smell of newly baked bread and roasting meat would bring a mouth-watering anticipation of pleasures soon to come, for everyone - guests, family and servants alike - would sit down together for the wedding feast, the only distinction of rank being the position at the table - above or below the salt.

Meanwhile upstairs, in one of the oak beamed bed-chambers, the bride was being dressed for her wedding. She was the daughter of Thomas Fairclough, the great-grandson of Sir Laurence Fairclough named in 1476 as one of the marshalls of the King's hall. Her bridal gown would have been made by one of the skilled needlewomen of the manor, but the cloth for this special occasion would have been bought in London. Not far away, at Dane End, the bridegroom was also putting on his wedding attire, which was even more splendid than that of the bride. Ceremonial dress always included the sword in its ornamental sheath, and the wedding garments would be of richly embroidered satin and velvet, with a great deal of fine lace, and silver buttons and buckles.

Some of the wedding guests would have been arriving over the past few days, for travelling was difficult, and anyone coming from a distance would set off in good time and enjoy the hospitality of the house for a day or two before the ceremony. There may have been relatives from Bedfordshire and more distant parts of Hertfordshire, but the guests would also include friends from the neighbouring manor houses - the Kymptons from Howells, the Wilsons of Walkern and Willian, the Clarkes of Benington, and perhaps the Nedhams from Little Wymondley Priory. The Pomfrets of Baldock may also have been invited and there would no doubt have been members of the Barre family - relations of Elizabeth's mother Millicent.

We have no record of the wedding feast at Fairclough Hall, but in a similar establishment, at Ingatestone Hall in Essex, Sir William Petre was keeping a detailed record of all his household expenditure. His step-daughter, Catherine Tyrrell, was married in June 1552, and the description of the feast can give us some idea of the kind of food which was being prepared for Thomas and Elizabeth and their guests.

On the eve of Catherine Tyrrell's wedding the dinner consisted of: 4 lings; 5 couple haberdins; 16 mackerels; 2 congers, one boiled and one baked; 15 couple soles; a thornback; 2 pikes; 4 mullets; 40 flounders; 3 dishes of butter (4½ lbs); a lead of cheese (56 lbs) and a score of eggs. Although it was a Saturday (not Friday) this was obviously one of the extra 'fish days' and there were severe penalties for anyone who ate meat on fish days - wedding or no wedding!

On the following day the dinner included a whole ox and a quarter, 4 veals, 6 lambs, 2 kids, 2 bucks, 22 geese, 2 cygnets, 24 capons boiled and roasted, 7 pheasants, 16 rabbits, 2 dozen chickens, 6 'brewers' (a kind of snipe), 7 partridge, 8 heronshews and 5 dozen quails. We are not told how many guests, servants and villagers sat down to the feast, but it must surely have been a vast number. For supper on the wedding day they consumed 5 muttons, 4 lambs, 1 kid, 1 buck, 16 capons, 3 pheasants, 3 dozen chickens, 36 rabbits, 20 pairs of pigeons, 4 peachickens and 2 dozen quails.

In addition to the meat, fish and fowl there would have been bread but probably no vegetables. In Tudor times vegetables tended to be used in soups and salads but not often eaten with the meat. A great variety of herbs and spices would have been used. The Petre accounts mention mace, cloves, saffron, ginger, cinnamon, pepper and caraways. The herbs are not listed, because these would have been brought in straight from the kitchen garden.

The acater also made some unusual purchases that week - 'an hundred marchpane bread - 6d, a quarter gold - 16d, 1lb turnsole for jellies - 2s'. Marchpane was a confection of sugar and almonds, similar to marzipan, while the gold was real gold-leaf, used for gilding some of the sweetmeats, including the gingerbread and probably the march-panes. The 'turnsole' refers to linen rags steeped in the juice of the turnsole plant, which were put into the hot liquid when making jellies, in order to give the violet or purple colouring.

There is no record of the puddings and desserts which were provided for the wedding feast, but the list of provisions for the week includes 6 hundred eggs and 8 gallons of cream, suggesting that vast quantities of syllabub and custard were being made for the occasion.

The sweet dishes at this time were often very elaborate, for the cooks were highly skilled, and cooking was a work of art. Many of the country house cooks received their training in the great kitchens of the royal palaces. One speciality known as a 'subtlety', was made from finely spun sugar, perhaps in the shape of a swan, or something appropriate to the occasion. It is all too easy, when thinking of our 16th century ancestors, who ate with fingers rather than forks, from heavy pewter dishes and platters, to imagine that their food was equally plain and simple. But this was certainly not the case on festive occasions.

When all the festivities were over Thomas and Elizabeth left Fairclough Hall, probably on horseback, and returned to Dane End. If Thomas was the son of John, which seems likely, his parents and young sister Joan would still have been living in the family home. But the manor houses were big enough to accommodate several generations. Thomas would continue to help his father in the management of the estate, while Elizabeth would be trained by her mother-in-law to become an efficient Lady of the Manor.

A great deal of information about life in a Tudor country house can be found in the 'Paston Letters'. The Paston family of Norfolk (who were related to several branches of our family in the 'network') left a large collection of letters extending over several generations. From these letters the social historian Trevelyan draws a picture of the woman's role in the running of the country house. He writes:

> When once a lady was married, she entered on a sphere of activity, influence and even authority. The Paston letters tell the tale of several generations of matrons by no means slaves to their husbands, but rather their counsellors and trusted lieutenants. They seem utterly devoted to their lords' interests, to which their numerous children must be sacrificed ... Their letters show them taking part in the legal and business interests of the family, as well as the purely domestic sphere where they ruled supreme. To organise the feeding and clothing of the inhabitants of one or more manor houses, was in itself a task for life, requiring the same sort of administrative ability as ladies in our day so often devote to public work or professional employment. The household requirements

could not in those days be met by hasty shopping. Everything that could not be supplied by the estate must be ordered months beforehand - wines of France, sugar grown in the Mediterranean, spices, pepper, oranges, dates and the better kinds of cloth ... As to home produce, the preparation, curing and storing of the meal, meat and game off the estate and the fish from the ponds, besides the command of the dairy, the brew house and the kitchen with its fire of logs roaring up the great chimney, were all under the supervision of the lady Chatelaine. Much of the clothing too ... was spun and woven, cut out and made up in the house or the neighbourhood under the lady's orders.

So Thomas and Elizabeth settled down to their married life at Dane End. Their first child, Lucie, was baptised in Weston church on 22nd August 1557. Two years later they had another little daughter, Elizabeth, followed by Joanne in 1561 and Anne in 1563. At last, in October 1565, Elizabeth gave birth to their first son. He was named Thomas after his father and also after his Fairclough grandfather, and there would have been great rejoicing at the safe arrival of the son and heir. In November 1567 a second son was born. We have already met him, for this was John of Baldock, whose will has provided so much interest and information for his 20th century kinsmen.

The next child was another daughter Mylicente, born in 1569, followed by Bridgette in 1572 and finally George in 1577. Mylicente was named after her maternal grandmother, Millicent Fairclough, formerly Barre, a descendant of Sir Thomas Barre, Lord of the Manor of Ayot St Lawrence and Knebworth. He was a Member of Parliament in the reign of Henry V and Sheriff of Hertfordshire in 1415. There is a monument, sadly mutilated, to Sir Thomas Barre and his wife Elizabeth in the church at Ayot St Lawrence.

The six little girls, Lucie, Elizabeth, Joanne, Ann, Mylicente, and Bridgette would have been taught by their mother to read and write, to sew and perhaps to spin. Music also played an important part in Elizabethan family life, and the children would have been encouraged to sing and to play the spinette or the virginal.

Young Thomas, John and George would have had lessons from the parish priest. Latin was the most important subject for boys at this time, for this was the language of the law, the church, medicine and literature.

It was also important to be skilled in country pursuits - hawking, hunting and shooting. The age of Elizabeth was on the whole a peaceful one, but every gentleman knew that in times of trouble he would be required to fight to defend his Queen and Country. Horsemanship and swordsmanship were skills in which the young squire would be expected to excel from his earliest years. This was the age of chivalry and courtly love, even though a man could seldom marry the lady of his choice.

Thomas and Elizabeth had almost certainly known each other since childhood. Their marriage would have been arranged by their parents and they may have been betrothed at a very early age. It is to be hoped that it was a happy marriage, because it was certainly a very long one, lasting over fifty years. Both Thomas and Elizabeth lived to see their sons married, and the birth of at least thirteen grandchildren - (Thomas had 9 children and John of Baldock had 4). Thomas died in 1608, and Elizabeth lived on for another eight years. In her old age, the death of her son John of Baldock, at the age of 46, must have brought great sadness.

KYMPTON.   *Azure a pelican between three fleurs de lis or.*

When his father died, the young Thomas Harmer would have inherited the estate, and his mother may have moved to a dower house nearby. Even if she stayed on at Dane End, she would have handed over her duties as Lady of the Manor to her daughter-in-law. This would have been Elizabeth, Thomas's second wife, daughter of George Clarke of Benington.

But it is Thomas and his first wife, Jane Kympton, who form the next step in the direct line of descent. Before we continue with their story however, we turn to the Kympton family, and their ancestors the Hydes of Throcking, who were connected with several of the leading families of Hertfordshire.

David Wright born 1954

Susan Wright born 1955

Peter Wright born 1958

Patrick Wright born 1959

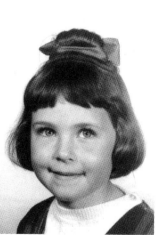

Andrew Wright born 1963

Annette Castle born 1963

The 9x great-grandchildren of Thomas Harmer and Elizabeth Fairclough

David, Susan, Peter, Patrick and Andrew are the grandchildren of Thomas Harmer and Mercy Galbraith. Annette is the great-granddaughter of Mary-Ann Harmer and Alfred Penn of Aston, and the great-niece of Alice Penn mentioned in Chapter 17.

Chapter 4

The Hydes of Hertfordshire

In 16th century Hertfordshire there were two families bearing the name of Hyde, always distinguished in the history books as the Hydes of Aldbury and the Hydes of Throcking, from which our family was descended. At first it seemed that there was no connection, because their arms were completely different. But they obviously knew each other, and were frequently marrying into the same families. Eventually Cussons solved the problem when he showed that the Hydes of Throcking were using two alternative sets of arms, one of which was almost identical with that of the Aldbury family. So we now know that they were branches of the same family, although the exact relationship is still unclear.

There was also in the 17th century a third family of Hydes, taking a prominent part in the political history of the period. Edward Hyde was the Earl of Clarendon and his son Laurence, Earl of Rochester. To the Earl of Clarendon, who was Lord Chancellor and a close friend and adviser to Charles II, fell the task of explaining to Charles's new wife, Catherine of Braganza, the presence of the king's mistress, Barbara (Villiers) Palmer, at the court at Whitehall. When the Queen found that Barbara's name was also on the list of 'Ladies of the Bedchamber' she had a fit of hysterics, and Lord Clarendon, a kind and compassionate gentleman, had great difficulty in calming her. This episode, known as 'the Crisis of the Bedchamber', was one of many crises through which the faithful Clarendon supported the King.

Later Lord Clarendon's daughter, Anne Hyde, became the first wife of James II and the mother of Mary and Anne, both of whom in due course became Queen. His son, Laurence Hyde, Earl of Rochester and President of the Council, was one of the seven signatories of the petition which brought William of Orange to the throne in 1688. Since William was married to Laurences's niece Mary his involvement in this matter must have been, to some extent, personal as well as political.

Although Edward Hyde (Lord Clarendon) and his son Laurence had Hertfordshire connections (Laurence was Lord Lieutenant of Hertfordshire from 1687-89) there is no evidence that they were closely related either to the Hydes of Aldbury or the Hydes of Throcking. Edward Hyde was born at Dinton near Salisbury, and was the third son of the local squire. But once again their arms are almost identical with those of the Aldbury and Throcking families, showing that all three were descended from a common ancestor.

The Aldbury Hydes came from Hyde in Dorset. John Hyde bought the manor of Aldbury in 1544, but died the following year. He was succeeded by his son Thomas, and then by his three grandsons, George, Robert, and Nicholas (later Sir Nicholas) who married Bridget, the daughter of Miles Sandys of Latimers in Buckinghamshire. Nicholas died in 1625 leaving the manor to his son Sir Thomas Hyde, who later bought North Mimms Park from the Coningsbys. When Thomas died in 1665 Aldbury went to his daughter Bridget who was married to Peregrine Osborne 2nd Duke of Leeds.

In Aldbury church there are monuments to many of the Hyde family and also the Brays and Verneys who were their kinsmen. The Hyde memorials are to John 1545, Thomas 1570, George 1580, and Sir Thomas 1665, who left the grand sum of £120 (at least £12,000 in today's money) for the poor of the parish. There are also the arms of the Hydes and the Botelers, the latter suggesting further links with the Hydes of Throcking.

The Hydes of Throcking were descended from William Hyde who acquired the manor from the Boteler family about 1395. It descended through his son Laurence and down through two more generations to Leonard, who died in 1508 leaving the manor to his son George who was married to Alice Roper of Eltham in Kent. Alice was the sister of William Roper, the son-in-law of Sir Thomas More. She was related to Trevor Roper Lord Dacre, and also to Peregrine Osborne who married into the Hyde family of Aldbury.

George and Alice Hyde had two sons, Leonard the heir, who married Ann Boteler of Watton Woodhall, and William, married to Elizabeth Shipman. They also had three daughters, Elizabeth, Lucy and Audrey. Elizabeth was married first to Thomas Fyshe of Ayot St Lawrence, and afterwards to William Perient. Lucy married Edmund Kympton of Clothall, and they were the grandparents of Jane Kympton who married Thomas Harmer in 1592. Later Elizabeth's great-great-grandson, Leonard Fyshe, married Lucy's great-great-granddaughter Rebecka Harmer. But before we follow Lucy and her descendants we go back to the somewhat involved history of the Hydes of Throcking and their various manors, Throcking Hall, Hyde Hall, and Daniels.

The manor of Throcking, as we have seen, came into the family in the 14th century. Around 1540 George Hyde decided to replace the old manor house of Throcking Hall with a grand new mansion house which is mentioned in his will in 1553. In 1692 this mansion was pulled down by the Elwes family and replaced with a 'modern' house, described by Chauncy as 'a curious and neat fabric'.

The manor of Sandon, later known as Hyde Hall, came to the Hyde family in 1492. It had previously been held by eight trustees, including Sir William Clifford, Sir William Say, John Boteler and Ralph Jocelyn. It is interesting to note that a Jocelyn was connected with the manor which became known as Hyde Hall, and that the Jocelyn (or Josselyn) family later held an estate in Sawbridgeworth with the same name.

The third manor, known as Daniels (or Danyells), no doubt from the name of a previous owner, was the smallest and least important of the Hyde estates, and was usually granted to a younger son. Judging by the beautiful manor house which still survives to this day, the younger son would have considered himself very fortunate to inherit this lovely home, with its moated garden, and views across the rolling Hertfordshire countryside.

Cussons gives some interesting extracts from George Hyde's will in which he asks 'to be buryed in the chaunsell of the parishe churche of Throckyng by the little dore on the north side of the said chaunsell as nyghe the place where the course or bodye of Leonard Hyde my father lyeth buryed as may be conveniently'

George Hyde died in 1553, but his eldest son Leonard had predeceased him. There emerges here a rather sad story. Leonard was only 28 years old when he died in 1549 leaving a young widow, Ann Boteler of Watton Woodhall, and three little daughters, Ellen, Mary and Grissell. (Mary was later to become Lady Mary Hunsdon). Leonard's death may perhaps have been the result of a hunting accident which, though not immediately fatal, caused serious injury. His will dated 30th May 1549 certainly seems to indicate that he knew he had not long to live.

He makes small bequests to various neighbours whom he names, and to the poor of Ashwell, Baldock and Watton. To his three little

The manor of Daniels or Danyells was usually granted by the Hydes to their youngest son. This is a 17th century rebuilding of an earlier manor house, extended in the 19th century. Much of the original house, including the moat, still remains

A present-day view of Hyde Hall, showing part of the ancient moat, and the barns built by the Hyde family in the 17th century. The present farmhouse is an 18th century rebuilding of the house built by William Hyde around 1565.

daughters he leaves £30 each on attaining the age of eighteen, and releases his brother William of the payment of 40 marks owing to him. He leaves his sword to his brother-in-law Thomas Fyshe (husband of his sister Elizabeth), and to each of his cousins a bow 'to be taken at their choyse of my boos lying at Plummers of Baldock and my arrows to be devyded betwene them'. He leaves rings to his father, mother, Lady Elizabeth Butler, his brother William, Thomas Fyshe, Edmund Kympton, John Pratte, William Butler and their wives. The remainder of his rings go to Ann his wife.

Leonard died in October 1549, five months after making his will, and a few weeks later Ann his wife gave birth to their first and only son. He was named William, no doubt after Leonard's only brother, of whom he seemed to be very fond. But this brother William was later to cause problems in the family, though it is not clear whether or not he was really to blame.

When their father George died in 1553 his estates at Throcking and Sandon went to his grandson William (Leonard's son) who was now just four years old. It was obvious that young William was the rightful heir, being the son of George's elder son Leonard who had died four years earlier. George's younger son William inherited Daniels. But for some reason, in 1561, all of young William's estates were conveyed to this uncle William.

Soon after acquiring these estates, William re-built the old manor house at Hyde Hall, replacing it with a 'mansion house' which he granted to his eldest son Leonard who was about to be married. Chauncy accuses Leonard of paving his kitchen at Sandon with the gravestones from Throcking church. A later historian repeating this accusation adds, 'It is a curious fact that no memorials to the Hydes now remain, although they were all buried in Throcking church'. It must have been rather fun having the names of the ancestors written in letters of stone on the kitchen floor!

When uncle William died in 1590 he left Hyde Hall, and all his other property, to his son Leonard. But now young William who had originally inherited it from his grandfather, seems to have claimed a right to the estate. Obviously something had gone wrong with the legal transactions - perhaps a confusion with all the Leonards and Williams! Young William never recovered the estate, and from now on it was the heirs of his cousin Leonard who inherited Hyde Hall. But when

William died sometime before 1592, Leonard, we are told, had to pay £60 a year as dower rights to the young widow Mary Bristow and £20 a year to her son Nicholas.

But it was not quite as simple as that. Cussons gives us some more information. He quotes an extract from a plea made in 1592 in the Court of Requests, by Leonard Hyde against his nephew Nicholas. According to this it appears that it is young Nicholas, not his mother, who has been demanding money. Leonard does agree to help (there is evidence that Mary and her children are desperately poor) but he is doing so out of charity, not because he feels that the money is due.

The will of uncle William, written in 1580 and proved in 1590, is extremely interesting, and shows that there really has been a tremendous family row over the whole inheritance. William was evidently being blamed for taking away his nephew's property, but he states that his conscience is clear.

One cannot help feeling sorry for William, because public sympathy was naturally with the nephew and later with the nephew's young widow and her children. Poor Uncle William protests that he **bought** the manor quite legally from his nephew. He writes '.. for the discharge of my conscience I do here before God .. purge and discharge myselfe of the forgerye untruly layed to my chardge, and do proteste that my saied nephew did seale and delyver ye same writing of release unto me as his deed in forme of law ...'

So William was actually accused of forgery! What really happened we shall never know, but it is significant that Mary Bristow, the young widow, never blamed anyone for her misfortune. She is described by the Court of Requests as 'a gentlewoman and very reasonable and inclined to peace and quiet, although she was greatly incited to be troublesome at law by Nicholas Hyde her son, a man very contentious, and one who would rather lose by law than gain by peace'. It seems that the Court did not uphold Nicholas's claim and it was Leonard's admiration and affection for Mary which persuaded him to make provision for her and her family.

We do however have some sympathy for Nicholas. Although Leonard had been generous and provided him with a comfortable income, his fortunes would have been very different had it not been for that hunting accident in 1549 which killed his young grandfather and deprived him of his rightful inheritance.

Leonard Hyde was now a very wealthy man, having inherited all the Hyde family estates, including the manors of Sandon, Throcking and Daniels. He was knighted by James I in 1603, just before his coronation. Perhaps his cousin, Lady Mary Hunsdon, had put in a good word for him to the King. If so it would seem that Mary, the sister of William Hyde, bore him no ill will over her brother's lost inheritance.

Mary, the second daughter of Leonard Hyde and Ann Boteler, was one of the three little girls left fatherless by Leonard's early death. She was married to Sir John Cary, later Lord Hunsdon, who was a close friend and courtier, and also a second cousin, to Queen Elizabeth. They lived in grand style at Hunsdon House, previously one of the royal residences of Henry VIII. They obtained it by gift from the Queen, probably in recognition of Sir John's services as Governor of the town and garrison of Berwick in Scotland - a key position at a time of uneasy relationships between the English and the Scots. Sir John and Lady Mary, before going to Scotland, were frequent visitors at Court, and when Queen Elizabeth died it was Sir John who had the privilege of escorting the Scottish King James VI to take possession of the throne as James I of England. There is a monument in Hunsdon church which is itself a piece of national and family history. The inscription reads as follows:

> Here resteth in Peace Sir John Cary, Knight, Baron of Hunsdon (being the fourth son to the Right Honorable Henry, Baron of Hunsdon) and the Lady Mary Hunsdon, his wife, daughter to Leonard Hide of Throcking in the County of Hertford Esqre. The said Sir John Cary was sent to Barwick by the late Queen Elizabeth of Famous Memory in the Year of our Lord 1593, to be Marshall of the Town of Barwick and Captain of Norham; afterwards he was made Governor of the said Town and Garrison of Barwick in Scotland and so he remained until he returned into England with the most famous King James, where he entered into the Possession of the Crown of England; and so having two sons and two daughters ended his transitory Life in assured Hope to rise again in Christ.

It was sad that Mary's father Leonard had not lived to see his children grow up - in fact he never did see his son William, whose lost inheritance caused such an upheaval in the family. But his widow Ann Boteler lived to a good old age and would have enjoyed visiting her daughter Mary at Hunsdon House and hearing stories of life at the court of Queen Elizabeth. Her niece-in-law Lucy Hyde would also have been an intimate friend of the Queen as she is recorded as one of the Ladies of the Bedchamber.

Sir Leonard Hyde, Ann Boteler's nephew-in-law (and brother of Lucy above), was now Master of Hyde Hall and all the other estates, but he seems to have handed over Hyde Hall to his son Robert, possibly at the time of his marriage. In 1608 Robert sold Hyde Hall to the Earl of Exeter, from whom it went to Sir Julius Adelmare (sometimes known as Julius Caesar). In 1656 it was sold to William Franklyn, from whom it went to his nephew-in-law Sir Nicholas Miller.

Throcking Hall followed a different descent. Robert Hyde inherited it on the death of his father Leonard in 1625, but sold it in 1630 to Sir Thomas Soame. Thomas was the son of Sir Stephen Soame who was Lord Mayor of London in 1598 and was related to our family through the Knightons and Underhills of Little Bradley in Suffolk. There is a large memorial slab to Sir Thomas on the floor of the chancel of Throcking church. About 1670 the manor of Throcking went to the Elwes family, possibly because of a connection with the Freemans, for we find that Thomas Soame was married to Joan Freeman and Robert Elwes to Elizabeth Freeman, her cousin. The Elwes are part of the family network. They are mentioned in Timpson's 'English Eccentrics', under the heading 'Oddness can run in the family'!

Lucy Hyde, our ancestor, was the second daughter of George Hyde and Alice Roper and the sister of Leonard who died so tragically in 1549. Like her sister-in-law Ann Boteler, Lucy was widowed at an early age, for we read that she was 'holding court' at Astwick when she was 24 years old, following the death of her husband Edmund Kympton. Edmund however, lived long enough to produce a son and heir, George Kympton, whose daughter Jane was to marry into the Harmer family. The Kymptons were squires and land owners in Hertfordshire and Bedfordshire, but they were also merchants, and their history now takes us into a new sphere - the world of trade and commerce in the City of London.

Chapter 5

The Kympton Family

George Kympton, the son of Edmund Kympton and Lucy Hyde, was probably born at the manor of Howells in Weston. The family also owned the manors of Astwick, just across the Bedfordshire borders, Kingswoodbury and Mundens, but Howells seems to have been the main family home. On 25th July 1568 George Kympton was married at St Leonard's Church, Bengeo to a certain Catherine Brooke, whose identity still remains something of a mystery. She is recorded as Catherine Brooke of High Cross, and it seems likely that she was the daughter of George Brooke, 9th Lord Cobham, and aunt of Elizabeth Brooke who married Robert Cecil, 1st Earl of Salisbury.

The Kymptons had already been established in Weston for several years for we are told that a messuage called The Lodge and certain lands, 'parcel of the late park of the manor of Weston' were leased to Edmund Kympton in 1541.

A manor called 'Kimptons' in Stanbridge near Dunstable was held by members of the Kympton family as early as 1400, but we hear no more of them until 1539, when Edmund bought Astwick and Kingswoodbury from John Poley and his brother-in-law Richard Sheldon. The Poleys and the Sheldons were already related to the Harmer ancestors through the Suffolk line and it is possible that they were also related to the Kymptons.

When Edmund Kympton died, in 1551, his wife Lucy (Hyde) 'held Court' at Astwick, and presumably managed the estate until her son George came of age in 1564. A few years later a certain George and William Kympton were possessed of the manor of Brickendon near Hertford. This was probably George Kympton, the son of Edmund and Lucy, in partnership with his cousin William. The exact relationships at this stage are a little difficult to work out, partly because the Heralds' Visitations give very few details, and as usual, they completely ignore the daughters unless they happen to be the heirs. We know for instance, from the Wilson pedigree, that Edmund Kympton had a daughter Elizabeth, who married Edward Wilson of Willian, but she does not appear on the Kympton tree. Things are complicated still further by the fact that some of the Kympton family were living in London.

In the 16th century many changes were taking place. Until this time most of the land was held by small country squires, who might have two or three manors which were occupied by various members of the family. But gradually, in the 16th and 17th centuries, the more enterprising gentlemen were buying out the small landlords and building up large estates.

These men were often merchants, who had made their wealth from wool or some other trade, and were now investing it in land. Both Richard Hale of King's Walden and William Hyde of Throcking were London grocers, or grossers, (general merchants) and many long-established families were becoming wool merchants.

The wool trade had been flourishing since mediaeval times, but was mainly in the hands of a few wealthy merchants who traded with France and belonged to an association known as the Staple. But now the number of wool merchants was increasing, and the cloth trade was beginning to emerge. The landowners were not only breeding sheep and producing wool, but were also employing local people as weavers and dyers to produce the finished cloth.

The rich merchants in the city were also commissioning their own ships. Until now the trading ships had been mainly Venetian, the exotic goods from the East being brought overland to Venice and then shipped to England. Now English ships would carry the wool or woollen cloth to the continent, and bring back spices, wine and silken goods which were more and more in demand by the English gentry and nobility.

The old Trade Guilds took on an even greater importance and gradually changed their character, so that each guild or Livery Company was made up of a group of powerful merchants who were not necessarily connected with the trade from which the Company took its name. They were often general merchants trading in a variety of commodities, and their wealth and influence became such that they were virtually in control of the country. The Sovereign and government relied on the merchants to create the wealth to run the country, to expand its industries, to finance grand new buildings and endow universities, schools and colleges.

Hertfordshire was very well placed for the London trade, not only for export, but also for the needs of the city itself. Large herds of cattle, fattened on the Hertfordshire pastures, would be driven up to London to supply the inhabitants. Geese were also reared and driven to London in large flocks, often passing through the county from areas further north, their feet having been dipped in tar to prevent them from becoming sore on the long journey. There was also grain and flour, produced on the local farms, and taken by ox cart to the capital. It is thought that Wheathampstead took its name from the wheat which was grown and milled there to supply the Abbots of Westminster.

While some local landowners began to accumulate wealth, others went into decline, and found it difficult to live on their incomes. There were a number of reasons for this, including the Civil War, which in the 17th century caused great hardship and loss of property. Land and possessions would be confiscated as a punishment for supporting the wrong side, and high taxes were demanded from both sides to pay the extra costs incurred by the war. Many of the wealthy families were also 'recusants' (faithful to the 'old religion', Roman Catholicism), and lost thousands of pounds and much of their land as a penalty.

Back in 1588 we find a list of gentlemen who contributed to the defence of the country at the time of the Spanish Invasion. Most, including Thomas Harmer and George Kympton, were required to pay £25 each (probably equivalent to about £2,500 in today's money), but a few, like Robert Hyde of Throcking, had to pay twice that amount. There were many such demands for extra taxes during the 16th and 17th century.

The Harmers and the Faircloughs, for various reasons, were among the families who lost most of their land in the 17th century, but the Kymptons were more fortunate because they were not relying solely on their rents, but were also city merchants. In the Victoria County History of Hertfordshire we find:

> More significant are the Londoners who took farms in Hertfordshire. In 1551 a clothworker of London held chantry lands in Bishop's Hatfield. **At the same time one Edward Kimpton of Westminster held a lease of the meadows, feedings and pastures of Clothall, Yardley and Rushden. In 1552 he sold them to William Kimpton, a London Merchant Tailor.**

This William Kimpton (more frequently spelt Kympton) would have been the brother of Edmund Kympton who married Lucy Hyde, and

Edward would have been their father. The family had probably been living in London for several generations for they do not appear in Hertfordshire until 1539, though there were earlier links with the area and the Kymptons were probably already part of the network. In the 16th century the family still had their house in Westminster as well as land and property in Hertfordshire and Bedfordshire. William was married to Jone Maryman at St. Margaret's Westminster in 1539, and there are several other family baptisms and marriages recorded at St. Margaret's.

William Kympton was Master of the Merchant Taylors Company for the year 1570, and there are many references to him in the Company's records. In 1576 he was elected Sheriff, only one step away from the very top position of Lord Mayor of London. Other local gentlemen are listed as members of the Merchant Taylors at this time, including Henry Palmer, Walter Fyshe, Andrew Osborne and Jeffery Elwes.

One very well-known Merchant Taylor from Bedfordshire was William Harpur. He was Master of the company in 1553 and Lord Mayor of London in 1561, after which, as was the custom, he was awarded a knighthood. He put his wealth to good use in the county, and is best remembered for the founding of the four Harpur Trust schools in Bedford. Every year on Founder's Day the pupils still give thanks for their founder Sir William Harpur and his wife Dame Alice.

William Kympton's two sons, Edward and William, were also members of the Merchant Taylors' company, and Edward was Master in 1596. Details concerning the life and character of William Kympton (the elder) which appear in Clode's 'Early History of the Guild of Merchant Taylors' are quite fascinating, and too numerous to record here. But reports of the actual words spoken by our great uncle more than 400 years ago are really exciting, even if they did get him into trouble! Clode records one episode, which took place in 1562:

> Some freeman complained of William Kympton's con-
> duct towards him. The offender ought to have known
> better manners, for he was Warden two years later and
> became (as we read in these pages) a well-known citizen.
> This is his case ... 29th August 1562 - William Kympton
> fined 40s for calling Stephen Myliney a 'craftie boye',
> whereupon the said William lefte in pawne with the
> Master a ring of gold in payment of the said 40s.

Nevertheless the Master and Wardens upon gentle submysion of the said Kimpton (sic) have remytted the moytee of the said fyne.

But that was not the end of the matter, William had to apologise in the presence of the assembled company in the following words:

I know I have offended you and not used myself well in speaking such evil words against you. I am sorry for them from the bottom of my heart, and do ask your hearty forgiveness, for they were uttered in coller, but rudely rashly and immoderately. I pray you that we may be friends and so continue.

Later, William is described as 'A man of reputation, who was Sheriff in 1570, but was brought before the Star Chamber in 1576'. When he was Senior Sheriff, William had to search the Charter House for Roman recusants, and there is a graphic description of the search:

On Sunday last, at six of the clock in the afternoon Mr Sheriff Kympton and Mr Sheriff Barnes and I (the Recorder) did repair to the Charter House and knocking at the gates no man answered ... Mr Sheriff Barnes, by agreement, went upon the backsyde to see that no Mass hearers should escape, and after divers knockings at the gate the porter comes ... The Porter answered us very stubbornly and at length he opened the gate, and being half in and half out ... he thrust the gate so sore upon my leg that I shall carry the grief thereof to my grave. Sittens that time my pain has been so great that I can take no rest, and if Mr Sheriff Kympton had not thrust the gate from me, my legge had been utterlie bruised into skyvers, and besides the porter began to bussel himself to his dagger, and tooke me by the throat, and then I thrust him from me, for indeed he was but a testy little wretche. And so I willed Mr Sheriff and his officers to stay the fellow from doing any hurte to any other in his furye.

Whether or not Sheriff Kympton and his companions found any Roman recusants, or whether they even managed to search the Charter House we are not told.

While William and his sons were enjoying the excitement and pageantry of life amongst the London merchants, Edmund's son

George was looking after the Hertfordshire estates, probably rearing sheep and producing wool for the London and overseas markets. He was still living in the beautiful manor house of Howells, and this is where all his children were born.

George and his wife Catherine Brooke had seven children, whose baptisms are all recorded in the Weston parish registers. Jane, the eldest was born in 1573, followed by Anne, Leonard, George, another George, another Anne, and finally a third George. This last George survived and became his father's heir. Leonard, named after his Hyde ancestors, evidently died, as we hear no more of him. The second Anne may have lived, but again there is no further record of her, so it seems likely that Jane and George, the oldest and the youngest, were the only surviving children.

Young George was later to marry Dorothy Becher, the daughter of Sir William Becher of Howbury Hall in Renhold, Bedfordshire. George and Dorothy lived in the beautiful manor house of Clothallbury, situated between Kingswoodbury and Quickswood (home of the Earl of Salisbury). Clothallbury is described by Cussons as 'a mansion of considerable importance, judging from the fishponds and extensive terraces and avenues which surrounded it'. Parts of the old 15th century house still survive, though it has been much altered and extended.

George and Dorothy probably had children to carry on the Kympton name, but from this point we leave them and follow the descendants of Jane and her husband Thomas Harmer who now represent the next generation on the Harmer family tree.

St Leonard's Church Bengeo where George Kympton and Catherine Brooke were married on 25th July 1568.

Chapter 6

Thomas and Jane

Thirty seven years have passed since the marriage of Thomas Harmer and Elizabeth Fairclough. It is now September 1592 and Thomas, their eldest son, is about to be married. It is a very suitable marriage, for the bride is to be the daughter of their friend and neighbour George Kympton of Howells. The marriage will mean that there will be links between the Harmers, the Fairgloughs and the Kymptons and more than half of Weston will now be in the family.

Jane Kympton's destiny was probably determined from the moment she was born - she was to be the wife of young Thomas Harmer, who was then 8 years old. Thomas had to wait for her to grow up, and they were married when she was just 19 and he was 27.

Thomas's younger brother, John of Baldock, had married earlier the same year. Although the parents were obviously happy to see their younger son married, it would not have been quite such an important occasion as the marriage of the eldest son and heir, who would in his turn be expected to produce suitable heirs for the future.

This was a time when the question of heirs would be very much to the fore in the minds of the people of England. Queen Mary, after many disappointments, had died childless, and when in 1558 she was succeeded by her sister Elizabeth there were renewed hopes that there might one day be a royal infant to become king or queen of England.

But Elizabeth seemed determined to preserve her reputation as the Virgin Queen, and now that she was nearly 60 years old, all hopes of marriage and motherhood had long since been abandoned. The question of who would succeed her would have been a subject for much discussion, especially amongst those who had connections with the Court or the City.

Jane's uncle, William Kympton, who was a merchant in the City of London, must have been well aware of the political events of the time, and her second cousin Mary Hyde, (now Lady Hunsdon) was frequently at Court and closely acquainted with the queen.

But while the royal family were having problems with succession, the Harmer family were more fortunate. In February 1593, John's wife Ann Pomford gave birth to a baby daughter, and in December Jane Kympton produced the son and heir. They named him George after his maternal grandfather, and he was baptised in Weston church on 9th December 1593. No doubt there was great happiness and relief both in the Harmer and the Kympton families. Birth was very dangerous for both mother and baby, and to produce a healthy baby boy in the first pregnancy was a cause for great rejoicing.

We can imagine a wonderful Christening party at Howells, with a large gathering of friends and relatives, and a feast with special delicacies brought from London by the merchant uncles and cousins. George and Catherine Kympton would have been particularly delighted with the new arrival, as Jane was now their only daughter. Their other surviving child was young George who was still only 10 years old.

Guests at the Christening would have included members of the Becher family of Renhold in Bedfordshire, including perhaps three-year-old Dorothy, who was later to become the wife of young George Kympton. The Bechers (or Beechers) were a well-known Bedfordshire family. Dorothy's brother William (later Sir William, a Member of Parliament for Bedford) was married to Elizabeth St John of Bletsoe. The Becher name is probably most well known today in connection with Becher's Brook, named after Captain Becher, a 19th century descendant of the family.

The domestic life of the Becher family has been well documented, and many details are recorded in Joyce Godber's 'History of Bedfordshire'. They seem to have had a fairly luxurious life style, and there was an element of 'keeping up with the Bechers' amongst the neighbouring gentry.

Travel at this time was usually on horseback, and even quite young children would travel long distances strapped to the saddle in front of their parents. But when the Becher family set off to visit their friends and relatives, the cavalcade would include the family coach, a heavy wooden structure on four wheels, with no springs, and leather curtains to draw over the windows when it rained. But it was only used by the very young or the very old, for it was considered quite inappropriate for able-bodied people to 'coddle' themselves in this way!

While most of the houses were still sparsely furnished, the Becher furniture included court cupboards, cushions of crimson velvet embroidered with gold, a painted cloth 33 yards long showing the story of the prodigal son, a picture of Queen Elizabeth, coverlets, curtains and chairs of silk, satin, velvet and dornix (Tornai) work. A great deal of money was spent on clothing, and the tailor's bill for William Becher in 1606 came to £37. His purchases included a variety of doublets and cloaks, one trimmed with silver lace and gold and silver buttons. There was also a hat with a pearled band. Hats were worn indoors for all formal occasions (except in the presence of the Sovereign) and also at meals. Gentlemen always wore their hats in church and women were never seen with their heads uncovered. Most of the Becher family clothes came from London, but gloves were bought in Northampton.

In 1624 the Bechers bought Howbury Hall, once the home of the Piggot ancestors. There were fires in most of the rooms, and twice a year 17 chimneys were swept at a cost of 17 shillings. Compared with the bill for food (£100 was spent during one year for meat, and £30 on bread, cakes and flour from the local baker) the bill for staff wages was very low. Sir William's man cook had £8 a year, Lady Becher's maid had £4, and Nan the washmaid had £2-10s. But even these wages appear to be above the statutory maximum which was laid down each year at the quarter sessions - the general rate for a washmaid being only £2.

We have no such domestic records of the Harmers of Weston, but their lifestyle in the early 17th century would have been similar to that of the Bechers. Thomas, as the son of the Lord of the Manor, would have been a well-respected member of the local community, probably a church-warden, and as such responsible for looking after the needs of the poor, the maintenance of the highways and the censuring of wrong-doers. It is unfortunate therefore that the only record we have of his character shows him in a somewhat different light.

The Quarter Session Records are one of the few sources of information at this time but they do give a rather one-sided view. Accusations are made and investigated but we are not told of the background or even the verdict. There may have been particular reasons for the anger and indignation which caused Thomas Harmer to act as he did in 1592. The accusation was as follows:

> Whereas from time immemorial there was a common
> way ...... in a field in Weston, on 18th December 1592,
> Thomas Harmer the younger, by force and armes,

knowingly and designedly stopped up and debarred ye commen gappe with a great and very deep ditch and a quick set hedge.

In 1594 Thomas was in trouble again, when, being taxed for the maintenance of the gaol and prisoners at Hertford Castle, he 'forcibly tore up the bill of assessment and furthermore erased his name out of the bill of the collection on behalf of the poor.' One of the Justices who would have heard his case would have been Henry Bull of Hertford, his son's future father-in-law. But Henry evidently did not think too badly of Thomas Harmer, otherwise he would not have allowed his daughter Rebecka to marry into the family.

In 1595, Thomas and Jane had their second child, a daughter whose name in the Parish Register is not clear but may have been Susan. Another daughter, Ann, was born in 1596. There was also another son Joseph, but we have no record of his birth, and only know of his existence because he is mentioned both in his father's will, and the will of his uncle John of Baldock.

Then in November 1598 came the tragic day when Jane gave birth to their third son Thomas. The baby survived, but Jane, like so many young mothers, died in childbirth. She was only 25 years old, and had produced five babies in the six years of her marriage. On November 2nd baby Thomas was baptised in Weston church and on the same day his mother was laid to rest in the churchyard.

It must have been particularly hard for the Kymptons to lose their only daughter, and young George, now 16 years old, would also sadly miss his sister who had been his devoted companion from the time he was born. But life in the manor house went on as usual. Elizabeth Fairclough would have taken charge of her motherless grandchildren, teaching and training five year old George and his brothers and sisters to read and write and to behave in a way appropriate to young ladies and gentlemen.

In 1601 Thomas married again. His wife was Elizabeth Clarke, the daughter of George Clarke of Benington and Elizabeth Bristow. Elizabeth's father, Nicholas Bristow of Ayot-St-Lawrence, was 'Clarke of the Jewells' to the Queen, and his father and grandfather had served in this way throughout the reigns of King Henry VIII, Edward VI and Queen Mary. Mary Bristow, the young widow of William Hyde mentioned in a previous chapter, was Elizabeth's sister.

George Clarke had property in Benington but was also Lord of the Manor of Therfield and Ashwell. He also held the manor of Chesfield, which was later absorbed into Graveley. There still remain the ruins of the old church at Chesfield, and also a farmhouse and another house called Rook's Nest. This was once the home of the writer E M Forster and was the setting for his well-known novel Howard's End. For many years Newberry Manor descended with the manor of Chesfield, so it is possible that Chesfield once belonged to the Harmer ancestors.

The Clarkes and the Bristows were already related to the Kympton family, and the Clarkes also had Bedfordshire connections. Sir Francis Clarke of Houghton and John Clarke of Henlowbury were part of the same family. They also had links with the Kents of Astonbury and the Josselyns of Hyde Hall in Sawbridgeworth.

We have a copy of the Marriage Settlement for Thomas Harmer and Elizabeth Clarke, an agreement drawn up by the two fathers to ensure that Elizabeth and her future children would be well provided for. From this document we discover, amongst other things, that Thomas had recently built a new 'mansion house' at Dane End, and the old home had now taken on the status of a farm house. But when Newberry Manor was sold in 1620 the mansion house went with it, and the Harmers returned to the old family home. The present Dane End farmhouse, a listed building, is recorded as being of 17th century origin with later additions and alterations, so it is not clear how this fits in with the historical facts.

In 1602 Thomas and Elizabeth had their first child, named Elizabeth after her mother, followed by Mary in 1604, John in 1606 and finally Benjamin in 1608. Benjamin is often mentioned as the heir, but presumably he inherited the property which came to Thomas through the Clarke family. It was George, the eldest son of the first marriage, who inherited what was left of the Harmer estates.

The Harmer family had now come upon hard times, and in 1620 Thomas sold Newberry manor to Sir Thomas Puckering, who had already acquired Weston manor. Thomas kept back part of the land including, as we have seen, Newberry Wood, the name acting as a reminder of the old family estate for many years to come. There were also other lands which Thomas was able to pass on to his son George, and a detailed account of George's inheritance is given in the Inquisition Post Mortem carried out after Thomas's death in 1625.

The term 'Inquisition Post Mortem' occurs frequently in old records. When a landowner died, the Crown often took an interest and made enquiries as to how the property had come into the owner's possession, hoping that some of it might possibly revert to the Crown. The Harmer properties were evidently quite complicated, and had to go before three different courts before they could be sorted out. The existing document gives us an interesting account of the property which Thomas still owned at the time of his death, which included:

> .. a capital messuage .. Dane Ende .. containing in all 240 acres in Weston juxta Baldock and Walkerne parcel of the manor of Lannock, 4 acres of wood called Newberry with appurtenances in Weston, one other messuage and 60 acres of land with appurtenances in Weston, 32 acres of land with appurtenances in Clothall and divers lands, tenements and heraditaments in Clothall and Norton.

Whether George was allowed to keep all this property, or whether some was forfeited to the Crown we are not told, but he seems to have lived very comfortably and was later able to provide suitable dowries to marry his daughters to wealthy husbands.

We hear nothing more of Thomas's sons Joseph and Thomas (except that they were mentioned in the two wills) but we know that his daughter Ann was married to John Payne. We also know that Elizabeth married Thomas Humberstone in 1621 and they lived at Tile Kiln Farm in Weston. The Humberstones were a well-known local family, Lords of the Manor of Walkern. In the Walkern church archives is a report of an incident which took place on Easter Sunday 1637, when Thomas Humberstone and his wife refused to go up to the altar rail for communion and insisted on kneeling in their own pew in the chancel. Bearing in mind Thomas Harmer's past record, we can conclude that Elizabeth had inherited some of her father's characteristics!

Thomas's son John married a lady called Timothae, and they had five sons, one of whom was called Timothy. This led to considerable confusion in wills and documents, especially as his mother's name was not always written with the female ending.

Thomas's will survives, and though it is short is does give one intriguing piece of information. It begins:

> In the name of God, Amen. I, Thomas Harmer of North Hawe, gent, in the countie of Hertford ...

Thomas and Jane

What was Thomas Harmer doing in North Hawe? Until now, we have never come across any of the family living in this part of Hertfordshire, although we later find members of the family at North Mimms Park and Potterells. It remains a mystery. Thomas asks that his body may be decently and orderly buried in the chancel of the parish church at Weston. Whether or not this request was carried out we do not know, for there is no memorial to Thomas Harmer in Weston Church. The church however has been much altered and rebuilt, so there may once have been a monument which has now disappeared.

Thomas leaves the very large sum of £200 to his youngest son Benjamin, and £3 to Elizabeth, but to each of his other children he leaves just twelve pence, a token amount to indicate that they had not been omitted inadvertently. They had probably already received their inheritance when Thomas moved away from Weston. Thomas is generous to the poor of the parish (in spite of refusing as a young man to pay his subscription!). The usual amount to be left to the poor seems to have been 40 shillings, but Thomas's will states:

> To the poore of the Parrish and Towne of Weston where
> I was borne, the somme of six poundes of lawfull English
> monye.

If, as suggested, we multiply by 100 to get a rough equivalent in present-day values, it would mean that the poor of Weston benefited on this occasion by about £600.

Thomas's heir, George Harmer, married Rebecka Bull of Hertford in 1623, and he came into his inheritance two years later. But it seems that Thomas had already handed over the property at Weston before he retired to North Hawe.

George and Rebecka form the next step in the family descent. But before we continue we look at the Bull pedigree, which includes another very well-known family - the Piggots. It also leads us back to our ancestors the Knightons of Bayford whose history opens up another large group of related families in Suffolk. These include the Harveys of Ickworth Hall, and here we come full circle, for the Harveys were descendants of the Harmers of Thurleigh, way back in the 13th century.

Chapter 7

The Knightons of Hertfordshire and Suffolk

In the quiet Suffolk village of Little Bradley stands the ancient church of All Saints. Arthur Mee, writing in 1941, gives the following description:

> The cluster of cottages and a farmhouse share the quiet of a country lane, and amid finely wooded fields stands the little church, its walls and chancel arch Norman, the top of its tower mediaeval.
>
> On the chancel wall is a figure of Richard le Hunt, kneeling here in his armour since 1540, with his headless family. There are many brasses to folk who were baptised long ago at the big 14th century font. An early 16th century Underhill kneels with his wife; and Thomas Knighton, who must have known them both, is near, armoured but headless, with two sons and a daughter.

Yes, Thomas Knighton certainly did know them both! They were his grandparents, Thomas and Thomasine Underhill. The writer goes on to say that there are portraits of two other early 17th century families, John le Hunt with his wife Jane Colte (her shield showing three prancing colts) and Thomas Soame with his wife, five sons and two daughters. All these families were ancestors or kinsmen of the Harmers of Weston, the link being Thomas Knighton of Bayford near Hertford.

Thomas Knighton of Bayford was the father of the headless Thomas in Little Bradley Church, and he was married to Ann Underhill, daughter and co-heiress of Thomas Underhill of Little Bradley Manor which is also known as 'Harveys'. The name 'Harveys' is interesting, for not far away is Ickworth Hall, the home of the Suffolk branch of the Harvey (or Hervey) family. So far we have found no direct link between the Harveys of Ickworth and the Knightons of Harveys, but they certainly intermarried, because the Harvey arms appear on one of the Knighton family memorial brasses in Little Bradley church.

Clutterbuck tells us that 'the vill of Beyford', together with Essingdon, Hertingfordbury and the Castle of Hertford, belonged in the

14th century to the Duchy of Lancaster, and descended from John Duke of Lancaster to his son King Henry IV. In the early 1500's the manor of Bayford was bought by John Knighton from Henry VIII for £317 13s 9d. It was John's son Thomas who married Ann Underhill of Little Bradley. When his father died Thomas Knighton inherited Bayford, but seems to have chosen to go and live on his wife's estate in Suffolk. All his children were born there, but his eldest son, Thomas, married a Hertfordshire lady, Alice Bull of Hertford. This Thomas is described in the Hertfordshire Visitations as Thomas Knighton of Brickendon (a manor near Bayford which was later held by the Kympton family). But in the Suffolk Visitations he is described as Thomas Knighton of Harveys in Little Bradley, and as we know, his memorial is in Little Bradley Church.

There were still however strong links with Hertfordshire, and particularly with the Bull family. Thomas Knighton's sister Jane married Alice Bull's brother Charles, and while Thomas and Alice stayed in Suffolk, Jane and Charles lived in Hertford, where Charles was soon to inherit considerable estates from his father Richard Bull.

Both the Suffolk and the Hertfordshire Visitations describe the Knighton family arms. The Suffolk account is as follows:

> Quarterly, 1 and 4, Barry of eight Or and Azure on a canton Gules a ton of the first (Knighton) 2 and 3 Underhill, impaling Browne.

This was obviously granted to Thomas the younger and included his mother's family, Underhill, which we now learn also included the Browne family. This was almost certainly the family from Abbess Roding in Essex, related to Ann Browne, the first wife of Sir William Petre of Ingatestone Hall. The arms of Thomas the elder, given in the Hertfordshire pedigree, are simply those of the Knighton family.

Thomas Knighton and Alice Bull of Little Bradley had a daughter, Ann, and two sons, but we only know of the second son because he appears on Thomas's memorial brass. The daughter, Ann Knighton, was married first to Richard le Hunt, of Hunt's Hall in Ashen, Essex, and secondly to Thomas Soame of Beetley in Norfolk. The eldest son of this marriage, also Thomas Soame, is pictured with his wife Elizabeth Alington and their 7 children on a brass in Little Bradley church. One of the other sons of Ann Knighton and Thomas Soame was Sir Stephen Soame, Lord Mayor of London in 1598. It was

Stephen's son Thomas who bought Throcking Hall from the Hydes in 1630, and who is mentioned in chapter 4.

HERE LYETH BVRYED Ẏ BODIE OF THOMAS SOAME OF LITTLE BRADLEY IN Ẏ COVNTY OF SVFF: GENT: HE DIED Ẏ 12 OF OCTOB 1606 ÆTATATIS SVA 64 HE MARRIED ELIZABETH ALINGTON DAVGHTER OF ROBERT ALINGTON OF HORSHEATH IN THE COVNTY OF CAMBRIDGE ESQVIER BY WHOM HE HAD ISSVE 5 SONNES AND 2 DAVGHTERS W^CH SAID ELIZABETH ERECTED THIS SMALL MONVMENT FOR A PERPETVALL MEMORYE OF HIS NAME Ẏ 15 OF MAY A° DNI 1612

QVIS EST HOMO QVI VIVET ET NON VIDEBIT MOREM PS 88

Returning to Thomas Knighton and Alice Bull, we find that their elder son and heir was Francis, who lived at Barnardiston Manor, in Suffolk. There were links here with the Barnardistons of Northill in Bedfordshire, who were related to the Fyshe family and to several other Bedfordshire families. Francis Knighton was married to Katherine, the daughter of Sir Weston Browne of Abbess Roding, a family already linked with his Underhill ancestors.

The Underhill family name had died out two generations earlier, when Thomas Underhill and his wife Thomasine had produced only female offspring - Ann (married to Thomas Knighton the elder) and Thomasine, who married Thomas Stuteville of Dalham. The Stutevilles, like so many of the Suffolk families, had connections with the Bedfordshire families who were part of the network.

Thomasine Underhill took her name from her mother, Thomasine Caldebeck, who was first married to John Turnor of Haverhill. It is in the Caldebeck pedigree that some enthusiastic 17th century genealogist gets quite carried away, and takes us right back to Sir Payne Peverell, a

14th century ancestor who was living in Suffolk in the reign of Edward II. Weaving our way backwards and forwards between the maternal and paternal lines we encounter delightful names such as Sir Thomas Notbeame and Hammond Lord Peche, while other names link us with some of the well-known Suffolk families including Aspall of Aspall, Gedding, Grey, and Waterville.

Ickworth Hall, the home of the Suffolk branch of the Harvey (Hervey) family, was very close to 'Harveys' at Little Bradley, and the Caldebecks, Underhills and Knightons must have married into the Harvey family at various times. The Suffolk Harveys (whose name is now associated with a popular brand of sherry) were descended from the Harveys of Thurleigh who were descended from the Bedfordshire Harmers in the 14th century. The arms of the Suffolk Harveys remind us that they were also descended from the Poleys of Boxted, Poley being a name which has already appeared in connection with the Kymptons and the manors of Astwick and Kingswoodbury.

The Harvey pedigree in the Suffolk Visitations starts in Bedfordshire when John Harvey of Thurleigh married Joan, daughter of Sir John Nyernute of Fleetmarston in Buckinghamshire. Their son John married Joan, the daughter of William Paston of Norfolk, whose family archives include the famous 'Paston Letters' so often quoted by social historians. One daughter of John Harvey and Joan Paston was Elizabeth, Abbess of Elstow, whose effigy can still be seen in Elstow Abbey.

We come down through several more generations of Bedfordshire Harveys, including Sir George, High Sheriff of Bedfordshire and Buckinghamshire in 1510, who left all his estates to his illegitimate son Gerard, ignoring his wife and children who he denied were his!

From this point the Harvey pedigree continues with George's uncle Thomas, a lawyer at Lincoln's Inn. He married a Suffolk heiress, Jane Drury of Ickworth, thus founding the Harvey family of Suffolk. Many members of the Harvey family are buried in St Mary's church at Bury St Edmunds.

During this time the Knightons of Bayford continued to hold lands in Hertfordshire. When Thomas left Bayford to go and live at Little Bradley, his younger brother John took over the Bayford estate, and John's son Sir George Knighton inherited in 1585. Sir George's eldest son George predeceased him, and the estate went to his daughter Ann,

Philip Harmer born 1988

Johnathan Harmer
born 1992

Stephen Harmer born 1988

Jennifer Wright born 1986

Emily Wright born 1982

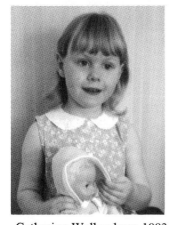

Catherine Walker born 1993

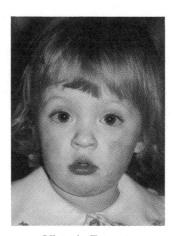

Victoria Frampton
born 1995

Sarah Walker born 1990

The 21x great-grandchildren of Sir Payne Peverell
who lived in Suffolk in the reign of Edward II.
Philip, Stephen, Johnathan, & Victoria are the grandchildren of John and Mary Harmer of Redbourn.
Emily, Jennifer, Sarah, & Catherine are the great-grandchildren of Thomas and Mercy Harmer of Suffolk

who married Sir John Ferrers of Markyate Cell. Their eldest son and heir was Sir Knighton Ferrers, who inherited the estate but died soon afterwards, just before the birth of his only daughter Katherine.

This was the time of the Civil War, and the widow now married Sir Thomas Fanshawe of Ware Park, an ardent Royalist. Katherine Ferrers and her mother were forced by the Parliamentarians to flee from their home and take refuge with relatives in Huntingdonshire. When she was only 12 years old, Katherine was forced, much against her will, to marry Fanshawe's son Symon, though she never seems to have taken his name, and we hear no more about him.

By the time Katherine and her mother were able to return to their home in Markyate, Katherine, now Lady Katherine Ferrers, was an angry and rebellious young woman of eighteen. From then on she proceeded to earn herself the reputation of The Wicked Lady, which has followed her right down to the present day.

According to the legend, she joined Ralph Chaplin, a local farmer, and, dressed in man's clothing, held up wealthy travellers on Watling Street which passed near her home. After Chaplin was killed during a robbery on Finchley Common, Katherine continued her life as a highwaywoman. Then one night, on Nomansland Common, she herself was shot and fatally wounded. She managed to ride back to her home at Markyate Cell, where she died alone in a secret room, which is still said to be haunted by her ghost. Markyate Cell has been much altered and rebuilt since the 17th century, but part of the old building remains, presumably enough to enable Katherine's ghost to find its way around!

Highwaymen, and especially highwaywomen, have always been seen as romantic figures, even though their objective was robbery and murder. In the popular films which have dramatised her story, Lady Katherine Ferrers emerges a beautiful and fearless young woman. Although we cannot condone her ruthless deeds, we may perhaps feel that the violence and bloodshed which had surrounded her from the moment she was born accounted to some extent for her wild behaviour.

But whatever our views about her dramatic exploits we now leave Katherine Ferrers, The Wicked Lady, as we encounter a very different character, an Elizabethan poet whose name we can be proud to include on our family tree.

Chapter 8

The Chapmans of Hitchin

When Thomas Chapman died in 1589, he left to his son George one hundred pounds and two silver spoons. Had it not been for this legacy, one of John Keats's most famous poems might never have been written. It begins, 'Much have I travelled in the realms of gold', and describes his feelings on first reading George Chapman's translation of Homer. Although Chapman himself was a well-respected playwright, poet and scholar, he is now best remembered because of Keats's poem.

The Chapman family lived in Tilehouse Street in Hitchin. In his will Thomas describes himself as a yeoman, but his family owned the manor of Mardocks near Ware, and their pedigree is recorded in the Heralds' Visitations. Thomas was married to Joan, the daughter of George Nodes who was Lord of the Manor of Shephallbury.

Although Thomas was not a wealthy man he managed to give his sons a good education. The oldest son, Thomas, seems to have inherited some of the original family estates so that he could live on his income, but John and George both went to university and followed a professional career. John went into the Church, and for a time was rector of Willian. George studied either at Oxford or Cambridge - or possibly both. For a time he earned his living as a schoolmaster, but as soon as he received his legacy he went to London, where he became a successful playwright.

He belonged to the group of Elizabethan poets and playwrights which included Ben Jonson, Edmund Spenser, Christopher Marlowe and William Shakespeare. He worked closely with his friend Ben Jonson, and they collaborated in several plays including Eastward Hoe in 1605. Eastward Hoe gives a vivid picture of old London, which is said to have inspired Hogarth's famous engravings. But the play caused offence to the newly crowned King James I because of satirical references to the Scots. This landed them in the Fleet prison, and Ben Jonson wrote to his patron the Earl of Salisbury for help:

> I am here, my most honoured lord, unexamined and unheard, committed to a vile prison, and with me a

gentleman, whose name may have come to your lordship's notice, Mr. George Chapman, a learned and honest man ...

The same year Chapman was in trouble again for unfortunate references to the French queen in his play 'The Conspiracie and the Tragedie of Charles, Duke of Byron'. But it was not in George's nature to stir up trouble, and many contemporary writers remarked that his personal character stood very high. He was described as 'of most reverent aspect, religious and temperate'. His plays were well received and one entitled 'All Fools' was described by Swinburne as 'one of the most faultless examples of high comedy in the whole rich field of Elizabethan drama'. Swinburne quotes the following lines as one of the most delicate and evocative passages in the portrayal of Love:

> I tell thee Love is nature's second sun:
> Causing a spring of virtues where he shines,
> And as without the sun, the world's great eye,
> All colours, beauties, both of Art and Nature,
> Are given in vain to men, so without Love
> All beauties bred in women are in vain:
> All virtues born in men lie buried,
> For love informs them as the sun does colours,
> And as the sun, reflecting his warm beams
> Against the earth, begets all fruits and flowers:
> So love, fair shining in the inward man,
> Brings forth in him the honourable fruits
> Of valour, wit, virtue, and haughty thoughts,
> Brave resolution, and divine discourse:
> Oh, 'tis the Paradise, the heaven of earth.

While his plays showed a witty and lively mind, it was in his poetry that his genius was most widely acclaimed. It was much admired by later critics such as Lamb and Coleridge, while in his own day Shakespeare describes him as '.. a spirit by spirits taught to write above a mortal'.

But the main work of Chapman's life was his translation of Homer, in which he claimed to be inspired by the spirit of Homer himself. It took him 26 years, and when he had finished he wrote, 'The work that I was born to do is done.' He would have been gratified to know what effect it had on one of the greatest poets of the 19th century. Keats came upon a borrowed copy, and remained out of bed all night to read it, such was its vitality and force. He shouted with delight when some passage of special energy pleased him, and straight away he wrote his famous sonnet declaring that he had never experienced the full force of Homer's genius, until he heard Chapman 'speak out loud and bold':

> Then felt I like some watcher of the skies
> When a new planet swims into his ken.

Chapman had many friends both in London and in his home town of Hitchin, where he was a familiar figure walking the cobbled streets or wandering in the surrounding countryside when he returned home to visit his family.

But he never lived in Hitchin again. His life was in London, where he had several distinguished patrons, including Prince Henry. The prince had promised him a pension while he was working on his translation of Homer, but unfortunately died long before it was completed. Another of Chapman's patrons was Sir Henry Fanshawe of Ware Park who had been one of Prince Henry's confidants. When he had finished the first twelve books of the Odyssey in 1614, Chapman sent a presentation copy to Sir Henry, with the following inscription - 'For my righte worthie Knighte, my exceeding noble friende, Sir Henry Fanshawe, a poore Homericall new yeare's gift.'

But the money forthcoming from his various patrons was not enough to live on, and although he made a certain amount from his plays and published books of poetry, he spent the latter years of his life in poverty. When he died in 1634 he was buried in the churchyard of St Giles in the Fields. A monument was erected over his grave, designed by his beloved friend Inigo Jones. The monument still stands, but the inscription has been changed. The original, which was in Latin, is translated thus:

> D.O.M. Here lies George Chapman, a Christian Philoso-
> pher and Homerical poet. He lived 77 years and died 12
> of May 1634, for whose worth and memory to posterity
> Inigo Jones, Architect to the King, for ancient friendship
> made this.

In more recent times T S Eliot referred to him as 'potentially the greatest artist of the Elizabethan dramatists.'

It has been asked why George Chapman's wealthy brother Thomas did not help him when he was in dire poverty, but perhaps the family did not appreciate the situation. Unlike many poets, Chapman was famous in his own lifetime. His plays were being produced in London, and several books of poetry were published, but fame did not necessarily bring fortune. His brother John, who was a parson, would certainly have helped had he known that his brother was near to starvation. John was the rector of Willian for one year 1606 - 07. In spite of this short incumbency, there is a memorial to him in Willian church, possibly because of the reflected glory of his famous brother. The communion silver in Hitchin church also holds a reminder of the family. On the patten is the inscription 'the gift of Anne Chapman, widow of John Chapman late rector of Willian.'

All the Chapman family were generous to the poor, (though not to their own brother!). Thomas in 1595 set aside £10 'to be laid out in barley and converted into malt, the yearly income thereof to redound to the use of the poor of Hitchin.'

Both John and Thomas had sons, several of whom went into the church. In 1668 Thomas Chapman, Clerk, of Little Wymondley, settled an annual rent charge of five shillings on a house in Stevenage, the amount to be distributed among the poor in bread on St Andrew's Day by the Vicar and churchwardens.

There is a brass in Walkern church to Edward Chapman, another of George Chapman's nephews. George himself never married, though he fell in love several times, and wrote poems in praise of womanly beauty. But the Chapman name lived on for many years in Hitchin, the literary tradition being perpetuated by a descendant who founded the firm of Chapman and Hall, publishers of such well-known authors as Dickens, Trollope and Mrs Gaskell.

All of Thomas Chapman's three daughters were married by the time he made his will in 1581, (he died 8 years later). They are named as Margaret Chambers, Joan Monk, and Elizabeth Piggot, and to each of them he leaves £10 and two silver spoons.

The Monks were evidently a well-known Hitchin family, for in his 'History of Hitchin', Reginald Hine specifically mentions them, when he tells how the Parish Registers can give a moving story of the life of the local inhabitants. He writes:

> ... in their pages one may gravely and profitably study the
> rise and fall of families, the havoc of plague and civil
> war, the whims and oddities of nomenclature, the

occupations and immoralities of the poeple, the peculiarities of the incumbents, the carelessness of the scribe and the deadly working of the worm ... You can grieve to see the rich and flourishing family of Monk gradually decline from their timbered mansions in Bancroft into the Dead Street slums ... You come with delight and refreshment upon such names as Katherine Jolleyfellow, Greediana Tarboys and Affabel Battel.

We do not know if Joan Monk and her husband lived in one of the timbered mansions of Bancroft, or whether the family fortunes had even then begun to decline. But we do know that her sister Elizabeth Piggot, in her will of 1616, leaves Joan some of her clothing, though this does not necessarily mean that she was poor.

In his will Thomas Chapman asks to be buried at Hitchin near his wife Joan who, he records, died in 1566. This tells us that George would have lost his mother when he was only seven years old. Perhaps it was his older sister Elizabeth, our ancestor, who looked after him in his early motherless years, and as they walked together in the beautiful countryside around Hitchin, helped to nurture in her brother that love of beauty which was later to find expression in his life's work in the realms of poetry and literature.

GEORGE CHAPMAN.
Facsimile of an old Engraving.

The will also mentions his grandchildren, Rebecca Piggot (the daughter of Elizabeth), Joan Chambers, and John and Thomas Monk. They each receive 40 shillings - quite a large sum of money at this time.

Elizabeth Chapman died in 1616, six years after her husband Thomas Piggot whom she had married in October 1571. Thomas died in 1610 and was buried in the church at Tewin where, according to his memorial inscription, his family had lived for more than 300 years. So now we go to Tewin, to try to discover something of the history of the village, and of our Piggot ancestors.

Chapter 9

In search of the Piggots of Tewin

Tewin in the 16th and 17th century, with its wooded hills, and its meadows running down to the river Mimram, was a very desirable place to live. There were no less than five mansion houses, each with its own extensive gardens, as well as substantial farmhouses and attractive cottages.

The little church of Tewin is full of history. Around its walls are monuments and memorials of men and women long since dead and forgotten. But they are not quite forgotten. Many of the names are familiar, and are already recorded on the pages of our family history.

Clutterbuck gives a long and detailed account of all the memorials, which include Boteler, North, Warren, Fleet and Collet. He also describes the memorial to our ancestor Thomas Piggot. It is a small but rather beautiful brass, showing Thomas in armour with a full-length cloak, standing with his hands piously folded in prayer. Above the figure are the family arms (a shield with 3 pick-axes), and beneath is the following inscription:

> Here lyeth buried the body of Thomas Pygott gent, whose ancestors have remayned dwellinge in this towne this 300 years and upwards. He died the 11 of January 1610 and in the 70 yeare of his age and lefte behinde him 2 daughters Rebekah the wife of Henry Bull of Hertforde gent, and Elizabeth the wife of Beckingham Boteler of this towne of Tewinge gent.

The brass is on the floor in the south aisle of the church. It is now covered with carpet for protection, so unless one knew where to look it would never be seen. The inscription is interesting but somewhat puzzling, for we find no indication in the history books that Thomas Piggot ever lived in Tewin. It was not until recently, when we found a copy of Thomas's will, that the story began to make sense.

But even if the Piggots had never lived here, Tewin would still be important. All of its five mansions were in some way linked to the

St Peter's Church Tewin

Memorial brass on the floor in the
south aisle of the church.

Thomas Piggot lived at Tewin Water.
His wife Elizabeth was the sister of the
poet George Chapman.

family, and apart from Weston, it probably has more ancestral connections than any other parish in Hertfordshire.

The manor of Tewin, before the dissolution, belonged to the monastery of St Bartholomew in Smithfield. About 1540 it was bought by the Wroth family from whom it went to the Botelers or Butlers. The manor, known as Tewin Bury, descended to Beckingham Butler who married Elizabeth, the younger daughter of Thomas Piggot and Elizabeth Chapman. In the 17th century it was sold to Richard Hale, from whom it went to William Cecil, 2nd Earl of Salisbury. After this it seems to have come back into the family when it was bought by James Fleet, son of Sir John Fleet who was Lord Mayor of London in 1692. It then descended to his great-nephews, John and Edmund Bull. In the 18th century Tewin Bury, like several other properties in Tewin, was bought by George the 3rd Earl Cowper.

Not far away from Tewin Bury was the mansion known as Tewin Water. In the 17th century this also belonged to Beckingham Butler, and seems to have followed the same descent as Tewin Bury. It was certainly in the possession of James Fleet in the 18th century and he is said to have 'repaired and beautyfyed' it, before bequeathing it to his great-nephews John and Edmund Bull. Finally, like Tewin Bury, it went to the Cowper family.

On high ground just over a mile to the north-east of the church was Queenhoo Hall, built in 1550 by Edward Skeggs. The Skeggs (or Skegg) family were ancestors of Ann Warren who married John Harmer in 1698. The Victoria County History describes Queenhoo as 'a small house of red brick, very little altered, and there are no indications that it has ever been larger.' There follows a very detailed description of the house, together with plans of the ground and upper floors, but we are given no indication of its history. We find, however, from other sources, that Queenhoo was once the home of Aphabelle Partriche, a London goldsmith. Later, as we know from the memorials in Tewin church, it went to the Boteler family, and then to the Abel Smiths of Watton Woodhall. There is a theory that Queen Elizabeth once stayed here, using it as a hunting lodge, hence the name Queenhoo Hall.

Just to the east of the church, on a site adjacent to the churchyard, was Tewin House, built by John Mountford, Doctor of Laws and Residentiary of St Paul's London. John Mountford was the son of Dr Thomas Mountford, rector of Tewin in 1633, and brother of James Mountford who followed his father as rector, but was turned out of the living in 1643. James Mountford was presumably a friend of Thomas Piggot as he is named as one of the executors of his will. The house built by John Mountford was later pulled down and replaced in 1715 by a 'handsome modern house', which was demolished in 1807.

Marden, or Marden Hill, was perhaps the grandest of the five mansion houses of Tewin. It stood on high ground about half a mile to the east of the church, and the park and gardens ran down to the river. The estate belonged to Edward North, Master of the Harriers to King Edward VI. It descended to his son Edward, then to his grandson Edward who was Serjeant at Arms to Charles I. It then went to his great-grandson Hugh, who sold it to Richard Hale. Thomas Piggot in his will left a bequest to 'my welbeloved brother in Christ, Edward North the elder of Marden.'

In 1672 Marden was bought by Edmund Field, who was Member of Parliament for Hertford from 1671 until his death in 1676. From Edmund Field, the estate went to his kinsmen the Warrens and the Collets of Hertford Castle. One of the Collet (or Colet) family was Dean of St Paul's and founder of the famous Colet's school.

In describing the memorials in Tewin Church, Clutterbuck gives details of many of the families who lived in these stately homes of Tewin. The name of Affabel Battel of Tewin Berry (sic) turns up yet again, and we also learn that Julyan Dewhurst, the daughter of Beckingham Butler of Tewin Bury, died at Cheshunt Nunnerie in 1637.

This information was at first rather puzzling. Perhaps in old age Julyan became a nun, spending her declining years in the tranquility of a religious community. But there were no nuns or nunneries in 1637; they had all been swept away by Henry VIII a hundred years before. The answer, of course, was quite simple. Cheshunt Nunnerie was now the private home of the Dewhurst family, but had retained its original name. Robert Dewhurst, Julyan's husband, had bought it from the descendants of Sir Anthony Denny, to whom it was granted in 1537. Robert Dewhurst is still remembered in Cheshunt as the founder of the Dewhurst School, which bears his arms and initials on the east wall.

Among the many Botelers buried here are: Sir George (a Gentleman of the Privie Chamber to Charles I), Edward (of the Honourable Order of the Bath), and Ralph of Queenhoo Hall (who is buried with his wife Susannah, and their infant grandson George). In the churchyard lies the body of Lady Ann Grimston, wife of Sir Samuel Grimston of

Queenhoo Hall, probably built by Edward Skeggs about 1555. The home of Aphabelle Partriche, a London Goldsmith; the Boteler family; and in the 18th century Captain William Sabine, 2nd husband of Lady Cathcart.

Tewin Bury, the home of Beckingham Butler and his wife Elizabeth Piggot in the 17th century. This 18th century house replaces the earlier manor house, but the original chimneys and fireplaces remain.

Gorhambury. She is remembered because of the tree which grew up through her gravestone as a direct result, it is said, of her challenging the doctrine of the resurrection.

But without doubt the most remarkable character to be buried at Tewin was the Right Honourable Dowager Lady Cathcart, who died at Tewin Water in 1789. She had been married four times (no offspring) and after the death of her 4th husband she inscribed as a 'poesy' on her wedding ring 'If I survive I will have five'.

She was married first to our kinsman James Fleet of Tewin Bury, then to Captain William Sabine of Queenhoo Hall, next to Lord Cathcart, and finally to Hugh Macguire, for whom she bought a Lieutenant Colonel's commission in the British Service. She was soon to discover, however, that he only wanted her money! She plaited some of her jewels into her hair and quilted some into her petticoats. She also hid her will, but Macguire's mistress managed to find it, and Macguire proceeded to alter it in his own favour, threatening to shoot her if she tried to stop him. Then things got even worse. Clutterbuck quotes the following account from her obituary in the Gentleman's Magazine for 1789:

> One morning when she and her caro sposo were out to take an airing from Tewin in the coach, she proposed to return but he desired to go a little further. She remonstrated that 'they should not be back by dinner-time'. At length the Colonel told her ... they should not dine at Tewin, for they were on the high road to Chester.

When her friends found out what had happened they sent an attorney chasing after her with a writ of Habeas Corpus. The attorney caught up with them at the inn at Chester.

> The attorney found him and demanded a sight of my lady but he did not know her person. The Colonel told him that he should see her immediately and he would find that she was going with him to Ireland with her own free consent. The Colonel persuaded a women, whom he had properly tutored, to impersonate her. The attorney asked the supposed captive if she were going to Ireland....of her own free will? 'Perfectly so.' Astonished at such an answer, he begged her pardon, made her a low bow, and set out again for London.

Lady Cathcart remained a prisoner in Ireland, but after a time her husband died and she returned in triumph to her house in Tewin. She is said to have danced at Welwyn Assembly with the spirit of a young woman when she was over 80 years old! She died at Tewin at the great age of 97.

> What her Ladyship had to leave she left among her domesticks. Her body was dressed in linen and laid in a leaden coffin; the outside coffin was covered with velvet trimmed with gold, on which was a gold plate, whereon were engraven the names of her husbands, her age etc. She was carried in a hearse and six, followed by two coaches and six...to the church of Tewin, where she was buried in a vault near her first husband. Hatbands and gloves were given in general to all those who chose to attend and a sumptuous entertainment was provided ...

This must surely have been the most spectacular funeral that Tewin was ever likely to witness! There is a memorial with her arms and an inscription on the south wall of the church, and her mortal remains are interred in a vault below.

Clutterbuck has no such story to tell about the Piggots of Tewin. The only references to the family (apart from the mention of the memorial brass and Thomas's generous bequests to the poor) are connected with Thomas's daughter Elizabeth, who as the wife of Beckingham Butler became Lady of the Manor of Tewin. But the inscription on the memorial clearly states that Thomas's ancestors had lived here for 300 years and upwards. So who were they, and where did they live?

It was not until we came upon Thomas Piggot's will, and then took a closer look at the memorial inscription, that things became a little clearer. First we discovered that Thomas not only died in Tewin, but he really did live there. This is the relevant passage: '... after my decease the messuage or mansion house called the Waterside ... to the use of Elizabeth Piggot my wief for the term of her life'. He goes on to say that Waterside will finally pass to Beckingham Butler and his wife Elizabeth and their heirs for ever. It is obvious that Waterside is Tewin Water, which we know was inherited by Beckingham Butler in the early 17th century. So Thomas and Elizabeth lived at Tewin Water, probably moving there at the time of their marriage, and this is where

Marden Hill, once the home of Edward North, Master of the Harriers to Edward VI.
Later it passed to the Warren family. In 1785 Arthur Warren sold it to Robert
Mackey, who built the present house about 1790. Fragments of the earlier house built
by Hugh North in 1650 still remain

Tewin Water, home of Thomas Piggot and his family in the 16th and 17th century.
In the 18th century it went to James Fleet who 'repaired and beautyfyed' it. Later it
passed to his kinsmen the Bulls, and then to the Cowper family.

their daughters Rebecka and Elizabeth were born and brought up. Tewin Water was, for a generation at least, the Piggot family home.

But what about the inscription? Where were all the Piggots during the past 300 years? Again the will gives us a clue. Thomas writes: 'I will that my said executors shall cause to be laid over and upon my body one faire marble stone with inscriptions thereon **shewing the continuance of me and my ancestors abiding and dwelling in Tewinge.**'

So the inscription was at the express wish of Thomas himself. There can be no doubt that Thomas had long associations with Tewin, which would account for his deep attachment to the parish. But nowhere does it say that it was his **Piggot** ancestors who had lived here for 300 years. It now seems probable that Tewin was the home of either his maternal ancestors, or perhaps his father's maternal line. There are certain indications that there could have been links with the Bull or Knighton family - one being the mention of 'my cousin Bull' in an earlier Piggot will, and also the fact that Thomas's first daughter Rebecka was baptised at Bayford, the Knighton family home.

Thomas's will indicates that he was an extremely wealthy man, and owned a great deal of property in the area. He specifically mentions his manors and lands in Tewin and Digswell which he leaves to Sir Henry Cork and William Warren.

Rebecka, Thomas's elder daughter, is not mentioned in the will - everything seems to be left to the younger daughter Elizabeth. In the Butler pedigree, however, Elizabeth is described as **'co-heiress'** to Thomas Piggot, so we can assume that Rebecka had already received her share.

Thomas's will includes an inventory which lists two rather unusual items. One is a sheath of arrows, reminding us of the sporting or perhaps warlike habits of our ancestors, and the other is a bath! It is good to know that our early 17th century relations paid some attention to their personal hygiene. It was shortly before this that Queen Elizabeth was reported to have told one of her ministers that she took a bath twice a year whether she needed it or not!

Thomas's wife Elizabeth (Chapman) also leaves a will in which she states that all her goods and chattels are to be divided equally between her two daughters. To her sister Monk she leaves her best hat, her best gown, her best petticoats and her taffeta cape. All the rest of her wearing apparel is to be given to the poor. There are several bequests to various servants of Beckingham Butler, which suggests that she spent the last years of her life at Tewin Bury with her daughter and son-in-law. Thomas Piggot died in 1610 in his 70th year, and Elizabeth lived on for six more years and died in May 1616.

Here the search for the Piggots of Tewin comes to an end. But before we leave Tewin, we take one more look at Thomas and Elizabeth, living with their two little daughters, Rebecka and Elizabeth at the beautiful riverside mansion of Tewin Water. They would have had visits from various relatives including, perhaps, Elizabeth's brother George Chapman the poet. The Butlers were living nearby at Tewin Bury, so Elizabeth would have known her future husband Beckingham Butler from childhood. Rebecka, seven years older than her sister, would also have known her future husband Henry Bull, and was possibly already related to him. The Bulls lived in Hertford, but also had estates in Stapleford and probably in Tewin itself. We know they were related to the Fleet family and that John and Edmund Bull eventually inherited both Tewin Bury and Tewin Water.

There is no doubt that Tewin has many family connections - the Bulls, the Fleets and the Botelers, the Skeggs, the Warrens, and the Piggots. But to find the Piggot ancestors it seems that we must go elsewhere, and the search takes us first to the village of Little Wymondley and then across the border into Bedfordshire.

PIGGOT. *Argent three picks sable.*

Chapter 10

The Piggots of Hertfordshire and Bedfordshire

In the village of Little Wymondley stands a beautiful Grade I listed house, dating back to the late 14th century. It is still known as Wymondley Bury, the name by which John Piggot and his family would have known it when they came to live here 400 years ago. It was originally the Manor House for Great and Little Wymondley, and was probably built by William de Argentein around the year 1380.

Much of the original house remains, but there were once two more bays which have now disappeared. The 13-foot-wide fireplace with its massive carved beam above, would have been put in by a member of the Piggot family soon after they bought the property in 1544. They would also have built the fine solar on the upper floor, which would have been used for various forms of recreation - perhaps as a shovelboard room. There is a cellar under the dining room (the old hall) which has brick niches round the walls, probably once used for storing wine flasks.

The Victoria County History (written about 100 years ago) gives not only a detailed account of the house but also of the surrounding gardens and grounds:

> Close to the house on the north is an old brick dovecote which still contains some 300 nests, and a little to the south-east of the house stands a fine Spanish chestnut of great age but still flourishing. Gilpin refers to it in his 'Forest Scenery' about the year 1798.

This tree is also described by Cussons who says that the trunk is 44 feet in circumference. Chauncy also remarks on it, so it must already have been renowned for its size and antiquity as early as 1700.

At the present time, although the tree has split into several parts, it is still sending out new growth from its gnarled and twisted trunks, and the ancient dovecote still stands in the garden beside the moat, where a bridge marks the site of the original drawbridge.

The 'capital messuage of Wymondley Bury', we are told, belonged originally to the Priory and in 1544, at the time of the dissolution, it

Wymondley Bury, built by William de Argentein around 1380. The picture above shows the north front with gables at each end forming part of the extensive cross-wings. On the right is the dovecote built by John Piggot in the 16th century. The studded oak door also dates from this period. Inside, there remain the massive arcade posts, crown posts and beams of the original 14th century hall.

The church of St Mary the Virgin Little Wymondley, just to the north of Wymondley Bury. It was built in the 2nd half of the 15th century on the site of an earlier church dedicated to St Peter, built by Richard de Argentein in the 13th century.

was bought by a certain Thomas Piggot for his son John who was about to be married. But although the Piggots bought Wymondley Bury and lived there for several generations, they were never Lords of the Manor. The Lordship of Wymondley was granted soon after the Conquest to the Argentein family and was passed down through their descendants, the Alingtons and the Grosvenors, in an unbroken line until the 18th century.

Thomas Piggot obviously bought a lease or a tenancy which would have been almost identical to a freehold of today, but did not include all the manorial rights and privileges. One of these privileges was the office of Cup-bearer to the King, which was granted to the Lords of Wymondley in the 13th century. The duty of presenting the first cup of wine at the Coronation feast was carried out by members of the Argentein family and their successors for seven centuries, the last occasion being the coronation of George IV in 1820.

The Argenteins almost certainly lived at Wymondley Bury, and the house which William de Argentein built around 1380 probably replaced an even older manor house on the same site. But the Alingtons who inherited in 1429 never made Wymondley their permanent home. They had a much grander house at Horseheath in Cambridgeshire, and only came to Wymondley two or three times a year to hold the Manor Court. It was probably about this time that Wymondley Bury was handed over to the Priory, which had been founded by the Argentein family in the 13th century. Then, at the time of the dissolution, it was bought by Thomas Piggot for his son John who was about to marry Margaret Grainger.

John, as we have seen, carried out extensive alterations to the house, adding the chimney and fireplace, and building the upper floor. But he did not have many years to enjoy his new home. He died in 1558, and the property reverted to his father, although the widow Margaret, and later her second husband John Palmer, continued to live in the manor house with their young family.

Thomas Piggot, John's father, died in 1581 and his grandson Maurice inherited the property. Maurice died in 1609, presumably without a direct heir, and Wymondley Bury went to our Thomas Piggot of Tewin.

This link with Wymondley Bury takes us one step further forward in our search for Thomas's ancestors. We can now assume that the

Thomas Piggot who bought Wymondley Bury in 1544 was his father, and Maurice from whom he inherited the property was his nephew. But there is still no indication of who this other Thomas might be, or where he came from. Although we know that there were Piggots in many parts of Hertfordshire from the 13th century onwards, there are surprisingly few references in the Hertfordshire archives and no Piggot pedigrees are recorded in the Heralds' Visitations. But surely there must be a link somewhere! So the search begins.

One of the earliest Piggots to be mentioned in Hertfordshire was Peter Piggot (or Picot) who held the manor of North Mimms from 1239. A manor known as Piggots remained in the area until the 15th century when it was part of the estate of Thomas Knollys. Throughout the 13th century we find references to Picot or Piggot in Wheathampstead where there was also a manor known as Piggots. It is in connection with this manor of Piggots in Wheathampstead that we first come across the name of Baldwin Piggot who owned the manor in 1307.

Baldwin was succeeded by his son John, but after this the manor went to the Casterton and Colville families. Baldwin Piggot held vast estates over a wide area of Hertfordshire and Bedfordshire, and he seems to be the ancestor of most of the Bedfordshire Piggots, many of whom also held land in Hertfordshire.

In the 15th century there were strong Piggot connections in the parish of Wallington. In the church is a 15th century altar tomb bearing the arms of Piggot and Prysot, and in the north window of the Lady Chapel are fragments of 16th century glass, also bearing the Piggot arms. These were probably memorials to members of the family who owned the nearby manor of Kingswoodbury in 1481, and also the manor of Astwick, both of which later passed to the Kympton family.

The Thomas Piggot who was Sheriff of Hertfordshire in 1445 was probably a member of this family, but there seem to be no further references to him or his family.

This is as much as we know about the early Piggots of Hertfordshire. But across the border in Bedfordshire it is quite a different matter. There are many references in the various histories and there are Piggot pedigrees in the Heralds' Visitations.

The Piggots of Bedfordshire were one of the oldest and most prolific families in the county (prolific perhaps because many of the 16th and

17th century gentlemen seem to have had two or even three wives). There were Piggots or Picots on the Bedfordshire borders as early as 1224 when young Hugh Piggot brought a case before the court stating that he had been wrongfully deprived of 20 shillings of rent which his father William, recently deseased, had been in the habit of receiving from tenants in Luton. It is thought that the family held land in Stopsley before the Conquest, and their descendants have remained in the area up to the present day.

In the 14th century there was a Baldwin Piggot at Cardington who had a son John, and this must certainly be the same Baldwin Piggot who held the manor of Wheathampstead. Baldwin, we are told, took his name from his grandfather, Baldwin Lord Wake, who married Ela de Beauchamp of Bedford Castle. Their daughter Joan married John (sometimes referred to as Michael) Piggot, and Baldwin Piggot was their son. Their great-grandson, Sir Baldwin Piggot of Cardington, was a Member of Parliament for Bedfordshire.

Sir Baldwin served in three parliaments from 1381 to 1401. He also left a very interesting will, from which we learn quite a lot about his character. Joyce Godber in her 'History of Bedfordshire' tells us:

> From his will we get some idea of the kind of man he
> was - attached to his family, his servants and his tenants.
> He mentions his sister Margaret, a nun of Elstow Abbey,
> and two sisters 'in religion at Sempringham'. He refers to
> six servants by name, one of whom was to have a cow;
> and to all servants unnamed he left 40d each; to the poor
> 40s; and to the fabric of Cardington Church 40s; while
> his tenants were to be excused rent for one term.

The history of Howbury Hall in Renhold (later the home of the Becher family) was closely bound up with the history of the Piggots of Cardington. We go back to the year 1265, when John de Beauchamp, the youngest son and last male heir of William de Beauchamp, was killed in the battle of Evesham. The estate was divided among his three sisters, Maud, Beatrice, and Ela. Maud, an ancestor of the Mowbray family, held the smallest portion which later became absorbed into the other two. Beatrice held the largest portion known as Renhold Manor, which descended to the Latimers and Nevills, and Ela had the manor later known as Howbury Hall.

Ela, as we know, married Baldwin Lord Wake, and their daughter and heir Elizabeth married John de Hoobury - whence the manor took its name. Elizabeth had no children so the manor of Hoobury (or Howbury) Hall went to her sister Joan, who was married to John (or Michael) Piggot. The manor was held by their grandson John Piggot until 1351, when he exchanged it with Elizabeth Latimer for the manor of Cardington. In this way the Latimers and Nevills were able to unite Howbury with the larger manor of Renhold.

In the 16th century the combined estates went to the Becher family, who were linked by marriage with the Kymptons, who were linked through the Enderbys to the Piggots of Astwick and Kingswoodbury which were later owned by the Kymptons!

The Piggots also had links with Houghton Conquest. Through his wife's grandfather, William de Beauchamp, John Piggot inherited one of the manors of Houghton. The other manor had also been in the Piggot family until the 15th century, when Baldwin Piggot sold it to the Conquest family. When Lewis Conquest died around 1640 the whole manor, including Houghton House, came once again to the Piggots. Later they sold it to Robert Bruce Earl of Ailesbury from whom it went to the Duke of Bedford.

By the 16th century there were many branches of the Piggot family in Bedfordshire, probably all descended from the Beauchamps and Baldwin Lord Wake, and also from the Piggots of Wheathampstead. In 1518 Totternhoe Manor was acquired by a certain Thomas Piggot, Sergeant-at-Law. He died in 1521 and was suceeded by his son William, who was suceeded by Robert in 1575 and Francis in 1587.

In 1570 a Thomas Piggot and George Fyshe were responsible for supplying armour and weapons in the Hundred of Wixamtree. George Fyshe, who was the King's Surveyor for Bedfordshire, held the manor of Holme Hill Grange from Warden Abbey. Long before this, however, there had been Piggots at Stratton and Holme, who served as Sheriffs as early as 1408. Meanwhile a Francis Piggot was holding the manor of Southill with Rowney, land later held by the Whitbread family. The rabbit warren at Rowney Grange was sold by Sir Michael Fisher to Francis Piggot in 1544 for £698 6s.

Going forward a few generations we find that in 1609 the rectory of Studham descended to a Thomas Piggot and his father-in-law Thomas Sankey and their heirs for ever. They sold it to William Halsey (who was related to our family through the Hare and Roberts ancestors of Thrales End).

We hear less of the female members of the Piggot family, but several seem to have been drawn (or pushed) towards the nunneries. In addition to Margaret, who was Abbess of Elstow from 1392 to 1409, there was also Eleanor who was Prioress of Harrold in 1501 until her death in 1509.

All these Piggots were certainly part of the family, but it is not easy to find out exactly where they fit in. There is one line however, the Enderby line, which definitely deserves further investigation because it almost certainly leads us towards Thomas of Tewin.

In the 16th century John Enderby owned the manor of Edworth, and also the manor of Beeston-Caldecote or Trumpingtons. From 1300 this latter manor had been in the Trumpington family, passing with Moggerhanger to the Enderby and Lucy families in the 15th century.

The history of the manor of Edworth is more complicated, and has interesting connections with the Suffolk ancestors. In 1307 it was owned by the Earls of Pembroke, and was held by Walter de Langton, bishop of Lichfield and Coventry until his death in 1321, when it went to his brother-in-law Edmund Peverell. Edmund, whose daughter Margaret was married to William de la Pole, was already linked to the family through both the Brooke and the Underhill ancestors.

From Edmund Peverell we come down through four generations to Alice Furtho, daughter of William Furtho of Furtho, who married John Enderby. Their daughter Eleanor Enderby married Francis Piggot and they had a son Thomas who was later knighted and served three times as High Sheriff of Bedfordshire - in 1552, 1557 and 1571. Thomas died in 1581, leaving the manor to his sons John and Lewis (Michael the eldest son is said to have been disinherited because his father disapproved of his marriage).

At this point the Visitations and the history books give slightly conflicting accounts of dates and relationships. But it now appears that Thomas the son of Francis Piggot and Eleanor Enderby must have been the same Thomas who bought Wymondley Bury for his son John in 1544. When Thomas Piggot of Edworth died in 1581 (all sources agree on this date) he is said to have left his property to his sons Lewis and John. But in fact, if our theory is correct, John had already died in 1558. The manor of Edworth, it seems, went to Lewis, and John's share (Wymondley Bury) went to John's son Maurice, who definitely inherited in the year 1581.

The links already established are strengthened still further (or even confirmed) by the information on a memorial plaque in the church at Lower Gravenhurst. The memorial is to Benjamin Piggot who died in 1606 at the age of 55. It gives a long and detailed account of the descent of the Piggot family over nine generations.

Benjamin's grandfather was Thomas, Sergeant-at-Law to Henry VIII, the same Thomas who acquired Totternhoe Manor in 1518. His father was Francis and his mother was Margery St John, daughter of Sir John St John of Bletsoe. It also lists Benjamin's three wives. The first was Mary Astry of Harlington, the second was Anne Wiseman of Essex and the third was **Bridget Nedham of Little Wymondley** in Hertfordshire!

One thing that the plaque does not tell us (because it was not relevant to Benjamin's descent) was that his father Francis Piggot had two wives. Benjamin was the son of the second marriage to Margery St John, but the first marriage was to **Eleanor Enderby**. So now we find that Michael, John, and Lewis, the grandsons of Francis and Eleanor, are the nephews of Benjamin. There seems no doubt that nephew John was the John Piggot who lived at Wymondley Bury and that the Nedhams and Piggots were friends and neighbours - hence the marriage between Bridget and Benjamin.

Thomas of Tewin would have been John's younger brother. He is not actually mentioned in the Visitations, but it is not unusual to find omissions. One would certainly expect to find a son called Thomas named after his father. Benjamin would have been considerably younger than both his nephew John and his nephew Thomas, which is understandable since Benjamin was the son of the second marriage.

As a child young Benjamin Piggot of Gravenhurst would have visited his nephew John (who would have been more like an uncle) at Wymondley Bury. We can imagine him exploring the gardens and perhaps climbing the famous Spanish Chestnut tree, then running across the meadows to the Priory to play with the Nedham children, Juliana, Thomas, James, and Bridget, who was later to become his wife.

The clothes these little Tudor children were wearing must have been quite restrictive, but we can be sure that they somehow found a way of doing all the things that children do today. The great barn at the Priory, which is now used for parties and wedding receptions, would have been a wonderful place for hide-and-seek.

When Thomas of Tewin died in 1610, only a year after inheriting Wymondley Bury from his bother John's son Maurice, the estate, together with Tewin Water, went to his daughter and son-in law, Elizabeth and Beckingham Butler. Later both properties and also Tewin Bury, went to James Fleet and then to John and Edmund Bull.

So perhaps we have solved the mystery of Thomas and his Tewin ancestors. The Piggots, Bulls, Fleets and Botelers were all part of the network, and any or all of these families could be the ancestors who were referred to in Thomas's memorial. His immediate Piggot ancestors however came from Bedfordshire, though further back there were links with Wallington and possibly with Wheathampstead.

No doubt many of Thomas's other ancestors are buried in Tewin church, close to the spot where he lies, but exactly who they are we shall probably never know.

Bletsoe Castle, home of Benjamin Piggot's mother, Margery St John

Chapter 11

The Bull Family of Hertford

Towards the end of January 1603, in a handsome timbered house in St. Andrew's Street Hertford, a baby girl was born. Her name was Rebecka, and she was the daughter of Henry Bull, one of the Chief Burgesses of Hertford, and his wife Rebecka Piggot of Tewin. The birth of a new baby was always a cause for rejoicing, but at this time the thoughts of Henry Bull and his friends were occupied with graver matters. The great Elizabethan age was coming to an end, and already King James VI of Scotland was preparing to travel south to take his place as James I of England.

Queen Elizabeth died on 24th March 1603 and the whole country mourned the loss of one of the greatest monarchs it had ever known. For the people of Hertfordshire it was almost like a personal bereavement. Elizabeth had spent much of her early life at the Royal Palace in Hatfield, whence she had been summoned in November 1558 to return to London as Queen of England. Throughout her reign she was a frequent visitor to the county, staying with her cousin Henry Cary at Hunsdon, and with William Cecil in his magnificent house at Theobalds.

There were state visits too, as in 1561 and again in 1581, when during an outbreak of plague in London, her parliament met in Hertford. But from now on things would be very different. The new King would visit the stately homes of Hertfordshire, but his preference was for the flat open countryside on Royston Heath, where he could indulge his passion for hunting and horse-riding. He did, however, much admire Cecil's great house at Theobalds and persuaded him to exchange it for the old brick palace of Hatfield.

Meanwhile, in the family home in St Andrew's Street, the new baby was flourishing. There had been four previous children, two by Henry's first wife Cecily who died giving birth to their second child in 1593. The baby, their first son, died a few weeks later. Henry remarried in 1596 and the following year they had Alice, who also died in infancy. The next baby, the son and heir, fortunately survived. They called him

Richard after his grandfather, and also after the little brother who died. Young Rebecka, Henry's fifth child, was probably strong and vigorous from the moment she was born. She was to grow up to become one of the most dominant characters in our family history and lived to a grand old age.

Although she was born and brought up in the town house in Hertford, Rebecka probably spent part of her childhood at Benwick Hall, a beautiful house on the banks of the River Beane at Stapleford, which had been the country home of her grandparents and great grandparents for over a hundred years. There is now no trace of the old house, but for many years the water-mill remained, giving its name to the hamlet of Bullsmill, which still serves as a reminder of the family who lived there 400 years ago.

The pedigree in the Visitations takes us back to Rebecka's great-great-grandparents, Richard Bull of London and Hellen Skipwith of St Albans. When he left London, Richard may have lived for a while in St. Albans. He certainly owned land in Hertfordshire in 1483, when it is recorded that the manor of Halfhyde or Westmill was in the possession of Richard Bull.

When Richard died, his property went to his son Charles who was married to Jane Knighton of Bayford. By this time the family was well and truly established in Hertford, where Charles owned a great deal of property which was later described in his son Richard's will. The Bull family were very closely associated with the Knightons, who in turn had strong links with many Suffolk families, including the Underhills, Caldebecks, Stutevilles, Turnors, Hunts and Brownes.

Charles Bull was married to Jane Knighton, and his sister Alice married Jane's brother Thomas Knighton, so their children were closer than most cousins. Two of these cousins went on to marry into the Hunt family of Hunts Hall in Ashen, on the Suffolk-Essex borders, after which the Hunt cousins married each other! Thus the Bulls, Knightons and Hunts were related in many directions.

When Charles Bull died his son Richard inherited most of the property. Richard, like his two Knighton cousins, had married into the Hunt family. His wife is described as 'Alice Hunt of Stanford', Stanford being a hamlet adjoining the parish of Southill in Bedford-shire. Alice was almost certainly the sister of Richard Hunt who married Ann Knighton. We know that members of the family held the manor of Stanford, which was very close to Northill and Ickwell where the Barnardiston, Piggot and Fyshe families were living.

Richard Bull was closely involved in the civic life of Hertford, and in 1578 was elected Bailiff. (This office was later known as Mayor, but until 1605 the official title was Bailiff). As one of the Chief Burgesses Richard would have been responsible for making ready the Castle to receive the official guests, including the Queen and her retinue, when parliament met in Hertford in 1581.

It was perhaps because of their experience in writing reports and keeping records that the pedigrees which both Richard and Henry Bull prepared for the Heralds' visits were so much more detailed than many of the others. In the 1572 Visitations, Richard very kindly tells us that 'Henry Bull is five years old' and 'Richard Bull is seven weeks old.' Little details like this are particularly moving, making our distant ancestors seem much closer, and compelling us to believe that 8 x great grandfather Henry was once a little boy of five.

As it happens, we also have a record of Henry's baptism in the St Andrew's parish registers, and the dates do not quite agree. Henry was growing up faster than his father realised, and was seven years old, not five. But father was not mistaken about the age of the baby who was probably still keeping him awake at night! The recorded 'seven weeks' seems to be quite correct.

Richard Bull the father died in 1585 and his burial is recorded in the St Andrew's parish registers:

> 15 Sept. Mr. Richard Bull, gent. and sometime one of the Burgesses of Hertford.

Richard left a detailed will, and most of his estates went to his elder son Henry. The will is interesting as it includes several place names which still exist in Hertford today.

> ... The capital messuage wherein I now dwell in the parish of St Andrews, and that tenement thereunto belonging adjoining in the occupation of Rafe Lee with all the houses, backsides and other appurtenances thereunto belonging ... two messuages or tenements in the....occupations of Richard Crowche and Thomas Wrattinge in the said town of Hertford nigh unto the mill, with all the houses, edifices, buildings and other appurtenances thereunto belonging ... a messuage or

tenement situate at the west end of the town of Hertford
... now in the occupation of Anthony Garland or his
assignes, and all houses, edifices, buildings, orchards,
grounds, meadows, pastures, feedings and other profits
and hereditaments appertaining to the said messuage and
the two pightels at the said town's end now in the tenure
of Robert Hitchcock, and one pightell lying in Blakemore
and another pightel adjoining unto Castle Mead and that
close or croft called Rafes Close adjoining nigh unto the
common meadow called Hartham ... also my four
messuages or tenements now in the several tenures or
occupations of Leonard Halford, John Prinsdiche, William Ford and Cuthbert Stevenson, situate and being in
the said town of Hertford, with all the edifices, buildings,
orchards, backsides and other hereditaments to the same
pertaining.

This sounds like quite a large slice of Hertford, which would have been
very much smaller than it is today. To those who know Hertford well,
some of the place names may still be familiar. There may even be
descendants of the Lees, Crowches, Wrattings, Garlands, Hitchcocks,
Halfords, Prinsdiches, Fords, or Stevensons still living in the town. In
addition to the property in Hertford, Richard also mentions:

My messuage or tenement called Bouwiche (Benwick)
Hall situate in the parish of Stapleford ... with all lands,
tenements, meadows, pastures, feedings, woods, groves,
springs, fishings and other effects thereunto belonging
and lying in the parish of Stapleford and Bengeo ... and
all my lands tenements etc ... known by the name of
Bakers or by any other name whatsoever in the said
parish of Stapleford and Bengeo (except my messuage
and tenement in the tenure of George King) and those
grounds holden of the manor of Russells ..., and all that
messuage or tenement called Baldwins in Waterford ...

Having disposed of his estates, Richard bequeaths £50 to his ten-
year-old daughter Alice to be paid at the age of twenty-one or on the
day of her marriage. Alice also receives a bed with blankets, pillows,
bolsters and coverlets - all great luxuries at this time. Richard also
inherits a bed with similar bedding, but he is not to have this until he
reaches the age of 24. (He is only 13 at this time.) He leaves only £5 to

his married daughter Elizabeth, who has probably already received a good dowry. Although Henry is 20 years old he is included in his father's instruction to his wife Alice to 'have a care to the well bringing up of my two sons Henry and Richard, and my daughter Alice in godly learning in the fear of God.'

Henry Bull not only inherited his father's property, but also his interest in local government. In addition to his position as Chief Burgess, he was also a Justice of the Peace, and in 1600 he was Bailiff (Mayor) of Hertford at the age of only thirty-five.

It is likely that the various generations of the Bull family spent the early part of their adult lives at Benwick Hall, where their young children could grow up and play in the pleasant woods and meadows of Stapleford. Later, as their administrative duties became more numerous, they would have moved back to the town house in Hertford.

Henry was probably born at Benwick Hall but we know that his father was later living in Hertford, so we can assume that Henry spent his formative years in the town, witnessing the pomp and pageantry in which his father would be taking a prominent part. Henry would have been 13 years old when his father served his year as Bailiff, and at the age of 16 he would have witnessed all the grandeur of the occasion when the queen and her parliament assembled in Hertford.

Henry himself was very much a townsman, and probably never went back to live at Benwick Hall. It was Henry or possibly his son Richard who finally sold the family home. By the end of the 17th century Benwick Hall had passed to the Goldesborough family, from whom it went to the Wilsons. Between 1795 and 1803 it was the home of Thomas Blore the topographer, who during this time collected a vast mass of material referring to the topography and antiquities of the county, which was afterwards used by Clutterbuck in his history.

With Benwick Hall went the manor of Russells, partly in Stapleford and partly in Bengeo and Hertford. Besides the general right of common, Benwick Hall had attached to it two acres in Brocket's Bush. All this belonged to Henry Bull and was later acquired by the Wilson family. Benwick Hall and Russells finally went to a certain Richard Emmot who pulled down the house and built a dog kennel in its place. But now even that is gone. It seems likely that Henry also sold much of the Hertford property, because it does not appear in his will, although he may already have handed it over to Richard before he died.

Henry Bull died in 1637 and his will is interesting but again slightly puzzling. He not only leaves the usual bequest to the poor of his own parish of St Andrew's Hertford, but there is also a bequest to the poor of the parish of Harston in Cambridgeshire. We have no knowledge of any connections with this parish, though Little Bradley, the home of his Knighton ancestors, is not far away.

Henry leaves to his younger son Edward a house and land on the Heath in the parish of St. Andrews, which is in the occupation of John Rogers. To Richard he leaves part of a farm called Rowney, lying in the parishes of Great Munden, Little Munden and Sacombe. He names the various pieces of land as Redding Field, Redding Grove, and Collier's End. This was purchased from Henry's niece and nephew, Helen and William Butler (presumably the children of Beckingham Butler of Tewin Bury). He still owes £250 to his niece Helen and states that if Richard fails to discharge this debt, then the property will go to Edward - plus the debt!

Henry then turns to matters nearer home. To his son Richard he bequeaths 'my great presse standing in the chamber wherein I usually lodge, and the brewing copper, brewing vessell and all other ymplements belonging to the brewhouse.' At first it seems that the 'great presse' might have been a printing press on which Henry produced posters and news-sheets for the town of Hertford. But since he goes on to talk of brewing implements, it seems more likely that it was a cider or wine press - although it was odd to have it in his bedroom. Richard inherits the house and all that remains in it, and Henry particularly reminds his executors not to allow the house to be stripped bare before Richard gets it. He says that Richard will receive the specific bequests and also 'whatever else my executors shall think good to leave in my dwelling house for comeliness'.

Henry's daughters Cecily and Elizabeth receive money and a share of the goods and chattels, but Rebecka is not mentioned at all. The executors were his brother Richard and his son Edward, and for their pains he gives to his brother a 'gold ring with the death's head' and to his son Edward 'the old silver ball called mother's ball'. It is interesting to speculate where the gold ring and the silver ball are today. Are they lost in the earth, melted down, or tucked away in an old jewel box in some dusty attic?

Henry's will is dated 29th November 1637, but according to the St. Andrew's parish registers he was then already dead. On this occasion we must believe the will, and assume that the clerk at St. Andrew's had got his records in a muddle. The records state that Mr. Henry Bull was buried on October 3rd, and that his wife Rebecka was buried a week earlier, on 26th September. It seems likely that the year is correct and that Rebecka and Henry both died within a few weeks of each other towards the end of the year 1637.

There are still a few unsolved mysteries in the history of the Bull family. In 1615 we find that Henry Bull and a certain John Cason were in possession of the mansion house and manor of Brent Pelham. This is surprising because the Pelhams were near the Essex borders, away from the usual Bull territory. Whether Henry was related to the Casons, or was just a friend or business partner we have not discovered, but it seems likely that there were family connections, possibly through the Mannocks of Stoke-by-Nayland in Suffolk.

Chauncy in his delightful conversational manner, tells us all about the Cason family. Edward Cason, son of Thomas of Steeplemorden in Cambridgeshire, was one of the Masters of the Bench in the Middle Temple. He made a Learned Reading there in 8 James I (1611) and later married Jane, daughter of Sir Henry Boteler of Hatfield Woodhall. Their son, Sir Henry Cason, married Susan Oxenbridge, by whom she had issue Edward and John, who with Henry Bull inherited the manor of Brent Pelham. We soon discover why Chauncy was so interested in this family. He had a deep admiration for Susan Oxenbridge! When Henry Cason died, Susan married Sir Thomas Cecil, son of Robert Cecil, 1st Earl of Salisbury. Chauncy continues with a fulsome account of the lady in question:

> And not long after, Sir Thomas Cecill died; his lady surviving; she was a proper comely Lady, endowed with a most rare and pregnant wit, a florid and ready Tongue, very sharp, but witty in her Repartees; her common Discourse did much exceed the ordinary Capacity of her Sex; and she dying at a great Age.

Chauncy was of course writing in the early 18th century, long before the rules of sexism had been invented!

The manor of Brent Pelham previously belonged to Edward Newport, and his son John Newport, a well-known royalist. John was married to Katherine, daughter of Sir Francis Mannock of Gifford's Hall in Stoke-by-Nayland. The Mannocks were related to the

Chapmans and to the Dacres family of Cheshunt. The Newports were also part of the network.

With all these connections there is bound to be a story here, but the details remain a mystery.

Another unidentified character is Major Richard Bull of Marwell, near Southampton. He too married into the Dacres family of Cheshunt, who were related to the Trevor Ropers and to the Hydes of Throcking. The name Richard Bull suggests he was a fairly close relation, and could well have been Rebecka's uncle (Henry's brother).

A certain William Bull, Clk. M.A. is listed as Rector of St Andrew's, Hertford in 1633. He took over from Edward Baynes who is said to have 'resigned', but was in fact turned out by the House of Commons. The connection with St. Andrews suggests that William was a relative but we have not yet placed him on the family tree.

Finally, going forward into the 18th century, we come across two sculptors, Thomas and Richard Bull. They were based in London, but did a great deal of work in the Hertforshire churches, so there is probably a family connection. Thomas's work can be seen in the church at Redbourn, which is particularly interesting as this is the home of some of the 20th century members of the family.

So with several questions still unanswered we leave the Bull family of Hertford and return once again to Weston to follow the history of Rebecka and her Harmer descendants.

Giffords Hall, Stoke-by-Nayland

Chapter 12

George and Rebecka

On 28th April 1623, George Harmer and Rebecka Bull were married at St. Andrew's Church in Hertford. Rebecka was an autocratic and strong-minded young lady, well aware of her distinguished ancestors. But it was to be a long and apparently happy marriage, and Rebecka was a devoted mother and grandmother.

We have no record of where George and Rebecka spent the early years of their married life. George's father, Thomas, now a widower, was probably still living at the family home with his younger children. When he made his will just before his death in 1625 he was living at North Hawe but this may have been the home of a sister or a married daughter, where he spent the last few months of his life.

The family home would now be the old manor house at Dane End, the new 'Mansion House' and most of the land which comprised Newberry Manor having been sold to Thomas Puckering a few years earlier. It would not therefore be quite so easy to accommodate two or three generations of the family, and George and Rebecka may have lived elsewhere.

The Harmer family had at some time owned property at Welwyn, near to, or perhaps part of the ancient manor of Lockleys. The area is now known as Harmer Green, and although many attempts have been made to identify the member of the family from whom it took its name, nothing definite has been discovered. The most likely theory is that it was part of the extensive lands owned by the Harmers in the 16th Century or earlier, even though the name Harmer Green does not appear until the 17th century.

It is possible that George and Rebecka went to live there at the time of their marriage, and sold it a few years later when they moved back to Weston. It may not have been until after the family moved away that it took the name of Harmer Green, to identify it as the land which 'from time immemorial' belonged to the Harmers.

In 1634 the Hale family were at Harmer Green. This comes as no surprise, because it is a general rule that wherever there are Hales, the

Harmers have been there before! There is almost an air of defiance in the heading which appears in the Visitations of 1634 - 'Hales of Harmer Green'. But there are certainly no hard feelings towards the Hales, who in any case are reputedly related to our family through the 19th century Hare and Weatherley ancestors. They also intermarried with the 17th century family on several occasions. Richard Hale of Tewin, son of Richard Hale of London, married the daughter of Sir Thomas Dacres of Cheshunt, and his cousin John married the daughter of Sir Humphrey Browne of Essex, who belonged to the Browne family from Abbess Roding. It was this John who bought Harmer Green for his 20-year-old son who was about to be married.

George and Rebecka had their first child, Rebecka, in February 1623/4. The baptism record gives no clue as to where the family was living, because Rebecka, like many first babies, was baptised in her mother's home parish - St Andrew's Hertford.

There were possibly other babies who did not survive because the next to be recorded was John, baptised at Weston in 1628. This was the notorious John who caused so many problems in our family research that the whole project was held up for nearly two years! By the time John was born, his grandfather Thomas had died and the young family were back at Dane End. George and Rebecka went on to have four more sons, George, Thomas, Edward and William, and another daughter, Mary.

Although his father had sold off a large part of the family estate, George was still able to live the life of a country gentleman. In general he seems to have been a good law-abiding citizen. He was one of the churchwardens at Weston, and would have been responsible for administering the poor-law, and maintaining law and order in the parish. But there does seem to have been a long-running dispute between the Harmers and people of Weston concerning the common rights. In 1652 George had to appear at the Quarter Sessions, accused of 'digging up the waste and common land.' We do not know the outcome, but we can be sure that George would not give up easily! The dispute had been going on for at least 60 years, and it probably continued for many years to come.

Unlike his father-in-law Henry Bull, George Harmer was very much a countryman, and his time would have been fully occupied with outdoor pursuits and with the management of his estates and the fulfilling of parish duties. Rebecka also would have been kept busy with the organisation of the home, the children and the servants, as well as caring for the sick and needy in the parish. She was a very devout lady and would have been very strict about daily prayers and Sunday church attendance for all her household.

George died in 1655 at the age of 62. The marriage had lasted for 32 years, quite a long time by 17th century standards. He lived to see his elder daughter Rebecka married to Leonard Fyshe, who was already related to the family through the Hyde ancestors. George, like his father, requested that his body should be decently buried at Weston, either in the church or the chancel as his executors should think fit. Once again no memorial remains, but this is probably due to the fact that the church was extensively 'restored' during the Victorian period.

George's will gives useful information about the family. His first concern is for his two youngest sons, Edward and William, to each of whom he leaves £120, of which £20 is to apprentice them to a 'good trade or exercise'. The remaining £100 they each receive at the age of twenty-one, and until this time they also have a £6 a year allowance for their maintenance. It was always a problem to know what to do with younger sons. Some would go into the army, like Rebecka Fyshe's son, Captain Leonard Fyshe, or Henry Bull's brother, Major Richard Bull. Some, like many of the Chapman family, would go into the church, or study law at the Inner Temple or Grays Inn, while others would be apprenticed to some useful craft or trade. Trevelyan, in his English Social History, remarks on this as a particularly English trend:

> The younger son of the Tudor gentleman was not
> permitted to hang idle about the manor-house, a drain on
> the family income, like the impoverished nobles of the
> continent who were too proud to work ...

George's younger daughter Mary is to receive £150 at the age of twenty one with an additional maintenance allowance of £7 a year (surprisingly a pound more than her brothers). To his son Thomas, he bequeaths £100, of which £50 is to be paid on the feast of the Annunciation immediately following his death, and the other £50 two years later. Young George is to have £50, but not until the year 1658 (three years hence).

It is likely that Thomas and George had already received houses and land from the estate. Rebecka also had probably already received her share of the inheritance at the time of her marriage.

Next we come across another example of a trend we have noticed before - that of transferring a debt from one member of the family to another. George's son-in-law Fyshe (Rebecka's husband) owes £120 to George's daughter Mary, and she is to transfer this debt to John, who will be paying her allowance.

The debt, if and when he could recover it, would help to reimburse him for the money he was paying out. Presumably John, as the heir, would now be responsible for keeping his mother, his unmarried sister, and all the dependent members of the family.

The dowry which a wife would bring to her husband's family at the time of her marriage was intended partly to make sure that her children were well provided for, and partly to ensure that if she was left a widow she would receive a suitable allowance from the family estate. This would include a dower house, and one third of the family income. Thus, while his mother was alive, the young heir would be required to pay out a third of his income, which could be quite a burden, especially if the old lady lived on well beyond her three score years and ten! This situation seems to have caused quite a few problems to poor John, as we shall see later.

Rebecka lived on for another thirty years after George's death. She would have spent her time happily and profitably, doing good works, helping to teach her grandchildren and training them to grow up to be good God-fearing men and women. She would also visit her many friends and relations. There were some long journeys which would have been made on horse-back, even at an advanced age. A journey to visit her cousins at Little Bradley in Suffolk would have taken at least two days. She would be accompanied by a maid and a man servant and would spend the night at an Inn or at the home of a friend or relative.

One of her most frequent visits would have been to North Mimms - again quite a long journey - to the home of her daughter Rebecka and her son-in-law Leonard Fyshe. Rebecka and Leonard were fourth cousins, both being the great-great-great-grandchildren of George Hyde of Throcking. The Fyshe family were for many generations Lords of the Manor of Ayot Mountfitchet (Ayot St Lawrence), and Leonard himself was a wealthy landowner with property in Hatfield and North Mimms. Rebecka's home at North Mimms (possibly Potterells) is described in the inventory which has survived with Leonard's will. It was a three-storey house, with at least eight bedrooms and extensive living rooms, including the main hall, two parlours and a 'shovelboard room'. The contents of the home included fifteen beds with all the bedding, three court cupboards and numerous chairs, curtains, cushions, chests and tables.

While young Rebecka was living in comfort and luxury, her sister Mary, who had married a certain Robert Offley, was having problems, and her mother was very concerned for her welfare. She had recently been left a widow with several young children and an inadequate income, and Rebecka was doing all she could to help her. This is why she was so distressed when her son John didn't pay her 'thirds', which meant that she couldn't help poor Mary as she would have wished.

It is unlikely that Rebecka would have visited her son George, because he was now living in Ireland. He had previously been married, but his wife Mary had died early in the marriage, probably in childbirth. One of the Fairclough uncles was a priest in Ireland, so it is possible that George, overcome with grief at the loss of his wife and baby, decided to go and join him.

Thomas, one of the younger sons, was married the year after his father's death. The marriage to Ann Tucke took place at St Albans Abbey in September 1656. It seemed at first that there was no reference to the Tucke family in any of the history books, but then it became apparent that Tucke was an alternative spelling for Tooke, the family who held the manor of Popes between Hatfield and Essendon. There are many memorials to the Tooke family in Essendon church.

We hear no more of the youngest son William, so it may be that he died at an early age. But we do have information about Edward, who eventually married in 1692 when he would have been more than fifty years old. His wife was Elizabeth Flindell, and they were married at Ayot St. Lawrence, and later went to live at Aston. They had two daughters - Ann who died in infancy and Mary who later married William Chalkley, and whose 20th century descendants are now living in Epsom. Edward died at Aston in 1718. In his will he describes himself as a gentleman, so he had obviously acquired some property. Rather than taking an apprenticeship he had possibly used his £120, a very considerable sum, to buy more land, and had enough income to remain independent.

By the time Edward married, his mother Rebecka had died, so she never knew her little grand-daughter Mary. We do not know whether Thomas and Ann Tooke had any family but we do know that Rebecka and Leonard Fyshe had at least two children who would have known and loved their grandmother. There were also plenty of grandchildren in the family home at Weston, although by the time the family were growing up, Rebecka would have moved to her house in St Andrew's Hertford, where she remained until her death. This was probably a house which she had inherited from her father's estate. There would also at some time have been a dower house on the estate at Weston, but there is a suspicion that John may have sold this in order to pay off some of his debts.

Young Rebecka Harmer, by marrying into the Fyshe family, reinforced the already existing links with several other families including the Harveys, who now had the manor of Potterells, and also the Botelers, Hydes and Coningsbys. Rebecka and Leonard's two children were Leonard, later Captain Leonard Fyshe, and Mary, who married into the Coningsby family.

To understand the complex relationship between the Coningsbys, Botelers, Fyshes, Harveys, Hydes and Harmers we must go back to Sir Humphrey Coningsby who was a judge under King Henry VIII. His son John inherited the manor of North Mimms by his marriage to Elizabeth Frowick, and their son Sir Henry Coningsby was in possession when he died in 1590.

Both Henry Coningsby and his sister Ann married into the Boteler family of Watton Woodhall - Henry married Elizabeth, and Ann married Sir Philip. Henry and Elizabeth had a son, Sir Ralph Coningsby, who was Sheriff of Hertfordshire in 1596.

In 1601 Sir Ralph built a grand brick mansion, later known as North Mimms Park, to replace the old manor house, and his arms, three rabbits (or coneys), can still be seen over the front entrance. Sir Ralph and his wife Jane had a daughter who married Ralph Coney of St Albans (whose arms are similar to those of the Coningsbys, except that they have four coneys instead of three). Ralph Coney's daughter Frances married a John Harmer who is certainly a member of the family, but has not yet been identified.

Sir Ralph Coningsby also had a son Thomas, born in 1591, who was High Sheriff of Hertfordshire in 1638 and again in 1642. He was an ardent supporter of Charles I and was arrested by the Parliamentarians at St. Albans in 1643 and imprisoned in the Tower for seven years. Meanwhile, all his property at North Mimms was confiscated, and his wife Martha and their four children, Harry, Ralph, Thomas and Elizabeth, had to leave their home and take refuge with royalist relations. At the Restoration, the property was returned to the family, but Thomas died soon afterwards, and his son Harry sold the estate to the Hyde family of Aldbury.

Harry, who later became Sir Harry Coningsby, is recorded in 'Who was Who'. He was well-known as a translator, and he also wrote an account of his father's sad career.

In the British Museum is the manuscript of a letter dated 30th March 1665, addressed to Sir Thomas Hyde, the son of the purchaser of North Mimms, requesting him to 'allow this little booke a little roome in the house which was so nearly associated with the glorious and honest deportment of my most dear father'.

According to 'Who was Who', Sir Harry was the only son of Thomas, but there were in fact two other sons, Ralph and Thomas. Ralph probably died in childhood, but Thomas married and had a son Roger, who later married Mary Fyshe, and lived at Potterells.

Mary was the daughter of Leonard Fyshe and his wife Rebecka Harmer, the daughter of George and Rebecka. Roger and Mary Coningsby had a son Roger, who was George and Rebecka's great-grandson, but he died without issue so there were no more Coningsby descendants from the Harmer family.

Rebecka Harmer, George's widow, died in 1685 at the age of eighty two. She begins her will, 'I, Rebecka Harmer of the town of Hertford in the county of Hertfordshire, being very ancient but of sound mind and memory, praised be to God for it, but knowing my time in this world to be short, do therefore make my last will and testament in manner following ...'

The tone of her will suggests that she is still a spirited and determined lady, expressing her exasperation towards her son John **'who has always been very backward in paying my rents'**. She goes on to say that although she has recently taken him to court and sued him for her 'thirds', he still has not paid up, neither has he paid the damages which the court awarded her. The amount owing from the rents and the damages comes to more than she has been able to give to all her other children, so even if she 'forgave' him the debt, he would still be getting more than his share. But she really does love her wayward son, and now we hear her softening a little towards him. If he will pay the money quietly to her executors after her death, she will forgive him £5 of it.

To her son Edward, not yet married, she gives half of all her household goods. There is a suspicion that John did not pay Edward all of the money which should have come to him at the age of twenty-one, and Rebecka is trying to help him. Her daughter Mary has the other half of her household goods, plus 'Harvey's debt of £20, if she can get it'. We do not know who Harvey is, but he could well have been a relative. One branch of the Harvey family owned the manor of Potterells quite close to North Mimms, where Mary's married sister Rebecka Fyshe was living. To her son George, Rebecka leaves £5, 'if he comes home from Ireland to collect it'.

In a codicil written a year later, Rebecka softens even more towards her son John. She says she will 'forgive' him £40 of the £80 which he owes her, if he will pay the other £40 to his sister Mary. It may be that Rebecka realised that John himself was having problems, and simply could not pay all the allowances and bequests which were set out in his father's will. His wealth, which was considerable, was all tied up in land and property, and if he was having difficulty in collecting his rents, it might be impossible to meet all the demands of the family. His own children were growing up, and presumably there were certain expenses for their education and training.

Rebecka does not mention her son Thomas, who was married to Ann Tooke. Ann would certainly have brought with her a good dowry, and Thomas, as the third son, had also inherited property from his father, so he was probably quite comfortable. Neither does she mention William, who had possibly died, or Rebecka who was now part of the wealthy Fyshe family and would need no more help.

The story of the Harmer family now continues with John, the eldest son and heir of George and Rebecka. But before we go back to Dane End, where the young family are growing up, we take a brief look at two other families, the Nedhams and the Warrens who are soon to take their place on the family tree.

Chapter 13

The Nedham family of Wymondley Priory

In the church at Little Wymondley is a brass plaque in memory of James Nedham and his son John. It tells us that James was advanced by King Henry VIII for his service in England and France, and lies buried in the church of Our Lady at Boulogne, where he was killed in 1545. The memorial was erected in 1605 by James's grandson George Nedham, and it was George's grand-daughter Mary who later married John Harmer of Weston.

John Harmer had two wives, and both were descended from the ancient family of Nedham, of Nedham Grange in Derbyshire. John's second wife, Ann Warren, was a distant cousin of his first wife, Mary (or Margaret) Nedham. Although James Nedham came from Derbyshire in 1536 there had been a branch of the family in Hertfordshire many years earlier. There is a reference to Luke de Nedham in 1312.

James Nedham was 'accountant, surveyor general, and clerk' to King Henry VIII, and in 1536, in return for services to the King, he was granted the Augustinian Priory at Little Wymondley with all its extensive lands and properties. The priory was founded by Richard de Argentein in the reign of Henry III, and owned land and property in many parts of Hertfordshire, including the manor of Marden at Tewin, and the water-mill at Ickleford. In addition to acquiring all these properties, James Nedham was also able to buy the entire contents of the Priory, which were valued at a sum total of only £13-12s-9d. Cussons quotes the original inventory, which was drawn up by the king's commissioners, one of whom was Thomas Perient Esquire, a familiar name in our family history.

It seems that the commissioners may have tried to keep the cost as low as possible, for they were very dismissive about some of the items. For example:

In the Kitchen 3 kettles (very old) 4 pence. 2 spits (little worth) 4 pence. 3 platters, 3 dishes, 6 porringers, 2 sauces 2 shillings.

In the Buttery or Pantry 3 salts of pewter 3 pence. A chaffing dish 2 pence. 2 candlesticks 2 pence.

The sale of the contents of the Priory chapel seems at first even more ludicrous, but perhaps not if we remember to multiply by a factor of about 100. In the Quire we find the alabaster altar valued at 2 shillings, 2 old linen altar cloths at 2d, a Mass Book 4d, sanctuary bell 1d, a vestment of blue silk (very old) 20d, one pair of 'orgaynes' (very old) 5 shillings, 2 crosses with a cross cloth 6d, one old senser 2d, 2 vestments, one of Bawdekyn and one of red silk 3d, one old Cope 8d.

At Our Lady's Altar was a 'table of alabaster of the resurrection' valued at 8d, and a Holywater Stoppe at 2d. At St Laurence's Altar a 'table of alabaster of the Trinity' was valued at 6d. But a pair of silver chalices at 24 shillings and 4 pence seems nearer the present-day value. In the farmyard things were in general rather more expensive, probably because they were more useful. A cart-horse and harness was 25 shillings, and the cart 3 shillings and 4 pence, though the plough was only valued at 8d.

Chauncy, writing about the Priory 150 years later, after it had been converted into a 'mansion' by James Nedham or his son John, gives the following description (spelling modernised):

> A fair old building with cloisters; there was a Chapel consecrated since the Dissolution. Almost surrounded with a moat, situated upon the side of a small hill, encompassed with near 400 acres of rich meadow, pasture and arable land enclosed to it, with a very fair orchard and garden, yielding the best sort of fruit. The house is supplied from a conduit, with sufficient water to turn the spit in the kitchen upon all occasions.

Cussons, writing in the late 19th century says, 'Nothing of the old religious house now remains'. But this is not quite true. Although James Nedham pulled down most of the original building, he did leave the 13th century chapel, and incorporated it into his new house. As we have heard, the chapel was re-dedicated, and it was in this chapel that some of our family were baptised and married. According to Chauncy, it seems that the cloisters also remained until the 18th century.

Extensive alteration in the 1970's uncovered considerable 13th century remains including the original high-pitched seven-sided rafter roof of the chapel nave, two south lancets, and the original north doorway. A 16th century wall painting of Roman soldiers was found in the North East corner, and all this has now been carefully preserved.

The conduit which supplied water to the mediaeval priory, and which turned the spit in the kitchen where our ancestors roasted their Sunday joint, is also carefully preserved, and is listed by the Department of the Environment as an Ancient Monument.

The ancient tithe barn, built around 1400, has been restored, and the architectural detail of the nine-bay structure with its magnificent raftered roof, is probably more appreciated now than at any time in its long history. The dovecote, again a listed building, has now been converted into a house known as Dove Cottage.

One other very interesting feature, which would have been familiar to our family when they lived there 400 years ago, is the grove of box trees about thirty feet high, claimed to be the oldest in England. They are almost certainly the descendants of those which are known to have been here in ancient times. Some box leaves were found with a Roman burial urn nearby, and it could well be that the original trees were introduced by the Romans nearly two thousand years ago.

The pedigree of the Nedham family has been documented by various historians, but as usual there are slight discrepancies. We are not sure whether John Harmer's wife was baptised Mary or Margaret, but we do know that she was the daughter of Eustace Nedham and his wife Frances Wingate, whose father was Lord of the Manor of Lockleys at Digswell. The Wingate family came originally from Harlington in Bedfordshire, and included Edmund Wingate, a renowned mathematician, who went to France to teach English to Princess Henrietta Maria, the future wife of King Charles I.

Eustace was the son of George Nedham, the grandson of James who acquired the Priory in 1536 and built the house which we see today. George's brother James, and his two sisters Juliana and Bridget, all had connections with our family. James was married to Elizabeth, sister of Beckingham Butler of Tewin Bury, whose wife Elizabeth was sister of Rebecka Piggot. Bridget Nedham married Benjamin Piggot of Gravenhurst in Bedfordshire - a member of the same Piggot family, and Juliana married William Warren, alias Bygrave, of whom we shall hear more later. The Warrens of Bygrave were almost certainly the ancestors of Ann Warren, John Harmer's second wife, from whom our line descended.

Frances Wingate was the second wife of Eustace Nedham, and the Priory now descended through his eldest son George, the son of his

Wymondley Priory, built by Richard de Argentein in the 13th century and converted into a 'mansion house' by James Nedham about 1540. The old Priory Chapel was incorporated into the house and re-dedicated for use as a private chapel. Several of the Harmer ancestors were baptised and married here.

The 600-year-old tithe barn was one of the original Priory buildings. It is over 100 feet long and 39 feet wide. Leading from the barn is a medieval wall which enclosed the monks' cemetery.

first wife, Ann Norton. George died in 1669, and was succeeded in turn by his son and grandson, both named George. But there were to be no more Georges or any other male heirs. The third George had only daughters - Susan, Barbara and Martha, who jointly inherited the property. Martha married Thomas Browne, an eminent surveyor, who later became Garter King of Arms. They lived for a time at Wymondley Priory, and then moved to Camfield Place in Essendon. Martha died in 1773 and Thomas died seven years later at the age of 79. They were buried in Essendon church where there are monuments to their memory.

Barbara Nedham married John Sherwin of Nottingham and their son Robie Sherwin became Rector of Ashwell. The third sister, Susan, seems to have remained unmarried, and later went to live at Graveley, possibly with her aunt Elizabeth Nedham, whose husband, Simon Degge, was Lord of the Manor.

Around 1733 the Priory, which had been the home of the Nedhams for nearly 200 years, was finally sold. It was bought by Samuel Vanderplank, and descended to his son-in-law, Gilbert Joddrell, and then to the Clitherow family of Essendon. In 1806 they sold it to Samuel Heathcote of Shephallbury who had recently bought Wymondley Bury and was now Lord of the Manor of Wymondley. Samuel Heathcote was a direct descendant of the Nodes family of Shephallbury and was therefore, although he may not have been aware of it, a kinsman of Elizabeth Chapman, whose husband Thomas Piggot had inherited Wymondley Bury 200 years before.

It is clear that the 17th century Harmers and Nedhams were well known to each other. Young John Harmer would probably have met Mary Nedham at Tewin Bury, the home of Elizabeth and Beckingham Butler. Elizabeth was John Harmer's great-aunt, and Beckingham's brother-in-law, James, was Mary's great-uncle. Both families, as we have seen, were also related to the Piggots of Gravenhurst.

We have no record of John and Mary's marriage, probably because it took place at Little Wymondley and the parish registers are incomplete. Most of the early ones have been lost, those that remain being little more than notes on particular families. Fortunately, one of those families was the Nedham family, and the fragments which have survived are quite useful. All of the baptisms took place in the private chapel of Wymondley Priory, and one marriage is also recorded - that of Joanna Nedham to Francis Taverner (a family which was linked with the Docwra family). It is likely that John Harmer and Mary (or Margaret) Nedham were also married here, and that the record was never entered in the Little Wymondley parish registers.

We are not certain whether John's wife was Mary or Margaret because there are two possible baptism entries in the registers. The first one states that 'Mistress Margaret Needham (sic), daughter to the right worshippfull Mr Eustace Nedham was baptised 21st May 1629'. The second simply records, 'Mary Nedham baptised 23 February 1636/7.' The second entry seems the more likely, as the Weston parish registers later refer to John's wife as Mary, although there is still some doubt because one of John's daughters is baptised Margaret. All we can say for certain is that John Harmer's wife was the daughter of Eustace Nedham, and that she was baptised in the chapel at Wymondley Priory either in May 1629 or February 1636/7.

Several of the entries in the Nedham family records give the actual date and time of birth, which somehow seems to bring the history to life. The record of Mary's great-nephew, another Eustace, is one of those given in detail:

> Eustache the sonn of George Nedham Esq and Lidia his wife was baptised in the chapell at the Priory June 20 and born June 14 about six in the morning 1675.

It was Juliana, the aunt of Eustace Nedham, who was almost certainly the ancestor of John Harmer's second wife, Ann Warren. Juliana, the sister of Bridget who married Benjamin Piggot, and of James who married Elizabeth Butler, was married to a certain William Warren, alias Bygrave, who had taken the name of Bygrave in order to inherit estates be-longing to that manor. So now we turn to the history of the Warren family, which takes us first to Bygrave and Baldock, before returning once again to the old familiar haunts in the parish of Tewin.

NEEDHAM. *Argent a bend engrailed azure between two harts' heads caboshed sable.*

Chapter 14

The Warren Family.

There were several branches of the Warren family in 16th century Hertfordshire, all bearing the distinctive arms described as 'Checky or and azure, a quarter gules with a lion argent therein'. Going back to the 14th century we discover that Sir John de Warren, natural son of John Earl of Surrey Sussex and Warenne, who died in 1347, bore a canton of the arms of his mother Alice de Nerford (Gules, a lion rampant ermine) over the checky shield of Warren. Earlier still, in the 13th century, there were connections with the Earls of Warwick, when Waleran added his mother's arms (Warren) to his own. The house of Howard still bears a Warren quartering on its shield, which is perhaps explained by the following entry in the Guide Book to Peveril Castle:

> In 1310 Edward II granted Castle and Honour to John de Warrenne Earl of Surrey. Later it was taken back into the king's hands, but re-granted to John in 1314. Taken back again in 1327 and granted to Queen Isabella for life. Later the Warrens lost the title Earl of Surrey because in the 15th century the eldest son of the Duke of Norfolk (Howard) held the title.

In the 16th century the arms of Warren were quartered with those of George Nevill, Baron Abergavenny, so we know the Warrens were related to many of the great families of England, and it is likely that Ann Warren was one of the descendants. There are strong indications that she belonged to the branch of the family who bought the manor of Bygrave, near Baldock, in the first half of the 16th century.

The manor of Bygrave lay below the northern slopes of the Hertfordshire chalk hills, in the angle formed by the Icknield Way and the Great North Road, which met at the adjacent town of Baldock. The church stood in the highest part of the village, and adjoining the churchyard on the south side was the old fortified manor house surrounded by moats, which at one time also enclosed the church.

In the 13th century the manor was held by the de Somery family, and in the 14th century it was sold to Sir John Thornbury, who obtained a licence to crenellate his two houses within the manor of Bygrave. From the Thornbury family it passed to Laurence Warren of Poynton in Cheshire and his wife Joan.

Laurence bought the manor of Bygrave in 1550, but he died in 1556, leaving the manor to his son William, who apparently took the name of Bygrave for the Visitations of 1586. This William Warren (alias Bygrave) married Juliana Nedham of Wymondley, the great-aunt of Mary Nedham - later Mary Harmer. They had several children, but in 1589 William died leaving a young family, with his eldest son still only five years old. He had left an annuity for Juliana to help her bring up the children, but the manor was held in trust for his heir, also named William, to inherit when he came of age at eighteen.

During his long minority there was evidently some bad management, for the debts accumulated, and when he took over the manor in 1602, things were in a very bad way. Not only was William burdened with debts, but he also had to support his young brothers and sisters. In 1613, in order to make fitting provision for them, he sold the Bygrave estate to William Whettall of Thetford and Sir John Heveningham of Norfolk, 'endeavouring to raise the price by hinting that the estate was desired in high quarters'.

After all these years the details have been lost, but it seems that somewhere here is a rather sad story. William, having sold the estate, now moved to London, where he possibly became a merchant. But he really did not want to part with the family home. He offered to retain the mansion house, dovehouse, buildings, gardens and orchards on a ten-year lease. But Whettall refused, even though he complained that he did not want to live there himself because it was too far from his home, and tried to get William to reduce the price on this account.

So Juliana and the children would have had to move out of their home and find somewhere else to live. It seems likely that William may have managed to buy a small estate at Ashwell, not far from Bygrave, where he settled his mother and family while he himself returned to London, desperately trying to earn money to pay off the debts and revive the family fortunes.

At this stage we leave William and his family for the moment while we look at the other branches of the Warren family and try to discover how the jig-saw puzzle fits together.

There are three Warren pedigrees in the Heralds' Visitations - Warren of Harpenden, Warren of Colney, and Warren alias Waller of

Ashwell, all descended from Sir John Warren of Poynton in Cheshire. In the 17th century there were Warrens holding the manor of Marden in Tewin, and these can be fitted onto the Ashwell pedigree.

The Harpenden pedigree too contains some interesting links with the Warrens of Tewin. We find the name 'Field' (married to Bridgett Warren) and also Jeremy Thornton whose daughter married Bridgett's brother Gregory. Both these names occur later in the history of Marden. The Harpenden pedigree includes marriages with the Booth family who were connected with the Newports of Pelham, the Snagges of Letchworth and Marston Moreteyne, and the Skipwiths of St Albans (ancestors of the Bull family). The Booth family lived at Shrublands Hall in Suffolk - a mansion which in the 20th century had connections with the de Someries, the family who held Bygrave in the 13th century.

The Colney pedigree includes the marriage of Gilbert Warren to Margery, daughter of Thomas Hickman, haberdasher of London. This is interesting, because the sanctus bell in the church at Aldenham bears the inscription 'Thomas Waller Ralph Hickman 1647'. The Wallers were connected with the Warrens on the Ashwell tree (not the Colney tree as one might have expected) but this simply indicates that all the branches were closely connected.

Henry Hickman who died in 1594, and his son George who died in 1635, were Lords of the Manor of Bushey from 1568. Thomas Hickman was probably the son of George, and followed his father as Lord of the Manor. Thomas Hickman's other daughter Alice (the sister of Margery Warren) married Nicholas Tooke of Essendon Parsonage, who was the great-uncle of the Ann Tooke who married Thomas Harmer, the brother of John who married Ann Warren.

Although these three Warren pedigrees all had various connections with the family, they do not give any definite link with the Warrens of Bygrave. But now the clues lead us back to Tewin and to the manor of Marden, where we find a family of Warrens who could well form the link between William of Bygrave and Ann, the wife of John Harmer.

Clutterbuck tells us that around 1670 the manor of Marden passed from the North family to Edmund Field Esq. who was Member of Parliament for the Borough of Hertford from 1671 until his death in 1676. He continues:

> In the year 1692 this estate was possessed by **Richard Warren**, Rector of South Warnborough in the County of

Southampton, Clerk, LL.D. He devised it by will, dated in that year, to his son Richard Warren, who in 1728, upon his marriage with Mary, one of the four daughters and co-heiresses of Joseph Collet, then late of Hertford Castle, Esq. settled this estate on the issue of that marriage, under which settlement it passed to his only son Arthur Warren Esq.

He goes on to say that on Christmas Day 1785 Arthur Warren sold Marden to Robert Mackey of Tewin House who pulled down the house in 1790 and built a handsome modern mansion on the site, (the house which we see today). In 1809 it was sold to Richard Flower of Hertford. He sold it in 1817 to Claude-George Thornton Esq., Governor of the Bank of England. (There was a Joan Thornton who married Gregory Warren in the 17th century who may well have belonged to the same family.)

Clutterbuck's account gives a great deal of interesting information, but not yet enough to link the Warrens of Marden with the Warrens of Bygrave. The Victoria County History states that Marden went from Edmund Field to **Edward** (not Richard) Warren who was holding it in 1700. From Edward it went to his son Richard who died in 1768 and was succeeded by his son Arthur. This does not quite agree with Clutterbuck but it does link up with the Ashwell tree where we find an Edward who had a son Richard.

The only problem now is that one of the burials in Tewin church indicates that Richard was the son of Richard. We are told that '... not far off lies the body of Dr Richard Warren and Catherine his wife, only child of Sir Anthony Vincent of Stoke, in Surrey, Bart, and **underneath**, the body of Richard Warren Esq. and Elizabeth his wife.' This Richard and Elizabeth must surely be the parents of Dr Richard Warren - it is not likely that he would be buried on top of someone else's parents! We must therefore conclude that Marden went from Edmund Field to **Richard** Warren (his fourth cousin), then to Richard's son, Dr Richard Warren, before going to his grandson Richard and his great-grandson Arthur.

The memorials in Tewin church give us more information about the Warren family. First we have on the north wall of the Nave, the arms of Warren quartered with Collet and underneath the following inscription:

> In a vault in this church lies ye body of Mary Warren, wife of Richard Warren of Marden, Esq. daughter of Joseph Collet of Hertford Castle, Esq. a woman of extraordinary sweetness of temper, great probity, and extensive knowledge; she died December 28th 1733 in the 31st year of her age leaving two sons, Arthur and Collet.

Underneath is a verse in praise of Mary Warren who was wise, humble, fair and 'chaste as a Roman dame'. This is followed by the reference to Dr Richard Warren already quoted. Underneath this is the Latin inscription 'Ricardus Warren ortus comitibus de Warren et Surrey, natus A.D. 1686, obiit 1768', confirming that the family was descended from the Earls of Surrey.

It will be remembered that Clutterbuck states that Marden passed from Richard Warren to his 'only son' Arthur Warren, so it appears that the other son, Collet, died in infancy. We have one more reference to Arthur Warren and to his wife Mary, whose children are buried in the churchyard at Hertingfordbury. The inscription reads:

> Here are interred Arthur Warren, son of Arthur Warren Esq. and Mary his wife, late of Marden in this County, who died January 28 1762 aged 9 years. Likewise Louisa Warren, their daughter, who died August 25 1762 aged two years. Also, Frances-Maria Warren their daughter, who died Sept. 14 1762 aged three years. Mary Warren, wife of the above mentioned Arthur Warren, died the 11th of November 1787 aged 57.

It must have been a very sad time for Mary and Arthur, losing three of their children in one year. The two little girls probably died of smallpox, which was the most frequent cause of death until the introduction of vaccination in the 19th century.

There are very few further references to the Warren family of Hertfordshire - the only significant entries being in the Hitchin Parish Registers:

> 20th August 1688 - baptism of Jacob son of William Warren als. Wood de Gosmore

> 5th March 1688/9 - marriage of Edward Warren de Clothall and Elizabeth Wood of Bigrave.

This shows the Warren family once again taking an alias (we already have Waller and Bygrave). There is almost certainly a family connection here, but it does not give the necessary link between William of Bygrave and the Richard who inherited Marden from Edmund Field.

The most likely theory is that the first William on the Ashwell tree was the son of William and Juliana Nedham, (young William who had to sell the manor of Bygrave to pay his debts). He married Elizabeth Hammond and they had a son Edward and also a son William. Edward was the grandfather of Dr. Richard Warren of Marden and William was the grandfather of Ann Harmer. We know that Ann's grandfather was William, and that he married Ann Skegg in 1638. Their son John was born in 1639, and his daughter Ann was born in 1676.

This would mean that Ann was the second cousin of Dr. Richard Warren of Marden, and the second cousin twice removed of Mary Nedham. The fact that Ann is two generations further down the Nedham family tree than Mary, is due to the fact that John Harmer's second marriage took place more than 40 years after his first marriage, when he was 70 years old. And so the story continues.

Marden Hill, Tewin, home of the Warren family 1692-1785

Chapter 15

John Harmer 1628 - 1711

John Harmer, the eldest son of George and Rebecka, was married to Mary Nedham of Wymondley Priory sometime between 1655 and 1658, but we have no record of the marriage. One possibility is that it took place in the private chapel at the Priory, and the record never found its way to the Parish Registers. Alternatively it could have taken place outside the county - possibly a clandestine marriage, like that of his daughter Frances some years later.

There is already the mystery of George's will, and how John could possibly have managed to get it proved within 17 days of his father's death. This was the time of the Commonwealth and strange things were happening in high places. The bishops had been dismissed, and all wills had to be sent to London to be proved. George Harmer made his will on January 4th 1655, died on the 6th, was buried on the 8th, and the will was proved on the 25th. John must have been desperate for money, and the moment his father was buried he possibly took off for London, galloping down the Great North Road, changing horses at Barnet, and arriving in London before nightfall. There he perhaps persuaded one of his influential friends to put the will on the top of the pile, and within three weeks it was proved and John was able to claim his inheritance.

After the marriage John and Mary settled down in the family home at Dane End, where John would now be head of the household, responsible for looking after his widowed mother, his younger brothers and sisters, and his new wife. Having obtained access to his father's estate he would now be able to pay off some of the debts which had been accumulating in recent months. There would also have been a good dowry from Mary's father, Eustace Nedham, which would help the financial situation. In July 1658 Mary gave birth to their first child - a daughter, who was named Frances after her grandmother Frances (Wingate) Nedham, and her great-great-grandmother Frances Docwra.

After this, babies arrived in quick succession. George was baptised in September 1659, Barbara in November 1660 and Nedham (named after his grandfather) in 1661. During this time there was great rejoicing throughout the country. The bleak days of the Commonwealth were over, and on May 29th 1660, on his 30th birthday, the young prince came back in triumph to take his place as Charles II of England. The theatres were re-opened and soon a new generation of playwrights, including Wycherley, Congreve and Farquhar, were producing plays which delighted their audiences, but would have shocked even the most broad-minded of the Puritans.

What John and Mary felt about all these political, religious and moral controversies we do not know, but George Nedham, Mary's brother, later felt it his duty to tell tales about Sir John Docwra's political views. In the Quarter Sessions of 1689, when William and Mary had recently taken over the throne from James II, the following case is recorded:

> Mr. George Nedham maketh oath that Sir John Docwra said that King William was no King and that the parliament now sitting was no parliament, till King James should get his throne at Whitehall again.

The Docwras, like the Coningsbys, were staunch royalists during the Civil War, and were later supporters of James II, who fled to the continent because of opposition to his Roman Catholicism. This opposition became especially strong when he had a son by his second wife Mary of Modena, (he had only daughters by his first wife Anne Hyde). The baby, James Edward, would have been heir to the throne, with the possibility of continuing the Catholic monarchy.

It is unlikely that John and Mary had much time for politics, though they still had relatives who were taking an active part in the affairs of state, and they would have been very aware of all that was going on at Westminster and Whitehall. But John was busy with his estates, while Mary was running the house and looking after the family.

As in the previous century, there was a great deal of organising to be done in the country house, especially during the winter months. The outside servants would see that the dove-cote and stew ponds were well stocked, and the warrener would ensure an adequate supply of coneys - but the lady of the house would have to plan all the meals, and supervise the kitchen and the brewhouse.

Once again the Becher family archives give an idea of the kind of food which would haver been prepared for special occasions. The menus in Mrs Becher's 'Dinner Book' for 1709 include: Buttock of beef, chine of mutton, Pigg, roast tongue and udder, Scotch collops, scorseneroe pye, a jole of sturgeon, snipes, larks, and Hogee Pogee (perhaps an early version of Lancashire Hot Pot!) The favourite vegetable seems to have been boiled or roasted 'heartychoaks', but they also had 'spinnage' and cabbage.

Wool from the sheep would still be spun and probably woven in the manor house to provide cloth for household needs, though as they moved towards the 18th century, some of the crafts were becoming more specialised. Various commodities like furniture and cloth which were previously made at home would now be bought in the local towns. Many gentlemen obtained licences to hold a Fair once or twice a year, and here the local people, both from the manor house and the cottages, would stock up with items which could not be produced at home. One very famous fair was the Barnet Horse Fair, which continued right up to the beginning of the present century.

Only one baptism is recorded between 1661 and 1669. This was Thomas, baptised at Weston in 1665. But there were two sons, Eustace and Edward, who do not appear in the registers, and it is likely that they were born during this period.

In December 1669 another daughter was born. She was baptised Rebecka, a name which had appeared in four successive generations, going back to her great-grandmother Rebecka Piggot of Tewin. The next child, Margaret, was baptised in 1671, and another baby, probably still-born, in 1673. Joseph was born in 1674 and finally Dorseus in 1675. Poor Mary had now given birth twelve times during the eighteen years of her marriage, and all but one of the babies had survived. A few years later Mary herself died, but we have no record of her burial.

We now come to the point where some of the events in the family history seemed too strange to be true. The general rule with family research is to begin with the most recent ancestors and work backwards. This we did quite successfully with help from parish registers, wills and Land Tax Assessments. But it is also possible at the same time to discover some of the more distant ancestors, assuming from their names and places of birth that they will eventually fit in somewhere. There comes a time when the two pieces of research will meet, and with any luck join neatly together to form a continuous family tree. But in the case of the Harmers, the two halves just would not fit together. There seemed to be a missing generation which had completely disappeared.

We had worked our way back to 4 x great grandfather John Harmer, who was born in 1701, and forward to John Harmer who was born in 1628. Now we were looking for the son of the older John, who must be the father of the younger. No such person could be found and it seemed that we should never get back beyond 1701. But from time to time a thought occurred - could the John born in 1628 be the father of the John born in 1701? It seemed most unlikely but finally we were able to prove that he was. Our 4x great grandfather was born when his father was 73 years old! At last the tree fitted together, and we had a continuous line right back to 8x great-grandfather Thomas, who was born about 1530.

If Mary Nedham died about 1676, John would have been forty-eight years old. He had eleven living children, ranging from eighteen-year-old Frances to Dorseus who was only a baby. It would have been understandable if at this stage John had looked for another wife, to help run his home and care for the children. But this was not the case. His second marriage did not take place until twenty-two years later.

It would have been a hard time for the older girls, Frances and Barbara, who with the help of the servants, looked after their younger brothers and sisters. For a few years their grandmother Rebecka would have been alive to give help and support, but she was now an old lady, probably living in Hertford, so the young family would have had to manage mainly on their own.

Quite soon came the time when Frances would expect to be married to some wealthy young squire. Girls were often married at sixteen or seventeen, and if they reached the age of twenty without finding a husband, there was cause for concern. Perhaps John could not afford to provide a suitable dowry, or perhaps he simply wanted to keep Frances at home to run the house.

By the age of twenty-five Frances was getting desperate, and decided to take matters into her own hands. On August 2nd 1683 she ran away to London with a certain James Oldham, and they were married at St James's Duke Place. A note in one of the many Guide Books on genealogy gives the following information, which is particularly interesting in view of the fact that a member of our family formed part of the statistics:

> From 1660 so-called clandestine marriages (i.e. without
> banns or licence) took place, especially in London - at

Fleet Prison Chapel, at 'marriage houses' in the Liberties of the Fleet etc. **Some 40,000 marriages took place at St. James's Duke Place between 1664 and 1694.**

The priests in charge of these various churches or chapels were unscrupulous enough to waive the rules in order to obtain the often substantial fee which was demanded, and young couples would come from all parts of the country.

We hear no more of Frances, except that she is mentioned in her father's will, so he obviously forgave her. He left her only £5 (equivalent to £500 today), but this was quite usual for a married daughter, who would have already received a dowry of some kind. Frances was to receive the £5 only if she came personally to demand it. This was to make sure that she really did receive it herself, and that it did not disappear into someone else's pocket.

The second daughter, Barbara, perhaps also seeing visions of lonely spinsterhood looming on the horizon, found her own way of dealing with the situation. Not a clandestine marriage this time, but an illegitimate baby! Her daughter Joanna was baptised at Weston on 2nd May 1697. Later that year, on November 1st, Barbara was married at Ayot St Peter to Thomas Stanton, presumably the father of her child. Again John remembers her in his will, and leaves her £5 to be paid at the rate of 4 shillings a year. It would therefore be twenty-five years before she received the final payment, by which time she would be seventy-six years old (if she lived that long).

It seems that John provided Barbara and her husband with a cottage on the estate, because in his will he mentions three cottages, one of which is occupied by Thomas Stanton. These cottages sound very pleasant, with orchards, buildings and four acres of pasture land, so Barbara and her family probably lived very comfortably, even if it was not a 'mansion house', which she might have expected if she had been provided with a good dowry and a wealthy husband. We know nothing of Thomas Stanton or his family, but Nicholas Pevsner in his 'Buildings of England', makes frequent references to Edward and William Stanton who were very talented sculptors, and whose work can be seen in many Hertfordshire churches. It is possible that Thomas Stanton was a member of the same family.

Less than a year after Barbara's marriage to Thomas Stanton, John himself decided to embark on a second marriage. His new wife was

Ann Warren and, as we have seen, she was a distant cousin of his first wife Mary Nedham. The marriage took place on August 2nd 1698 at Ayot St Peter, where Barbara had been married the previous year. It may be significant that Ayot St Peter at this time was performing marriages from all over the county, for those who for some reason did not wish to be married in their own parish. We get the impression that these marriages were carried out quietly, perhaps even secretly, and the situation later presented to family and friends as a 'fait accompli'. The fact that Barbara had an illegitimate daughter, and John was a seventy-year-old widower with eleven grown-up children, may account for the fact that in both cases a quiet wedding seemed more appropriate.

The following year John and Ann had their first child - a daughter Elizabeth, baptised at Aston in May 1699. Sadly the baby died the following year and was buried at Weston in March 1700/01. By this time Ann was expecting her second baby, and in July 1701 a son John was born. He was our 4x great grandfather.

It is surprising that John the father, being the sort of person he so obviously was, had not already given his name to one of the sons of his first marriage, but apparently not. This son was to become his heir, which again is rather surprising, when he already had five sons from his first marriage. It may be that these older sons were to inherit considerable wealth from the Nedham family - possibly one of the reasons why two of them had been given Nedham names.

The next child, born in 1703, was another daughter - again named Elizabeth, which seems to suggest that this was the name of Ann's mother. This Elizabeth also seems to have died, because she is not mentioned in her father's will. In 1705 there was a son Joseph, suggesting that at some time between 1674 and 1705 the first Joseph had died (though sometimes two or more living children had the same name). In 1706 there was another son, a second George, who later married Rose Watts of Ickleford, and then Mary Lanton of Ashwell. Finally, John and Ann had another daughter Phyllis who was born in May 1711. John was now eighty three years old, and he died a few months later, after a full and very eventful life. He was buried at Weston, probably in the family vault, but again no memorial remains.

John's will was made in September 1711 and proved in January 1711. From this it appears that the death took place before the will was made - but we have to remember that until the calendar was changed in

1751, September came before January. (To save confusion, the months from January to March are often written with two year-numbers, the year that ends in March followed by the year that begins in April.) It is a lengthy and detailed will, almost certainly written entirely in John's own hand. The writing is bold and clear, indicating that at the age of eighty-three he was showing no sign of physical or mental frailty.

In addition to the bequests to Frances and Barbara already mentioned, he leaves £8 to his daughter Welles (probably Margaret), £10 to Eustace, 40 shillings to his brother Edward (married to Elizabeth Flindell), and just one shilling to his son Edward. Edward was married to Sarah Jepps, a member of a well-known family of millers who owned land in and around Weston. One of their descendants married into the equally well-known Bonfield family, some of whose 20th century descendants live in Southampton, and others in Toddington in Bedfordshire.

The 'daughter Welles' may have married into the Welles family of Gaddesden. The 1593 list of contributors to the defence of the kingdom mentions Thomas Welles of Gaddesden, while the 1590 list mentions Thomas Welles of the Howe. John of Baldock also speaks of a debt owed by a certain 'Welles' so there may already have been family connections.

John's largest bequests go to the four surviving children of his second marriage - John, Joseph, George and Phyllis, who each receive £100, to be paid at the age of twenty one. There is also an extra £20 for each of the boys, to apprentice them to a good trade. John is included in this bequest, even though he is to inherit all his father's property in Weston and Walkern.

Newberry Wood is specifically mentioned in the will, also a pasture called Duffads near the tile kiln. John's widow Ann has the three cottages for her life-time, after which they also go to John. These three cottages were still known as 'Harmer's Row' right up to the beginning of the present century. Newberry Wood later became known as Harmer's Wood, and another meadow, part of the old Dane End Farm, was known as Harmer's Close, names which are still in use today.

In addition to the rents from the cottages, Ann is to have an income of £5 a year, to be paid to her by her son John at the rate of £1-5s every quarter. It is to be hoped that young John behaved better than his father, and paid up without being taken to court.

John has now brought us into the 18th century. The age of the Tudors and Stuarts is coming to an end, and from now on there will be rapid changes in the economic and social history of the country.

King William, of whom Sir John Docwra so strongly disapproved, has now been succeeded by his sister-in-law Queen Anne. Although John Docwra and his fellow Jacobites are still hopeful, neither James Edward Stuart (the Old Pretender) or his son, Bonnie Prince Charlie, will ever occupy the British throne.

For the Harmer family too it is the end of an era. It is apparent from John's will that he is still a wealthy man - the £500 in bequests alone would be equivalent to at least £50,000 today. But it is also apparent that he is now splitting up the estate. Much of the property has been sold, and the proceeds divided amongst his children. Although young John is the heir, and will have Dane End farmhouse and probably a good sized farm in Weston, he will now have to earn his living. He will no longer be a 'gentleman' living on the income from his estates, but will join the ranks of that very worthy section of society - the yeoman farmers.

From now on we shall find no more family details in the history books and for this reason we know less about the 18th and 19th century Harmers than about their Tudor and Stuart ancestors. But the story goes on, and we now follow the family into the final chapters, which lead us through the 18th and 19th centuries and up to the present day.

Wymondley Priory, the home of John Harmer's first wife, Mary Nedham.

This view shows part of the mansion house built by Mary's great-grandfather in the 16th century.

Chapter 16

The Yeoman Farmers

John Harmer, the eldest son of John's second marriage, was only ten years old when his father died in 1711 at the age of eighty-three. Although there were several sons of the first marriage, it was John who was named as the heir, and at twenty one he would inherit Dane End, together with various cottages and lands in Weston and Walkern - remnants of the Newberry Manor estate.

Meanwhile, life at Dane End would have continued much as before. There were no financial problems for the moment, because the recent sales of land had provided enough capital for Ann and her young family to live quite comfortably. Ann remarried in 1714. Her husband was Samuel Mead, a tailor, and they had one son, Samuel.

In 1733 John was married to Mary Ralphs, the daughter of Daniel Ralphs, a yeoman farmer who had property in Baldock and Sandon. The marriage took place at Therfield, probably Mary's home church, and the young couple settled at Sandon, where they either owned or rented a good-sized farm. The Land Tax Assessments for Sandon, of which only a few have survived, show John Harmer in 1745 paying a yearly land tax of £17-12-0, which indicates a farm of several hundred acres. John Harmer was one of the Assessors, and his signature appears on all the Assessment schedules until 1755. After this there are no more surviving records until 1780, when the Assessors were William Harmer, (John's son) and John Skegg, who was probably a relation of John's mother Ann Warren.

A year after their marriage John and Mary had their first child - a son called John. He was baptised at Weston in October 1734, but died a few months later. The next two children, Elizabeth and Ann, were also baptised at Weston, but the three youngest were all baptised at Sandon - William in 1741, Margaret in 1747, and John in 1752.

The youngest son, John, our ancestor, was to be the next heir. This followed an established custom amongst the yeoman farmers - a trend frequently observed in our own family research, and later confirmed as a widely established practice known as Borough English. The yeoman farmers would expect their older offspring to go out into the world and seek their fortune. Many would go on from the local grammar school to university and enter one of the professions. Some would become merchants or businessmen, millers, brewers or bankers, while others, like some of the younger sons of the gentry, would be apprenticed to a 'good trade'. Sometimes they would acquire land by marrying the daughter of a farmer or gentleman who had no sons, and others might inherit from an uncle who had no heirs of his own. Meanwhile, the youngest son would stay on at home, working on the farm and gradually taking over from his father. Finally, when his father died, he would inherit the property.

The definition of a yeoman is 'a man owning and cultivating a small landed estate', but in fact he was not necessarily the owner. There were many kinds of tenancy at this time, and some were almost identical to a freehold. The basis of English land law was that all land was owned by the Crown. A small part was in the Crown's actual occupation, while the rest was held by tenants either directly or indirectly from the Crown. 'Nulle terre sans seigneur' (no land without a lord) - this was the law, and it can be traced back to 1066 when William I regarded the whole of England as his by conquest. Most of the 'tenants' were in fact powerful Land Lords, who had been granted control of the land by virtue of some favour done for the sovereign. The Land Lords would divide the land into smaller estates, and their tenants would probably do the same.

There were three types of tenancy. The land might be granted **for life** (as long as the tenant lived), **intail** (as long as the tenant or any of his descendants lived) or in **fee simple** (as long as the tenant or any of his heirs, whether descendants or not, were alive). Each of these lengths of tenancy was know as an 'estate' (from the word 'status'). Thus a man could own an estate, yet never own any of the land itself. Ownership of an estate in fee simple has come more and more to resemble ownership of the land itself, but even today it is technically true to say that all the land in England is owned by the Crown.

To confuse matters even more, one could add yet another kind of tenancy - **in male-tail**. This rather bizarre term simply means, as one might expect, that only male descendants were eligible to inherit, and if there were no sons or grandsons, the property might revert to the Crown. This was one of the possibilities investigated in the Inquisitions Post Mortem, which have been mentioned several times in previous chapters. The Crown would grasp every possible opportunity to acquire some of the property when a wealthy landowner died.

One of the main differences between the prosperous yeoman and the country gentleman, was that the yeoman would normally have only one property where he lived and took an active part in the work of the farm. He might employ a large number of labourers, but he, and certainly his sons, would work alongside the men, as well as doing all the organising and accounts.

The 'gentleman' would probably do none of these things - certainly not the manual labour. Apart from the home farm, which would produce food for the manor house, all the properties would be let to tenants, and the gentleman would live entirely on his rents. This was sometimes a precarious livelihood, as we have seen in past generations.

On the whole the 18th century yeoman's sons tended to be more highly educated than the sons of the gentry, who would not expect to earn their own living. Many of the leading doctors, lawyers and theologians came of good yeoman stock, though the politicians and statesmen, as well as the country parsons, were more often drawn from the gentry and nobility.

Although it was John, the younger son of John and Mary, who was to inherit the family farm at Dane End, the elder son, William, did inherit the farm at Sandon, which was probably part of his mother's dowry from the Ralphs family. We discover from the Land Tax records that William took over the Sandon property around 1765 (probably at the time of his marriage to Ann Hazard) and soon afterwards the parents, John and Mary, moved back to Weston.

By this time the two older daughters were already married. Ann was married in 1756 to John Doo, whose signature appears on the Land Tax Assessments for Therfield and who had several properties there. Elizabeth was married the following year to John Knight, who also had land in Therfield.

It is difficult to picture exactly what had been happening at Dane End since John Harmer's death in 1711. It was still the main family home, and Ann, John's widow, was entitled to live there for the rest of her life. For much of this time she probably managed the farm, with the help of some of her sons and step-sons, but by the time she died in 1749 most of the children had married and moved away. It is possible that John may have put a bailiff in charge of the farm until he was ready to come back and take over his inheritance. If, as we can assume from the Land Tax Assessments of Weston and Sandon, John and Mary moved back to Weston in 1765, they would have been in their early sixties, and only their two youngest children were still living at home. Margaret would have been eighteen and John, the heir, about thirteen, having been born in 1752 when his mother was 49 years old.

But although John and Mary were no longer young, the old house at Dane End was soon to become a real family home once again - perhaps for the very last time.

In 1773 Margaret was married to Robert Farr. Once again the marriage took place at Sandon, where there were obviously strong family ties, but the Farrs seem to have been a long-established Weston family. According to the Land Tax records, Robert owned a small property in Weston, while a certain Thomas Farr, probably his father, rented a very large farm (taxed at £30-12-0) from William Hale.

Then in 1776 young John Harmer was married to Sarah Fisher. Again the marriage took place at Sandon, which was probably Sarah's home. The Fisher family had been Lords of the Manor of Therfield until 1714 and still held land in the area. But there is no evidence that the young couple ever lived at Therfield or Sandon, even though their first two children were baptised there. It seems likely that John, with his young family, stayed on at Dane End, gradually taking over from his father as he grew older.

By the time John the elder was writing his will in 1780 it was quite clear that he had handed over the property to his son, with the knowledge that there was now a new generation to continue the line of succession.

At this time there would have been three grandchildren, Penny, four years old, John aged three, and Mary just a baby. George, our great-great-grandfather, was born three years later.

All the children would have known and loved their grandparents. We can imagine them walking together through the beautiful woodlands and pastures which surrounded the Dane End farmhouse, and on Sundays making their way across the fields to the old church where their ancestors had been baptised, married and buried from far-off times, even before records began.

John lived on for another seven years, dying in 1787 at the age of 86. His will shows that young John has inherited not only the manor house and farm, but also a cottage in Warrens Green (occupied by William Humberstone), 'my acre of land in Walkern' (which seems to have had some special significance), and a silver tankard. Elizabeth inherits a cottage with outbuildings and land in Weston Town, while Ann, the wife of John Doo, gets his silver boat and silver pint mug. Margaret, the wife of Robert Farr, gets five guineas. He leaves an annuity of £15 to 'my loving wife Mary'. Mary died two years later in 1789, having lived, like John, to be 86 years old.

Young John and Sarah went on to have a large family, 4 sons and 6 daughters, and they were the last generation of Harmers to be born and brought up in the old manor house at Dane End. They were a healthy family, and all grew to maturity except for Martha, the youngest, who died in 1818 at the age of twenty, just a year after her father, and two years before her mother. All three are buried in one grave in Weston churchyard, where their memorial stone still remains.

The Weston Land Tax Assessments now give a record of how the family land was finally dispatched. The records from 1780 onwards give both the name of the proprietor and that of the occupier.

In 1780 we find that the proprietor of the Weston property is John Harmer senior, and the occupier John Harmer junior. From 1781 to 1794 the proprietor is John Harmer and the occupier is 'self' - so this means that John the elder actually handed over to his son between 1780 and 1781. There are no records between 1794 and 1798, but during this time John evidently sold the farm to John Pryor who was now Lord of the Manor of Weston.

The Pryor family were originally brewers from Baldock, and for many years they had been anxious to buy up the remaining properties in Weston. But a few of the very old families, including the Harmers, had tried desperately to hang on to at least a small part of their ancestral lands. Now however, the family obviously needed the capital, so they reluctantly agreed to sell, and remain as tenant farmers. As we have seen, some of the old tenancies were almost identical to freehold possession, but this would not be the case with the new tenancies.

In 1798 the Tax Assessment document shows that the last of the Harmer lands have gone. It states 'Proprietor - John Pryor. Occupier John Harmer'. From 1799 to 1811 the entries are the same, after which there are no more records until 1826, when the two Johns have been succeeded by two Thomases. It states 'Proprietor Thomas Pryor.

Occupier Thomas Harmer'. The final entry in 1831 states 'Proprietor - widow of Thomas Pryor. Occupier Thomas Harmer. Rent £39. Tax £4.11.0.' Thomas was the third son of John and Sarah, not the youngest or the oldest, but he was the one chosen to inherit the tenancy.

Sometime between 1831 and 1841 Thomas seems to have exchanged his tenancy of Dane End for the tenancy of Hall's Green Farm - formerly known as Fairclough Hall. This was now also in the possession of the Pryor family. The census of 1841 and also 1851 shows Thomas Harmer living at Hall's Green Farm, the home of his Fairclough ancestors, and his two brothers George and Joseph are working on the farm.

Thomas was married to Martha Ballard and they had four daughters, including Sarah, a doiley-maker, who married William Aylott, a farmer from Walkern. There had been one son, Thomas, but he seems to have died in infancy. So when Thomas Harmer died there would be no more Harmers owning or occupying the farms of Weston.

George and Joseph, our two great-great-grandfathers, inherited no land, although they each had a cottage from the original estate, and probably a small share of the capital which came from the sale of Dane End. George was able to afford an apprenticeship for his son William, who was later able to buy his own house and workshops at Aston, where he built up a successful wheelwright's business.

George was married in 1806 to Elizabeth Goldsmith of Baldock. The Goldsmith family owned property in and around Baldock, and they were also tallow-chandlers. Elizabeth seems to have inherited money from her Goldsmith and Gilbert ancestors, and appears in the 1851 census as a widow of independent means.

George and Elizabeth had five sons, John, George, Joseph, Thomas and William (the wheelwright). There was also one daughter, Sarah, married to James Breed of King's Walden.

Thomas was married to Mary Palmer, and several of their descendants have been traced, two in Australia, and others in Maidenhead, Basingstoke and St Albans. Joseph married Elizabeth King, and they had twin daughters, Sarah and Elizabeth, born in 1838. George married Susan Turner whose family were carpenters at Weston, and John married Charlotte Green. Charlotte was the daughter of a London merchant, and came to Hertfordshire as a governess. Their descendants now live at Redbourn, where they are not only carrying on the family tradition of farming, but also preserving the family name, with three Harmer sons born within the past nine years.

About our other great-great-grandfather, Joseph Harmer, we know very little. He was married in 1813 to Ann Dearmer, a member of a local family who were previously connected with the wealthy Underwood family, and in the 19th century were blacksmiths in Weston. Joseph had a son John and two daughters, Sarah and Mary. Mary later married her cousin William (George's son).

Although we know so little about Joseph there is one thing which makes him seem very real. His name appears on the 1871 census, when at the age of eighty he was living with his daughter Mary, our great-grandmother, at Aston. We have a photograph of Mary, and when we look at this little old lady, we realise that she would have known all about Dane End, and probably loved to listen to stories told by her father Joseph, of his childhood in the old family home.

William Harmer son of George, and Mary Harmer daughter of Joseph, were married at Weston in 1839, but moved away two years later. During the next thirty years the Harmer name in Weston gradually died out. It is still remembered because of field and place names such as Harmer's Wood and Harmer's Close, but apart from this all trace of the family has now disappeared. In the archives, however, and among those who study them, the parish of Weston will always be remembered as the Harmer family home.

Dane End, Weston, home of the Harmer family for 300 years

Chapter 17

The Wheelwrights.

In 1835, towards the end of the reign of William IV, William Harmer, son of George and Elizabeth and grandson of John and Sarah, began his apprenticeship to Thomas Lawman, the village wheelwright at Weston. The original indenture certificate has survived, and was passed on to us recently by our cousin Maurice Castle, the grandson of William's younger daughter Mary-Ann. The apprenticeship in the Art of a Wheelwright was to last for a term of five years during which time, '... the Apprentice his master faithfully shall serve, his secrets keep, his lawful commands everywhere gladly do.'

The sum of eighteen pounds was paid, and for this the master promised to teach and instruct his apprentice, provide him with tools, lodgings and sufficient meat and drink and other necessaries except clothes and medical attendance in case of sickness or accident. The contract also stated that the apprentice:

> ... shall not commit fornication nor contract Matrimony within the said Term, shall not play Cards or Dice Tables or any other unlawful games ... he shall neither buy nor sell, he shall not haunt Taverns or Playhouses nor absent himself from his said Master's service day or night unlawfully.

Presumably William fulfilled these conditions to the satisfaction of his master and became a fully-qualified wheelwright. The census for Weston village in 1841 has the following entry: 'William Harmer - Age 25 - wheel.' It also records that he has a wife Mary age 20, and two little sons - Thomas age 2, and Eli - 6 months. But since the apprenticeship would not have been completed until 1840, it seems that Thomas Lawman must have bent the rules slightly. We know that William was married in April 1839 to his cousin Mary Harmer and that their son Thomas was baptised two months later. William at this time was actually 26 and Mary 22, (ages in the 1841 census were calculated to the nearest 5 years) so they probably felt they had waited long enough!

Ten years later, according to the 1851 census, the family had moved to Aston. By now they had six children, though baby Eli had died. Thomas was eleven, and then there was Noah eight, Sarah six, Charles four, William two, (our grandfather) and another little Eli, just three months old. As eight-year-old Noah was baptised at Aston, we assume they moved there from Weston sometime between 1841 and 1843.

In the 1861 census there were four more children: George, Mary-Ann, Joseph and Frederick, and the family was now complete - eight sons and two daughters. The two eldest sons were already described as wheelwrights, and all the other children were 'scholars', even three-year-old Frederick.

By 1871 Mary was a widow, and she herself was described as a wheelwright, as well as Head of the family. Charles, William, Eli and George were also wheelwrights, presumably all working in the family business, or perhaps having workshops in neighbouring villages and living at home. The two eldest sons, Thomas and Noah, seem to have gone away. William their father had died in 1870, at the age of 56.

But as we mentioned in an earlier chapter, there was now one other member of the household, whose name links us with the far-off days of Weston Dane End where he was born. This was Joseph Harmer, wrongly described in the census as 'father-in-law'. His relationship to Mary was of course father, but the enumerator was probably confused because his name was Harmer. Joseph died two years later, and was buried at Aston.

In 1881 there were just three names in the census, Mary and two of her sons, George and William. Mary is still 'Head' of the family, but is no longer described as 'wheelwright'. At the age of sixty three she had presumably retired from active participation in the business.

We have now come to the point where we can draw on the reminiscences of two remarkable people - William John Harmer, (our Uncle) and his cousin Alice, the daughter of Mary Ann Harmer and William Penn. Alice was born and brought up in Aston, where her parents kept the Rose and Crown Inn. She spent a great deal of time with her grandparents, William and Mary, who lived nearby.

When they first moved to Aston, William and Mary kept the inn, now the Rose and Crown but then known as The Boot, and ran their wheelwright's business from there. As trade increased they needed bigger premises, and bought a cottage with buildings and land just

Mary Harmer born at Weston 1817.
Died at Aston 1905

May and Alice Penn photographed
outside the Rose and Crown about 1910

The Rose and Crown at Aston, probably a few years later than the photograph above.
The McMullen's sign over the door perhaps indicates that it has now been sold to the brewers.

across the road. It was a large and rambling cottage with two staircases, one rather wider than usual leading up from a lobby off the main living room. There were three storeys, providing plenty of room for the growing family.

The old family home, now known as Wisteria Cottage, still stands in Aston. It is thought to date back to Tudor times, and may at some stage in its history have been used as a place of worship. Recently some old wall paintings were discovered in one of the upper rooms and they have been carefully preserved behind glass panels. Presumably the Harmer family had no idea they were there, unless of course they were the ones who papered over them in the first place!

Cousin Alice told us many stories about her grandmother, Mary Harmer of Aston, whom she loved very dearly. 'Grandmother Harmer always worked hard, both in the house, and when necessary in the workshop. Grandfather and all the boys wore white shirts, and Grandmother used to make them herself, and laundered them with great care. You can imagine the washing and ironing! She had a woman to help her, but never trusted her with the shirts.

'She cooked wonderful meals for the family using a big kitchen range, but she never used the Dutch oven. That was where she kept all her valuable papers and documents. One day someone lit the fire under the Dutch oven, and all the papers went up in smoke! But Grandmother didn't blame anyone. They were only old bits of paper, she said, and it was no use crying over spilt milk. She was a very sweet lady, always kind and gentle. Many people would come to her for advice, because of her wisdom and understanding.'

We only knew Cousin Alice during the last few years of her life, but it seemed that she had inherited many of the same qualities which she described in her grandmother. We met her for the first time when we went to fetch the old oak dining table, reputedly made by our great-grandfather, which she wanted us to have because she knew we had a large family, (four sons and one daughter, exactly half the size of great-grandmother's family). The table is roughly made (unlike the beautiful carts and carriages made in the Harmer workshops) but it is greatly valued because of its family associations. It is made of solid oak planks which were probably lying around in the workshop at Aston, and was perhaps put together in a hurry when great-grandmother suddenly decided she could no longer fit all the children round the existing table. She may even have made it herself. She certainly sawed off all the corners at one stage, because the younger children kept bumping their heads on them.

We were also given several other family heirlooms including a hundred-year-old paisley shawl, two 'witch balls' and great-grandmother's **best** bellows, which her family were never allowed to poke into the fire! One of the witch balls, made of blue glass, has been passed on to our grand-daughter Emily who will probably pass it on to future generations.

Alice lived to be 94 and died on Christmas Eve 1981, her active and intelligent mind undimmed right to the end. She had a premonition that she would die on that day, and was quite happy to face death, as she had faced every crisis in her life, without fuss or drama. Her mother had also died at the age of 94, and she too had died on Christmas Eve.

The other source of information was William John Harmer (known as Jack), the son of William Harmer and Mary Hare, and the older brother of our father Thomas. He himself was a wheelwright, and when he died in 1987 at the age of 99, we found in his workshop a book in which he had started to record his memories, mostly incidents from his boyhood and early manhood in Hertfordshire. Some were recounted in detail; others were just headings, tantalising hints of stories which now will never be told.

As children we loved to visit him in his workshop, with its special smell of new wood and turpentine. We would play with the curly shavings which fell from his plane and sometimes he would light up the forge just for us, so that we could pull on the bellows, and see the coals glow red and the sparks fly up like a golden fountain.

Like his cousin Alice, Jack had a wonderful memory, and all the details which he told us, when checked with the records, were invariably found to be correct. Just before he died he talked to us about his early life at Aston and Watton-at-Stone.

'I understand my grandfather moved to Aston in the 1840's and took the Inn, now the Rose and Crown. Later he moved to premises just across the road. The house is still there, I am told, and that is where my father and my aunts and uncles were born, and I was born there too.

'My father and all of my seven uncles were wheelwrights. Most of them set up businesses in the surrounding villages, but Uncle Joe took a job in London as a wheel-maker, piecework, and took on his younger brother Frederick as a dowel and wedge-maker as soon as he was old enough to leave home. Later on he took over the business and became a successful coach-builder, making beautiful coaches and carriages for the London tradesmen and gentry.'

When Jack was about two years old they moved from Aston. 'The Woodhall estate always kept a full-time wheelwright, so Uncle Noah, and then Uncle Charlie took the job at different times. When Uncle Charlie left, father took over, leaving Uncle George to look after the Aston shop with one nephew.

'We went to live at Tonwell and the first thing I remember is going to Tonwell school equipped with a little green bag and a slate, and being rolled over in the road by one of the bigger boys on my way home. Then we moved to Sacombe to be nearer the Woodhall works, and I had two miles to walk to Sacombe school.'

Jack recalled some of the early Christmases of his childhood, 'We used to walk up to Sacombe House for the school treat. When we arrived we had to stand in line and Sir Samuel Smith gave us all a silver threepenny bit. On one occasion he missed me. I was in a real stew! I couldn't eat my tea. So later in the afternoon I plucked up courage and told Sir Samuel he had missed me out. He promptly put his hand in his pocket and gave me sixpence!

'Then came the time to stay with grandmother and grandfather Hare for the Christmas holidays. We travelled with the carrier, Walter Hornett, who lived near our grandparents at Aston End. Walter had a small-holding and took his produce to Ware about twice a week. As our house at Sacombe was near the main road he always used to call and have a cup of tea and rest his horse, as that was about half-way. He had a covered cart, so brother Tom and I were snugly packed in for the journey to Aston End. When he got home we had to go into his house and wait until he put his horse up and unloaded. Then he would walk with us to grandmother's house - about a quarter of a mile. Grandmother would say "You will surely stop and have some supper with us, Walter." Walter never refused, and then he gave them all the town talk and various news he had heard on the journey.

'When he had gone grandmother made the beds lovely and warm with a copper warming pan filled with hot embers from the fire. There was a huge open fireplace, seven or eight feet wide with a blazing log fire. Brother Tom used to sit one side and I the other, and look up at the stars.

'We used to spend the harvest holidays at Aston End too. No doubt we were very useful to take messages and carry cans of beer to the men. One extra helper for harvest was a very strong man known as Plunkey Will. He used to do a lot of scythe work on the hills to save the horses pulling the heavy old sail reaper. Plunkey Will used to take on piece-work, hedging, ditching and draining for the surrounding farms. A week or so before harvest he would call and see grandmother and tell her what wonderful crops they had got, and would they want him this year? Her reply was "Of course, you know you always come for harvest." He would then explain how he had set out that morning at 9 o'clock to collect a little money, but all his customers were out and he hadn't had a mite to eat or drink all morning. That brought a response from grandmother, "Fetch Master Maynard a jug of beer."

'There was always a quart jug on the dresser, so Master Maynard was lucky. It was my job to make sure the jug was kept full. I had to tap the barrel and if it began to "sound" I had to report that it was getting empty.

'There was only one shop in Aston End, and it was a great treat to go with grandmother to Liza Newland's general store and help carry the various "goodies" home, and then save up to buy something we had seen, on our next trip to the shop. We used a short cut up Lanterns Lane, and on a summer afternoon it was a lovely country walk.'

When Jack was about eight Uncle Joe in London wanted extra help with the expanding business, so it was decided that Uncle Eli and his two grown-up sons should join the London shop and Jack's father would take over his shop at Watton-at-Stone.

'My only dread of going to Watton was that there was a schoolmaster there - we had a lady teacher at Sacombe - but I needn't have worried. Mr Richards was strict but always kind and just. He was also choirmaster and organist and he got me to be his organ-blower which carried a salary of £1 a year plus special occasions. Once a year we had to go to Woodhall House to play the hymns for the missionary service. As the organ was in the next room I had to listen and hear if we were in time with the congregation. The butler, who was a choir member, always said we were quite in time. My worst job was to keep from falling down on the highly polished floors.'

As Jack grew up he began to learn the trade. He could make a wheelbarrow body before he left school, but the art of making a wheel would not be learnt until a little later, when he became a full-time apprentice. Both his sisters went to Ware Grammar School but Jack and Tom seem to have had a very sound education at the village school, where the standards were remarkably high. Both boys stayed at school to the age of 15, and learnt algebra, geometry and trigonometry.

As soon as he left school Jack joined the other two apprentices in the workshop, but three years later William Harmer died as the result of a tragic tree-felling accident, and at 18 Jack had to take over the business. Fortunately his father had lived long enough to give him a good basic training and he had a natural talent for the work.

The wheelwright was one of the most skilled of the country craftsmen. Not only did he have to be good with his hands, but he had to have the eye of an artist, and a sound understanding of mathematics. Every measurement had to be deadly accurate - a wheel that was less than perfect was completely useless.

In later years the segments of the wheel (felloes) were machine-made and bought in, but at this time every part of the wheel was made by hand - including the iron rim. Most of the wheelwrights had some 'smithing' skills and could carry out all the complicated procedures involved in making a wheel, but they would often employ a smith who would specialise in the metal work. The wheelwright would not only make and repair carts and carriages but would also make ploughs and harrows and repair other farm machinery.

Artistic skills were needed in the designing and finishing of each piece. Farm wagons were real works of art, with their gracefully curved sides and elegantly painted wheels with the spokes outlined in yellow or gold.

Sign-writing was another skill required by the wheelwright, for every farmer or tradesman would have his name and address in beautiful lettering on the sides of his carts and wagons. Jack had a special talent for this and became well known in the district for his workmanship.

The wheelwrights would go round the countryside and choose their wood while it was still growing. They looked for trees which would give the correct curves for shafts or sides. Sometimes they would tie the branches so that they would grow to a certain curve - then they would have to wait a year or two before they could be used. It has been said that one generation of wheelwrights prepared the wood to be used

Above:
William Harmer born at Aston 1849.
Died at Watton 1907.

Left:
Alice Penn age 22. Born at Aston 1887.
Niece of William above.

The Wheelwright's shop at Watton-at-Stone in 1911, with Jack (left) and Thomas, the sons of William above. On the far right are the two daughters May and Emma.

by the next. Different kinds of wood were used for each part of the wheel - oak for the spokes, elm for hubs and beech for felloes. The wheelwright would not only need to know his trees, but also understand the habitat, as different soils affected the nature of the wood.

The travelling sawyer would usually do the felling. There would be a pair of sawyers to every four or five villages and they had their own saws, between 5 and 8 feet long, and their own sharpening tools and equipment. The wheelwright would get one of his farmer customers to cart the tree to the workshop, where he would have his own saw-pit.

Then the sawyers would come and saw the wood into planks. It would then be stacked, with little pegs between the planks to let the air circulate, and left to season for a year or two before it was ready for use. The wheelwrights did some of their own sawing - with the young apprentice in the pit. It was very tiring work and the youngster couldn't stop and rest, except when the saw needed oiling.

Thomas always remembered working in the saw-pit, pulling on the heavy saw hour after hour after hour, with the saw-dust cascading down and sticking to his sweaty face and arms.

The 1914 war was to bring changes to the family. Tom by now had a small but thriving herd of cows, and the wheelwright's business was employing several men and training new apprentices. Both Tom and Jack were in reserved occupations because the farmers could not function without the wheelwright to mend carts and implements. But it was felt that one of the brothers should go and fight for King and Country, so Tom volunteered.

At home Jack and his mother coped with the business and with Tom's cows and milk-round. Both the village blacksmith and their own smith had gone to France, and they were left with a retired farrier to do all the shoeing of both horses and wheels.

Jack was kept busy from early morning to late at night. Sometimes after dark there would be a knock on the door - and there was a ploughman with a broken whippletree which was urgently needed first thing in the morning. So Jack would go out and light up the forge - and sometimes work until the early hours to get it finished.

Fortunately Tom survived the war and came back to take over his cows and horses, while Jack was able to concentrate once again on his carts and carriages. But things were getting very difficult for the wheelwright. Jack recalls the problems of the post-war years:

'After the war things were never the same again. Some farmers were going out of business and told us "Don't do too much to that cart - by this time next year I shall be finished."

'One thing that hit us hard was an end to the yearly credit. Ever since my grandfather's time we had had a yearly account with the wholesale ironmongers in Hitchin. Then they gave up and we had to deal with the London houses. They gave us a monthly account, so it was a case of a friendly visit to our customers saying "Please can you pay us a little off your account, as we have to settle our bills before next week". We used a good many tons of iron in those days. All the wheels had iron rims, each weighing about 70lbs.'

With the coming of motor transport things became even worse, as there were fewer wheels to be repaired. There was also one practical difficulty which Jack describes. 'Our workshop at Watton was right on the main road, and with the coming of motor traffic we got a lot of dust blowing in. When we heard a heavy lorry coming it was a case of "Quick, shut the paint-shop doors" or hours of work would be ruined.'

For the Harmer family 1927 marked the end of an era. The small country wheelwright was finding it more and more difficult to make a living, and Jack and his mother decided to sell up and move to Suffolk where Tom was farming and the two sisters were teachers. 'I didn't like the idea of parting with the tools that had been in the family for so many years so I railed them all down to Suffolk and set up the forge and wheelwright's shop there.'

But he never built up a real practice again. The demand for skilled wheelwrights was gradually dying out as tractors and metal-wheeled trailers replaced the horse and cart. In any case, the Suffolk villages already had plenty of craftsmen of their own. Every county had its own traditions, and a Hertfordshire wheelwright would not necessarily be acceptable to the Suffolk farmer.

After his mother died Jack moved several times in Suffolk and Norfolk. His sisters retired early from teaching and together they bought and restored several beautiful old farmhouses. But every time Jack moved - the tools moved with him - even the forge, the lathe and the metal shoeing plate! And it was here, in his workshop amongst his precious tools that we found his book of memories.

It was here too that we found a half-finished wheelbarrow, started not so very long ago, just before old age and frailty forced him to put down his beloved plane and chisel for ever. A wheelbarrow was probably the first thing he ever made. It was also the last. The wheel had come full circle.

William John Harmer was the last of the Hertfordshire Harmers, certainly in our branch of the family. Some of his uncles and their sons lived on in the county and carried on as wheelwrights for a few more years. But by 1939 the trade was almost dead.

Our story, however, is not quite finished. Thomas Harmer, the last name on our tree, has not played an important part in this chapter because he was not a wheelwright. He decided to follow his mother's family tradition and become a farmer, not knowing that he was also following the tradition of his distant Harmer ancestors as well. He spent most of his young life at Watton-at-Stone and, like his brother Jack, he had many memories of Watton and Woodhall Park, the 'big house', where so many of his Boteler relations had lived in earlier generations. So now we go back once more to Watton-at-Stone, for one last glimpse of the Harmers of Hertfordshire.

Watton Church about 1871. As restored by J Clarke, Esq., Architect

Chapter 18

Memories of Watton-at-Stone

William Harmer, our grandfather, born at Aston in 1849, was a fully-qualified wheelwright by the age of twenty. For several years he worked for the family firm, and later took over from his brother Charles as estate carpenter for the Abel Smiths at Woodhall Park. In 1883 he married Mary Hare, the daughter of William and Eliza Hare of Aston End, whose ancestors had been farmers at Thrales End, near Harpenden, since the seventeenth century.

The marriage, for some reason which we have never discovered, took place in London, at Emmanuel Church, St Marylebone. The address for both William and Mary is given on the marriage certificate as 35 Lyons Place, which may have been the town house of the Abel Smith family. When the Squire went to London for the 'Season' some of his staff would go with him including, perhaps, the estate carpenter who would look after the carriages and the daily carts which would come up from Watton, bringing fresh vegetables from the Woodhall gardens, and milk, butter and cream from the home farm. At the time of the marriage Mary was already expecting their first child, (Eliza, who died two years later) so they possibly decided to get married quietly in London, before returning to Aston with the new baby.

We knew and dearly loved our grandmother Mary. She was a wonderful lady, whose mind and memory were alert and clear right up to the time she died at the age of 99. She often told us stories of Thrales End Farm where she spent her childhood, but she never talked about the early years of her married life.

Our father, Thomas Hare Harmer, was the second son, born at Tonwell near Ware in 1891. His older brother was William John (Jack), born in 1888, and there were two sisters, Emma, born in 1893, and May in 1895. The family moved to Watton-at-Stone when Thomas was about five years old, and he lived here until his marriage in 1923.

Mercy Galbraith, our mother, seems to have come to Watton quite by chance, and the story of how she and Thomas met and fell in love has been re-told many times in the family.

Watton-at-Stone was one of the larger villages in the area, with three inns, various shops and small businesses, a Wesleyan Chapel and a handsome parish church. Most important of all was the 'Big House', Woodhall Park, the home of the Squire, Colonel Abel Henry Smith. All the village children used to curtsy or bow when the squire drove past, all except our mother, who flatly refused!

The parish church played an important part in the lives of all the inhabitants. All the Woodhall estate employees, (and that meant most of the village) were obliged to go to church, whether they were Christian or agnostic. Our grandparents would probably have gone anyway - grandfather and young Thomas sang in the choir, and for many years Jack was the organ-blower.

The history of the church goes back to 1221, when the first rector is recorded, but there was probably a Saxon church on the site before the conquest. The earliest brass is to Sir Philip Peletoot who died in 1361, and there is a brass effigy of a priest about 1370. There is also a large marble memorial to John Boteler of Woodhall, who died in 1774. The Harmers must often have looked at this memorial, little knowing that John Boteler was one of their kinsmen.

Our parents often talked about Watton, and many of the names became quite familiar to us in our childhood. It was interesting recently to read the well-known names in the Hertfordshire Directory for 1906. Good old Dr. Hodges was listed as 'Herbert Chamney Hodges LRCP Lond. of Watton Cottage, surgeon, medical officer and public vaccinator'. The rector was the Revd. John MacInnes MA of Pembroke College Cambridge. The curate was the Revd. Allen Ellison MA and he lived at Ardoyne House.

In the Commercial Section of the directory are the names of tradespeople who were neighbours and friends of our grandparents. Grandfather is listed as William Harmer - wheelwright. There is also George Jepps - tailor; William Bonnet - baker; Harry Wilson - grocer, draper and furniture dealer; Charles Penn - tobacconist and cycle agent; Walter Scowen - miller (water mill); William Hedger - Fly proprietor; and Cecil Peck - relieving officer, vaccination officer and registrar of births and deaths. There was also Arthur Parker who kept a coffee tavern. Perhaps he was an enthusiastic supporter of the Band of Hope, which our mother joined when she first came to Watton as a child.

Drink was a serious problem at this time, and many good, hard-working people were ruined by alcohol addiction. Several of the

Mercy Galbraith and Thomas Harmer 1916.
Thomas served in the 5th Lancers from
1916-1918

Thomas's sisters, Emma and May Harmer - about 1916

maiden ladies of the village, including Miss Mercer, Miss Pritchard and the Misses Newman, as well as the ladies from Woodhall, would spend their time doing 'good works'. This would include running Bible Study classes, sewing classes, Girls' Friendly Society, and Band of Hope. Our mother 'signed the pledge' at the age of 10, and took the promise so seriously that she never drank alcohol (except Communion wine) throughout her life.

The farmers of Watton named in the 1906 Directory were Frederick Newman of Watton Place, Richard Gubbin of Bardolf's Farm, and Kenneth Douglass of Broom Hall. The Douglasses, a delightful Scottish family, were great friends of our mother, and we had tea with them at Broom Hall on one of our childhood visits to Watton.

The Harmer family was very much part of the local community. Grannie was a great character, well known in the village as a no-nonsense type of woman, but always ready to help anyone in need. She was renowned for her generosity, while at the same time having a reputation as a shrewd business woman, refusing to pay a penny more than she thought the goods were worth. The tradespeople and wholesalers in Hertford and Ware came to know her, and treated her with respect. She tended (right to the end of her life) to buy groceries in bulk as far as possible, thus paying wholesale prices.

Uncle Jack once told us, 'Mr Raiment of Hertford supplied us with all our groceries for the year, and my father looked after all his delivery vans and carts. At the end of the year we settled the accounts and we usually had about £50 to take.'

The wheelwright's shop at Watton was at the far end of the village, right opposite the Waggon and Horses, and this was the end of the round for various tradespeople. The baker would call on Grannie and she would buy up any cakes and rolls he had left over - at a bargain price of course! The family were always pleased if there was gingerbread, which was particularly good.

Thomas Harmer had always planned to be a vet, like his uncle Thomas Hare, but when his father died this was not possible. He would have to stay at home and help run the wheelwright's business. But Tom was still determined to work with animals. He already had a horse and two ponies, and now he began to build up a herd of cows. He bought some buildings next door to the wheelwright's shop, and rented the meadow opposite, which ran down to River Beane. Soon he was able to start his own milk round in the village. His mother was delighted - she was re-living her old life at Thrales End. Jack was now running the wheelwright's business, and Grannie was helping both Tom and Jack, besides looking after the house, and cooking for her four children and two apprentices.

The two girls were at Ware Grammar School, and times were hard for the family. There were occasions when a calf had to be sold to pay the school fees and Auntie May remembered doing her homework whilst looking after the cows on Watton Common. In the winter the girls lodged in Ware and came home at weekends. They had only one bicycle between them, so one would ride a certain distance, then leave the bike by the roadside and walk on. The other sister would pick up the bike and ride on until she caught up with, and overtook the other, and the whole process would be repeated all the way home.

Grannie always had a great admiration for Miss Brough, the headmistress of Ware Grammar School who was always so supportive and encouraging. Probably Miss Brough also had a great respect for Mrs Harmer, the widow who was determined to give her daughters a good education.

To us as children the most familiar of the Watton names were the Scowens and the Hedgers. They were good friends of the Harmer family and also had close connections with our mother.

Emmeline Scowen was a Hedger before she married, and her mother, old Mrs Hedger, had been nanny to the Abel Smith children, possibly for two generations. The family and all the village were very fond of her. She was a woman of wisdom and insight, and people came to her with their troubles, though she had plenty of troubles of her own, poor lady. Her husband, William Hedger, had been coachman at Woodhall, but sadly he became addicted to drink. When he became too unreliable to continue as coachman the Squire provided him with a cottage, from which he ran his own business as a Fly Proprietor.

There was always a demand for transport to Ware and Hertford for the London trains, or for business and shopping. Mr Scowen, the miller, also kept several horse-drawn vehicles for hire. Whenever Mr Hedger or Mr Scowen were particularly busy they would ask young Thomas Harmer to help out. From the age of thirteen Thomas had been driving the governess cart, and he much preferred this to helping in the wheelwright's shop.

One summer's day in 1905 a message came from Mr Hedger, asking if Tom could go to Ware to meet the London train. Fourteen-year-old Tom as usual was only too pleased to oblige. But as he set off from Watton in the pony cart that afternoon, he could not have guessed that this would be a journey he would remember for the rest of his life. The visitors he was about to pick up from the London train were a rather stern middle-aged lady and a little girl called Mercy - who would one day become his wife.

Our mother, Mercy Galbraith, came to Watton when she was ten years old. For as long as she could remember she had lived at Brookleaze House, a small private orphanage in Bath. There were only ten little girls who had all grown up together, and they were lovingly cared for by Miss Palmer and Miss Phillips, with Miss Fennal the cook, and two young maids called Marie and Miriam. They were brought up strictly, but there were plenty of treats too. There were picnics at Little Salisbury Hill, summer holidays at Weston-super-Mare, and Christmas outings to Evans and Owens to look at the toys, with the excitement of riding home in a cab. In fact, they had to take **two** cabs, and even then they had to sit on each others' laps.

When the Home closed early in 1905, it seemed to Mercy as if her whole world was coming to an end. All the other children were to be adopted, some by local families, and the others were to sail with Miss Palmer to Canada. Mercy's aunt did not wish her to be adopted and hoped to find a home for her within the family.

There were tearful 'Goodbyes' as one by one the little girls left for their new homes. The saddest time of all was when dear Miss Palmer left with the last of the children. Mercy loved Miss Palmer more than anyone else in the world. Miss Phillips was rather severe, and Mercy was very much in awe of her. Both ladies, however, remained life-long friends, and I remember them as sweet old ladies, dressed in black satin and lace, who often came to stay with us during my childhood.

Miss Phillips and Mercy were the last to leave Brookleaze House. Mercy remembered going round the empty rooms, so quiet and strange now that all the lively little girls had gone. Then the cab arrived at the door, and Mercy and Miss Phillips set off on the first stage of their journey to London.

They stayed at various places in London, a few weeks with Mercy's Aunt Marion, and several months with an Italian family called Stopani, and then, for some reason which remains a mystery, Mercy was sent to stay with the Miss Goodwins at Watton.

And so it happened that my mother and father met for the first time at Ware station that summer afternoon in 1905. Tom was not usually very interested in the visitors he fetched from the station, but he always remembered the little girl in the sailor suit, with a boater hat and long golden curls, who never stopped talking all the way home! He had no idea of course that she would one day be his wife, or that the rather forbidding lady who accompanied her would become a close family friend. Miss Phillips stayed a few days to see Mercy settled, then went back to London, presumably to take up a new appointment as nanny or governess. It was many years before Mercy was to see her again.

Miss Goodwin and Miss Kitty Goodwin were genteel maiden ladies. They seem to have had no experience of children, but Mercy was happy there. Her own impression was that she was very naughty, and they were surprisingly tolerant. She remembered putting the cat in the bath to see if it would swim. It jumped out and ran all over the house, leaving a trail of water on precious carpets and furniture.

The ladies must have become very fond of her because years later, when they died, they left her the wicker-backed rocking chair which she loved to sit in when she first came to live with them. The chair which came from Watton so long ago is still in the family, and Mercy's great-grandchildren now love to rock in it.

Although Mercy's stay with the Goodwins was not intended to be permanent, arrangements had been made for her to go to the village school. On the first morning of the autumn term, two little girls came to escort her. One was the headmaster's daughter, Gwennie Richards, and the other the daughter of Mr Peck, the Relieving Officer. These two little girls, and Ina Douglass from Broom Hall, became Mercy's best friends. The Pecks were a large, happy family and Mercy was often invited there for tea, or for birthday and Christmas parties. I think some of the wonderful Christmas parties which our mother organised when we were children were modelled on the parties she enjoyed so much with the Peck family at Watton.

The Miss Goodwins were friendly with Mrs Scowen at the Mill House, and sometimes visited there, taking Mercy with them. The Scowens had one little girl, Marjorie, who was about seven years old. Mercy was so good at playing with Marjorie, and inventing games to

Left:
Mercy Galbraith aged 2
at Brookleaze House. Bath.

Below:
Mercy's granddaughter Susan
also aged 2.

Below left:
Great- granddaughter Emily
in the rocking chair where
Mercy loved to sit when she
came to Watton in 1905.

keep her amused, that she was frequently asked to come and keep her company.

Early in 1906 Mercy's aunt wrote to say that she had not been able to find a home for her and she would have to go to Canada after all. Soon came the time for more sad farewells. Mercy had made many friends during her eight months in Watton and was just beginning to feel settled. Her dear friend Ina Douglass gave her a parting present. It was a small green address book. My mother used it all her life, and fortunately it has survived to this day. Inside the cover a childish hand has written with great care:

From Ina Douglass to Mercy. Apr. 17 (06).

Mercy would never forget that journey back to London. This time there was no Miss Phillips to accompany her, and she travelled alone in the care of the Guard. She was very frightened, and desperately worried that there would be no-one to meet her. Her imagination conjured up visions of White Slave Traders, who would kidnap her, and subject her to unspeakable horrors!

Mercy spent the next few weeks in London with her aunt, buying clothes and getting ready for the journey to Canada. Then one day Aunt Marion told her they were going to Liverpool Street to meet someone. When the train arrived, to Mercy's surprise, there was Mrs Scowen from Watton.

Mercy remembered the two ladies walking backwards and forwards up and down the platform for what seemed like hours. She knew they were discussing her future, but had no idea what was being planned. Later she was told that the Scowens had kindly offered to adopt her.

I think my mother was pleased to go back to Watton, but the thing that concerned her most was the address book. Ina Douglass never ceased to tease her about accepting a parting present, and then coming back again. Although she knew it was only in fun, Mercy was very embarrassed, and never forgot it.

The next few years were not easy. Mercy had to get up early to clean the fireplaces and prepare breakfast before she went to school, and was kept busy in the evenings until she went to bed. But it is possible the various duties were no more than would have been expected from a daughter in a busy household. Mercy had no experience of ordinary family life. At Bath there was a Cook and two maids, and the children were never allowed in the kitchen. The new life certainly came as a shock. She had no idea how to peel potatoes or prepare vegetables, and the cold water made her fingers ache. When she asked for warm water she was told not to be such a baby.

Incidents like this, which my mother remembered more than seventy years later, would probably have gone unnoticed in the security of a normal home. But Mercy's past life had made her sensitive and vulnerable, and she was hurt because she felt she was not really treated as a member of the family.

She was never legally adopted and refused to be called Mercy Scowen. The Scowens instructed the school about the change of name, but Mercy absolutely refused to answer to any name except Galbraith, and I think Mr Richards understood, and didn't insist. In all the changes of her young life, her name was the only thing that really belonged to her.

Mercy left school at the age of thirteen. Children were allowed to leave provided they could pass an examination. This meant that some of the brighter children missed out on education which could have been valuable to them.

When she was seventeen Mercy decided she would like to become a hospital nurse. She wrote to The London Hospital, but was told she could not begin her training until she was eighteen. Feeling that she really needed to move away and become independent she took a job as a Nursery Maid with the Kindersley family at The Mill House, Codicote. There were five children, Edmund, Ruth, Bridget, Hallam and Barnabus. Mercy was now happier than she had been since she left her childhood home in Bath.

After several years as Nursery Maid she was ready to take a post as a Nanny. She had four happy years looking after little Peter Seebohm, son of the Quaker banking family at Harpenden, and stayed with him until he went away to school. Next she looked after Betty Snook, another loveable little girl, and finally she went to the Goldings at Upton House in Hertford.

Mr Golding was a Vet, and they were a delightful family. Mercy really went there to look after four-year-old Janie, but there were two slightly older children, Mary and Jimmy, who had the reputation of being very naughty. Mary had even been known to **swear**! It seems to have been a 'Mary Poppins' situation, though I never heard that they put pepper in Nanny's tea! They soon became good friends and grew

Thomas and Mercy in 1927 with their daughters Mercy and Evelyn.
The first harvest at Laurel Farm, Brundish, Suffolk.

Right:
Thomas with his grandson Patrick
in 1963.

Below:
John and Evelyn Wright
Christmas 1995.

Evelyn Harmer, the younger daughter of Thomas
and Mercy, married John Wright in 1952. They
have 5 children: David, Susan, Peter, Patrick and
Andrew; and 4 grandchildren: Emily Jennifer,
Sarah and Catherine

Apologies to any future grand-children who have
not found a place in this book.

very fond of each other. Mercy was extremely happy there, and only left to get married in 1923.

Mercy was surprised when she received a letter from Tom Harmer in 1916, saying he would like to come and say 'Goodbye' before he went away to join the army. They had known each other since Mercy came to Watton ten years earlier, and Mercy was a great friend of Tom's sisters, Emma and May, but never had any particular feelings about Tom. She mainly remembered him galloping down the lane and round the corner at break-neck speed, riding one pony and leading two others, when he came to water them at the pond opposite the Mill House where she lived.

But Thomas had always had a special affection for Mercy, the little girl he fetched from the station when she was ten years old.

As the war entered its third year, there was great pressure on the young men to join the army, even if they were not conscripted, and Thomas, the gentlest and most unwarlike of men, had volunteered because he felt it was his duty. Being an experienced horseman he was drafted into a cavalry regiment, the 5th Lancers, and was sent for training to the Curragh Camp in Ireland. When he came home on leave for Christmas 1916, Tom and Mercy became engaged.

After the war Tom returned to Watton. His mother had looked after the livestock while he was away, and now he started to raise a herd of pedigree Dexter cows. But it was several years before he could afford a farm where he could settle down and support a wife and family. Tom's two sisters were by now teaching in Suffolk, and they suggested that Tom might look for a farm there, where property was less expensive.

On November 24th 1923 Thomas and Mercy were married at Watton Church. They left the same afternoon for their new home in the depths of rural Suffolk, where Mercy, with typical enthusiasm, set about adapting to her new role as a farmer's wife. They lived happily in Suffolk for fifty years. Thomas died in 1973 at the age of eighty two, and Mercy lived to be ninety one.

And that really is the end of the story. Thomas and Mercy had no sons to carry on the family name, but they have many descendants, who will perhaps read this history and hand it on to the next generation, helping to keep alive the memory of our Hertfordshire ancestors.

Appendix A

Pedigrees and Biographies of inter-related families in Hertfordshire, Bedfordshire, Suffolk, Essex, Kent and Sussex.

Contents

Some of the names have alternative spellings with variations occurring within
a single document but in general one spelling only has been used in these pedigrees.

Pedigrees are arranged in alphabetical order as far as possible, with
exceptions in some cases to accommodate a double page when necessary.

Abbreviations:

osp - obit sine prole (died without offspring); **M.I.** - Memorial Inscription; **m** - married
d - daughter or died (according to context)

↓ with name of pedigree in brackets indicates that the line continues in the named tree.
If there is only a reference, with no continuation, the note (see ---- tree) is used

The Anderson Family
of Eyworth, Bedfordshire

SIR EDMUND ANDERSON, Lord Chief Justice, sat in trial of Mary Queen of Scots. Bought the manor of Eyworth in 1594.
Married Magdalen Smyth of Annables Manor. Magdalen's nephew, Sir George Smyth, married the daughter of Sir Rowland Lytton of Knebworth. (see Lytton tree)
Sir Edmund Anderson bought the manor of Edworth and also Stratton & Holme from the Piggot family in 1588. He died there in 1605.
There is an altar tomb in Eyworth church.

SIR FRANCIS ANDERSON, d. 1616 (Monument in Eyworth Church)

m.① Judith, d. of Sir Stephen Soame, a relative of the Hunt and Knighton families. (see Soame tree)

m.② Audrey (or Etheldred), d. of Sir John Boteler of Hatfield Woodhall and Elizabeth Villiers (Sister of the Earl of Buckingham)

WILLIAM ANDERSON

ELIZABETH ANDERSON

GRIZELL ANDERSON
m. Sir George Booth of Shrublands, Suffolk

MARGARET ANDERSON
m. Sir Richard Gadbury.
d. 1624 (Brass on the chancel floor at Eyworth)

EDMUND ANDERSON
of Stratton. d. 1638
m. Alice, d. of Sir John Constable, Viscountess Verulam and Baroness of St Albans. d. 1656

SIR STEPHEN ANDERSON
Created Baron 1664
m. Mary ... who died 1667.

SIR JOHN ANDERSON
osp

MARY ANDERSON
Died young

The Anderson Family
of Pendley in Aldbury, Hertfordshire

SIR JOHN ANDERSON, Sheriff of London.
m. Elizabeth, d. of Sir Francis Bowyer, Alderman of London
(Her sister Margaret m. Sir William Spencer)

FRANCES ANDERSON
m. Robert Nedham of Shropshire

MARY (or SARAH) ANDERSON
m. Sir John Spencer of Offley
(see Spencer tree)

SIR RICHARD ANDERSON. d. 1632.
Sheriff of Herts 1610.
m. Margaret, d. of Robert Spencer, baron of Wormleighton, Northamptonshire (see Spencer tree)

ANDERSON. *Argent a cheveron between three crosses paty sable.*

SIR HENRY ANDERSON
m. Jacomina, d. of Sir Charles Caesar of Benington (see Caesar tree)

ELIZABETH ANDERSON
m. Robert, s. of Sir John Peyton of Dunnington, Isle of Ely

ROBERT ANDERSON

JOHN ANDERSON

WILLIAM ANDERSON

RICHARD ANDERSON

MARY ANDERSON

FRANCES ANDERSON

MARGARET ANDERSON

CATHERINE ANDERSON

DOROTHY ANDERSON

PENELOPE ANDERSON

ANNE ANDERSON

BRIDGET ANDERSON

2 April 1629 - Henry Bull married Katherine Anderson.

Date unknown c.1600 - Edmund Bressey married Katherine Anderson.

Descent of the Argenteins and Alingtons
Lords of the Manor of Wymondley and Cupbearers to the King

DAVID DE ARGENTEIN a Norman who served under William the Conqueror

JOHN DE ARGENTEIN, m.Ellen Fitzteck. Fought with King Stephen (1135-54) against the Empress Matilda, and is thought to have built Great Wymondley Castle. (Earthworks to the east of the parish church)

REGINALD DE ARGENTEIN. d. c1217. A grave slab in Baldock church possibly commemorates this Reginald, though some think it was his great-grandson

RICHARD DE ARGENTEIN. d.1246. Sheriff of Herts and Essex, Governor of Hertford Castle. In 1225 his name appears as one of the witnesses to the Statute of Magna Carta, which set out the provisions made in 1215. It was this Richard who founded the Priory of Austin Canons at Little Wymondley.

GILES DE ARGENTEIN, d.1283. Fought with Henry III in Wales, but later rebelled and fought against the King at Evesham. He was later pardoned and his lands restored. The Inquisition Post Mortem mentions his office as Cup-bearer to the King

ARGENTEIN. *Gules three covered cups argent.*

REGINALD DE ARGENTEIN 1240-1307. Inherited all the family lands, including at least 17 manors in Cambs, Suffolk, Norfolk and Herts. m. Laura de Vere, sister to the Earl of Oxford. (This could be the Argentein who is commemorated in Baldock church - opinions differ.)

JOHN DE ARGENTEIN. d.1318. Described as 2nd Baron Argentein. he m. Agnes Beresford. His tombstone was once on the floor of Little Wymondley Church, but was removed, or covered up, in the restoration of 1875. It is likely that John was originally buried in the Priory Chapel, but was re-buried in the parish church when the Priory was suppressed in 1537.

JOHN DE ARGENTEIN 1318-83. Performed the office of Cup-bearer at the Coronation of Richard II in 1377. He m. Margaret Darcy and had 3 daughters. He also had an illegitimate son William, who managed with difficulty to gain the right to inherit his father's property.

WILLIAM DE ARGENTEIN, d.1419. He re-built the Hall (Wymondley Bury) and this is mainly the building which we see today. His son John predeceased him and he was succeeded by his granson John - 5 years old

JOHN DE ARGENTEIN, 1414-20. He only outlived his grandfather by one year, dying at the age of 6. He was the last of the Argenteins to be Lord of Wymondley. His two heirs were his sisters, Joan, aged 13 and Elizabeth, aged 12..

JOAN DE ARGENTEIN m. Robert Alington, osp, Joan's sister Elizabeth inherited the manor.

ELIZABETH DE ARGENTEIN m. William Alington. Inherited the manor of Wymondley

JOHN ALINGTON, d.1480. m. Mary Cheney

SIR WILLIAM ALINGTON, c1449-1485, m. Elizabeth Wentworth. Killed in the battle of Bosworth

SIR GYLES ALINGTON, 1483-1521. Until he came of age Wymondley was controlled by his guardians Richard Gardiner and Sir Gilbert Talbot. m① Margaret Spencer of Althorpe (see Spencer tree), m② Mary Gardiner, d. of his guardian

SIR GILES ALINGTON, 1500-86, m① Ursula Drury (see Soame tree), m② Alice Middleton. He outlived his son Robert and grandson Giles

SIR GILES ALINGTON, 1572-1638, succeeded his great-grandfather at the age of 14. m①, 1594, Dorothy Cecil, m② the daughter of his half-sister. For this "incestuous match" he was fined £32,000 by the Star Chamber and pardoned "on condition that he did not live with his niece of the half blood". His daughter Ann m. Sir Thomas Fanshawe of Ware Park (see Note (*2) on Soame/Alington tree)

WILLIAM ALINGTON 1610-48, m.Elizabeth Tollemache. Created Baron Alington of Killard by Charles I in 1642.

WILLIAM ALINGTON d.1684, Created Baron Alington of Wymondley by Charles II in 1682. m. Diana Russell (who later sold the manor of Wymondley).

HILDEBRANDE ALINGTON became 4th Baron of Killard on his nephew Giles' death. He bought back the manor in 1704. He died childless in 1722 and the manor went, in equal shares, to his 3 nieces.

GILES ALINGTON 1681-91. 3rd Baron of Killard & 2nd Baron of Wymondley. At his death, aged 10, the Wymondley title became extinct. His uncle Hildebrande inherited the Irish title. Due to a faulty will Giles' mother, was able to sell the land, which had been in the family since the Norman Conquest, to Elizabeth Hamilton (d. of Lord John Culpepper - see Roper tree)

JULIANA ALINGTON m. Viscount Howe

DIANA ALINGTON m. Sir George Warburton. Their d. Diana (*1) m. Richard, Lord Grosvenor, who acquired the other two thirds of the manor

CATHERINE ALINGTON m. Nathaniel Napier

(*1) Diana's husband Richard became Lord of the Manor but it is unlikely that members of the Grosvenor family ever lived at Wymondley. Sir Richard Grosvenor sold the manor in 1767. It went to the Wilshere family, and William Wilshere was the last to perform the ceremony of Cup-bearer at the Coronation of George IV in 1820. The house and land had already been sold (in 1806) to the Heathcote family, who were descendants of the Nodes family of Shephall (see Nodes tree).

The Barnardiston Family
of Suffolk and Bedfordshire

THOMAS de BARNARDISTON, of Barnardiston in Suffolk, lived in the reign of Edward II (1307-27). m. Margery, d. of William Willoughby of Suffolk

SIR THOMAS BARNARDISTON lived in the reign of Edward III (1327-77). m. Lucie, d. of Robert Havering of Norfolk

BARNARDISTON.
Azure a fesse dancetty ermine between six cross-lets argent

WALTER BARNARDISTON lived in the reign of Richard II (1377-99)m. Frances, d. of Thomas Kingsman

THOMAS de BARNARDISTON

JOHN BARNARDISTON of Keddington and Barnardiston. (osp)

ROGER BARNARDISTON of Grimsby, d. about 1440 m. Elizabeth, d. of Sir Edmund Perpoint

THOMAS BARNARDISTON of Suffolk. m. Joan Vavasour

WALTER BARNARDISTON - Clarke of the Church of Keddington, Suffolk at the time of Henry VI

SIR THOMAS BARNARDISTON of Keddington at the time of Edward IV, Edward V and Richard III. m. Elizabeth, d. of John Newport of Pelham in Hertfordshire (connected with Bulls and Casons)

SIR THOMAS BARNARDISTON of Ketton (Keddington). m. Ann, d. of Thomas Fitz Lucas of Saxham.

A daughter, m. Thomas, Lord Audley, Chancellor of England

GEORGE BARNARDISTON, m. Elizabeth, d. of Thomas Burley of Lynn in Norfolk. In 1543 he acquired Ickwell Bury in Northill, Bedfordshire

SIR THOMAS BARNARDISTON, m. c1520, Mary, d. of Sir Edward Walsingham, Lieutenant of the Tower. (Mary later m. Francis Clopton of Kentwell)

JOHN BARNARDISTON of Ickwell Bury, m. Joan, d. of Thomas Mellor (or Miller) of Lynn in Norfolk. Joan d. 1568. John d. 1587 (buried in the aisle of Northill Church)

ELIZABETH BARNARDISTON m① ... Brookesbye. m② Francis Clopton (see note 1 below)

SIR THOMAS BARNARDISTON m① Elizabeth Hanchett m② Ann Bygrave (alias Warren) of Hertfordshire

ANN BARNARDISTON m.1610, William Clopton (brother of Elizabeth's second husband, Francis)

GEORGE BARNARDISTON of Ickwell Bury. d.1577. m. Mary, d. of Sir George Perient of Digswell. (see Perient Tree)

MARGARET BARNARDISTON, m. 1573, William Fyshe of Stanford Manor in Southill. The Old House at Ickwell Green came to the Fyshe family from the Barnardiston estate.

SIGISMUND BARNARDISTON m. 12th June 1582 at Northill to Mary Wynche (d. 1594)

① ②

SIR THOMAS BARNARDISTON m. Mary, d. of Sir Richard Knightly of Fawsley.

GYLES BARNARDISTON of Clare in Suffolk m. Philippa, d. of Sir William Waldegrave of Smallbridge in Bures, Suffolk (see Waldegrave Tree)

ROBERT BARNARDISTON of Ickwell Bury. m. Katherine, d. of George, son of John, the first Lord Mordaunt of Turvey. (see Mordaunt Tree)

SIR WILLIAM FYSHE of The Old House, Ickwell Green m. Elizabeth, d. of Sir Thomas Barnardiston of Suffolk (his 3rd cousin once removed) (Fyshe Tree ↓)

↙

HANNA BARNARDISTON m. John Brograve of Hammels in Hertfordshire, (Related to the Leventhorpes of Shingle Hall and to the Brownes of Abbess Roding)

SIR NATHANIAL BARNARDISTON m. Jane, d. of Sir Stephen Soame (Lord Mayor of London in 1598) and grand-daughter of Ann Knighton and Richard Hunt. (see Soame and Hunt Trees)

ELIZABETH BARNARDISTON m. Sir William Fyshe (her 3rd cousin once removed)

↗

HENRY BARNARDISTON of Ickwell Bury, d. 1640. m. Margaret, d. of Robert Hares of the town of Bedford

RICHARD BARNARDISTON of Ickwell. bapt 19th August 1604

ROBERT BARNARDISTON, d. 1652. In 1680 his son George conveyed Ickwell Bury to John Harvey

NOTE 1: There were many connections between the Barnardistons and the Cloptons of Kentwell Hall. Around 1540 Francis Clopton married Lady Mary Barnardiston, widow of Sir Thomas Barnardiston, and afterwards he married Sir Thomas's daughter Elizabeth (the widow of .. Brookesbye). His brother William Clopton married Sir Thomas Barnardiston's other daughter Anne.

From the Parish Registers:
In 1567 George Barnardiston married Mary Clopton at St Mary's, Bury St Edmunds.
In 1610 Ann Barnardiston, d. of Sir Thomas Barnardiston, married William Clopton at Clare.

Note from White's History of Suffolk: Sir Thomas Barnardiston of Keddington was created baronet in 1663. In the reign of Queen Anne two baronets of the family sat in Parliament at the same time - Sir Samuel and Sir Thomas.

The Barre Family
of Knebworth, Ayot St Lawrence and Panshanger

A DAUGHTER of Lawrence de Ayot m. ... Pembrugge of Ayot St Lawrence

SIR RICHARD de PEMBRUGGE
d. 4th August 1375

HAWISE PEMBRUGGE
m. Thomas Barre

ALICIA PEMBRUGGE
m. ... de Beurlee

HENRY de PEMBRUGGE
b. 1360. Inherited Ayot but died two months later, age 15.

SIR THOMAS BARRE (*1) m. Elizabeth ... Died 30th December 1421. Member of Parliament for Hertford in 1420. Inherited Ayot on the death of his cousin Henry in 1375. Also held the manor of Aldenham in 1391. Monument (mutilated) in Ayot St Lawrence Church to Sir Thomas and his wife Elizabeth.

RICHARD de BEURLEE
Jointly inherited Ayot but the whole estate later went to his cousin Sir Thomas Barre

THOMAS BARRE - predeceased his father

A SON - probably the ancestor of Milliscent Barre who m. Thomas Fairclough and was the grandmother of Thomas Harmer of Weston

SIR JOHN BARRE, d. 1482. Inherited Ayot from his grandfather. m. Indonea, d. of John Hotoft, from whom he inherited the manors of Knebworth and Panshanger.

JOAN BARRE
m. ... Delabere

ANCRET BARRE
m. ... Hanmer (or Harmer)

ISABEL BARRE (Isabel Countess of Devon) 1443-88

m① Humphrey Stafford, Earl of Devon who was beheaded for treason in 1469

m② Sir Thomas Bourchier, younger son of the Earl of Essex

RICHARD DELABERE

EDWARD HANMER

ISABEL BOURCHIER died before her parents and the manors descended to her mother's cousins Richard Delabere and Edward Hanmer

(*1): Sir Thomas Barre was a Justice of the Peace for Hertford in 1384, 1385 and 1401. He was Sheriff in 1415 and Member of Parliament for Hertford in 1420. He was also Surveyor of the King's hay, for which service he received 40 marks a year, plus 3 tuns of red wine. In 1394 he accompanied the king to Ireland, and was required to serve him and ride with him when called upon. He outlived his wife and son and died on 30th December 1421. He and his wife Elizabeth are buried in the church of Ayot St Lawrence. He was almost certainly the ancestor of Milliscent Barre and therefore of all the Harmer family from the 16th century.

DESCENT OF THE MANORS OF AYOT, KNEBWORTH AND PANSHANGER.
Thomas Bourchier survived his wife and daughter, and from him the estates went first to his wife's (Isabel Barre's) three cousins, Richard Delabere, Thomas Cornwall and Edward Hanmer (or Harmer). They sold them to Thomas Bourchier's nephew, Henry Bourchier, 2nd Earl of Essex, who married Mary, eldest daughter of Sir William Say. Their only child, Anne Bourchier, married Sir William Parr, who inherited the property, then divorced his wife and retained most of her estates. Soon afterwards his sister, Catherine Parr, became Queen Consort. Sir William was created Earl of Essex, and later Marquis of Northampton. He tried to advance Lady Jane Grey to the throne but failed and was committed to the Tower, and all his honours forfeited, though his life was spared. His lands were later returned to him by Queen Elizabeth who, in 1559, re-created him Marquis of Northampton, made him Privy Councillor and Knight of the Garter.

The manor of Ayot was the portion of the estate which was retained by the divorced wife and went to her niece Gertrude, daughter of Elizabeth Say and William, Baron Blount. Gertrude was the wife of Henry Courtenay, 2nd Earl of Devon and 1st Marquis of Exeter, who lived at Powderham Castle in Devon. In 1538, because of disputes about succession (Henry Courtenay was a relative of the king and had some claim to the throne) he was arrested and imprisoned in the Tower and was executed for High Treason in 1540. The manor was forfeited to the crown, and soon afterwards was granted to Nicholas Bristow. It remained in the Bristow family for 4 generations and was sold by the widow of William Bristow in 1714.

The manor of Knebworth went to Sir Robert Lytton, of Litton in Derbyshire, by his marriage to Agnes, another daughter of John Hotoft. The manor of Panshanger was granted in 1546 to Nicholas Throckmorton. In 1567 it went to Edward Skeggs (an ancestor of Ann Warren who married John Harmer in 1698) In 1693 it was acquired by Sir Gervase Elwes, whose family also acquired the manor of Throcking and the manor of Stoke College at Clare in Suffolk. His younger brother Sir John Elwes, knighted in 1665, was married to the daughter and co-heir of Sir Walter Raleigh. In 1719 Panshanger went to Earl Cowper, Lord Chancellor, who lived at Cole Green, and later built the mansion house known as Panshanger.

The Boteler Family
of Hatfield and Watton Woodhall.

SIR RALPH BOTELER, Lord of Woodhall, m. Hawise, d. and heir of Richard, son of Hugh Gobion. Died before 1300 (Inquisition 35 Edward I)

SIR JOHN BOTELER, m. Joan, d. of John de Argentein of Throcking, who d. in 1318 leaving his two daughters as heirs.	**WILLIAM BOTELER,** m. Elizabeth Argentein, sister of Joan	**RALPH BOTELER**, m. Katherine, d. of Sir Philip Peletoot who died in 1361. (Brass in Watton Church)

EDWARD BOTELER, b.1339, sold Throcking to William Hyde about 1395	**SIR PHILIP BOTELER** of Woodhall, d. 1421. m. Isabel ...

PHILIP BOTELER of Woodhall, d. 1425, m. Elizabeth Cockain (first wife)

JOHN BOTELER, m. Constance Downhall of Goddington, in the North.

JOHN BOTELER, d.1514, m. Dorothy, d. of William Tyrrell of Gipping, Suffolk. (see Tyrrell tree)

SIR PHILIP BOTELER, m. Elizabeth, d. of Robert Drury of Halstead. They had 19 children.

BOTELER. Gules a fesse checky argent and sable between six crosslets or.

THOMAS; WILLIAM; GEORGE; GRIFFITH; JOHN; THOMAS.	HENRY; ANTHONY; RICHARD; FRANCIS; PHILIP.	**SIR JOHN BOTELER** of Woodhall, m. Grizel, d. and heir of Sir William Roche of Lamer in Hertfordshire, who was Lord Mayor of London in 1540.	**ANN BOTELER** m. Leonard Hyde of Throcking-.(Hyde tree) ⬇	**ELIZABETH BOTELER** m. Henry Gill ------ **MARY BOTELER** m. John Harpham	**DOROTHY BOTELER** m. Anthony Browne ------ **KATHERINE BOTELER** m. Roger Potts	**MARGARET BOTELER** ------- **BRIDGET BOTELER**

WILLIAM; RICHARD; NICHOLAS. ------ **ELIZABETH BOTELER** d.1590, m. Sir Henry Coningsby of North Mimms (Coningsby tree ⬇)	**SIR PHILIP BOTELER** of Woodhall m. Anne, d. of John Coningsby of North Mimms (Coningsby tree ⬇)	**SIR HENRY BOTELER** of Hatfield Woodhall and Brantfield. High Sheriff 1603-4 m① Katherine Wallace of Hadleigh / m② Alice Pulter of Wymondley (Botelers of Queenhoo ⬇)	**MARY BOTELER** m. Thomas Shotbolt ------ **SARAH BOTELER** m. Roger Colte (connected with the Hunt family of Suffolk and Essex)	**SUSAN BOTELER** m. Julius Ferrers of Markyate. Their son John m. Ann Knighton whose son was Knighton Ferrers, the father of Kathleen Ferrers ('The Wicked Lady')	**MARGARET BOTELER** m. Nicholas Bristow (Bristow tree ⬇) ------- **MARTHA BOTELER** m. Sir George Perient (Perient tree ⬇)

SIR PHILIP BOTELER of Watton Woodhall m. Catherine, d. of Sir Francis Knollys	**SIR JOHN BOTELER**, of Hatfield Woodhall. Created Baron in 1620. m. Elizabeth Villiers, sister to George Villiers, Earl (later Duke) of Buckingham.

PHILIP BOTELER of Stapleford m. Alice, d. of John Shotbolt of Yardley, Herts.	SIR ROBERT BOTELER m. Frances, d. of Sir Drew Drury	SIR HENRY BOTELER osp ------ JOHN BOTELER osp	WILLIAM BOTELER osp. m. Joan Wingate of Lockleys (sister of Frances who m. Eustace Nedham)	AUDREY BOTELER m. Sir Francis Anderson of Eyworth, Beds (see Anderson tree)	ELEANOR BOTELER m. Sir John Drake	JANE BOTELER Duchess of Marlborough	ANN BOTELER Countess of Newport

PHILIP BOTELER	**SIR JOHN BOTELER**, Knight of the Bath, m. Ann (or Elizabeth) Spencer, granddaughter of Sir John Spencer of Althorpe. (see Spencer tree)	JOAN BOTELER sole daughter and heir. m. John, Lord Bellysis

SIR PHILIP BOTELER. Knight of the Bath. m. d. of Sir John Langham, Alderman of London	JOHN BOTELER, m. d. of Sir Edward Atkins, Lord Chief Baron	RALPH BOTELER	CATHERINE BOTELER m. Sir John Gore	ELIZABETH BOTELER m. Ralph Gore

SIR JOHN BOTELER, m. Elizabeth, d. of Sir Nicholas Gold of London	MARY BOTELER, m. Sir William Gostwick, Baronet, of Willington, Beds.	ANNE BOTELER unmarried	ELIZABETH BOTELER m. ... Copley Deputy Governor of Hull, later of Maryland

PHILIP BOTELER	ELIZABETH BOTELER

The Boteler Family
of Queenhoo Hall in Tewin

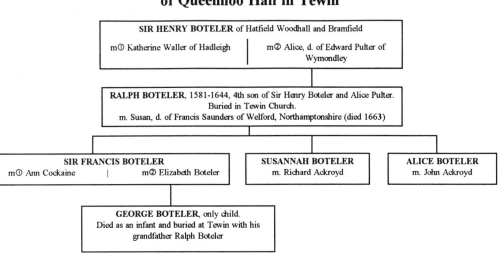

SIR HENRY BOTELER of Hatfield Woodhall and Bramfield

m① Katherine Waller of Hadleigh | m② Alice, d. of Edward Pulter of Wymondley

RALPH BOTELER, 1581-1644, 4th son of Sir Henry Boteler and Alice Pulter. Buried in Tewin Church.
m. Susan, d. of Francis Saunders of Welford, Northamptonshire (died 1663)

SIR FRANCIS BOTELER
m① Ann Cockaine | m② Elizabeth Boteler

SUSANNAH BOTELER
m. Richard Ackroyd

ALICE BOTELER
m. John Ackroyd

GEORGE BOTELER, only child.
Died as an infant and buried at Tewin with his grandfather Ralph Boteler

The Butler (or Boteler) Family
of Tewin Bury

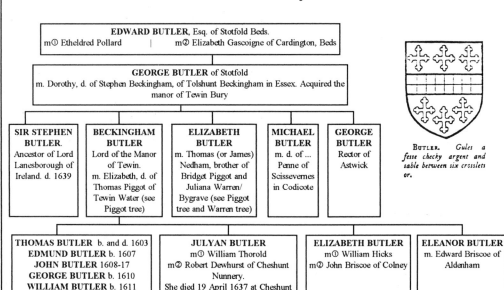

EDWARD BUTLER, Esq. of Stotfold Beds.
m① Etheldred Pollard | m② Elizabeth Gascoigne of Cardington, Beds

GEORGE BUTLER of Stotfold
m. Dorothy, d. of Stephen Beckingham, of Tolshunt Beckingham in Essex. Acquired the manor of Tewin Bury

SIR STEPHEN BUTLER.
Ancestor of Lord Lanesborough of Ireland. d. 1639

BECKINGHAM BUTLER
Lord of the Manor of Tewin.
m. Elizabeth, d. of Thomas Piggot of Tewin Water (see Piggot tree)

ELIZABETH BUTLER
m. Thomas (or James) Nedham, brother of Bridget Piggot and Juliana Warren/ Bygrave (see Piggot tree and Warren tree)

MICHAEL BUTLER
m. d. of ... Penne of Scissevernes in Codicote

GEORGE BUTLER
Rector of Astwick

BUTLER. *Gules a fesse checky argent and sable between six crosslets or.*

THOMAS BUTLER b. and d. 1603
EDMUND BUTLER b. 1607
JOHN BUTLER 1608-17
GEORGE BUTLER b. 1610
WILLIAM BUTLER b. 1611
JOHN BUTLER b. 1618

JULYAN BUTLER
m① William Thorold
m② Robert Dewhurst of Cheshunt Nunnery.
She died 19 April 1637 at Cheshunt Nunnery (memorial in Tewin church)

ELIZABETH BUTLER
m① William Hicks
m② John Briscoe of Colney

ELEANOR BUTLER
m. Edward Briscoe of Aldenham

THE BUTLERS sold the manor of Tewin to Richard Hale, who sold it to William Cecil, 2nd Earl of Salisbury (son of Robert Cecil and his wife Elizabeth Brooke). It went to his son, William Cecil, then to Robert Cecil, who served the Prince of Orange and accompanied him to England in 1688. He died possessed of the manor in 1705 and was buried at Hatfield. His son, William Cecil, sold the manor to James Fleet, son of Sir John Fleet. When James Fleet died in 1733 he left the manor (and also Wymondley Bury) to his great nephews John and Edmund Bull. (great grandsons of Richard Bull, brother of Rebecka). James Fleet was the first of the four husbands of Elizabeth Malyn, later Lady Cathcart (see Chapter 9).

The Butlers of Tewin Bury were not closely related to the Botelers of Woodhall and Queenhoo Hall although they lived on neighbouring estates in Tewin. They bore the same arms, so were presumably distant cousins.

The Brooke Family (Lords Cobham)
of Aspall Hall in Suffolk, Abbess Roding in Essex, Barkway in Hertfordshire, and Cobham Hall in Kent.

The manor of Aspall was held by ancestors of the Harmer family (the Peverells) from the time of Edward the Confessor. Later it passed to the Aspall family, who were descendants of the Peverells, and for a time it followed the descent of the manor of Little Bradley. The ancestral line comes down from Sir Payne Peverell, through Peche, Aspall, Notbeame, Gedding, Hinkley, Caldebeck, Underhill, Knighton, Bull and Harmer. The Brooke family acquired the manor of Aspall through the de la Poles, who are also on the Piggot tree. Catherine Brooke, who married George Kympton at Bengeo in 1568 almost certainly belongs to this family.

RANULF PEVERELL held the manor before 1066

↓

RALPH PEVERELL, Lord of the Manor of Aspall at the time of the Domesday survey (1086)

↓

EDMUND PEVERELL (*1) m. Alice, sister of Walter de Langton, Bishop of Lichfield and Coventry, who held part of the manor of Aspall in 1281. Edmund Peverell had probably inherited the other part of the manor, and by this marriage the two parts became united.

BRAYBROOKE. *Argent seven voided lozenges gules.*

JOHN PEVERELL osp | **MARGARET PEVERELL** m. William de la Pole (de la Pole and Piggot trees ↓)

SIR JOHN de la POLE m. Joan, d. of John, Lord Cobham

JOAN de la POLE Baroness Cobham, d. 1433. m. Sir Reginald Braybrooke

JOAN BRAYBROOKE Baroness Cobham, d. 1442. m. Sir Thomas Brooke, d.1439, MP for Somerset 1417-27. Became 5th Lord Cobham

CECIL, Marquess of Salisbury. *Barry of ten pieces argent and azure six scutcheons sable with a lion argent in each differenced with a crescent.*

EDWARD BROOKE of Aspall 6th Lord Cobham, d.1464. A zealous Yorkist who participated in the victory of St Albans in 1454. m. Elizabeth, d. of James. Lord Audley. | **REGINALD BROOKE**, d. 1482 m. Anne Everton. Inherited Aspall from his brother in 1464

JOHN BROOKE 7th Lord Cobham, m.① Eleanor Austell of Suffolk, osp; m② Margaret, d. of Edward Nevill Lord Abergavenny. | **EDWARD BROOKE**, Lord of the Manor of Aspall. d. 1541. (*2), m. Florence, d. of Robert Ashfield of Stowlangtoft, Suffolk.

THOMAS BROOKE 8th Lord Cobham, d.1529. m.① Dorothy, d. of Sir Henry Heydon m.② Dorothy, widow of ... Sothwell m.③ Elizabeth Hart	GEORGE BROOKE of Aspall, d. 1554. m. Ann, d. of John Carew of Somerset.	EDWARD BROOKE ------- JOHN BROOKE ------- WALTER BROOKE	RICHARD BROOKE ——— FRANCIS BROOKE ——— REGINALD BROOKE	ROBERT BROOKE m. Joan Pranell (see Brooke of Barkway tree)

GEORGE BROOKE 9th Lord Cobham, KG, 1497-1558. m. Ann, d. of Edmund Lord Bray. They had a d. Catherine who was probably the Catherine Brooke who m. George Kympton at Bengeo in 1568 (*3).	GEORGE BROOKE. d.1557 m.① Alice, d. of Sir John Tyrrell of Gipping Hall near Stowmarket in Suffolk (related to the Browne family). Monument in Stowmarket church.	m.② Elizabeth, d. of Edmund Withypoole of Ipswich

WILLIAM BROOKE 10th Lord Cobham, 1527-1596. m.① Dorothy, d. of George Nevill Lord Abergavenny m.② Frances Newton, Lady of the Bedchamber. Their d. Elizabeth m. Robert Cecil 1st Earl of Salisbury (*4).	GEORGE BROOKE, d. about 1580. m.① Mary, d. of Edward Jobson son of Sir Francis Jobson of Doniland in Essex	m.② Katherine, d. of George Jernegan MP for Orford and Eleanor Spelman (see Coningsby tree)

HENRY BROOKE 11th Lord Cobham, KG, 1564-1618, osp. Warden of the Cinque Ports. Imprisoned in the Tower with his brother George for complicity in the Raleigh conspiracy. m.1601, Frances, d. of Charles Howard 1st Earl of Nottingham. His nephew inherited	GEORGE BROOKE Imprisoned in the Tower. Executed 1603	EDWARD BROOKE, m. Agnes, d. of Thomas Fastolf of Pettaugh in Suffolk. (Brooke of Nacton tree ↓) (The Fastolf family probably built the famous 'Ancient House' in Ipswich in the late 15th century. Several members of the family served as MP for Ipswich.)

SIR WILLIAM BROOKE 12th Lord Cobham. Only son of George. Succeeded his uncle when his titles and lands were restored.	EDWARD BROOKE, d. 1679, buried at Aspall. m. Rebecca Wiseman, who died 12th August 1699 and is buried at St Margaret's, Ipswich

JOHN BROOKE, m. Mary, d. of George Green of Athlington. In 1702 John Brooke sold the manor of Aspall to Temple Chevallier of Jersey - a cider maker. Aspall Hall has since that time been famous for its cider.

The Brooke Family (Lords Cobham)
of Aspall Hall in Suffolk, Abbess Roding in Essex, Barkway in Hertfordshire, and Cobham Hall in Kent.

NOTES

(*1) Copinger states that Alice de Langton married Edmund Peverell, but the VCH suggests that she married Robert Peverell and Edmund was their son. Thomas Peverell DD (Oxford) and Bishop of Worcester was a member of this family. He died March 1419 and was buried in his own cathedral.

(*2) Edward Brooke d.1541 also held Abbess Roding in Essex and Barkway in Hertfordshire jointly with Sir John Petre of Ingatestone Hall ('Master John' whose baptism is mentioned in note (*1) of the Mordaunt tree). They sold Barkway to Henry Pranell whose daughter Joan was married to Robert Brooke, son of Edward, who appears on the Brooke of Nacton tree.

(*3) George Brooke 9th Lord Cobham had 2 daughters, Elizabeth who m. William Parr Marquess of Northampton, and Catherine who, according to the Visitations, m. John Jerningham. It seems likely however that this was the Catherine Brooke who married George Kympton (the other could have been a second marriage). The 2nd wife of William 10th Lord Cobham (brother of Elizabeth and Catherine) was Frances Newton, a Lady of the Bedchamber to the Queen. George Kympton's cousin Lucy was also one of the Ladies of the Bedchamber, so the two families would have been closely acquainted.

(*4) Elizabeth Brooke 1563-97 married Robert Cecil, Chief Secretary to Queen Elizabeth. In 1603 King James persuaded him to exchange his magnificent mansion of Theodalds near Cheshunt for the old brick palace of Hatfield. He was rewarded by being created Earl of Salisbury and Knight of the Garter. He became Lord Treasurer of England and Chancellor of the University of Cambridge.

(*5) The Brookes were one of the leading recusant families in the 17th century, related to the Mordaunts, Brownes, Throckmortons, and Wisemans. In 1603, two years before the Gunpowder Plot, Henry Brooke 11th Lord Cobham, and his brother George, together with Lord Grey de Wilton and Sir Walter Raleigh, were involved in a plot (the treason of the Main) to eliminate King James and his 'Cubs' and put Arbella Stuart on the throne.

The Brooke and Pranell Families
of Nursells Manor and Rushdenwell in Barkway, Hertfordshire

HENRY PRANELL of Barkway in Hertfordshire, Alderman of London, d.1594. m. Ann Baxter. Bought the manor of Barkway from Edward Brooke and Sir John Petre in 1583.

HENRY PRANELL m. Frances, late Countess of Hertford. osp 1599	**JOAN PRANELL** m. Robert Brooke, a London merchant of Copfield, Essex (son of Edward Brooke from whom his father-in-law bought the manor). He held the manor in 1595 when Henry Pranell died.	**MARY PRANELL** m. John, son and heir of Sir Francis Clarke of Houghton, Beds. (see Clarke tree)
ELIZABETH BROOKE m. Sir Robert Slingsby (He was made baronet by Charles II in 1660). Elizabeth inherited Barkway and sold it to Edward Chester	**MARY BROOKE** m. Thomas, s. of John Saunders of Long Marston in Hertfordshire and Mary Coningsby (d. of Sir Henry Coningsby of North Mimms). (see Coningsby tree)	**HENRY BROOKE** inherited Barkway, m. the d. of Lord Maltravers, s. of Thomas Howard Earl of Arundel and Surrey.

The Brooke Family of Nacton, Suffolk

THOMAS BROOKE of Leighton m. Joan, d. of John (or William) Parke of Copenhall, Chester.	**THOMAS FASTOLF**, MP for Ipswich in 1487.
SIR RICHARD BROOKE, d.1529, Recorder of London, Chief Baron of the Exchequer, represented the City of London in several parliaments. Built Crows Hall in 1526, m. Ann Leeds who d.1547	**JOHN FASTOLF**, d.1506, MP for Ipswich 1494
ROBERT BROOKE 1495-1578, m. Elizabeth Holgrave of Sussex, owned lands in Nacton, Foxholes, Bucklesham and Levington. His grandson Robert Brooke (d.1626) was Sheriff of Suffolk in 1623. Two generations later Sir Robert m. Ann, d. of Sir Lionel Tollemache.	**BRIDGET BROOKE** m. **GEORGE FASTOLF** (the Thomas Fastolf of Pettaugh whose d. Agnes m. Edward Brooke of Aspall was almost certainly a son of George and Bridget) (Brooke of Aspall tree ↓)

The Browne Family
of Abbess Roding, Welde Hall and Ridley Hall in Essex

THOMAS BROWNE inherited the manor of Abbess Roding from his brother John in 1467. m.Joanne Kyrkham of Devonshire

THOMAS (or Robert) BROWNE of Abbess Roding, b.1488 m..Mary, d..ofThomas Carleton

SIR WESTON BROWNE of Rookwood. Knighted by the King of Aragon at the time of Henry VII, m. Maud (or Elizabeth) d. of William Mordaunt of Turvey. (see Mordaunt Tree)

WILLIAM BROWNE a London merchant Lord Mayor of London in 1507 and 1513/14. He died in 1514 during his term of office.

SIR HUMPHREY BROWNE of Ridley Hall , Essex Justice of the Common Pleas at the time of Henry VIII (1509-47)
m① Ann, d. of Henry de Vere. (They had one child, George, who died without issue)
m ② Ann, d. of John, Lord Hussey. Her sister, Bridget Hussey, was the wife of Francis Russell, 4th Earl of Bedford, d.1641

JOHN BROWNE of Abbess Roding m. Audrey (or Etheldred) d. of Henry de Vere of Hedingham Castle in Essex and Great Addington, Northants. (Audrey was sister of Ann de Vere who m. Humphrey Browne and of Elizabeth who m. Lord Mordaunt)

SIR ANTHONY BROWNE 1510-67 of Welde Hall. Justice of the Common Pleas m. Joan Farrington (Sir Anthony was a guest at Catherine Tyrrell's wedding)

KATHERINE BROWNE m. Francis Knighton, son of Alice Bull and Thomas Knighton of Brickendon. (see Caldebeck tree and Hunt tree)

JANE BROWNE m ① Thomas Scroggs of Patmore m ② Walter Bridges of Patmore

ANNE BROWNE b. 1509 m.① John Tyrrell of Heron Hall (parents of Catherine Tyrrell of Ingatestone Hall) m② Sir William Petre of Ingatestone Hall (See Chapter 3, also Tyrrell tree and Petre tree)

ELIZABETH BROWNE m. John Hale who bought Harmer Green for his son John. (Hale tree ↓)

CATHERINE BROWNE m① Richard Townsende m② Sir William Roper of Eltham, Kent, son and heir of Sir Thomas Roper, grandson of Sir Thomas More. (Roper tree ↓)

CHRISTIANA BROWNE m. John Tufton of Kent. Their son was Nicholas Lord Tufton
-----
MARY BROWNE m. Thomas Wilford s. of Sir James Wilford

GEORGE BROWNE of Clovills Hall, m. Elizabeth Leventhorpe, d. of Sir John Leventhorpe of Shingle Hall, Albury, Herts and his wife Joan Brograve of Hammels, Braughing. Sir John Leventhorpe was Sheriff of Herts in 1510

HENRY BROWNE of London. d. 1558 m. Elizabeth Lambert, d. of Bartholemew Lambert

WILLIAM BRIDGES of Ickwell, osp.

DOROTHY PETRE m. Nicholas Wadham (Founders Wadham College, Oxford)

WESTON BROWNE d.1580 of Rookwood (or Clovills) Hall. m① Mary, d. of Sir Edward Capell of Hadham, Hertfordshire (osp). m ② Elizabeth, d. of Giles Pawlett

JOHN BROWNE of Wickham Hall m. Ann Stanton of Somerset

ANN BROWNE m. Rowland Elliott of Stortford

ELIZABETH BROWNE m. Sir Henry, s. of Sir George Jernagen of Somerleton, Suffolk

ANTHONY BROWNE osp 1583

CATHERIN BROWNE m. Nicholas, s. of Edward Waldegrave of Borley, Essex. (Waldegrave tree ↓)

JAYNE BROWNE m① Edward Wyatt of Tillingham, Essex m② Sir Gamaliell Capell. son of Sir Henry Capell. (Sir William Capell, gr. gr. grandfather of Gamaliell, was a native of Stoke by Nayland. He was Lord Mayor of London in 1503 and 1509 and an ancestor of the Earls of Essex. (Capell tree ↓)

SIR ANTHONY BROWNE of Welde Hall m.Elizabeth Pirton. They had John (son and heir), Elizabeth, Mary and Catherine.

WESTON BROWNE osp

WILLIAM BROWNE m. Mary, d. of Sir John Sulyard of Wetherden, Suffolk, widow of Thomas Tyrrell

ANN BROWNE m..Thomas Perient of Burgh, Essex (Perient tree ↓)

SIBBEL BROWNE m. John Christmas of Colchester

ELIZABETH BROWNE m. Thomas Cheney of Chesham Boyes Buckinghamshire
-----
JANE BROWNE m. John Filleal of Rayne Hall in Essex.

The Browne Family
of Abbess Roding, Welde Hall and Ridley Hall in Essex

The Manor of Abbess Roding (including Rookwood)

The manor of Abbess Roding or Abbess Hall belonged originally to Barking Abbey, but was taken over at the time of the Conquest by Geoffrey de Mandeville, one of the Norman barons. Later Barking Abbey regained part of the manor and held it until the Dissolution, when it was granted by Henry VIII to Thomas Cromwell. When Cromwell was disgraced and executed Henry VIII gave the manor to Ann of Cleves. Richard Lord Rich (later Lord Chancellor) was her Steward (*1). Later that year (1540), probably when Ann was divorced, the manor seems to have been in the possession of Richard Lord Rich and Oliver St John of Bletsoe. In 1541 it was acquired by Edward Brooke of Aspall Hall in Suffolk, a cousin of Lord Cobham. Edward Brooke also had estates at Barkway and St Pauls Walden in Hertfordshire which he held jointly with Sir John Petre, son of Sir William Petre of Ingatestone Hall.

The other part of the Abbess Roding estate, which was not regained by Barking Abbey, passed in 1086 to Aubrey de Vere, ancestor of the Earls of Oxford and also of the Browne family who later inherited it. It was known as Rookwood or Brownes. Thomas Browne was holding the manor in 1467, and it passed to his son Thomas (or Robert), then to Sir Weston Browne and to his son Sir Anthony Browne, Chief Justice of the Common Pleas. Here we have a great deal of confusion. This gentleman is referred to in some sources as Lord Montague, but Lord Montague was in fact an entirely different Anthony Browne, who lived at Cowdray in Sussex. To add to the confusion they were marrying into the same families. The Ropers of Eltham, Capells of Hertfordshire, and the Petres of Ingatestone Hall all had connections with both the Brownes of Sussex and the Brownes of Essex.

Around 1599 the manor of Rookwood (now sometimes referred to as Clovills), was acquired by the Capell family; presumably through the marriage of Sir Gamaliel Capell and Jayne, the daughter of Weston Browne and his second wife Elizabeth Pawlett. (His first wife was Mary Capell, Gamaliel Capell's niece). At this stage Nicholas Waldegrave, whose family had married into both the Brooke and the Browne families, seems to have had a share in the property, but finally the whole manor came to the Capells.

Mrs Sarah Capell, who was buried at Abbess Roding in 1698, was probably the last member of the family to live there. About 1700 Sir Gamaliel Capell, the great-grandson of the first Gamaliel, sold or mortgaged the manor to John Howland of Streatham, whose daughter and heir married Wriothsley Russell 2nd Duke of Bedford. His son, John 4th Duke of Bedford, sold Abbess Roding in 1739 to the Skinner family.

In the 19th century the Reverend Capel Cure, a descendant of the Capell family, bought the advowson of the Rectory. He did a great deal for the parish at his own expense, providing a village school and restoring the church.

(*1) Richard Lord Rich had a daughter Ann who was married to Sir Thomas Piggot (see Chapter 10 and Piggot tree). He later bought Wymondley Bury for his son John (the son of his second marriage, to Elizabeth Thynne).

The Brownes, Lords Montague of Cowdray
and Battle Abbey in Sussex

SIR ANTHONY BROWNE, created KB in 1377 at the Coronation of Richard II

SIR RICHARD BROWNE

SIR STEPHEN BROWNE, Lord Mayor of London 1439

SIR THOMAS BROWNE of Beechworth Castle in Surrey. Sheriff of Kent 1444 and 1460. m. Eleanor, d. of Sir Thomas Fitz-Alan, alias Arundel.

SIR GEORGE BROWNE.
Beheaded 1483 by Richard III. m. Elizabeth Paston of Norfolk, relict of Richard, Lord Poynings.

SIR ANTHONY BROWNE, Standard bearer of England 1485, Constable of Calais 1503, d. 1506 and buried at Calais. m. Lucy, d. and heir of John Nevile, Marquis of Montague

SIR ANTHONY BROWNE of Cowdray, Lieutenant of the Isle of Man 1526, ambassador to France 1533, Standard bearer and Master of the Horse to Henry VIII 1547, d. 1548 and buried at Battle Abbey. m. Alice, d. of Sir John Gage KG (died 1540)

LUCY BROWNE
m. Sir Thomas Roper of Eltham (grandson of Sir Thomas More - see Roper tree), they had 10 children.

SIR ANTHONY BROWNE of Cowdray, c1528-92, created 1st Viscount Montague 1554.
m① Jane, d. of Robert Radcliff, Earl of Surrey (*1) | m② Magdalen, d. of William, Lord Dacre

MARY BROWNE
m① Lord John Grey of Pirgo, Essex | m② Sir Henry Capell of Hadham, Herts. (see Capell tree)

SIR ANTHONY BROWNE, d.1592, 5 months before his father Knighted at Cowdray by Queen Elizabeth in 1591. m.Mary, d. of Sir William Dormer of Wing, Buckinghamshire

MARY BROWNE, d.1607
m①, 1565, Henry Wrothesley, Earl of Southampton. m② Sir Thomas Heneage, vice-chamberlain to Queen Elizabeth. m③ Sir William Harvey

ANTHONY-MARIA BROWNE, 1574-1629, 2nd Viscount Montague, m. Jane, d. of Thomas Sackville, Earl of Dorset. (see notes on the Gunpowder Plot)

JOHN BROWNE m. Ann Gifford

WILLIAM BROWNE, 1576-1637, osp. Became a Jesuit lay brother at the College of St Omer.

DOROTHY BROWNE
m. Edmund Lee of Stantonbury, Bucks.

FRANCIS BROWNE
———
ANTHONY BROWNE
———
Both died young

FRANCIS BROWNE
3rd Lord Montague m. Elizabeth, d. of the Marquis of Worcester

MARY BROWNE
m① Lord St John
m② Lord Arundel

CATHERINE BROWNE
m. William Tyrwhitt of Kettleby

MARY BROWNE
1603-84 m. 1620, Robert, 3rd Lord Petre. They were both buried at Ingatestone (see Petre tree)

STANISLAUS BROWNE
of Easebourne, living in 1687, m. ...

ANTHONY BROWNE
died young

FRANCIS BROWNE
4th Viscount Montague osp 1708

HENRY BROWNE
5th Viscount Montague, m. Barbara Walsingham of Essex.

ELIZABETH BROWNE
m. Christopher Roper, Lord Teynham. (see Roper tree)

STANISLAUS BROWNE
m. Honor, d. of .... Malbrantee, a merchant of Cadiz.

ANTHONY BROWNE 1686-1767
6th Viscount Montague m. Barbara, d. of Sir John Webb

HENRIETTA BROWNE
m. Richard Harcourt, a merchant at Boulogne

MARK BROWNE Lord of Methley, m. Anastasia, d. of Sir Richard Moore of Fawley, Berks

MARY BROWNE m. Sir Roger Langley of Higham Gobion, Beds

ANTHONY JOSEPH BROWNE
1728-87, 7th Viscount Montague, m. Frances Markworth, widow of Baron Halkerton of Scotland.

MARY BROWNE
1733-67, m. Sir Henry Bedingfield of Oxborough in Norfolk.

MARK ANTHONY BROWNE
1744-97, osp, 9th (and last) Viscount Montague.

ANASTASIA BROWNE
b.1749, m.1780 Sir Thomas Mannock of Giffords Hall, Stoke-by-Nayland, Suffolk (see Mannock tree)

GEORGE SAMUEL BROWNE
1769-93
8th Viscount Montague
Died unmarried aged 24

(***1**) The Brownes of Sussex were described as one of the most influential Roman Catholic families in the country. Anthony Browne, 1st Viscount Montague, was the only temporal peer to vote against the Act of Supremacy in 1559, and his houses at Cowdray and Battle Abbey, and Montague House in London, were resorts for deposed Marian clergy and later for the seminary priests. Midhurst and Battle became Catholic communities with their own priests, schoolmasters and doctors. Yet at the same time he was a trusted and influential public servant. As a mark of her trust Queen Elizabeth paid a week-long visit to Cowdray in 1591, when she knighted Montague's son.

Family connections with
The Gunpowder Plot

The 'network' included many families who in the 16th and 17th centuries remained faithful to the old religion - Roman Catholicism and several were suspected of having connections with the Gunpowder Plot. Most closely involved were: the Brownes of Sussex, the Mordaunts, Petres, Ropers, Brookes, Throckmortons, and Lord Monteagle.

The Brownes of Sussex
One of the most influential of the 'recusant' families. About 15 years before the Gunpowder Plot, Sir Anthony Browne, later 2nd Viscount Montague, had briefly employed Guy Fawkes as a footman. This situation became embarrassing in 1605 when Fawkes was arrested. It was also known that Sir Anthony had planned to be absent from Parliament on 5th November, and it was thought that he had probably been warned by Catesby. All this was enough to implicate him in the Plot. He was questioned by his father-in-law, Thomas Sackville Earl of Dorset, but denied all knowledge of the conspiracy. He escaped trial, but paid a fine and served a term in prison. His grandmother, Magdalen Viscountess Montague, a courageous old lady and loyal Catholic, held to her faith through all the searches and persecutions. She remembered happier days, when as a young Maid of Honour she had walked in the bridal procession at the marriage of Mary Tudor and Philip of Spain in Winchester Cathedral. She died in 1608 at her home near Battle, where there were five priests in the house to say Mass. William Byrd, a good friend of the family, wrote an elegy to mark her death.

The Three Brothers Browne and their Servant 1598
This miniature by Isaac Oliver (d.1617), is now at Burghley House, Stamford. It shows Anthony-Maria, the heir, with John on the left and William on the right. The significance and identity of the servant is unknown.

The Mordaunt Family
One of the conspirators, Robert Keyes, was closely connected with the Mordaunt family. Robert's wife Christiana was governess to the Mordaunt children, and Lord Mordaunt was Robert's patron and friend. Because of this involvement Lord Mordaunt was imprisoned in the Tower, tried in front of the Star Chamber, and fined £10,000. The mother of Robert Keyes was a member of the Tyrwhitt family of Lincolnshire. Robert's cousin, Elizabeth Tyrwhitt, was married to another of the conspirators, Ambrose Rookwood of Coldham Hall in Suffolk.

continued →

Family connections with
The Gunpowder Plot
(continued)

The Petre Family
Robert Wintour, another of the conspirators, was married to Gertrude Talbot, a member of a well-known recusant family at Grafton Manor near Bromsgrove. Her mother was Katherine Petre, daughter of Sir William Petre of Ingatestone Hall in Essex (see Chapter 3). The Petres were neighbours and patrons of William Byrd, who wrote a Mass to mark the occasion when John Petre, William's son, was created 1st Baron of Writtle in July 1603. William Byrd had a Catholic wife, Elizabeth Throckmorton, and was probably himself a Catholic at heart, but as Court Musician it would have been unwise to publicise the fact. He once said of Ingatestone Hall, 'It is a house truly most friendly to me and mine'. Here many of his Masses were sung. They were invariably written for small numbers since they could only be used secretly in private houses and chapels.

The Roper Family
Eliza Vaux (formerly Eliza Roper of Eltham in Kent) was one of the most courageous women at this time, when the Catholic families were suffering great hardship and persecution. She was the sister of Alice Roper who was married to George Hyde of Throcking, and sister-in-law of Sir Thomas More's daughter Margaret. Eliza was the widow of George Vaux, who died in 1594 when Eliza was only about 30 years old, leaving her with six young children as the sole head of a large Catholic house, Harrowden Hall, near Wellingborough. Eliza was the daughter of Sir John Roper, Clerk of the Common Pleas. Because of his position it was important to show absolute loyalty to the king, and his daughter's recusancy and possible involvement in the Plot (she was imprisoned for a short time in the Tower) caused problems in the family. Eliza was a highly-educated woman with many talents, but devoted her life to her children and also to the rebuilding of Harrowden Hall to include ingenious hiding places for the many priests who found refuge there. She was known with respect and affection (even by non-Catholics) as 'Eliza Vaux, the Dowager of Harrowden'. Ann Vaux, sister-in-law of Eliza, remained unmarried so that she could devote all her energy to the Catholic cause, and played a vital part in the circumstances surrounding the Gunpowder Plot. From 1590 onwards she protected and managed the affairs of Father Henry Garnet, Superior of the Jesuits.

The Brooke Family (including Lord Cobham)
In 1603 when King James failed to give the Catholics the tolerance which had been promised, discontented priests and laymen began to plot against him. The laymen included Henry Lord Cobham and his brother George, and also Sir Walter Raleigh. One plan was to imprison the king and demand concessions, and a second plan included an attempt to put Arbella Stuart (1st cousin of the king) on the throne. As a result of his involvement in these plots George Brooke was executed, but Lord Cobham and Raleigh were released on payment of heavy fines. Lord Cobham's titles were forfeited, but they were restored to his heir some years later. Robert Lord Salisbury, who was responsible for ordering these punishments, was married to Elizabeth Brooke, the sister of Lord Cobham and George Brooke.

The Throckmorton Family of Coughton Court in Warwickshire
This was another leading Catholic family. Ann Vaux had a Throckmorton grandmother and a Tresham stepmother, and Robert Catesby and his cousin Francis Tresham of Rushton Hall in Northamptonshire both had Throckmorton grandmothers. Sir Thomas Tresham, the father of Francis, had been fined frequently and spent many years in prison, and his cousin Thomas Throckmorton had been executed in 1584 for taking part in a plot to free Mary Queen of Scots. Sir Walter Raleigh's wife was Elizabeth Throckmorton, a cousin of Robert Catesby.

Lord Monteagle and Morley
William Parker Lord Monteagle and Morley was married to Elizabeth Tresham, daugher of Sir Thomas Tresham and first cousin to Robert Catesby. On 26th October 1605 Lord Monteagle received an anonymous letter warning him not to attend Parliament on 5th November. Because of this letter, known as 'The Monteagle Letter', the Plot was discovered and disaster averted. This 'dark and doubtful letter' is preserved in the Public Record Office. Lord Monteagle's daughter Catherine was married to John Petre, the grandson of Sir William Petre of Ingatestone Hall.

The Brocket Family
of Wheathampstead

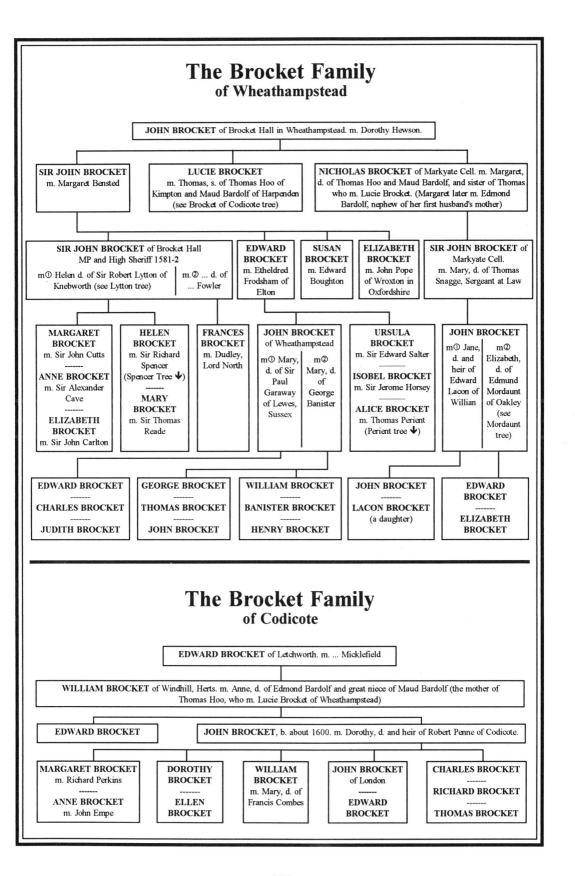

JOHN BROCKET of Brocket Hall in Wheathampstead. m. Dorothy Hewson.

SIR JOHN BROCKET
m. Margaret Bensted

LUCIE BROCKET
m. Thomas, s. of Thomas Hoo of Kimpton and Maud Bardolf of Harpenden (see Brocket of Codicote tree)

NICHOLAS BROCKET of Markyate Cell. m. Margaret, d. of Thomas Hoo and Maud Bardolf, and sister of Thomas who m. Lucie Brocket. (Margaret later m. Edmond Bardolf, nephew of her first husband's mother)

SIR JOHN BROCKET of Brocket Hall
MP and High Sheriff 1581-2
m① Helen d. of Sir Robert Lytton of Knebworth (see Lytton tree) | m.② ... d. of ... Fowler

EDWARD BROCKET
m. Etheldred Frodsham of Elton

SUSAN BROCKET
m. Edward Boughton

ELIZABETH BROCKET
m. John Pope of Wroxton in Oxfordshire

SIR JOHN BROCKET of Markyate Cell.
m. Mary, d. of Thomas Snagge, Sergeant at Law

MARGARET BROCKET
m. Sir John Cutts

ANNE BROCKET
m. Sir Alexander Cave

ELIZABETH BROCKET
m. Sir John Carlton

HELEN BROCKET
m. Sir Richard Spencer
(Spencer Tree ↓)

MARY BROCKET
m. Sir Thomas Reade

FRANCES BROCKET
m. Dudley, Lord North

JOHN BROCKET
of Wheathampstead
m① Mary, d. of Sir Paul Garaway of Lewes, Sussex | m② Mary, d. of George Banister

URSULA BROCKET
m. Sir Edward Salter

ISOBEL BROCKET
m. Sir Jerome Horsey

ALICE BROCKET
m. Thomas Perient
(Perient tree ↓)

JOHN BROCKET
m① Jane, d. and heir of Edward Lacon of Willian | m② Elizabeth, d. of Edmund Mordaunt of Oakley (see Mordaunt tree)

EDWARD BROCKET

CHARLES BROCKET

JUDITH BROCKET

GEORGE BROCKET

THOMAS BROCKET

JOHN BROCKET

WILLIAM BROCKET

BANISTER BROCKET

HENRY BROCKET

JOHN BROCKET

LACON BROCKET
(a daughter)

EDWARD BROCKET

ELIZABETH BROCKET

The Brocket Family
of Codicote

EDWARD BROCKET of Letchworth. m. ... Micklefield

WILLIAM BROCKET of Windhill, Herts. m. Anne, d. of Edmond Bardolf and great niece of Maud Bardolf (the mother of Thomas Hoo, who m. Lucie Brocket of Wheathampstead)

EDWARD BROCKET

JOHN BROCKET, b. about 1600. m. Dorothy, d. and heir of Robert Penne of Codicote.

MARGARET BROCKET
m. Richard Perkins

ANNE BROCKET
m. John Empe

DOROTHY BROCKET

ELLEN BROCKET

WILLIAM BROCKET
m. Mary, d. of Francis Combes

JOHN BROCKET
of London

EDWARD BROCKET

CHARLES BROCKET

RICHARD BROCKET

THOMAS BROCKET

The Bull Family
of Hertford, Stapleford and Tewin

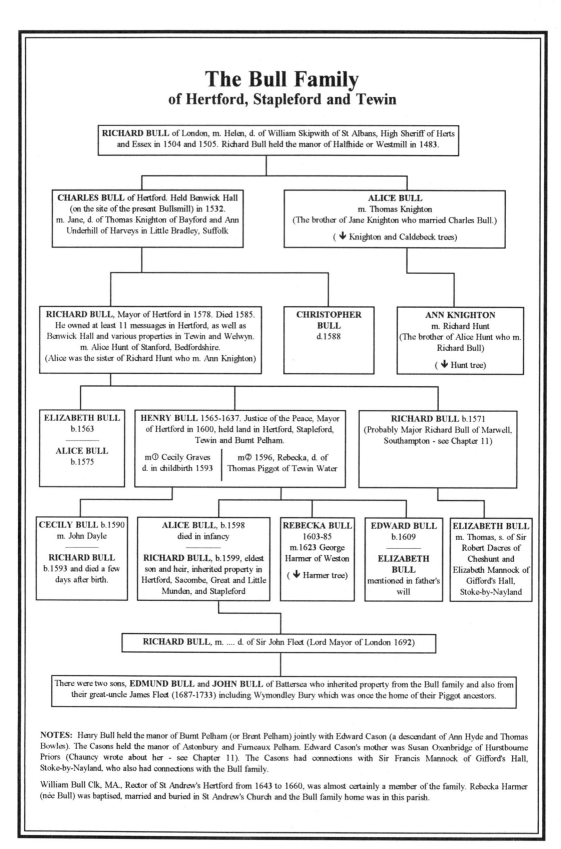

RICHARD BULL of London, m. Helen, d. of William Skipwith of St Albans, High Sheriff of Herts and Essex in 1504 and 1505. Richard Bull held the manor of Halfhide or Westmill in 1483.

CHARLES BULL of Hertford. Held Benwick Hall (on the site of the present Bullsmill) in 1532. m. Jane, d. of Thomas Knighton of Bayford and Ann Underhill of Harveys in Little Bradley, Suffolk

ALICE BULL
m. Thomas Knighton
(The brother of Jane Knighton who married Charles Bull.)

(↓ Knighton and Caldebeck trees)

RICHARD BULL, Mayor of Hertford in 1578. Died 1585. He owned at least 11 messuages in Hertford, as well as Benwick Hall and various properties in Tewin and Welwyn. m. Alice Hunt of Stanford, Bedfordshire. (Alice was the sister of Richard Hunt who m. Ann Knighton)

CHRISTOPHER BULL
d.1588

ANN KNIGHTON
m. Richard Hunt
(The brother of Alice Hunt who m. Richard Bull)

(↓ Hunt tree)

ELIZABETH BULL
b.1563
————
ALICE BULL
b.1575

HENRY BULL 1565-1637. Justice of the Peace, Mayor of Hertford in 1600, held land in Hertford, Stapleford, Tewin and Burnt Pelham.

m① Cecily Graves d. in childbirth 1593

m② 1596, Rebecka, d. of Thomas Piggot of Tewin Water

RICHARD BULL b.1571
(Probably Major Richard Bull of Marwell, Southampton - see Chapter 11)

CECILY BULL b.1590
m. John Dayle
————
RICHARD BULL
b.1593 and died a few days after birth.

ALICE BULL, b.1598
died in infancy
————
RICHARD BULL, b.1599, eldest son and heir, inherited property in Hertford, Sacombe, Great and Little Munden, and Stapleford

REBECKA BULL
1603-85
m.1623 George Harmer of Weston

(↓ Harmer tree)

EDWARD BULL
b.1609
————
ELIZABETH BULL
mentioned in father's will

ELIZABETH BULL
m. Thomas, s. of Sir Robert Dacres of Cheshunt and Elizabeth Mannock of Gifford's Hall, Stoke-by-Nayland

RICHARD BULL, m. .... d. of Sir John Fleet (Lord Mayor of London 1692)

There were two sons, **EDMUND BULL** and **JOHN BULL** of Battersea who inherited property from the Bull family and also from their great-uncle James Fleet (1687-1733) including Wymondley Bury which was once the home of their Piggot ancestors.

NOTES: Henry Bull held the manor of Burnt Pelham (or Brent Pelham) jointly with Edward Cason (a descendant of Ann Hyde and Thomas Bowles). The Casons held the manor of Astonbury and Furneaux Pelham. Edward Cason's mother was Susan Oxenbridge of Hurstbourne Priors (Chauncy wrote about her - see Chapter 11). The Casons had connections with Sir Francis Mannock of Gifford's Hall, Stoke-by-Nayland, who also had connections with the Bull family.

William Bull Clk, MA, Rector of St Andrew's Hertford from 1643 to 1660, was almost certainly a member of the family. Rebecka Harmer (née Bull) was baptised, married and buried in St Andrew's Church and the Bull family home was in this parish.

The Caesar Family
of Benington, Herts

SIR JULIUS CAESAR DELAMARE (or Adelmare)
Born in Venice, Doctor and Physician to Queen Elizabeth
m. Margery, d. and co-heir of George Perient of Digswell. (see Perient tree B)

SIR JULIUS CAESAR
Master of the Request to Queen Elizabeth and Master of the Robes to James I and Charles I. Lived at Tottenham in 1593 and Hackney in 1634. m. Dorcas, d. of Sir Richard Martin.

SIR THOMAS CAESAR
One of the Barons of the Exchequer.

m① Susan, d. of Sir William Ryder, Lord Mayor of London in 1600 | m② Ann, d. of George Lynn of Northampton

SIR JOHN CAESAR
acquired the manor of Hyde Hall. His son sold it to William Franklyn from whom it went to his brother-in-law Sir Nicholas Miller

HENRY CAESAR
Dean of Ely
_____
MARGARET CAESAR m. Nicholas Wright of East Mead, Southampton.

SIR HENRY CAESAR
osp in Italy

SIR CHARLES CAESAR
of Benington. One of the Masters of Chancery.

m① Ann, d. of Sir Peter Vanlore | m② ... d. of Sir Edward Barkham, Lord Mayor of London in 1621

ROBERT CAESAR
m. Elizabeth, d. of John Manning of Sussex

ELIZABETH CAESAR
m. Christopher Wright of Derby

AVICE CAESAR

SUSAN CAESAR

THOMAS CAESAR
m. Frances, d. of George Philipott of Thruxton, Hants.

MARY CAESAR

MARGARET CAESAR

ALICE CAESAR

JACOMINA CAESAR m. Henry Anderson of Pendley (See Anderson tree)

ANNE CAESAR

PHILADELPHIA CAESAR

The Cason Family
of Astonbury and Furneaux Pelham, Hertfordshire

THOMAS CASON of Steeple Morden, Cambridgeshire

EDMOND CASON of Hertford, m. Elizabeth, d. of Thomas Bowles of Wallington and his wife Anne Hyde of Throcking.

JOHN CASON
a London grocer
m. ... Edwards

EDWARD CASON made a learned reading in the Middle Temple in 8 James I (1611)

m① Jane Boteler d. of Sir Henry Boteler of Hatfield Woodhall | m ② Susan Oxenbridge of Hurstbourne Priors, Southampton (who later m. Sir Thomas Cecil, son of Sir Robert Cecil, Earl of Salisbury and his wife Elizabeth Brooke (see Brooke tree and also Chapter 11)

SIR HENRY CASON
of Astonbury and of Payton Hall in Suffolk. m. Dorothy, d. of Sir Thomas Tyringham of Tyringham, Buckinghamshire

EDWARD CASON
bought Furneaux Pelham

m① Mary Blechenden, d. of Thomas Blechenden of Kent | m② Martha Flyer, d. of Francis Flyer of Brent Pelham

JOHN CASON with his brother Edward and with Henry Bull (who was probably a kinsman) he bought Furneaux Pelham from Richard Meade

JOHN CASON
b. 1630
inherited Astonbury

JOHN CASON
2nd

HENRY CASON
inherited a share of Brent Pelham

EDWARD CASON
inherited a share of Brent Pelham

MARY CASON
m. Edward Newport and inherited Brent Pelham from her brothers
(By his marriage to Mary, Edward Newport inherited once again one of the manors which had belonged to his ancestors many generations earlier)
Mary was the only surviving heir of the Cason family (see Newport tree)

The Caldebeck, Underhill, Knighton, Ferrers and Bull Families
of Suffolk and Hertfordshire

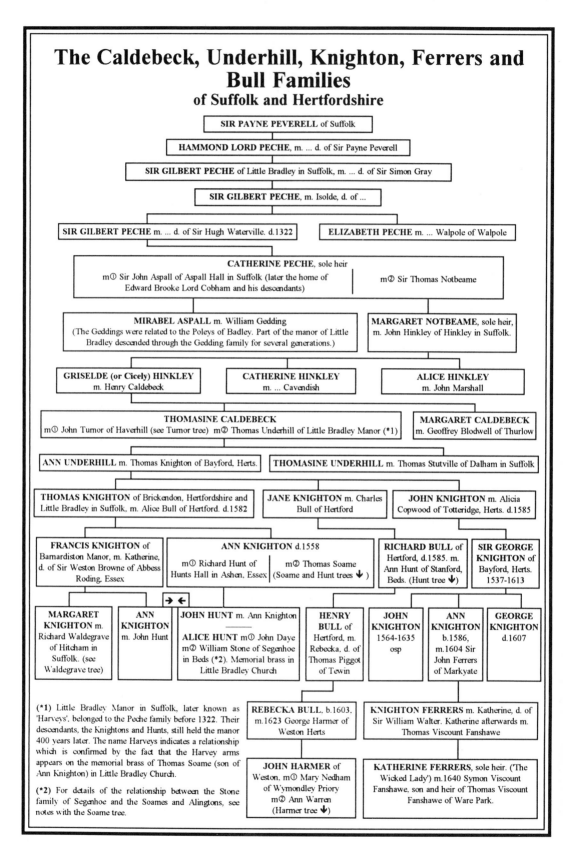

SIR PAYNE PEVERELL of Suffolk

HAMMOND LORD PECHE, m. ... d. of Sir Payne Peverell

SIR GILBERT PECHE of Little Bradley in Suffolk, m. ... d. of Sir Simon Gray

SIR GILBERT PECHE, m. Isolde, d. of ...

SIR GILBERT PECHE m. ... d. of Sir Hugh Waterville. d.1322

ELIZABETH PECHE m. ... Walpole of Walpole

CATHERINE PECHE, sole heir
m① Sir John Aspall of Aspall Hall in Suffolk (later the home of Edward Brooke Lord Cobham and his descendants)

m② Sir Thomas Notbeame

MIRABEL ASPALL m. William Gedding
(The Geddings were related to the Poleys of Badley. Part of the manor of Little Bradley descended through the Gedding family for several generations.)

MARGARET NOTBEAME, sole heir, m. John Hinkley of Hinkley in Suffolk.

GRISELDE (or Cicely) HINKLEY m. Henry Caldebeck

CATHERINE HINKLEY m. ... Cavendish

ALICE HINKLEY m. John Marshall

THOMASINE CALDEBECK
m① John Turnor of Haverhill (see Turnor tree) m② Thomas Underhill of Little Bradley Manor (*1)

MARGARET CALDEBECK m. Geoffrey Blodwell of Thurlow

ANN UNDERHILL m. Thomas Knighton of Bayford, Herts.

THOMASINE UNDERHILL m. Thomas Stutville of Dalham in Suffolk

THOMAS KNIGHTON of Brickendon, Hertfordshire and Little Bradley in Suffolk. m. Alice Bull of Hertford. d.1582

JANE KNIGHTON m. Charles Bull of Hertford

JOHN KNIGHTON m. Alicia Copwood of Totteridge, Herts. d.1585

FRANCIS KNIGHTON of Barnardiston Manor, m. Katherine, d. of Sir Weston Browne of Abbess Roding, Essex

ANN KNIGHTON d.1558
m① Richard Hunt of Hunts Hall in Ashen, Essex

m② Thomas Soame (Soame and Hunt trees ↓)

RICHARD BULL of Hertford, d.1585. m. Ann Hunt of Stanford, Beds. (Hunt tree ↓)

SIR GEORGE KNIGHTON of Bayford, Herts. 1537-1613

MARGARET KNIGHTON m. Richard Waldegrave of Hitcham in Suffolk. (see Waldegrave tree)

ANN KNIGHTON m. John Hunt

→ ←

JOHN HUNT m. Ann Knighton

ALICE HUNT m① John Daye m② William Stone of Segenhoe in Beds (*2). Memorial brass in Little Bradley Church

HENRY BULL of Hertford, m. Rebecka, d. of Thomas Piggot of Tewin

JOHN KNIGHTON 1564-1635 osp

ANN KNIGHTON b.1586, m.1604 Sir John Ferrers of Markyate

GEORGE KNIGHTON d.1607

(*1) Little Bradley Manor in Suffolk, later known as 'Harveys', belonged to the Peche family before 1322. Their descendants, the Knightons and Hunts, still held the manor 400 years later. The name Harveys indicates a relationship which is confirmed by the fact that the Harvey arms appears on the memorial brass of Thomas Soame (son of Ann Knighton) in Little Bradley Church.

(*2) For details of the relationship between the Stone family of Segenhoe and the Soames and Alingtons, see notes with the Soame tree.

REBECKA BULL, b.1603, m.1623 George Harmer of Weston Herts

KNIGHTON FERRERS m. Katherine, d. of Sir William Walter. Katherine afterwards m. Thomas Viscount Fanshawe

JOHN HARMER of Weston, m① Mary Nedham of Wymondley Priory m② Ann Warren (Harmer tree ↓)

KATHERINE FERRERS, sole heir. ('The Wicked Lady') m.1640 Symon Viscount Fanshawe, son and heir of Thomas Viscount Fanshawe of Ware Park.

The Caldebeck, Underhill and Knighton Families
and the Manors of Great Bradley, Little Bradley (Overhall or Harveys) and Netherhall in Suffolk

In 1305 the manors belonged to Sir John Botetourt and his wife Matilda who was grand-daughter of William de Beauchamp Baron of Bedford. By 1322 the manor of Little Bradley (Overhall or Harveys) was held by Gilbert Peche, ancestor of the Hunts, Underhills, Knightons, Bulls and Harmers. His descendants were there for nearly 400 years. Part of the manor passed down through the Gedding family, and during the minority of Robert Gedding it was held in trust jointly by John de la Pole Duke of Suffolk (related through the Peverell family), Sir John Heveningham, and Anthony Earl Rivers (Robert's guardian). Through the marriage of Robert's daughter, Constance Gedding, the manor passed to the Poley family of Badley. Henry Poley died in 1487 and it passed to his son Edmund, grandson John, and then to his kinsman John le Hunte of Hunt Hall in Ashen. The Hunts intermarried several times with the Knightons, Soames and Stutvilles, all of whom were connected with the manor of Little Bradley. As the alternative name 'Harveys' suggests, there were several connections with the Harvey family of Ickworth. In the 16th century the Underhills, direct descendants of Sir Gilbert Peche, were at Little Bradley, and their Knighton and Hunt descendants were there until the early 18th century. The last member of the family to live there was Thomas le Hunt who died age 76 in 1703.

The history of the manor of Great Bradley also has many familiar names. In 1491 it was held by Thomas Scroop, whose mother was a member of the Botetourt family (who held both manors in the 13th and 14th centuries). This Thomas was the father of another Thomas Scroop, a noted Carthusian monk, who inherited the estate. We are told in Copinger's 'Manors of Suffolk', 'He was a native of this parish and derives from the illustrious family of Scroope in Yorkshire. ... He became Suffragan to the Bishop of Norwich, and Vicar of Lowestoft, where he died in 1491 and was buried in the chancel of that church being nearly 100 years of age'.

In the 16th century the manor was vested in Bartholomew Brokesbye who died in 1524 when the manor went to his grandson, also Bartholomew Brokesbye. In 1561 it was bought by Francis Clopton, then Robert Peyton in 1565 and Peter Osborne in 1580.

In 1764 it went to Thomas Brand of Kimpton Hoo in Hertfordshire who on 20th April 1771 married the Hon Gertrude Roper, sister of Charles Trevor Roper 18th Lord Dacre. The Ropers were descended from the ancient family of Roper in Kent, who were also ancestors of the Harmer family. Thomas Brand died on 21st February 1794 and the manor passed to his eldest son Thomas Brand 20th Lord Dacre. He married in 1819 Barbarina, daughter of Admiral Chaloner Ogle, but died without issue and the manor passed to his brother Henry Otway Brand 21st Lord Dacre. He married Pyne, the daughter of the Hon and Very Rev'd Dean Crosbie, and sister of Lord Brandon. He assumed by sign manual in 1824 the surname of Trevor, and when he died in 1853 the manor passed to his son, Thomas Crosbie William Trevor 22nd Lord Dacre. He died without issue in 1890 and was succeeded by his brother Henry Bouverie William Trevor, MP for Lewes 1852-68, for Cambridge 1868-84, and Speaker of the House of Commons 1872-84. He was a Privy Counsellor and was created Viscount Hampden in 1884. He died in 1892 and his son, Henry Robert Brand 2nd Viscount Hampden and 24th Lord Dacre inherited. He was MP for Hertfordshire, and a Captain in the Coldstream Guards. He married in 1868 (2nd marriage) Susan Henrietta, daughter of Lord George Henry Cavendish.

During the years from 1771 the manor of Great Bradley had followed the same line as the manors of Kimpton and St Pauls Walden, once again reinforcing the link between these two localities.

The manor of Netherhall (presumably downhill from the manor of Overhall or Harveys) was held by the Hunt family in the 16th century, and followed the same line as Overhall until it was acquired by the Turnor family (also related to the Hunts, Knightons, Stutvilles and Underhills).

All Saints Church, Little Bradley, Suffolk

The Capell Family
of Little Hadham in Hertfordshire, and Abbess Roding and Raynes in Essex

SIR WILLIAM CAPELL, b. at Stoke by Nayland in Suffolk, Lord Mayor of London in 1504 and 1509, Knighted by Henry VII. Bought the manor of Walkern about 1510. He lies buried in a stately chapel built by him in St Batholomew's Church by the Exchange. m. Margaret, d. of Sir Thomas Arundell. They were ancestors of the Earls of Essex.

SIR GILES CAPELL of Hadham, d.1556 (buried beside his father at St Bartholomew's), m. ..., d. of Sir John Newton (alias Craddock)

ELIZABETH CAPELL, m. Sir William Pawlett, Knight of the Garter, Marquis of Winchester, d. 1571. Treasurer of the Household to Henry VIII,

SIR EDWARD CAPELL of Hadham, m. Ann, d. of Sir William Pelham of Burnt (Brent) Pelham.

MARGARET CAPELL, m. Robert Warde of Brooke (alias Kirkby), in Norfolk

SIR HENRY CAPELL of Raynes and Little Hadham Hall. High Sheriff 1585, Muster Master for Herts (see Capell notes)
m① Mary, d. of Sir Anthony Browne of Sussex and widow of Lord John Grey of Pirgo (see Browne of Sussex tree) | m② Lady Catherine, d. of Thomas Manners Earl of Rutland KG

MARY CAPELL, m. Weston Browne of Rookwood (or Clovills). She died childless (possibly in childbirth). Weston Browne then m. Elizabeth, d. of Giles Pawlett (a kinsman of Sir William Pawlett who m. Elizabeth Capell) and they had a daughter, Jayne, who m. Sir Gamaliel Capell. (see below) (Browne of Essex tree ↓)

ELIZA-BETH CAPELL m. John Wentworth of Bocking in Essex

SIR ARTHUR CAPELL of Little Hadham, 1558-1632, High Sheriff of Herts 1592, m. Mary, d. of Lord Grey of Pirgo

SIR EDWARD CAPELL b. 1559

JOHN CAPELL b. 1561, High Sheriff 1587, m. Helen, d. of Thomas Leventhorpe of Shingle Hall, Herts, and widow of John Longmore

AGNES CAPELL b. 1563

FRANCIS CAPELL and **ANN CAPELL** (twins) b. 1565. Ann m. Sir Robert Chester of Cockenhatch near Royston.

SIR GAMALIEL CAPELL of Raynes, 1566-1613, acquired Abbess Roding in 1692, knighted 1603, m. Jayne, d. of Weston Browne by his 2nd wife (Elizabeth Pawlett), and widow of Edward Wyatt of Tillingham in Essex. (Jayne was marrying her father's first wife's nephew) (Browne Tree ↓)

ROBERT CAPELL b. 1568

MARY CAPELL m. Henry Mildmay

SIR HENRY CAPELL son and heir, m. Ann Wentworth

DAUGHTER m. Constantine Lewin of Kent

DAUGHTER m. Sir John Corbett of Sproston in Norfolk. Their d. Bridget m. Brian Darcy of Tiptree, s. of Thomas Darcy of Tolshunt Darcy (Darcy Tree ↓)

SIR GAMALIEL CAPELL inherited Abbess Roding from his mother. His son and grandson (both Gamaliel) inherited. Finally sold to the Duke of Bedford about 1700.

MARY CAPELL ------ **PENELOPE CAPELL** m. Litton, s. of Edmund Pulter. (Pulter tree ↓)

ANN CAPELL m. Robert Wiseman of Canfield

ARTHUR CAPELL executed 1649, MP for Hertford 1641. At the Restoration his son Sir Arthur was created Earl of Essex

For Capell history see notes on Muster Books
For history of Abbess Roding see notes with Browne of Essex tree

Notes on the Muster Books 1580-1605
with reference to the Capell and Pulter families

Sir Henry Capell was Captain of the North and East Herts foot soldiers, and was responsible for recruiting and training a band of able men, who could be called upon at any time for the defence of the kingdom. The Captains or Commissioners of Array were also required to provide armour, arms and ammunition, sometimes at their own expense. Sir Henry's son, Sir Arthur Capell, was one of the Commissioners of Array, and was responsible for recruiting and helping to train the soldiers.

At this time there was no regular army, and the country relied on the County Militia, selected from the various bands of men between the ages of 16 and 60 who were required to do four days training a year under the command of the local Muster Captain. In 1588, when the country was threatened with invasion by the Spanish, a special levy was raised for the Defence of the Kingdon. The list of gentlemen who were required to pay £25 or more appears on page 234.

To give warning of invasion there was a chain of beacons along the south coast and across the country. They were guarded and maintained by specially trained and trustworthy Beacon Keepers and there was a very severe penalty for unauthorised firing. There were four beacons in Hertfordshire: on the tower of St Peter's in St Albans, on Hertford Heath, at Graveley, and at Therfield. Just across the county border there was a beacon on a high peak in the village of Ivinghoe. Four hundred years later Ivinghoe Beacon is a well-known local landmark, reminding us of the 16th century 'Early Warning System' which has now been replaced with rather more sophisticated methods!

The Hertfordshire Muster Books have been transcribed and published by the Hertfordshire Record Society. The earlier books in particular were meticulously kept, and were probably written by a professional scribe in the Capell household at Little Hadham Hall. They show that Henry Capell had at least 39 male servants. Some were probably sons of the gentry, who had been to university and were taking a year out to learn the skills of estate management before going on to the Inns of Court to complete their education.

The Hertfordshire Commissioners of Array, whose names appear in the Muster Books, were almost all related to each other, and several were related to the queen herself, ensuring a high degree of loyalty and commitment. There are many familiar names including: Boteler, Bowles, Brocket, Coningsby, Docwra, Horsey, Hyde, Leventhorpe, Lytton, Pulter, and Shotbolt.

Sir Henry Capell was succeeded as Muster Captain by Edward Pulter of Cottered and Wymondley (see Pulter tree). He was Muster Captain for 22 years. Like Henry Capell he received no pay for this public service, and willingly gave his time and money as one of the duties which went with privilege and wealth. We are told however that he was (understandably) a little resentful when asked to pay the extra levy which was demanded of all wealthy landowners in 1588. Later that year Edward Pulter had to march his selected band of soldiers to Tilbury, where an army was gathering in readiness to resist the expected Spanish invasion. Once the soldiers crossed the county boundary they were entitled to a maintenance allowance from the government, but during the 40 mile march through the Hertfordshire countryside Edward had to beg or buy their nightly board and lodging.

The Pulters were related by marriage to the Capells. Sir Henry Capell's granddaughter Penelope was married to Litton Pulter, the son of Captain Edward Pulter and his wife Mary who was the daughter of Sir Rowland Lytton of Knebworth.

Little Hadham Hall Hertfordshire 1893
Drawn by Maurice B Adams FRIBA

The Cary Family
of Aldenham, Hertfordshire

THOMAS CARY of Chilton in Devon, 2nd son of Sir William Cary, m. Margaret, d. of Sir Robert Spencer of Cople. (see Spencer tree)

JOHN CARY of Hackney, m. Martha, d. of Edmund Denny of Norwich and sister of Sir Anthony Denny of Herts (Privy Councillor to Henry VIII)

WILLIAM CARY, Esquire for the Body of Henry VIII. Died 1528. m. 1520 Mary, d. and heir of Thomas Bullen (Boleyn) Earl of Wiltshire, and sister of Ann Boleyn (2nd wife of Henry VIII and mother of Queen Elizabeth I). **(see important footnote)**

WYMOND CARY of Hackney. He had two daughters: Elizabeth, who m. George Dacres of Cheshunt, and Prudence, who m. Anthony Bridges of West Ham in Essex

SIR EDWARD CARY Master of the Jewell House. m. Catherine, d. of Sir Henry Knevett and widow of Henry, Lord Paget. She was the sister of Thomasine Knevett who m. Sir William Clopton of Kentwell Hall in Suffolk. (see Clopton tree)

SIR HENRY CARY 1524-96, Baron of Hunsdon, Lord Chamberlain (and first cousin) to Queen Elizabeth. m. Ann, d. of Sir Thomas Morgan of Kent.

CATHERINE CARY, a first cousin to Queen Elizabeth, m. Sir Francis Knollys (*1), counsellor and close friend of the Queen. Their d. Catherine m. Sir Philip Boteler. (↓ Boteler tree)

FRANCES CARY m. Ralph Bashe of Stanstead Bury, Herts
———
SIR ADOLPHUS CARY, m. Ann, d. of Sir Robert Corbett of Salop, osp. Buried at Aldenham
———
SIR PHILIP CARY, m. Elizabeth, d. of Richard Bland of Yorkshire. They had 2 sons and 2 daughters. There were five other daughters: **ELIZABETH; MURIEL CATHERINE; ANNE** and **ANNE.** who all married.

SIR HENRY CARY, Viscount Faulkland in Scotland, Died at Theobalds after breaking his leg in a fall. m. Elizabeth, d. of Sir Lawrence Tanfield, Lord Chief Baron of the Exchequer.

SIR GEORGE CARY, b.1556, Lord Hunsdon, m. Elizabeth, d. of Sir John Spencer. (See Spencer tree) He was Lord Chamberlain at the time of Queen Elizabeth's death. He died later the same year (1603). His brother John inherited the title. (*1)

SIR JOHN CARY 1563-1617, Lord Hunsdon, m. Mary, d. of Leonard Hyde of Throcking and widow of John Paston of Norfolk. There is a memorial plaque in Hunsdon church (See Hyde tree and Chapter 4)

SIR EDMUND CARY (*2) m① Mary Coker of Devon; m② Judith, d. of Lawrence Humphrey, DD, and widow of Sir John Rivers.
———
SIR ROBERT CARY (*3) Earl of Monmouth, m. .... Trevanion
———
PHILADELPHIA CARY m. Thomas, Lord Scroop of Bolton.
———
MARGARET CARY m. Sir Edward Hobby, Gentleman of the Privy Chamber
———
CATHERINE CARY m. Charles Howard, Earl of Nottingham and Admiral of England.

LUCIUS CARY
———
LAWRENCE CARY

EDWARD CARY
———
CATHERINE CARY

VICTORIA CARY
———
ANNE CARY

ELIZABETH CARY

ELIZABETH CARY b.1576.. Queen Elizabeth was one of her Godmothers. m. Thomas Barkley, s. and heir of Henry, Lord Barkley.

HENRY CARY, Lord Hunsdon, Viscount Rochford and Earl of Dover (*4) m. Judith, d. of Sir Thomas Pelham of Laughton, Sussex.

(***1**) Sir Francis Knollys, who had the task of looking after Mary Queen of Scots, tried to marry her to his nephew George Cary, hoping it would solve some of the problems, but unfortunately Mary was not interested.

(***2**) Sir Edmund Cary had 5 children: Robert, Ferdinando, Thomas, Anne and Catherine.

(***3**) Sir Robert Cary had 2 sons: ① Sir Henry Cary, Knight of the Bath at the creation of Charles, Prince of Wales, and ② Thomas Cary, died 1634, one of the Gentlemen of the Bedchamber to King Charles I. He m. Margaret, sole heir of Thomas Smythe, Clarke of the Parliament and Counsell. Sir Robert also had 3 daughters: Philadelphia, Frances and Elizabeth.

(***4**) Henry had no male heir so in 1617 King James granted the title to Sir John Boteler. It then went to Sir Thomas Dacres and in 1635 to the Earl of Elgin (the Bruce family, Lord Ailesbury).

Important footnote added as the book was going to press

New discoveries resulting from research by Anthony Hoskins, Librarian of the Newberry Library, Chicago, have been recorded in the official journal of the Society of Genealogists (report in The Daily Telegraph, 27th May 1997). Historians have always agreed that Henry VIII did have an affair with Mary Boleyn. the wife of William Cary, but hitherto the relationship was thought to be childless. Now there is strong evidence that Catherine and Henry Cary were in fact the children of Henry VIII. Catherine married Sir Francis Knollys, and their daughter Lettice (not shown on our tree) was an ancestor of Queen Elizabeth the Queen Mother. This would mean that Henry VIII's descendants did not die out with Queen Elizabeth I, but continued in an uninterrupted line to Queen Elizabeth II. From our own family point of view it means that the niece of our ancestor Lucy Hyde was married to the grandson of Henry VIII. (see Chapter 4)

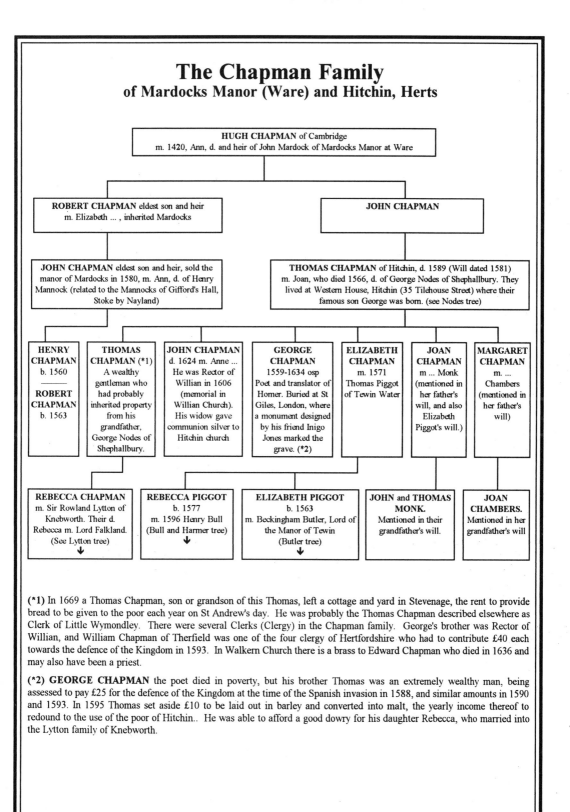

The Chapman Family
of Mardocks Manor (Ware) and Hitchin, Herts

HUGH CHAPMAN of Cambridge
m. 1420, Ann, d. and heir of John Mardock of Mardocks Manor at Ware

ROBERT CHAPMAN eldest son and heir
m. Elizabeth ... , inherited Mardocks

JOHN CHAPMAN

JOHN CHAPMAN eldest son and heir, sold the manor of Mardocks in 1580, m. Ann, d. of Henry Mannock (related to the Mannocks of Gifford's Hall, Stoke by Nayland)

THOMAS CHAPMAN of Hitchin, d. 1589 (Will dated 1581) m. Joan, who died 1566, d. of George Nodes of Shephallbury. They lived at Western House, Hitchin (35 Tilehouse Street) where their famous son George was born. (see Nodes tree)

HENRY CHAPMAN b. 1560
———
ROBERT CHAPMAN b. 1563

THOMAS CHAPMAN (*1) A wealthy gentleman who had probably inherited property from his grandfather, George Nodes of Shephallbury.

JOHN CHAPMAN d. 1624 m. Anne ... He was Rector of Willian in 1606 (memorial in Willian Church). His widow gave communion silver to Hitchin church

GEORGE CHAPMAN 1559-1634 osp Poet and translator of Homer. Buried at St Giles, London, where a monument designed by his friend Inigo Jones marked the grave. (*2)

ELIZABETH CHAPMAN m. 1571 Thomas Piggot of Tewin Water

JOAN CHAPMAN m ... Monk (mentioned in her father's will, and also Elizabeth Piggot's will.)

MARGARET CHAPMAN m. ... Chambers (mentioned in her father's will)

REBECCA CHAPMAN m. Sir Rowland Lytton of Knebworth. Their d. Rebecca m. Lord Falkland. (See Lytton tree) ↓

REBECCA PIGGOT b. 1577 m. 1596 Henry Bull (Bull and Harmer tree) ↓

ELIZABETH PIGGOT b. 1563 m. Beckingham Butler, Lord of the Manor of Tewin (Butler tree) ↓

JOHN and THOMAS MONK. Mentioned in their grandfather's will.

JOAN CHAMBERS. Mentioned in her grandfather's will

(*1) In 1669 a Thomas Chapman, son or grandson of this Thomas, left a cottage and yard in Stevenage, the rent to provide bread to be given to the poor each year on St Andrew's day. He was probably the Thomas Chapman described elsewhere as Clerk of Little Wymondley. There were several Clerks (Clergy) in the Chapman family. George's brother was Rector of Willian, and William Chapman of Therfield was one of the four clergy of Hertfordshire who had to contribute £40 each towards the defence of the Kingdom in 1593. In Walkern Church there is a brass to Edward Chapman who died in 1636 and may also have been a priest.

(*2) GEORGE CHAPMAN the poet died in poverty, but his brother Thomas was an extremely wealthy man, being assessed to pay £25 for the defence of the Kingdom at the time of the Spanish invasion in 1588, and similar amounts in 1590 and 1593. In 1595 Thomas set aside £10 to be laid out in barley and converted into malt, the yearly income thereof to redound to the use of the poor of Hitchin.. He was able to afford a good dowry for his daughter Rebecca, who married into the Lytton family of Knebworth.

The Clarke Family
of Walkern, Benington, Chesfield and Ashwell

CLARKE. *Gules three swords argent with their hilts or set fessewise with their points upwards.*

JOHN CLARKE of Stevenage, Herts

SIR EDWARD CLARKE of Reading, Berkshire

GEORGE CLARKE of Walkern and Benington m. ... Kympton

THOMAS CLARKE of Houghton, Beds

GEORGE CLARKE of Benington

WILLIAM CLARKE of Walkern. Died 1591, memorial in Benington Church. Bought Graveley in 1566.

JOHN CLARKE of Henlowbury, Beds. m. Jane, d. of John Kent of Astonbury

SIR FRANCIS CLARKE of Houghton, Beds m. Mary, d. of Henry Pranell of Barkway. (See Brooke tree)

JOHN CLARKE of Ashwell m. Marion, d. of Thomas Kympton of Myms

GEORGE CLARKE of Chesfield and Walkern m. Elizabeth Bristow (Bristow tree ↓)

EDWARD CLARKE

JOHN CLARKE

WILLIAM CLARKE of Therfield m. Susan Aylett of Maryland, Essex.

JOHN CLARKE of Ashwell. m. 1617, Judith, d. of Thomas Hawes of Bedford

WILLIAM CLARKE
m② Rebecca, d. of Thomas Taylor, Doctor of Phisick. No issue
m① Frances Bristow

ELIZABETH CLARKE m 1601, Thomas Harmer widower of Jane Kympton

MARY CLARKE m. ... Jackson

SUSAN CLARKE m. Thomas Joscelin of Hyde Hall, Sawbridgeworth

CATHERINE CLARKE m. Joseph Graves (See Bull tree)

THOMAS CLARKE of London m. Hester Anslow

RICHARD CLARKE m. Bridget Gates

ANN CLARKE

JOHN CLARKE

WILLIAM CLARKE

ROBERT CLARKE

AYLETT CLARKE

JUDITH CLARKE

ELIZABETH CLARKE

MARY CLARKE

LETTICE CLARKE

JOHN CLARKE b. 1620

THOMAS CLARKE

WILLIAM CLARKE

WILLIAM CLARKE

NICHOLAS CLARKE

FRANCIS CLARKE

ELIZABETH HARMER b. 1602 m. Thomas Humberstone of Walkern

MARY HARMER b. 1604

JOHN HARMER b. 1606 m. Timothae (Harmer 'B' tree) ↓

BENJAMIN HARMER b. 1609

The Bristow Family
of Sacombe and Ayot St Lawrence.

NICHOLAS BRISTOW of Ayot St Lawrence, Clarke of the Jewells to Henry VIII, Edward VI, Queen Mary and Queen Elizabeth, m. Lucy Barley (buried at Ayot St Lawrence)

NICHOLAS BRISTOW of Ayot St Lawrence, Clarke of the Jewells to Queen Elizabeth and King James, m. Margaret Boteler, daughter of Sir John Boteler of Hatfield Woodhall.

BRISTOWE of Ayot St. Lawrence. *Ermine a fesse cotised sable with three crescents or thereon.*

NICHOLAS BRISTOW m Elizabeth Pynder

ELIZABETH BRISTOW m. George Clarke of Chesfield and Walkern

MARY BRISTOW, m. 1572. William Hyde of Throcking, son of Leonard Hyde and Ann Boteler. (Hyde tree ↓)

FRANCES BRISTOW m. William Clarke (her cousin) (Clarke tree ↓ above) → ←

WILLIAM CLARKE m① Frances Bristow (his cousin) m② Rebecka, d. of Thomas Taylor, Doctor of Phisick

ELIZABETH CLARKE, m. 1601, Thomas Harmer, widower of Jane Kympton. (Harmer tree ↓)

NOTE: On the Fairclough tree we have ... Clarke who married Elizabeth Fairclough and went to Ireland to become a Dean. This may have been a brother of Elizabeth Clarke, the wife of Thomas Harmer, whose grandson, George Harmer, later went to Ireland, possibly to join his great-uncle.

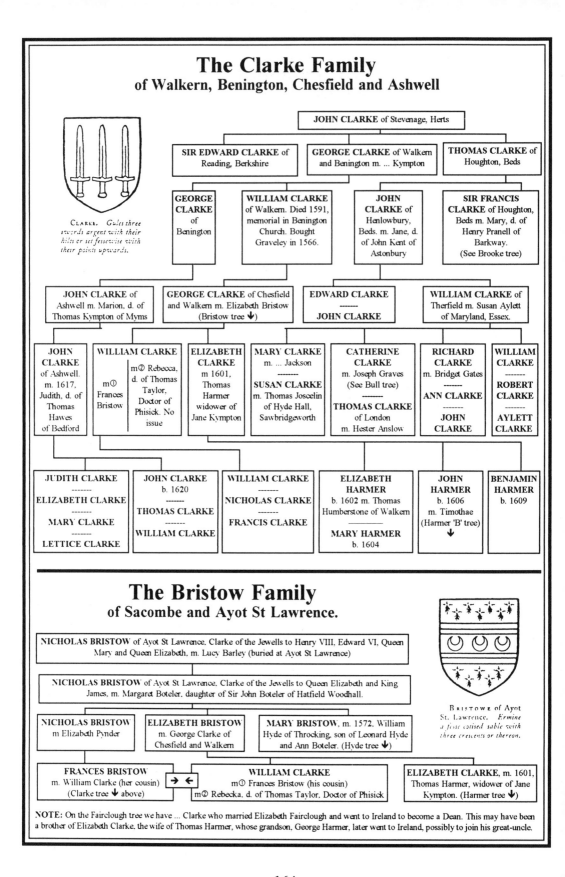

The Clopton Family
of Kentwell Hall, Long Melford and Kedington, Suffolk

SIR WILLIAM CLOPTON
m. ... Piggot

SIR THOMAS CLOPTON
m. Katherine Mylde of Clare, Suffolk (commemorated in NW window of the nave in Long Melford Church)

SIR WILLIAM CLOPTON of Kentwell Hall, d.1446

m① Margery (d.1420), d. of Sir Roger Drury of Rougham (memorial in Long Melford Church.)	m② Margery Francis, d.1424 (heraldic effigy in Long Melford Church)

ANNE CLOPTON ------- **MARGERY CLOPTON** Both died Oct 1420, only 4 months after their mother	**ALICE CLOPTON** 1410-40, eldest daughter (brass in floor of Clopton Chapel) m. John Harleston	**WILLIAM CLOPTON** d. March 1420, 3 months before his mother.	**KATHERINE CLOPTON**	**JOHN CLOPTON** d.1497. Largely re-built Long Melford Church, High Sheriff of Norfolk and Suffolk 1451, m. Alice, d. of Sir Robert Darcy of Maldon in Essex (see Darcy tree)

SIR WILLIAM CLOPTON

m① Joan, d. of Sir William Marrow of Stepney.	m② Thomasine, d. of Sir Henry Knevitt and sister of Catherine Knevitt who m. Sir Edward Cary

JOHN CLOPTON m. Elizabeth Roydon of Essex	**WILLIAM CLOPTON** of Kedington m. Elizabeth, d. of Sir Thomas Saye of Lyston Hall, Essex.	**ROBERT CLOPTON** a priest	**FRANCIS CLOPTON** m. Bridget Crane	**ANN CLOPTON**, d. 1550 m. Richard Poley of Boxted (Poley tree ↓)

WILLIAM CLOPTON d. 1562 m① Margaret Jermyn of Rushbrooke / m② 1550, Mary, d. of George Perient (see Perient tree)	**GEORGE CLOPTON** m. Alice, d. and heir of Sir Stephen Peacock, Lord Mayor of London 1532	**FRANCIS CLOPTON** m① Olyffe Gavel of Norfolk, m② Laura, d. of Sir Roger Wentworth, m③ Lady Barnardiston (Dame Mary) d. of Sir Edmund Walsingham, m④ Elizabeth Brookesbye (widow), d. of Sir Thomas Barnardiston and sister of Anne who m. Francis' brother William Clopton. (see Barnardiston tree)	**WLLIAM CLOPTON** of Lyston Hall m. 1610 Anne, d. of Sir Thomas Barnardiston of Kedington

ANN CLOPTON ------- **ELIZABETH CLOPTON** ------- **MARGARET CLOPTON** ——— **WILLIAM CLOPTON** ------- **FRANCIS CLOPTON** m. Agnes Crane	**GEORGE CLOPTON** ------- **THOMAS CLOPTON** ------- **BRIDGET CLOPTON**	**GEORGE CLOPTON** ------- **WILLIAM CLOPTON**	**EDMUND CLOPTON** ------- **FRANCIS CLOPTON**	**FRANCIS CLOPTON** of Lyston Hall, m. Ann Short of Wetheringset in Suffolk

FROM THE PARISH REGISTERS:

Mary Clopton m. George Barnardiston at Bury St Edmunds in 1567

John Clopton m. Elizabeth, d. of Thomas Meautis of Hertford and Elizabeth Coningsby of North Mimms

Kentwell Hall, Long Melford, Suffolk

The Coningsby Family
of North Mimms Park and Potterells

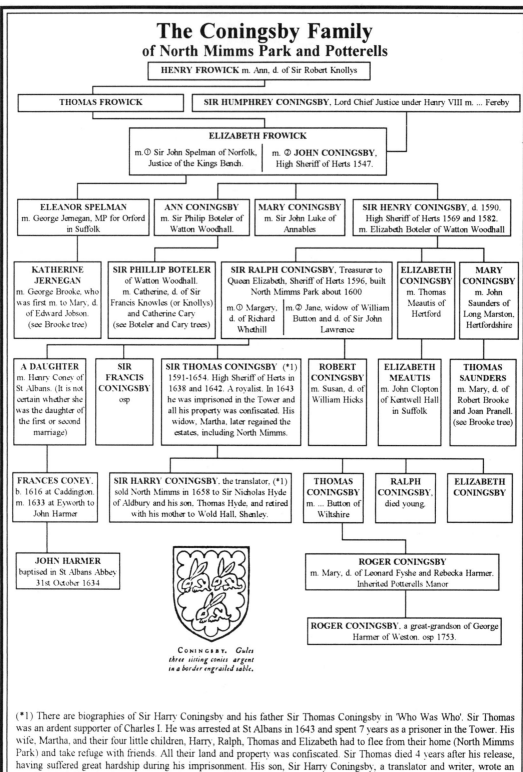

HENRY FROWICK m. Ann, d. of Sir Robert Knollys

THOMAS FROWICK

SIR HUMPHREY CONINGSBY, Lord Chief Justice under Henry VIII m. ... Fereby

ELIZABETH FROWICK
m. ① Sir John Spelman of Norfolk, Justice of the Kings Bench.
m. ② **JOHN CONINGSBY**, High Sheriff of Herts 1547.

ELEANOR SPELMAN
m. George Jernegan, MP for Orford in Suffolk

ANN CONINGSBY
m. Sir Philip Boteler of Watton Woodhall.

MARY CONINGSBY
m. Sir John Luke of Annables

SIR HENRY CONINGSBY, d. 1590. High Sheriff of Herts 1569 and 1582. m. Elizabeth Boteler of Watton Woodhall

KATHERINE JERNEGAN
m. George Brooke, who was first m. to Mary, d. of Edward Jobson. (see Brooke tree)

SIR PHILLIP BOTELER
of Watton Woodhall. m. Catherine, d. of Sir Francis Knowles (or Knollys) and Catherine Cary (see Boteler and Cary trees)

SIR RALPH CONINGSBY, Treasurer to Queen Elizabeth, Sheriff of Herts 1596, built North Mimms Park about 1600
m. ① Margery, d. of Richard Whethill
m. ② Jane, widow of William Button and d. of Sir John Lawrence

ELIZABETH CONINGSBY
m. Thomas Meautis of Hertford

MARY CONINGSBY
m. John Saunders of Long Marston, Hertfordshire

A DAUGHTER
m. Henry Coney of St Albans. (It is not certain whether she was the daughter of the first or second marriage)

SIR FRANCIS CONINGSBY
osp

SIR THOMAS CONINGSBY (*1)
1591-1654. High Sheriff of Herts in 1638 and 1642. A royalist. In 1643 he was imprisoned in the Tower and all his property was confiscated. His widow, Martha, later regained the estates, including North Mimms.

ROBERT CONINGSBY
m. Susan, d. of William Hicks

ELIZABETH MEAUTIS
m. John Clopton of Kentwell Hall in Suffolk

THOMAS SAUNDERS
m. Mary, d. of Robert Brooke and Joan Pranell. (see Brooke tree)

FRANCES CONEY,
b. 1616 at Caddington. m. 1633 at Eyworth to John Harmer

SIR HARRY CONINGSBY, the translator, (*1) sold North Mimms in 1658 to Sir Nicholas Hyde of Aldbury and his son, Thomas Hyde, and retired with his mother to Wold Hall, Shenley.

THOMAS CONINGSBY
m. ... Button of Wiltshire

RALPH CONINGSBY,
died young.

ELIZABETH CONINGSBY

JOHN HARMER
baptised in St Albans Abbey 31st October 1634

ROGER CONINGSBY
m. Mary, d. of Leonard Fyshe and Rebecka Harmer. Inherited Potterells Manor

ROGER CONINGSBY, a great-grandson of George Harmer of Weston. osp 1753.

CONINGSBY. *Gules three sitting conies argent in a border engrailed sable.*

(*1) There are biographies of Sir Harry Coningsby and his father Sir Thomas Coningsby in 'Who Was Who'. Sir Thomas was an ardent supporter of Charles I. He was arrested at St Albans in 1643 and spent 7 years as a prisoner in the Tower. His wife, Martha, and their four little children, Harry, Ralph, Thomas and Elizabeth had to flee from their home (North Mimms Park) and take refuge with friends. All their land and property was confiscated. Sir Thomas died 4 years after his release, having suffered great hardship during his imprisonment. His son, Sir Harry Coningsby, a translator and writer, wrote an account of his father's life, together with a letter to Sir Thomas Hyde (the son of the purchaser of North Mimms Park) which is now in the British Museum.

The De la Pole Family of Suffolk
showing links with the Brookes of Aspall and the Enderbys of Bedfordshire

WILLIAM DE LA POLE
Merchant of Hull

RICHARD DE LA POLE
Butler to the King [Edward III]

WILLIAM DE LA POLE, Merchant of Hull, d.1356, m. Catherine, d. of Sir John Norwich. (Effigy in the Church of the Holy Trinity, Hull)

WILLIAM DE LA POLE
m. Margaret, d. of Edmund Peverell and Alice Langton (sister of Walter de Langton, Bishop of Lichfield and Coventry)

MICHAEL DE LA POLE
1st Earl of Suffolk, Chancellor of England, d.1389, m. Katherine, d. and heir of Sir John Wingfield of Wingfield Castle in Suffolk.

JOHN DE LA POLE
succeeded to the manor of Everton in Bedfordshire in 1358, m.1362, Joan, d. of John 3rd Lord Cobham

KATHERINE DE LA POLE
m. John Bullok

MICHAEL DE LA POLE
2nd Earl of Suffolk, slain at Harfleur 1415 m. Katherine, d. of Hugh, Earl of Stafford (Effigy in Wingfield Church)

JOAN BARONESS COBHAM,
b. about 1378, d.1433 m. Sir Reginald Braybrooke, d.1405

ROBERT BULLOK
m. ... 1419

MICHAEL DE LA POLE
3rd Earl of Suffolk, slain at Agincourt 1415, m. Elizabeth, d. of Thomas Mowbray of Bedfordshire, Duke of Norfolk. (see Piggot tree)

WILLIAM DE LA POLE
1st Duke of Suffolk, beheaded 1450 (*1), m. Alice, d. of Sir Thomas Chaucer of Studham in Hertfordshire [now in Bedfordshire], and granddaughter of the poet Geoffrey Chaucer. Alice was previously married to the Earl of Salisbury.

JOAN BRAYBROOKE
Baroness Cobham, d. 1442, m. Sir Thomas Brooke of Aspall (d.1439), who became 5th Lord Cobham. (↓ Brooke tree)

ELIZABETH BULLOK
m. William Furtho of Furtho

JOHN DE LA POLE
2nd Duke of Suffolk, d.1491, buried at Wingfield, m. Elizabeth, d. of Richard Plantagenet, Duke of York, and sister of Edward IV. (Effigy in Wingfield church)

ALICE FURTHO
m. John Enderby of Edworth and Astwick, Beds, and of Kingswoodbury Herts, d.1457 (↓ Piggot tree)

JOHN DE LA POLE
Earl of Lincoln, m. Margaret, d. of Thomas Lord Arundel. Heir presumptive to the throne but when Richard III was killed at Bosworth in 1485, Henry VII became King.

EDMUND DE LA POLE
The last Earl of Suffolk, beheaded in 1513 because of his royal blood. m. Margaret, d. of Richard, Lord Scrope.

(*1) Among the Paston Letters is a very moving letter from William de la Pole to his son John. It was written at Wingfield Castle on 30 April 1450, and an extract is reproduced below:

> My dear and only well-beloved son, I beseech Our Lord in heaven, the maker of all the world, to bless you, and to send you ever grace to love Him and to dread Him ... And that also, wittingly, ye do nothing for love nor dread of any earthly creature that should displease Him ...

> Secondly, next Him above all earthly things, to be true liegeman in heart, in will, in thought, in deed, unto the King our aldermost high and dread sovereign lord, to whom both ye and I be so much bound to; charging you, as father can and may, rather to die than to be the contrary ...

> Thirdly, in the same wise, I charge you, my dear son, alway ... to love, to worship, your lady and mother; and also that ye obey alway her commandments, and to believe her counsels and advices in all your works.

> Furthermore, as father may and can, I charge you in any wise to flee the company and counsel of proud men, of covetous men, and of flattering men ... and to draw to you and to your company good and virtuous men, and such as be of good conversation, and of truth ...

> And I will be to you as good lord and father as my heart can think.

> Written of mine hand, the day of my departing fro this land. Your true and loving father, Suffolk.

The letter was written on the day when the King, at the instigation of the Commons, banished the faithful Duke from the country. On 2nd May, three days after writing this farewell letter to his beloved son, he was taken out to sea and beheaded. John's mother, whom his father commends to him so lovingly, was the granddaughter of the poet Chaucer.

The de la Poles and the Wingfield Connection

When Thomas Harmer married Mercy Galbraith in 1923 it was quite by chance that they came to live in the Suffolk village of Wingfield. Thomas immediately became interested in the historical connections with the de la Pole family, but was quite unaware that they were his distant kinsmen.

At this time the Vicar, the Rev'd Samuel Aldwell, was working on a history of Wingfield and Thomas Harmer soon became involved in the project. He drew up the ground plans of the church and college, and he also discovered the piscina which Mr Aldwell had hitherto been unable to locate. This is described in a note which was added just as the book was going to press:

> The old piscina in the Lady Chapel has at last been discovered and opened up. I had read in some old record of the Church that it was somewhere in the sill of the easternmost window on the south side of the Lady Chapel; so I asked Mr Harmer of Wingfield to remove the plaster and bricks with which the sill had been filled in. This he did most carefully, and we discovered that the window sill was originally flat, not sloping as it is now, but could not find any traces of a piscina. However, a few days after, Mr Harmer measured the distance of the piscina in the Chancel from the east wall, and then marked the spot on the Lady Chapel window sill a similar distance from the east wall; he went to work here and shortly after came across the piscina. It was uncovered on December 15th 1925 and is now being used for its original purpose.

The book, entitled 'Wingfield: Its Church Castle and College', was published a few weeks later. It is now out of print, but a few precious copies remain. The photographs opposite are reproduced from this book.

Thomas and Mercy spent the first three years of their married life at Wingfield, in the cottage called 'Buntings', on the hill overlooking the church and college. Buntings is now better known as the Swingletree Stables, and is the home of the famous Norwich Union coach and its equally famous driver John Parker.

There are three sets of effigies in the church. The earliest shows Sir John Wingfield, who died in 1361 leaving a bequest for the foundation of the Chantry College, which has remained an important feature of the village up to the present day. The second is of Michael de la Pole, 2nd Earl of Suffolk (died at Agincourt in 1415) with his wife Katherine Stafford, and the third is John de la Pole, 2nd Duke of Suffolk (died 1491) with his wife Elizabeth Plantagenet, the sister of Edward IV.

A present-day view of Wingfield, taken from the Buntings meadow. To the right of the church is a glimpse of the ancient college (now an arts centre). On the left is the public house, the de la Pole Arms. The signpost in the foreground directs us to Fressingfield and Laxfield (but beware of the unbridged ford!)

Wingfield Castle South Front

Wingfield Castle was the home of the de la Poles for over 100 years, from 1384 until it was forfeited to the Crown in the reign of Henry VIII. In 1532 it was granted to Charles Duke of Brandon, who probably built the house shown below. Both photographs were taken around 1924 by Mr J E Groom who was then living at the Castle

Wingfield Castle showing Tudor House and Courtyard

The Docwra Family
of Putteridge and Pirton, Hertfordshire

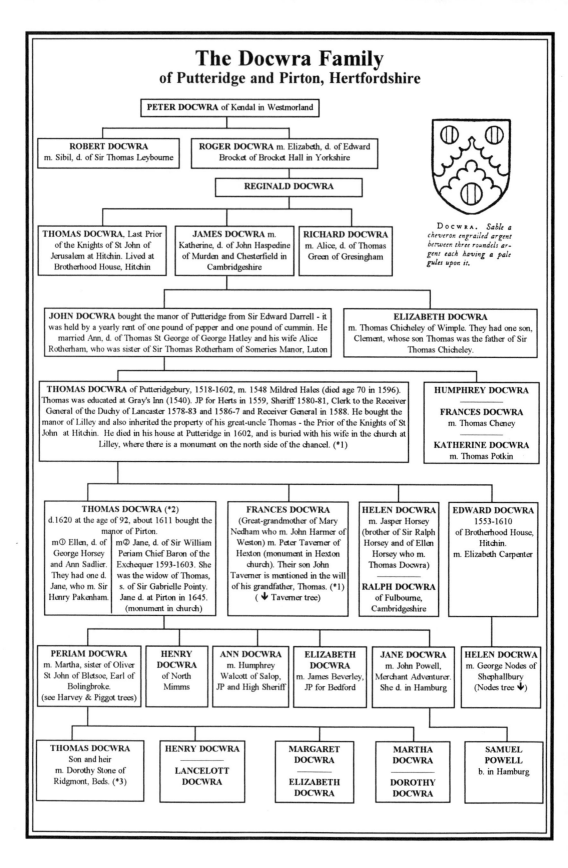

PETER DOCWRA of Kendal in Westmorland

ROBERT DOCWRA m. Sibil, d. of Sir Thomas Leybourne

ROGER DOCWRA m. Elizabeth, d. of Edward Brocket of Brocket Hall in Yorkshire

REGINALD DOCWRA

THOMAS DOCWRA, Last Prior of the Knights of St John of Jerusalem at Hitchin. Lived at Brotherhood House, Hitchin

JAMES DOCWRA m. Katherine, d. of John Haspedine of Murden and Chesterfield in Cambridgeshire

RICHARD DOCWRA m. Alice, d. of Thomas Green of Gresingham

Docwra. *Sable a cheveron engrailed argent between three roundels argent each having a pale gules upon it.*

JOHN DOCWRA bought the manor of Putteridge from Sir Edward Darrell - it was held by a yearly rent of one pound of pepper and one pound of cummin. He married Ann, d. of Thomas St George of George Hatley and his wife Alice Rotherham, who was sister of Sir Thomas Rotherham of Someries Manor, Luton

ELIZABETH DOCWRA m. Thomas Chicheley of Wimple. They had one son, Clement, whose son Thomas was the father of Sir Thomas Chicheley.

THOMAS DOCWRA of Putteridgebury, 1518-1602, m. 1548 Mildred Hales (died age 70 in 1596). Thomas was educated at Gray's Inn (1540). JP for Herts in 1559, Sheriff 1580-81, Clerk to the Receiver General of the Duchy of Lancaster 1578-83 and 1586-7 and Receiver General in 1588. He bought the manor of Lilley and also inherited the property of his great-uncle Thomas - the Prior of the Knights of St John at Hitchin. He died in his house at Putteridge in 1602, and is buried with his wife in the church at Lilley, where there is a monument on the north side of the chancel. (*1)

HUMPHREY DOCWRA
—
FRANCES DOCWRA m. Thomas Cheney
—
KATHERINE DOCWRA m. Thomas Potkin

THOMAS DOCWRA (*2) d.1620 at the age of 92, about 1611 bought the manor of Pirton.

m① Ellen, d. of George Horsey and Ann Sadlier. They had one d. Jane, who m. Sir Henry Pakenham.

m② Jane, d. of Sir William Periam Chief Baron of the Exchequer 1593-1603. She was the widow of Thomas, s. of Sir Gabrielle Pointy. Jane d. at Pirton in 1645. (monument in church)

FRANCES DOCWRA (Great-grandmother of Mary Nedham who m. John Harmer of Weston) m. Peter Taverner of Hexton (monument in Hexton church). Their son John Taverner is mentioned in the will of his grandfather, Thomas. (*1) (↓ Taverner tree)

HELEN DOCWRA m. Jasper Horsey (brother of Sir Ralph Horsey and of Ellen Horsey who m. Thomas Docwra)
—
RALPH DOCWRA of Fulbourne, Cambridgeshire

EDWARD DOCWRA 1553-1610 of Brotherhood House, Hitchin. m. Elizabeth Carpenter

PERIAM DOCWRA m. Martha, sister of Oliver St John of Bletsoe, Earl of Bolingbroke. (see Harvey & Piggot trees)

HENRY DOCWRA of North Mimms

ANN DOCWRA m. Humphrey Walcott of Salop, JP and High Sheriff

ELIZABETH DOCWRA m. James Beverley, JP for Bedford

JANE DOCWRA m. John Powell, Merchant Adventurer. She d. in Hamburg

HELEN DOCRWA m. George Nodes of Shephallbury (Nodes tree ↓)

THOMAS DOCWRA Son and heir m. Dorothy Stone of Ridgmont, Beds. (*3)

HENRY DOCWRA
—
LANCELOTT DOCWRA

MARGARET DOCWRA
—
ELIZABETH DOCWRA

MARTHA DOCWRA
—
DOROTHY DOCWRA

SAMUEL POWELL b. in Hamburg

The Docwra Family
of Putteridge and Pirton, Hertfordshire

NOTES

(*1) There is an entry for Thomas Docwra (Dockwray) in 'The History of Parliament' by P W Hasler. Thomas represented Clitheroe, one of the Duchy boroughs, and was clerk to the Receiver General of the Duchy of Lancaster. His son Thomas was married to the granddaughter of Sir Ralph Sadlier, Chancellor of the Duchy of Lancaster, by whose influence he obtained a number of posts and became very wealthy. He owned estates in Fulbourne in Cambridgeshire, and in St Albans, Pirton, Putteridge, Lilley and Kimpton. In his will (proved 1602) he mentions his grandson, John Taverner (see Taverner tree) to whom he leaves his books, urging him to concentrate on his studies and make good use of them.

(*2) In his History of Hitchin, Reginald Hine, writing in 1930, gives a great deal of information about Thomas Docwra, the son of Thomas above. He was Steward of the vast manor of Hitchin, a position which he took over from Sir Ralph Sadlier, his wife's grandfather.

Hine tells us that Sir Ralph Sadlier took his duties very seriously, and spent his whole life in the service of the State. As an old man he was thankful to hand over these responsibilities, which had included 'the thankless task of keeping Mary Queen of Scots in watch and ward'. Referring to his office as Steward of the Manor of Hitchin, Hine suggests that his successor, Thomas Docwra, was not quite so conscientious. He did 'hold court' occasionally, in 1590, 1591, 1592 and 1597, but 'there is reason to think it more for the sake of the dinner than from any sense of duty'. At one of the courts Docwra collected £8-0s-8d in fines, rents and fees, but of this no less than £2-11s-8d was spent on the dinner. The three course meal included venison, beef, mutton, rabbits, geese, capons, larks and pigeons, with 'Warden Pyes and fruit for pudding, all washed down with two gallons of wine and about as much beer as would flood out the river Hiz'. It is clear, he says, that Docwra neglected his duties as Steward, for in 1604 Sir Robert Cecil, the Lord Lieutenant, had to request him to hold a court 'to preserve order and to prevent disturbance of the deputy-bailiffs in their office'.

The offences which were tried at the court included: taking in a stranger to dwell without the consent of the Churchwardens; putting horses in the fields before all the harvest be home; buying up poultry before the market bell be rung; and building a pigeon house. (It was an infringement of the Lord's privilege to build a pigeon house. Only the Lord or gentlemen with a certain status were allowed to have pigeons 'which eat other men's corn')

(*3) In 1711, in the parish register of Ridgmont, Bedfordshire, is an entry concerning an affidavit made to the curate of Ridgmont and Crawley by Mrs Dorothy Docwra, widow and relict of Thomas Docwra, late of Putteridge, Herts. It states that she wishes to give everything to her two nieces, Dorothy and Catherine Stone of Ridgmont, spinsters, except one great china bowl, which she leaves to her granddaughter Isabella Warburton. She desires to be buried privately in the vault at Lilley beside her dear husband.

Dorothy was the great-granddaughter of William Stone who was Lord of the Manor of Segenhoe and Brogborough in the 16th century. His daughter Ann was married to Sir Stephen Soame of Suffolk and Hertfordshire, who was Lord Mayor of London in 1598. The family was also related to the Hunts and the Waldegraves of Suffolk (see chart with Soame notes)

In 1627 a certain Jasper Docwra, who was born at Hallwood in Codicote in 1607, made a sworn statement about Mr Penn's walnut tree (see Wingate pedigree). In 1689 Sir John Docwra was reported by George Nedham for speaking against William of Orange. Both these gentlemen belong to the Hertfordshire family, but it is not clear exactly where they fit onto the tree. Neither have we discovered the origins of William Docwra, a London merchant who in 1683 devised a new penny postal system in London 'for which he was alternately favoured and persecuted by the authorities'. He could possibly be William, the son of John Docwra and Martha Browne of Furneaux Pelham, who was born around 1660.

The Darcy Family
of Tolleshunt Darcy in Essex

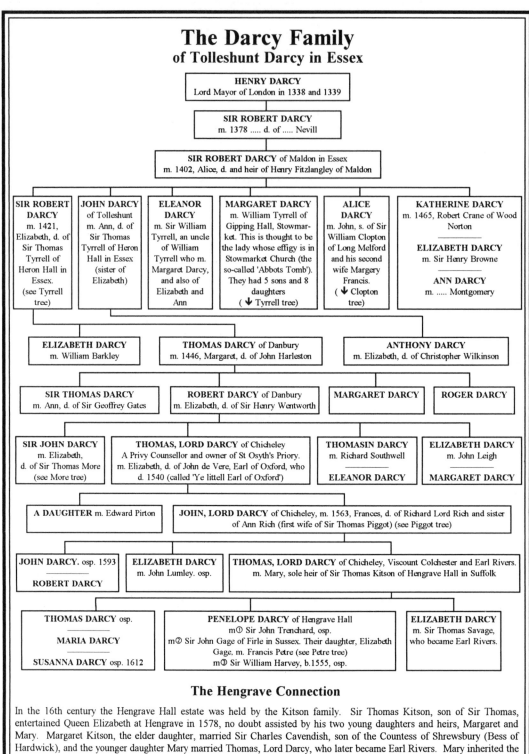

HENRY DARCY
Lord Mayor of London in 1338 and 1339

SIR ROBERT DARCY
m. 1378 ..... d. of ..... Nevill

SIR ROBERT DARCY of Maldon in Essex
m. 1402, Alice, d. and heir of Henry Fitzlangley of Maldon

SIR ROBERT DARCY
m. 1421, Elizabeth, d. of Sir Thomas Tyrrell of Heron Hall in Essex.
(see Tyrrell tree)

JOHN DARCY
of Tolleshunt
m. Ann, d. of Sir Thomas Tyrrell of Heron Hall in Essex
(sister of Elizabeth)

ELEANOR DARCY
m. Sir William Tyrrell, an uncle of William Tyrrell who m. Margaret Darcy, and also of Elizabeth and Ann

MARGARET DARCY
m. William Tyrrell of Gipping Hall, Stowmarket. This is thought to be the lady whose effigy is in Stowmarket Church (the so-called 'Abbots Tomb'). They had 5 sons and 8 daughters
(↓ Tyrrell tree)

ALICE DARCY
m. John, s. of Sir William Clopton of Long Melford and his second wife Margery Francis.
(↓ Clopton tree)

KATHERINE DARCY
m. 1465, Robert Crane of Wood Norton

ELIZABETH DARCY
m. Sir Henry Browne

ANN DARCY
m. ..... Montgomery

ELIZABETH DARCY
m. William Barkley

THOMAS DARCY of Danbury
m. 1446, Margaret, d. of John Harleston

ANTHONY DARCY
m. Elizabeth, d. of Christopher Wilkinson

SIR THOMAS DARCY
m. Ann, d. of Sir Geoffrey Gates

ROBERT DARCY of Danbury
m. Elizabeth, d. of Sir Henry Wentworth

MARGARET DARCY

ROGER DARCY

SIR JOHN DARCY
m. Elizabeth, d. of Sir Thomas More
(see More tree)

THOMAS, LORD DARCY of Chicheley
A Privy Counsellor and owner of St Osyth's Priory.
m. Elizabeth, d. of John de Vere, Earl of Oxford, who d. 1540 (called 'Ye littell Earl of Oxford')

THOMASIN DARCY
m. Richard Southwell

ELEANOR DARCY

ELIZABETH DARCY
m. John Leigh

MARGARET DARCY

A DAUGHTER m. Edward Pirton

JOHN, LORD DARCY of Chicheley, m. 1563, Frances, d. of Richard Lord Rich and sister of Ann Rich (first wife of Sir Thomas Piggot) (see Piggot tree)

JOHN DARCY. osp. 1593

ROBERT DARCY

ELIZABETH DARCY
m. John Lumley. osp.

THOMAS, LORD DARCY of Chicheley, Viscount Colchester and Earl Rivers.
m. Mary, sole heir of Sir Thomas Kitson of Hengrave Hall in Suffolk

THOMAS DARCY osp.

MARIA DARCY

SUSANNA DARCY osp. 1612

PENELOPE DARCY of Hengrave Hall
m① Sir John Trenchard, osp.
m② Sir John Gage of Firle in Sussex. Their daughter, Elizabeth Gage, m. Francis Petre (see Petre tree)
m③ Sir William Harvey, b.1555, osp.

ELIZABETH DARCY
m. Sir Thomas Savage, who became Earl Rivers.

The Hengrave Connection

In the 16th century the Hengrave Hall estate was held by the Kitson family. Sir Thomas Kitson, son of Sir Thomas, entertained Queen Elizabeth at Hengrave in 1578, no doubt assisted by his two young daughters and heirs, Margaret and Mary. Margaret Kitson, the elder daughter, married Sir Charles Cavendish, son of the Countess of Shrewsbury (Bess of Hardwick), and the younger daughter Mary married Thomas, Lord Darcy, who later became Earl Rivers. Mary inherited the Hengrave estate, which later went to their only daughter - Penelope. From her second marriage, to Sir John Gage of Firle in Sussex, Penelope became the ancestor of 9 generations of Gages. The last of the line, John Gage, lived at Hengrave Hall until the end of the 19th century. It was a member of this family, a keen botanist, who developed a new type of plum, known as a 'greengage'.

The Fairclough Family
of Weston

SIR LAWRENCE FAIRCLOUGH of Fairclough Hall

SIR RICHARD FAIRCLOUGH

SIR LAWRENCE FAIRCLOUGH, the King's Esquire in 1437

SIR RALPH FAIRCLOUGH

LAWRENCE FAIRCLOUGH, Marshall of the King's Hall in 1476, m. Elizabeth.

JOHN FAIRCLOUGH, eldest son and heir. osp   RALPH FAIRCLOUGH, heir to his brother

LAWRENCE FAIRCLOUGH

THOMAS FAIRCLOUGH, eldest son and heir, m. Milliscent, d. and heir of ... Barre

JOHN FAIRCLOUGH 1544-1630, (monument in Weston Church) m. Anne, d. of Thomas Spencer of Cople   ELIZABETH FAIRCLOUGH d.1616, m. Thomas Harmer of Weston who died 1608. (Harmer tree ↓)

THOMAS FAIRCLOUGH m.1602, Mary, d. of John Harvey of Thurleigh Beds	ANN FAIRCLOUGH m. Lawrence Fairclough ——— JANE FAIRCLOUGH m. Edward Kent of Aston Bury	MILLISCENT FAIRCLOUGH m. Andrew Bussy of Cheshunt	ELIZABETH FAIRCLOUGH m. ... Clarke (a Dean in Ireland) FRANCES FAIRCLOUGH m. ... of Riseley	ROSE FAIRCLOUGH m. Edward Underwood DOROTHY FAIRCLOUGH m. Robert Underwood

JOHN FAIRCLOUGH (*1), sold Fairclough Hall about 1665 to William Hale, m. Margaret, d. of Robert Herne of Tibbenham, Norfolk.   LITTON FAIRCLOUGH m.1637, his cousin Mary, d. of Oliver Harvey of Thurleigh.   CECIL BUSSY m. Elizabeth (died 1632 aged 27), d. of Sir Gerard Harvey of Cardington. (see Harvey tree)

THOMAS FAIRCLOUGH, son and heir - but Fairclough Hall had been sold. m. Ann, d. of Arthur Pulter of Bradfield. No issue. (see Pulter tree)   JOHN FAIRCLOUGH; LITTON FAIRCLOUGH; ELIZABETH FAIRCLOUGH; MARY FAIRCLOUGH. All named in the Will (1678) of their aunt, Elizabeth Harvey, d. of Oliver Harvey of Thurleigh

(*1) This John would probably be the Fairclough mentioned in connection with an incident at Walkern when there was a dispute between the Royalist rector, the Rev'd John Gorsuch, and his parishioners. (see (*3) on Harmer tree)

Holy Trinity Church, Weston.
On the chancel wall is a monument to John Fairclough who died in 1630.

The Fyshe Family
of Ayot Mountfitchet, Southill, Northill and Biggleswade

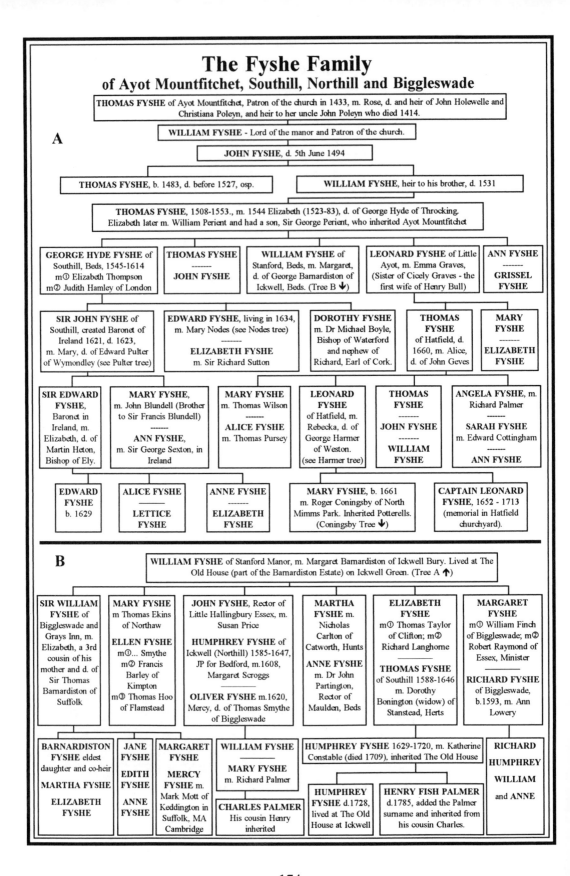

A

THOMAS FYSHE of Ayot Mountfitchet, Patron of the church in 1433, m. Rose, d. and heir of John Holewelle and Christiana Poleyn, and heir to her uncle John Poleyn who died 1414.

WILLIAM FYSHE - Lord of the manor and Patron of the church.

JOHN FYSHE, d. 5th June 1494

THOMAS FYSHE, b. 1483, d. before 1527, osp.

WILLIAM FYSHE, heir to his brother, d. 1531

THOMAS FYSHE, 1508-1553., m. 1544 Elizabeth (1523-83), d. of George Hyde of Throcking. Elizabeth later m. William Perient and had a son, Sir George Perient, who inherited Ayot Mountfitchet

GEORGE HYDE FYSHE of Southill, Beds, 1545-1614 m① Elizabeth Thompson m② Judith Hamley of London

THOMAS FYSHE

JOHN FYSHE

WILLIAM FYSHE of Stanford, Beds, m. Margaret, d. of George Barnardiston of Ickwell, Beds. (Tree B ↓)

LEONARD FYSHE of Little Ayot, m. Emma Graves, (Sister of Cicely Graves - the first wife of Henry Bull)

ANN FYSHE

GRISSEL FYSHE

SIR JOHN FYSHE of Southill, created Baronet of Ireland 1621, d. 1623, m. Mary, d. of Edward Pulter of Wymondley (see Pulter tree)

EDWARD FYSHE, living in 1634, m. Mary Nodes (see Nodes tree)

ELIZABETH FYSHE
m. Sir Richard Sutton

DOROTHY FYSHE m. Dr Michael Boyle, Bishop of Waterford and nephew of Richard, Earl of Cork.

THOMAS FYSHE of Hatfield, d. 1660, m. Alice, d. of John Geves

MARY FYSHE

ELIZABETH FYSHE

SIR EDWARD FYSHE, Baronet in Ireland, m. Elizabeth, d. of Martin Heton, Bishop of Ely.

MARY FYSHE, m. John Blundell (Brother to Sir Francis Blundell)

ANN FYSHE, m. Sir George Sexton, in Ireland

MARY FYSHE m. Thomas Wilson

ALICE FYSHE m. Thomas Pursey

LEONARD FYSHE of Hatfield, m. Rebecka, d. of George Harmer of Weston. (see Harmer tree)

THOMAS FYSHE

JOHN FYSHE

WILLIAM FYSHE

ANGELA FYSHE, m. Richard Palmer

SARAH FYSHE m. Edward Cottingham

ANN FYSHE

EDWARD FYSHE b. 1629

ALICE FYSHE

LETTICE FYSHE

ANNE FYSHE

ELIZABETH FYSHE

MARY FYSHE, b. 1661 m. Roger Coningsby of North Mimms Park. Inherited Potterells. (Coningsby Tree ↓)

CAPTAIN LEONARD FYSHE, 1652 - 1713 (memorial in Hatfield churchyard).

B

WILLIAM FYSHE of Stanford Manor, m. Margaret Barnardiston of Ickwell Bury. Lived at The Old House (part of the Barnardiston Estate) on Ickwell Green. (Tree A ↑)

SIR WILLIAM FYSHE of Biggleswade and Grays Inn, m. Elizabeth, a 3rd cousin of his mother and d. of Sir Thomas Barnardiston of Suffolk

MARY FYSHE m Thomas Ekins of Northaw
ELLEN FYSHE m①... Smythe m② Francis Barley of Kimpton m③ Thomas Hoo of Flamstead

JOHN FYSHE, Rector of Little Hallingbury Essex, m. Susan Price
HUMPHREY FYSHE of Ickwell (Northill) 1585-1647, JP for Bedford, m.1608, Margaret Scroggs
OLIVER FYSHE m.1620, Mercy, d. of Thomas Smythe of Biggleswade

MARTHA FYSHE m. Nicholas Carlton of Catworth, Hunts
ANNE FYSHE m. Dr John Partington, Rector of Maulden, Beds

ELIZABETH FYSHE m① Thomas Taylor of Clifton; m② Richard Langhorne
THOMAS FYSHE of Southill 1588-1646 m. Dorothy Bonington (widow) of Stanstead, Herts

MARGARET FYSHE m① William Finch of Biggleswade; m② Robert Raymond of Essex, Minister
RICHARD FYSHE of Biggleswade, b.1593, m. Ann Lowery

BARNARDISTON FYSHE eldest daughter and co-heir
MARTHA FYSHE
ELIZABETH FYSHE

JANE FYSHE
EDITH FYSHE
ANNE FYSHE

MARGARET FYSHE
MERCY FYSHE m. Mark Mott of Keddington in Suffolk, MA Cambridge

WILLIAM FYSHE
MARY FYSHE m. Richard Palmer
CHARLES PALMER His cousin Henry inherited

HUMPHREY FYSHE 1629-1720, m. Katherine Constable (died 1709), inherited The Old House

HUMPHREY FYSHE d.1728, lived at The Old House at Ickwell

HENRY FISH PALMER d.1785, added the Palmer surname and inherited from his cousin Charles.

RICHARD
HUMPHREY
WILLIAM
and ANNE

The Hale Family of Hertfordshire and Bedfordshire
(King's Walden, Tewin, Harmer Green and Clifton)

THOMAS HALE of Codicote (*1), m. Anne, d. of Edmund Mitchell of Codicote.

RICHARD HALE, grocer of London, d. 1620. Bought the manor of Kings Walden in 1576 from the Brooke family. Bought the manor of Edworth in 1614 for £3,000 from the Piggots (*2) and Marden Hill in Tewin from the North family. Richard was the founder of the grammar school in Hertford which bears his name.
m① Mary Lambert   m② Dyonisia Gifford of Somerset

WILLIAM HALE, d.1594, buried at St Paul's Walden, m. Alice, d. of Thomas Caulfield of St Paul's Walden

JOHN HALE of Codicote, m. ... d. of ... Rolte of Milton, Beds. Their son John bought Harmer Green (*3)

WILLIAM HALE of Kings Walden, 1568-1634, Sheriff of Herts 1621, m. Rose (1573-1648), d. of Sir George Bond Lord Mayor of London 1587. William bought the manor of Lannock (Weston) in 1621. Inherited the manor of Edworth, Bedfordshire.

RICHARD HALE of Marden Hill, Tewin Sheriff of Herts in 1631, m.1601 Elizabeth, d. of Sir Thomas Dacres of Cheshunt

HALE. *Azure a cheveron or battled on both sides.*

ROWLAND HALE 1600-69, Sheriff of Herts 1647, inherited Edworth, bought Clothallbury in 1656 for his son William, bought Kingswoodbury, m. Elizabeth, d. of Alderman Garaway of London

BERNARD HALE d.1663, Principal of Peterhouse College, Cambridge and Archdeacon of Ely

SIR JOHN HALE 1613-72, lived at Stagenhoe, Sheriff of Herts 1663

DYONISIA HALE 1611-83 m. Sir Thomas Williamson. Inherited Lannock

7 MORE CHILDREN (*4)

ROBERT HALE b.1610, bought Tewin Bury and Marden and sold them to the Cowpers, m. Anne, d. of Sir Frank Leventhorpe of Aldbury

6 MORE CHILDREN (*5)

WILLIAM HALE of Gray's Inn 1632-88, inherited Lannock in 1683 from his aunt Dyonisia. m. 1653 Mary, d. of Jeremy Elwes of Throcking. Inherited Kingswoodbury. Bought Fairclough Hall.

RICHARD HALE 1659-89, inherited Lannock and Kingswoodbury, m. Elizabeth, d. of Isaac Meynell, who afterwards m. The Honourable Robert Cecil 2nd son of the 3rd Earl of Salisbury

ROWLAND HALE b.1661 **7 MORE SONS** and **4 DAUGHTERS**

SIR BERNARD HALE 1677-1729, died in Red Lion Square, London, m. Anne Thursby of Northampton

WILLIAM HALE 1685-1717, MP for Sussex 1708, MP for St Albans 1715-17, inherited Lannock and Kingswoodbury, m. Katherine, d. of Peter Paggen of Wandsworth

BERNARD HALE, a General in the army, m. Martha Rigby of Mistley Hall, Essex

JOHN HALE, a General in the army, m. Mary Chaloner

WILLIAM HALE of Kings Walden, d.1793, m. Elizabeth, d. of Sir Charles Farnaby of Kent.

PAGGEN HALE, MP for Herts 1747-54, inherited Lannock, Edworth and Kings Walden, osp 1770

MARY HALE m. Sir Matthew Lamb. Their son, Peniston Lamb became Viscount Melbourne

WILLIAM HALE d.1829, m.1777, Mary (1753-1846) d. of James 2nd Viscount Grimston.

PAGGEN HALE

ELIZABETH HALE

CHARLOTTE HALE

SARAH HALE

ANNE HALE m. Sir Edward Deering

PAGGEN HALE b.1784 **CECIL HALE** 1786-1810 **HENRY HALE** 1791-1827

CHARLOTTE HALE b.1783, m.1809 her cousin Cholmley Deering

ELIZABETH HALE b.1789, m.1810, George Proctor of Mardocks in Ware. (Mardocks was once the home of the Chapman family)

WILLIAM HALE of Kings Walden, 1782-1852, Sheriff of Herts 1830, inherited in 1829.
m① 1815, Elizabeth, d. of the Honourable William Leeson   m② 1824, Charlotte, d. of Sir Richard Joseph Sullivan

CHOLMLEY DEERING m.1809, his cousin Charlotte Hale **EDWARD DEERING**

WILLIAM EDMUND BRAND HALE b.1816, osp 1848

EMILY HALE b.1818, m.the Honourable and Rev'd Philip Yorke Savile, son of the Earl of Mexborough

CHARLES CHOLMLEY HALE 1830-96. In 1896 Edworth was sold to John Inns and Lannock to Mr Pryor, thus uniting all the manors of Weston

CHARLOTTE HALE b.1832

(*1). Souces record a Richard Hale of Hexton who was probably a brother of Thomas. His son Thomas was a Counsellor of Law at Grays Inn. He married Elizabeth Symons and their son, Symon Hale of Clifton married in 1617 Judith, the daughter of Benjamin Piggot of Gravenhurst (see Piggot tree). They had a daughter, Bridget, who was named after her grandmother Bridget Nedham, and a son Oliver, named after his great-uncle Oliver St John of Bletsoe. (Benjamin Piggot's mother was Margery St John, sister of Oliver St John - see St John tree)

(*2). The descent of the manor of Edworth can be traced in a direct line from 1307 to 1896. The early part appears on the Piggot tree (Walter de Langford) and takes us to Lewis Piggot, who sold it about 1588 to John Spurling whose widow sold it in 1614 to Richard Hale.

(*3). This John (who bought Harmer Green) m. Elizabeth, d. of Sir Humphrey Browne of Abbess Roding (see Browne tree).

(*4). Richard 1596-1623; William 1597-1641; George b.1601; Alicia b.1603; Winefrida b.1604; Thomas b.1606; and Ann b.1609.

(*5). Dionysia m. Edward Coleman; John ; Mary m. Thomas Franklyn; Elizabeth m. George Gent; Martha; and Katherine b.1602.

The Harmer Family of Weston

John Harmer bought a messuage and land in Weston in 1541. He died in 1552 leaving lands in Clothall, Wallington and Rushden to his son John (*1). Thomas was probably a younger son, and inherited the Weston property.

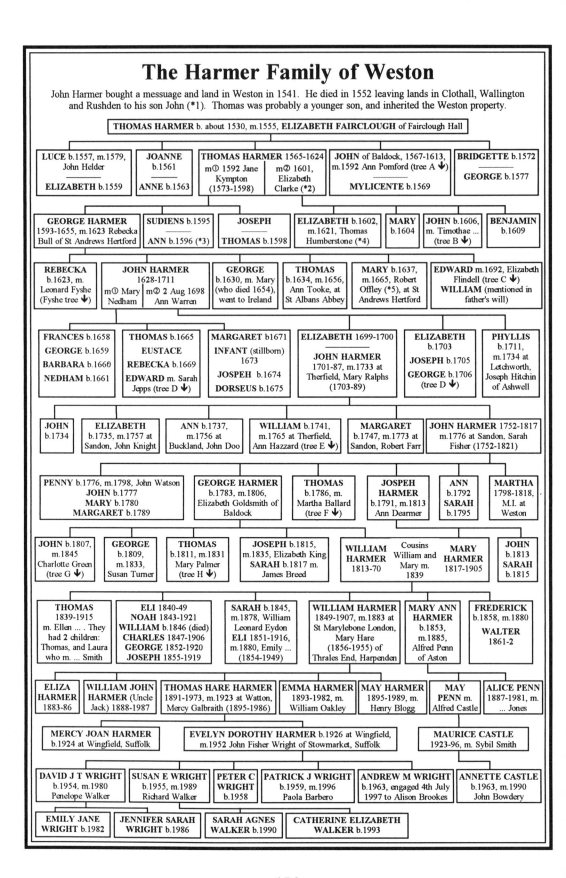

THOMAS HARMER b. about 1530, m.1555, **ELIZABETH FAIRCLOUGH** of Fairclough Hall

---

LUCE b.1557, m.1579, John Helder
———
ELIZABETH b.1559

JOANNE b.1561
ANNE b.1563

THOMAS HARMER 1565-1624
m① 1592 Jane Kympton (1573-1598)
m② 1601, Elizabeth Clarke (*2)

JOHN of Baldock, 1567-1613, m.1592 Ann Pomford (tree A ↓)
———
MYLICENTE b.1569

BRIDGETTE b.1572
———
GEORGE b.1577

GEORGE HARMER 1593-1655, m.1623 Rebecka Bull of St Andrews Hertford

SUDIENS b.1595
———
ANN b.1596 (*3)

JOSEPH
THOMAS b.1598

ELIZABETH b.1602, m.1621, Thomas Humberstone (*4)

MARY b.1604

JOHN b.1606, m. Timothae ... (tree B ↓)

BENJAMIN b.1609

REBECKA b.1623, m. Leonard Fyshe (Fyshe tree ↓)

JOHN HARMER 1628-1711
m① Mary Nedham m② 2 Aug 1698 Ann Warren

GEORGE b.1630, m. Mary (who died 1654), went to Ireland

THOMAS b.1634, m.1656, Ann Tooke, at St Albans Abbey

MARY b.1637, m.1665, Robert Offley (*5), at St Andrews Hertford

EDWARD m.1692, Elizabeth Flindell (tree C ↓)
WILLIAM (mentioned in father's will)

FRANCES b.1658
GEORGE b.1659
BARBARA b.1660
NEDHAM b.1661

THOMAS b.1665
EUSTACE
REBECKA b.1669
EDWARD m. Sarah Jepps (tree D ↓)

MARGARET b1671
INFANT (stillborn) 1673
JOSPEH b.1674
DORSEUS b.1675

ELIZABETH 1699-1700
———
JOHN HARMER 1701-87, m.1733 at Therfield, Mary Ralphs (1703-89)

ELIZABETH b.1703
JOSEPH b.1705
GEORGE b.1706 (tree D ↓)

PHYLLIS b.1711, m.1734 at Letchworth, Joseph Hitchin of Ashwell

---

JOHN b.1734

ELIZABETH b.1735, m.1757 at Sandon, John Knight

ANN b.1737, m.1756 at Buckland, John Doo

WILLIAM b.1741, m.1765 at Therfield, Ann Hazzard (tree E ↓)

MARGARET b.1747, m.1773 at Sandon, Robert Farr

JOHN HARMER 1752-1817 m.1776 at Sandon, Sarah Fisher (1752-1821)

PENNY b.1776, m.1798, John Watson
JOHN b.1777
MARY b.1780
MARGARET b.1789

GEORGE HARMER b.1783, m.1806, Elizabeth Goldsmith of Baldock

THOMAS b.1786, m. Martha Ballard (tree F ↓)

JOSPEH HARMER b.1791, m.1813 Ann Dearmer

ANN b.1792
SARAH b.1795

MARTHA 1798-1818, M.I. at Weston

JOHN b.1807, m.1845 Charlotte Green (tree G ↓)

GEORGE b.1809, m.1833, Susan Turner

THOMAS b.1811, m.1831 Mary Palmer (tree H ↓)

JOSEPH b.1815, m.1835, Elizabeth King
SARAH b.1817 m. James Breed

WILLIAM HARMER 1813-70

Cousins William and Mary m. 1839

MARY HARMER 1817-1905

JOHN b.1813
SARAH b.1815

THOMAS 1839-1915 m. Ellen ... . They had 2 children: Thomas, and Laura who m. ... Smith

ELI 1840-49
NOAH 1843-1921
WILLIAM b.1846 (died)
CHARLES 1847-1906
GEORGE 1852-1920
JOSEPH 1855-1919

SARAH b.1845, m.1878, William Leonard Eydon
ELI 1851-1916, m.1880, Emily ... (1854-1949)

WILLIAM HARMER 1849-1907, m.1883 at St Marylebone London, Mary Hare (1856-1955) of Thrales End, Harpenden

MARY ANN HARMER b.1853, m.1885, Alfred Penn of Aston

FREDERICK b.1858, d.1880
WALTER 1861-2

ELIZA HARMER 1883-86

WILLIAM JOHN HARMER (Uncle Jack) 1888-1987

THOMAS HARE HARMER 1891-1973, m.1923 at Watton, Mercy Galbraith (1895-1986)

EMMA HARMER 1893-1982, m. William Oakley

MAY HARMER 1895-1989, m. Henry Blogg

MAY PENN m. Alfred Castle

ALICE PENN 1887-1981, m. ... Jones

MERCY JOAN HARMER b.1924 at Wingfield, Suffolk

EVELYN DOROTHY HARMER b.1926 at Wingfield, m.1952 John Fisher Wright of Stowmarket, Suffolk

MAURICE CASTLE 1923-96, m. Sybil Smith

DAVID J T WRIGHT b.1954, m.1980 Penelope Walker

SUSAN E WRIGHT b.1955, m.1989 Richard Walker

PETER C WRIGHT b.1958

PATRICK J WRIGHT b.1959, m.1996 Paola Barbero

ANDREW M WRIGHT b.1963, engaged 4th July 1997 to Alison Brookes

ANNETTE CASTLE b.1963, m.1990 John Bowdery

EMILY JANE WRIGHT b.1982

JENNIFER SARAH WRIGHT b.1986

SARAH AGNES WALKER b.1990

CATHERINE ELIZABETH WALKER b.1993

The Harmer Family of Weston

(*1) John Harmer of Rushden and his son Edward are mentioned in the Hertfordshire Muster Books 1580-1605. Both men were fully trained and belonged to the 'Corselet' section of the Militia, which consisted of 'tall, well-built men who wore corselet armour ... the role for a courageous man'. They carried swords, daggers and pikes and were trained in sixteen postures of drill - three standing, five marching and eight charging. They formed ranks to protect the musket and caliver men, regrouping quickly when necessary and forming an impenetrable circle. John and Edward were each responsible for arming one other man. William Lane was furnished with John Harmer's caliver (a kind of musket) and John Wood was armed by Edward Harmer. John Harmer also provided one of the three riding horses for the Rushden militia.

(*2) Thomas Harmer's 2nd wife, Elizabeth Clarke, was first cousin to the troublesome young Nicholas Hyde mentioned in Chapter 4. (Their mothers were sisters, Elizabeth and Mary Bristow)

(*3) Ann Harmer was married in 1616 to John Payne of Rushden.

(*4) Thomas Humberstone and his wife are mentioned in the Walkern Church archives. There were bitter disputes between the parishioners and their priest, John Gorsuch, mainly because of his Royalist sympathies. On Easter Sunday 1637 he refused to administer the sacrament to Thomas Humberstone and his wife (Elizabeth Harmer) because they insisted on kneeling in their pew in the Chancel instead of coming up to the altar rail. Letters to the Archdeacon, the Bishop and finally to Archbishop Laud (who supported the priest) failed to settle the dispute, and eventually Gorsuch was ejected by Parliament in 1642. The following year John White published his 'First Century of Scandalous Malignant Priests', which included John Gorsuch, Rector of Walkern, 'who hath published a wicked libell against the Parliament, that some Lords whom he named were Fooles'. It also states that Gorsuch had provided a horse and rider to serve under Prince Rupert against Parliament, and had also 'denyed many of his Parishioners the sacrament of the Lord's Supper, without any cause shown, and refused to administer it to such as would not come up to the railes'.

Having been turned out of his benefice Gorsuch lived on in the parish, and continued to make himself a nuisance. Finally, in 1647, the authorities sent Fairclough of Weston with a body of men to eject him. In order to escape he hid in a haymow and was smothered. Thus ended the life of this turbulent, but probably well-meaning priest.

(*5) Mary Harmer's husband, Robert Offley, was the son of Edmund Offley, a burgess of Hertford and grandson of Sir Thomas Offley who was Lord Mayor of London in 1556. Edmund would have been a burgess at the time when Mary's grandfather, Henry Bull, was Bailiff (Mayor) of Hertford. Another of the burgesses at this time was William Tooke of Essendon, grandfather of Anne Tooke who married Thomas Harmer, Mary's brother.

Thomas Harmer and Mercy Galbraith were married at Watton Church on 24th November 1923 and on the same day moved into their new home in Suffolk. They lived in the county for 50 years, at Wingfield, Brundish and finally at Great Finborough near Stowmarket.

LEFT: Buntings, Wingfield where Thomas and Mercy spent the first 3 years of their married life. The pram indicates that the picture was taken about 1925 after the birth of their first baby.

BELOW: Two views of Laurel Farm, Brundish where they lived from 1926-37. (see Author's note)

[**Author's Note:** Laurel Farm is the setting for my children's book 'Six Weeks is Forever' (published 1996). The view on the left shows the horse pond and the window of the cheese loft above, which feature in the story.]

The Harmer Family of Weston

A

JOHN HARMER (John of Baldock) 1567-1613
m.1592 at Baldock, Ann Pomford (d. 8 Oct 1617)

ANN HARMER Bapt. 18 Feb 1593 at Baldock, m. John Milles	**THOMAS HARMER** Bapt. Jun 1597 at Baldock, died before 1613	**JONE HARMER** Bapt. Feb 1599 at Baldock m. James Maple	**ELIZABETH HARMER** Bapt. 12 July 1603 at Baldock

B

JOHN HARMER b.1606 Weston, m. Timothae ..... .

JOHN HARMER Bapt. 1633 Walkern	**EDWARD HARMER** Bapt. 1633, Benington	**THOMAS HARMER** Bapt. 1634, Benington	**GEORGE HARMER** Bapt. 1637, Benington	**TIMOTHY HARMER** Bapt. 1638, Benington

C

EDWARD HARMER d.1718 at Aston, (Will proved 1718), m.1692, Elizabeth Flindell of Ayot St Lawrence

MARY HARMER b.1694, m.1720, William Chalkley	**ANN HARMER** 1696-97

Mary and William are ancestors of Keith Walker of Epsom

D

JOHN HARMER of Weston, 1628-1711

m① Mary, d. of Eustace Nedham and Frances Wingate of Wymondley Priory | m② Ann Warren of Baldock, a grand-daughter of William Warren and Ann Skegg and a distant cousin of Mary Nedham, John's first wife.

EDWARD HARMER m. Sarah Jepps (died in childbirth 1709)	**GEORGE HARMER**, b.1706 m① 1728, Rose Watts (died 1733) | m② 1739, Mary Lanton of Ashwell

MARY HARMER b.1699	**ANN HARMER** b.1701	**THOMAS HARMER** b.1703	**SARAH HARMER** b.1705	**REBECKA HARMER** b.1707	**ROSE HARMER** b.1731	**MARY HARMER** b.1742	**ANN HARMER** b.1752, died 1753

MARY HARMER (illegitimate), Bapt. 3rd December 1743, m.1769, Robert Bonfield

Mary and Robert are ancestors of Cynthia Cox of Southampton and Patricia Martin of Toddington, Beds.

E

WILLIAM HARMER b.1741, m.1765 at Therfield, Ann Hazzard

WILLIAM HARMER b.1779, m.1806 Sarah Gundril

MARY HARMER b.1823	**RHODA HARMER** b.1824 m.1850, Richard Turner of Weston	**JOSPEH HARMER** b.1829

F

THOMAS HARMER b.1786, Farmer at Halls Green Farm, Weston (Fairclough Hall), m. Martha Ballard

MARTHA HARMER b.1823	**SARAH HARMER** b.1826, a doily maker, m.1848, William Aylott, a farmer of Walkern	**THOMAS HARMER** b.1827	**ELIZA HARMER** 1829-48	**MARY ANN HARMER** b.1831, m.1851 at Hitchin

The Harmer Family of Weston

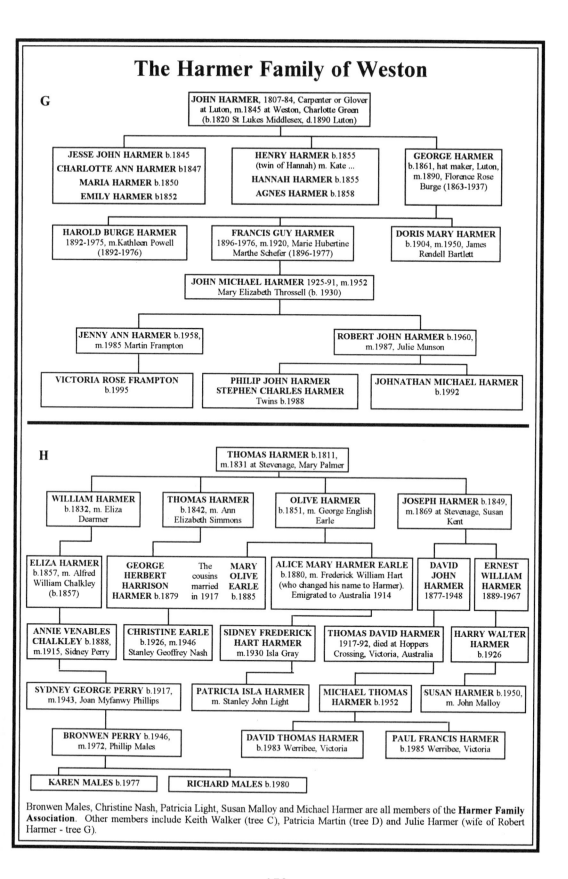

G

JOHN HARMER, 1807-84, Carpenter or Glover at Luton, m.1845 at Weston, Charlotte Green (b.1820 St Lukes Middlesex, d.1890 Luton)

JESSE JOHN HARMER b.1845
CHARLOTTE ANN HARMER b1847
MARIA HARMER b.1850
EMILY HARMER b1852

HENRY HARMER b.1855 (twin of Hannah) m. Kate ...
HANNAH HARMER b.1855
AGNES HARMER b.1858

GEORGE HARMER b.1861, hat maker, Luton, m.1890, Florence Rose Burge (1863-1937)

HAROLD BURGE HARMER 1892-1975, m.Kathleen Powell (1892-1976)

FRANCIS GUY HARMER 1896-1976, m.1920, Marie Hubertine Marthe Schefer (1896-1977)

DORIS MARY HARMER b.1904, m.1950, James Rendell Bartlett

JOHN MICHAEL HARMER 1925-91, m.1952 Mary Elizabeth Throssell (b. 1930)

JENNY ANN HARMER b.1958, m.1985 Martin Frampton

ROBERT JOHN HARMER b.1960, m.1987, Julie Munson

VICTORIA ROSE FRAMPTON b.1995

PHILIP JOHN HARMER
STEPHEN CHARLES HARMER
Twins b.1988

JOHNATHAN MICHAEL HARMER b.1992

H

THOMAS HARMER b.1811, m.1831 at Stevenage, Mary Palmer

WILLIAM HARMER b.1832, m. Eliza Dearmer

THOMAS HARMER b.1842, m. Ann Elizabeth Simmons

OLIVE HARMER b.1851, m. George English Earle

JOSEPH HARMER b.1849, m.1869 at Stevenage, Susan Kent

ELIZA HARMER b.1857, m. Alfred William Chalkley (b.1857)

GEORGE HERBERT HARRISON HARMER b.1879

The cousins married in 1917

MARY OLIVE EARLE b.1885

ALICE MARY HARMER EARLE b.1880, m. Frederick William Hart (who changed his name to Harmer). Emigrated to Australia 1914

DAVID JOHN HARMER 1877-1948

ERNEST WILLIAM HARMER 1889-1967

ANNIE VENABLES CHALKLEY b.1888, m.1915, Sidney Perry

CHRISTINE EARLE b.1926, m.1946 Stanley Geoffrey Nash

SIDNEY FREDERICK HART HARMER m.1930 Isla Gray

THOMAS DAVID HARMER 1917-92, died at Hoppers Crossing, Victoria, Australia

HARRY WALTER HARMER b.1926

SYDNEY GEORGE PERRY b.1917, m.1943, Joan Myfanwy Phillips

PATRICIA ISLA HARMER m. Stanley John Light

MICHAEL THOMAS HARMER b.1952

SUSAN HARMER b.1950, m. John Malloy

BRONWEN PERRY b.1946, m.1972, Phillip Males

DAVID THOMAS HARMER b.1983 Werribee, Victoria

PAUL FRANCIS HARMER b.1985 Werribee, Victoria

KAREN MALES b.1977

RICHARD MALES b.1980

Bronwen Males, Christine Nash, Patricia Light, Susan Malloy and Michael Harmer are all members of the **Harmer Family Association**. Other members include Keith Walker (tree C), Patricia Martin (tree D) and Julie Harmer (wife of Robert Harmer - tree G).

The Harvey Family
of Thurleigh and Northill in Bedfordshire and Ickworth in Suffolk

All the Harveys (or Herveys) of Thurleigh and Ickworth are said to be descended from **DE HARVEY, DUKE OF ORLEANS** who came to England with William the Conqueror. **HENRY HARVEY** was settled in Bedfordshire in the reign of Richard I (1189-99). He had a son **HENRY**, who lived in the reign of King John, and a grandson **OSBERT DE HERVEY** who died 1206. Osbert's son **ADAM** m. Julien, d. and heir of John Fitzhugh.

JOHN HARVEY (Hervic de Risely), son of Adam and Julien, died 1297, m. **JOAN**, d. and co-heir of **JOHN HARMER** of Thurleigh

WILLIAM HARVEY of Thurleigh, died 1376, m. Mary, d. and heir of Richard Folliot

SIR JOHN HARVEY of Thurleigh, m. Margaret (or Joan), d. and heir of Sir John Neyrnute of Fleetmarston, Bucks. John Harvey was Knight of the Shire 1386, Justice of the Peace for Bedford 1382-94.

JOHN HARVEY died 1426, m. Margery, d. of Sir William Calthorpe of Norfolk.

THOMAS HARVEY died 1475, Master of the King's Ordnance 1461, m. Jane, d. of William Paston of Norfolk.

ELIZABETH HARVEY, Abbess of Elstow, d.1500

THOMAS HARVEY of Thurleigh, m. Christian, d. of John Chicheley, Chamberlain of London

THOMAS HARVEY, admitted to Lincoln's Inn 1475, m. Jane, d. and heir of Henry Drury of Ickworth in Suffolk. Inherited the Suffolk estate which had previously belonged to the Harveys in the 13th century. (Harvey of Ickworth in Suffolk tree ↓)

JOHN HARVEY, Member of Parliament for Bedford 1472, died 1474, m. Alice, d. of Nicholas Morley. Alice later m. one of the Pastons of Norfolk

SIR GEORGE HARVEY 1474-1522, m. Margaret (or Elizabeth) Stanford

GERARD SMART died 1569, natural son (and heir by adoption) of Sir George Harvey, changed his name to Harvey, MP for Bedford 1554.

m① Elizabeth (widow), sister of John Lord Williams of Thame.	m② Ann (widow), d. of Nicholas Luke

H ᴀ ʀ ᴠ ᴇ ʏ of Thurleigh. *Gules a bend argent with three trefoils vert thereon.*

JOHN HARVEY m. Mary, d. of Sir John St John of Bletsoe. She was the sister of Margery St John who m. Francis Piggot of Gravenhurst (parents of Benjamin Piggot), and also of Oliver Lord St John. (see St John tree)

MARY HARVEY b.1580, m.1602 Thomas Fairclough of Weston	OLIVER HARVEY 1568-1627, eldest son and heir, m. Ann Browne of London. In 1605 King James I stayed with him for two nights at Thurleigh	SIR GERARD HARVEY of Cardington, 2nd son b.1569, knighted at Caddes by the Earl of Essex being the first to enter the town, m. Dorothy, d. of John Gascoigne of Cardington	JOHN HARVEY, 3rd son 1572-1619, described in the parish register of Thurleigh as 'Mr John, steward to ye Earle of Bullingbrooke, died at Knebworth at Sir William Litton's house there in the County of Hertford'	SAMUEL HARVEY of Shenfield, 5th son b.1576, m. Dorothy, d. of George Wingate. (George's grand-daughter, Frances Wingate, was the mother of Mary Harmer, née Nedham)
LITTON FAIRCLOUGH m.1637 his cousin Mary Harvey	**MARY HARVEY** m.1637 her cousin Litton Fairclough	**ELIZABETH HARVEY** 1606-78, left a bequest to her sister Mary Fairclough and her children. (*1)	**JOHN HARVEY** heir, m. his cousin Elizabeth, d. of Stephen Harvey of London. (clandestine marriage) (*2)	**ELIZABETH HARVEY** m. Cecil (d.1632 aged 27), s. of Andrew Bussy of Cheshunt and Milliscent Fairclough (sister of Thomas who m. Mary Harvey) / **GEORGE HARVEY** b.1627

JOHN HARVEY (*3), 1632-1715, left a cottage & land at Thurleigh for the poor (rents given at Christmas), sold Thurleigh to the Holts (*4)

(*1) Elizabeth's godparents were: her uncle, Sir Gerard Harvey; the Countess of Bollingbrooke (sic); and the Lady Becher.

(*2) The ceremony was at St James's, Duke Place, where about 40,000 clandestine marriages took place between 1664 and 1694.

(*3) In 1680 a John Harvey acquired Ickwell Bury from his kinsman, Robert Barnardiston, and the family lived there for nearly 200 years. They sold it in 1860 and bought The Old House on Ickwell Green from their kinsmen the Fish-Palmer family. At Northill there are several memorials to Harveys who are buried in the family vault beneath the church. But although they were related to the Barnardistons and to the Fyshe family the connection with the Harveys of Thurleigh is unclear.

(*4) In 1790 Rowland Holt sold it to the Duke of Bedford for £1,796. The next Duke sold it in 1880 to William Thompson.

The Harvey (or Hervey) Family
of Ickworth in Suffolk

THOMAS HARVEY of Thurleigh, admitted to Lincoln's Inn 1475, m. Jane, d. and heir of Henry Drury of Ickworth, Wordwell and Sapiston

WILLIAM HERVEY, admitted to Lincoln's Inn 1479/80, died 1538, buried in St Mary's Church, Bury St Edmunds (M.I.), m. Joan Cokett of Ampthill.

SIR NICHOLAS HERVEY of Bakenloo Manor, Bedfordshire, member of the royal household (Henry VIII), ambassador to Emperor Charles V in 1530, died 1532, buried at Ampthill, Beds. m① Elizabeth Fitzwilliam; m② Bridget Wiltshire (*1)

JOHN HERVEY d.1556 m.1511, Elizabeth, d. of Henry Pope of Mildenhall.

EDMUND HERVEY d. before 1560, member of the royal household (Henry VIII) granted part of the abbey of Elstow, Beds in 1541

WILLIAM HERVEY, eldest son and heir, d.1592, m.1554 Elizabeth, d. of John Poley of Boxted

14 OTHER CHILDREN including two named John - known as John the Elder and John the Younger

JOHN HERVEY, eldest son and heir, born about 1550, buried at Ickworth 1620, m.1582 Frances Bocking of Ashbocking

SIR WILLIAM HERVEY b.1555
m① Susan Jermyn of Rushbrooke | m② Penelope, d. of Thomas Lord Darcy (Earl Rivers) of Hengrave Hall. (no issue)

8 OTHER CHILDREN including another William (b.1557) known as William the Younger. The older children were baptised at Boxted, the later ones at Ickworth.

SIR THOMAS HERVEY m. Isabella, d. of Sir Humphrey May and Judith Poley (see Poley tree)

ISABELLA HARVEY 1659-97 m. Gervase Elwes of Stoke by Clare (*2) | **JOHN HARVEY** 1st Earl of Bristol

(*1) Bridget was the d. of Sir John Wiltshire of Stone Castle in Kent. She was the widow of Sir Richard Wingfield of Kimbolton Castle, a descendant of Sir John Wingfield of Wingfield Castle.

(*2) Isabella and Gervase had a son, Sir Harvey Elwes who, with his nephew, John Elwes, were known as 'The Misers of Ashen' and are mentioned in John Timpson's 'English Eccentrics'.

Ickworth Hall, home of the Suffolk branch of the Harvey family from about 1475 until John Hervey 7th Marquis of Bristol vacated in 1996.

The Hyde Family
of Throcking and Sandon

WILLIAM HYDE, a citizen and grocer of London, bought Throcking from the Botelers and de Argenteins in 1398. He d. about 1460. m.1414, Joyce ....

LAWRENCE HYDE b.1415

WILLIAM HYDE osp

Hyde. *Azure a cheveron between three lozenges or.*

ROBERT HYDE Lord of the Manor in 1486

GEORGE HYDE b.1443, m.1468, Agnes ...

Hyde. of Throcking. *Azure a saltire engrailed or and a chief ermine.*

LEONARD HYDE 1469-1509, m. Elizabeth Lyster of Norfolk. In 1492 acquired the manor of Sandon, sometimes known as Olivers, which was later known as Hyde Hall. Asked to be buried 'by the little dore on the north side of the chaunsell of Throcking Church'. One of his executors was John Knighton.

GEORGE HYDE 1495-1553, built mansion house at Throcking. Asked to be buried as near to his father as possible in Throcking Church.
m① Alice Roper of Eltham, Kent (see Roper tree)   m② Alice Brocket of Wheathampstead

LEONARD HYDE 1521-49, m.1546, Ann Boteler of Watton Woodhall, died just before the birth of his only son. In his will, dated 1549, he leaves his sword to his brother-in-law Thomas Fyshe, and his bows and arrows to his cousins.

LUCY HYDE, b.1527, m.1546 at Weston, Edmund Kympton. 'Held court' at Astwick at the age of 24 after the death of her husband. (Kympton tree ↓)

ELIZABETH HYDE 1528-83, m.① Thomas Fyshe, and m.② William Perient, both of Ayot Mount Fitchet. (Fyshe tree and Perient tree ↓)

WILLIAM HYDE 1533-90, m. Elizabeth Shipman, acquired Hyde Hall in 1561 from nephew William. In his will (written 1580, proved 1590) he states that his conscience is clear concerning the acquisition of Hyde Hall (*1)

MARY HYDE m. Sir John Cary Lord Hunsdon (memorial in Hunsdon Church)

ELLEN HYDE

GRISSEL HYDE

WILLIAM HYDE b.1549, m.1572, Mary Bristow, inherited Hyde Hall from his grandfather, but it was handed over to his uncle William in 1561

SIR LEONARD HYDE 1555-1624, High Sheriff of Herts 1606 (*2), m. Ann Tryce

LUCY HYDE Lady of the Bedchamber to Queen Elizabeth, m. Sir Robert Osborne (*3)

DUDLEY HYDE (a daughter) b.1559, mentioned in her father's will. (Probably named after Robert Dudley, Earl of Leicester who was a friend of the family and executor of her father's will.) (*4)

ANN HYDE m. Thomas Bowles of Wallington (brother of Richard Bowles who m. Alice Perient - see Perient tree) (*5)

NICHOLAS HYDE, named after his Bristow ancestors. (see Bristow tree)

ROBERT HYDE inherited Hyde Hall but sold it in 1609

WILLIAM HYDE m. Grissell, d. of Thomas Stutville of Dalham, Suffolk (a relative of the Caldebecks and Knightons)

MARGARET HYDE m. Captain Henry Lane, Esquire of the Body to King James I

ELIZABETH BOWLES m. Edward Cason (see Cason tree)

(*1) About 1565 William built a grand new mansion house to replace the old Hyde Hall, and he granted it to his son Leonard who was about to be married.

(*2) Leonard inherited all his father's estates. Around 1608 he granted Hyde Hall to his son Robert, who sold it in 1609 to the Earl of Exeter. It then went to the Caesars and the Franklyns, and then to Sir Nicholas Miller and his descendants.

(*3) Bridget Hyde of Aldbury (see Hyde of Aldbury tree) m. Peregrine Osborne.

(*4) Robert Dudley, 1532-88, was the son of the Duke of Northumberland, and was created Earl of Leicester in 1564. He was a favourite of the Queen, who would have liked to marry him, but he was already married. When his wife died he married again (secretly), and when the Queen found out she was furious and sent him to the Tower.

(*5) Mary, the grand-daughter of Ann Hyde and Thomas Bowles, m. Sir John Spencer of Althorpe (see Spencer tree)

Both sets of arms above were used by the Hydes of Throcking (see Chapter 4)

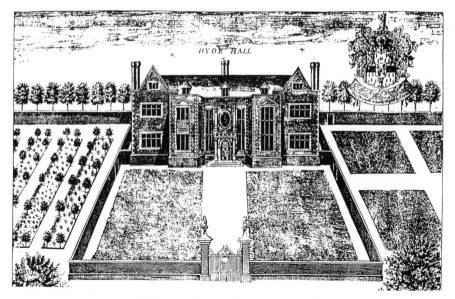

Hyde Hall Sandon, built by William Hyde about 1565

Drawing by John Drapentier, reproduced in Chauncy's Historical Antiqities of Hertfordshire c.1700

The Hyde Family of Aldbury

JOHN HYDE of Aldbury came from Hyde in Dorset and bought the manor of Aldbury in 1544. Died in 1545 (monument in Aldbury Church). He was an officer of the Court of the Exchequer.

THOMAS HYDE. d.1570, his eldest son George d.1580 (monument on N wall of Aldbury Chucrh to Thomas and George). Thomas had a d. who m. ... Bardolf of Harpenden, and two more sons. Robert, the 2nd s. inherited from his brother George but died 1607 and the property went to 3rd s. Nicholas

SIR NICHOLAS HYDE d. 1625 m. Bridget, d. of Miles Sandys of Latimers in Buckinghamshire

SIR THOMAS HYDE, d. 1665. Bought North Mimms Park from the Coningsbys. (Monument in Aldbury Church)

BRIDGET HYDE, only daughter, d. 1733. m. 1682 Peregrine Osborne, 2nd Duke of Leeds (d.1729). They had a son, Peregrine Hyde Osborne, and a grandson, Thomas Osborne, who m. Mary Godolphin.

HYDE OF ALDBURY.
Or a cheveron between three lozenges azure and a chief gules with an eagle or therein.

The Hyde Family - Earls of Clarendon

EDWARD HYDE EARL OF CLARENDON b.1608, the son of Henry Hyde of Wiltshire and Mary, d. of Edward Langford. He m. Frances, d. of Sir Thomas Ailesbury. In 1662 he became Lord Chancellor to Charles II. He died 1675 and was buried in Westminster Abbey

ANNE HYDE m. James Duke of York (later James II), younger brother and heir to Charles II. They had 2 daughters: Mary, b.1662, and Anne, b.1665, both of whom later became Queen. Mary m. William of Orange, and Anne m. George Prince of Denmark. When Anne Hyde died James m. Mary of Modena

LAURENCE HYDE, Earl of Rochester, President of the Council and Lord Lieutenant of Herts. He was one of the 7 signatories of the petition which brought William of Orange to the throne in 1688 (to replace James II and his son James, the heir apparent, who were unacceptable to many because they were Roman Catholics). His allegiance to William of Orange must have been strengthened by the fact that William's wife, Mary, was his niece.

King James II and his second wife, Mary of Modena, were Roman Catholics, and when they produced a male heir, James Edward Stuart, who would take precedence over his Protestant half-sisters, they were exiled. They fled to France with their baby son, and a few days later William of Orange and his wife Mary Hyde were proclaimed King and Queen. King James's supporters still hoped to restore the Stuart dynasty, setting their hopes first on young James Edward (later known as The Old Pretender) and then on his son Charles Edward - The Young Pretender (Bonnie Prince Charlie). All attempts failed and when Queen Anne died without producing an heir (after 17 pregnancies) the throne went to the Hanoverians.

All three of the Hyde families have similar arms, which indicates they were part of the same family, but the exact relationship is unclear

The Hunt Family
of Suffolk and Essex

JOHN LE HUNT lived in Suffolk at the beginning of the 13th century. His son, **SIR WARREN LE HUNT** succeeded him, followed by **EUSTACE LE HUNT** and **ROBERT LE HUNT** who was succeeded in 1310 by his son **JOHN LE HUNT.**

JOHN LE HUNT of Springfield in Essex, m. Anne, d. and heir of Sir William Rushbrooke of Rushbrooke in Suffolk.

ABELL LE HUNT m. Mary, d. of William Clopton of Kentwell Hall, Long Melford, Suffolk

JOHN LE HUNT m. Frances, d. and heir of ... Topsfield of Yeldham in Essex.

ROBERT LE HUNT m. ... d. of Henry Mackwilliams of Stamborne in Essex

JOHN LE HUNT of Hunts Hall in Ashen, Essex (on the Essex-Suffolk borders)

WILLIAM LE HUNT m. Agnes, d. of Sir William Waldegrave of Smallbridge, Suffolk. (Waldegrave tree ↓)

RICHARD BULL m. Hellen Skipwith

THOMAS KNIGHTON of Bayford, m. Ann Underhill of Little Bradley

WILLIAM HUNT m. Ann, d. and co-heir of Roger Fotheringer

ALICE BULL m. THOMAS KNIGHTON of Hertford Brickendon and Little Bradley (Memorial in Little Bradley Church)

CHARLES BULL of Hertford m 1532 JANE KNIGHTON of Bayford

ALICE HUNT m. Richard Bull → (cousin of Ann Knighton)

RICHARD HUNT m ANN KNIGHTON (Memorial in Little Bradley Church) Ann later m. Thomas Soame (see Soame tree)

FRANCIS KNIGHTON lived at Barnardiston Manor, m. Katherine, d. of Sir Weston Browne. (Browne tree ↓)

RICHARD BULL ← m. Alice Hunt.

HENRY BULL m. Rebecka Piggot. (Harmer tree ↓)

ALICE HUNT m① John Daye the printer who d. in 1584 (*1). m② William Stone of Segenhoe in Beds. (see Soame notes)

JOHN HUNT, d.1606, m. Jane Colte of Colte's Hall, Cavendish, Suffolk

MARGARET KNIGHTON, d.1589, m. Richard Waldegrave of Hitcham in Suffolk

GEORGE HUNT, eldest son and heir, m. Barbara, d. of Sir Rolfe Shelton of Shelton Hall in Norfolk

MIHI VITA CHRISTVS

JOHN HUNT. In 1644 he offered the whole Little Bradley Estate to Parliament in order to discharge himself from sequestration, but it seems to have been recovered later by members of the family (probably at the Restoration)

herre lies the Daye that darknes could not blynd
when popish fogges had our'd the sunne.
this Daye the cruell night did leave behynd
to wyn and spred what blouddi Actes wearye done
he set a Foxe to wright how Martyrs runne
By Death to lyfe. Fox hentur'd paynes: & health
to gyue them light Daye spent in print his wealth.

But God with gayn returnd his wealth agayne
and gaue to hym: as he gaue to the poore.
Two wyu'rs he had prrtakers of his payne
each wyfe twelue babrs and each of them one more
als was the last enrreaser of his storre
who mourning long for beyng lft alone.
Set vpp this toombe her self turnd to a Stone.

obiit 23 Iulii 1584.

SIR GEORGE HUNT

THOMAS HUNT d.1703

(**1**) John Daye was the foremost printer of his time. He produced the first English Church Book with tunes accompanying the words. John Foxe lodged in his house, and Daye printed the famous 'Foxe's Book of Martyrs'. He printed Queen Elizabeth's prayer book in six languages. He was born in Dunwich in 1522, died in 1584 and was buried in Little Bradley Church. The memorial brass above is on the north wall of the chancel and shows John with his wife Alice Hunt and their 13 children. In 1880 the Stationers Company, of which he had been Master 300 years before, set up a window in his memory, showing the three great martyrs, Andrew, Stephen and Paul.

The Knighton Family
of Bayford Herts and Little Bradley in Suffolk

JOHN KNIGHTON d.1559. In 1545 he received from Henry VIII the manor of Bayford, for which he paid £317. 13s. 9d.

THOMAS KNIGHTON of Bayford, m. Ann, d. and co-heiress of Thomas Underhill of Harveys in Little Bradley, Suffolk

THOMAS KNIGHTON of Brickendon. d.1582. m. Alice, d. of Richard Bull of Hertford and Helen Skipwith of St Albans. Thomas inherited his mother's estates in Suffolk and went to live there (↓ Knightons of Suffolk on Hunt tree)	JOHN KNIGHTON of the Inner Temple. d.1585. Lived at Aldbury. Acquired the manor of Kimpton in 1579 (*1) m. Alicia Copwood of Totteridge, Herts.	JANE KNIGHTON m. Charles, s. of Richard Bull of Hertford and Helen Skipwith of St Albans, and brother of Alice Bull who m. Thomas Knighton (Bull tree ↓)

DOROTHY KNIGHTON ——— URSULA KNIGHTON d.1605	JOYCE KNIGHTON ——— RALPH KNIGHTON	SIR GEORGE KNIGHTON of Bayford. 1537-1613. (*2) m.① Johanna Cadwell / m.② Susan White (no issue)	DIANIS KNIGHTON d.1616 ——— PHILIPPA KNIGHTON m.1559

JOHN KNIGHTON 1564-1635 m. Elizabeth Vaughan osp	GEORGE KNIGHTON eldest son and heir. d.1607 (pre-deceased his father - estate went to his nephew Knighton Ferrers)	ANN KNIGHTON 1586-1630 m. 1604, Sir John Ferrers of Markyate (Gentleman of the Privy Chamber to Queen Elizabeth. and James I - memorial in Bayford Church)	A DAUGHTER m. ... Spring of Norfolk

KNIGHTON FERRERS m. Katherine, d. of Sir William Walter. Knighton Ferrers died 1628, just before his d. Katherine was born, and his widow m. Thomas, Viscount Fanshawe of Ware Park (who may previously have been m. to Ann Alington. - see Soame note 2)

KATHERINE FERRERS m. 1640 (at the age of 12) Symon, Viscount Fanshawe (her step-father's son). Katherine became famous as The Wicked Lady (see Chapter 7)

(*1) Clutterbuck tells us that the Manor of Amwell Bury, alias Rushden, in the parish of All Saints, was held in the 19th year of Queen Elizabeth (1577) by John Knighton of Aldbury, his wife Alicia, and his son George. He also held the manor of Revell's Hall in Bengeo, and gave this to Henry Gardiner and his wife Mary (John's sister's daughter). John and George Knighton at this time also held Kimpton, Bayford and Brickendon.

(*2) There is a memorial to George Knighton in Bayford Church showing a knight in armour on an altar tomb.

The Kympton (or Kimpton) Family
of Westminster, Clothall and Weston

Held land in Herts and Beds, including the manor of Kimptons in Stanbridge, from the 14th century. By the 16th century they were also city merchants, but still held their estates in Hertfordshire. There is no apparent link with the manor of Kimpton Hoo in Hertfordshire.

EDMUND KYMPTON of Westminster, held land in Clothall, Yardley, Rushden and Astwick. He was probably related to the Poley and Sheldon families, from whom he acquired Astwick in 1539.

WILLIAM KYMPTON, Merchant Taylor, b. about 1515, m. 1539 Joan Mayman at St Margaret's Westminster, became Freeman of the Merchant Taylors Company in 1544 and Master of the Company in 1570. (*1)	EDMUND KYMPTON of Clothall, 1527-51, m. 1546 (at Weston) Lucy, d. of George Hyde of Throcking and Alice Roper of Well Hall, Eltham in Kent. (see Hyde and Roper tree) When Edmund died his wife held court until her son George came of age.

WILLIAM KYMPTON, Merchant Taylor, Freeman of the Company 1575, m. 1577 Cecily Burse at St Margarets Westminster. Possibly m. first to Jane Nodes of Shephallbury	EDWARD KYMPTON, bapt. 1556. Merchant Taylor, Master of the Company 1596.	GEORGE KYMPTON c.1546-1608, of Clothall and Weston (Howells). m.1568 at Bengeo, Catherine Brooke of High Cross (see Brooke tree). George and his cousin William also held the manor of Brickendon near Hertford

EDMUND KYMPTON m. 1619 Joanna Chaukell at St Margarets Westminster	JANE KYMPTON 1573-98 m. Thomas Harmer of Weston (Harmer Tree ↓)	ANNE b.1574; LEONARD b.1576; GEORGE b.1577; GEORGE b.1580; and ANNE b.1581. All died young	GEORGE KYMPTON b. 1583, only surviving son and heir, m. Dorothy, d. of Sir William Becher of Howbury Hall, Renhold, and lived at Clothallbury. He sold Astwick in 1420 for £2,100 to John Hudson (or Hodgeson) of London.

WILLIAM KYMPTON bapt. 1621 at St Margarets Westminster.

(*1) One of the most well-known local members of the Merchant Taylors Company was Sir William Harpur of Bedford, who was Master in 1553 and Lord Mayor of London in 1561.

The Descent of the Manors of Kimpton
with reference to the Hoo, de Vere, Knighton, and Brand families

Under the lordship of the Say family Kimpton was divided. Part was acquired in the 15th century by the Hoo family, Lords of St Paul's Walden, and in addition there were three manors: Hockinghanger, Parkbury and Leggats, which descended separately through the de Vere family and the Knightons. All were finally united under the the Hoo family who subsequently sold them to the Brands of Turvey.

THE DE VERE FAMILY AND THE MANOR OF HOCKINGHANGER

Baldwin de Vere of Northampton held the manor in 1235 under the lordship of William de Say. He was succeeded by his son Baldwin, who died before 1303, when his widow Matilda held the manor. It descended to their son John and their grandson Robert. In 1351 Robert settled the manor on himself and his wife, Elizabeth, in tail. The manor descended in the family to Henry de Vere, who died in 1493. The de Vere family were Earls of Oxford; one of the family seats was Castle Hedingham.

THE HOO FAMILY OF ST PAUL'S WALDEN

Robert de Hoo lived at the time of Edward I (1272-1307). His main seat was Lindley (or Lilley), which took the name of Lilley Hoo. In 1289 Robert also held the manors of Panshanger and Knebworth. In 1380 his kinsman, Sir William Hoo, had the manors of Luton Hoo, Offley and Cokernhoo. The Hoo family held all these manors during the 13th and 14th centuries, and they were the ancestors of Sir William Hoo, Lord of St. Paul's Walden in the 15th century.

> **SIR WILLIAM HOO**, died 1410, Lord of St Paul's Walden, m. Alice, d. of Sir Thomas St Omer

> **THOMAS HOO**, m. Dorothy Norwood. Acquired part of the manor of Kimpton (which became known as Kimpton Hoo). Buried at Kimpton Church in 1480

> **HENRY DE VERE**, d.1493, of Great Addingham, Northants

> **THOMAS HOO**, m. Maud, d. of Edmund Bardolf of Harpenden. Buried at St Paul's Walden 1516

ANNE DE VERE m. Sir Humphrey Browne of Abbess Roding.	**AUDREY (or Etheldred) DE VERE** m. John Browne of Abbess Roding (a nephew of Anne's husband Humphrey) (↓ Browne tree)	**ELIZABETH DE VERE** m. John Lord Mordaunt of Turvey. Elizabeth and her two sisters each inherited a third of the estate, but the whole manor finally went to Elizabeth's husband. (↓ Mordaunt tree)	**THOMAS HOO** d. 1551. m. daughter of John Newman of Hatfield

CATHERINE BROWNE m. William Roper of Eltham in Kent. (↓ Roper tree)	**LEWIS LORD MORDAUNT** of Turvey, d 1601. He was a judge at the trial of Mary Queen of Scots and of Thomas Duke of Norfolk. He sold Hockinghanger in 1596 to Thomas Hoo of St Paul's Walden	**THOMAS HOO** m. Luce, d. of John Brocket of Wheathampstead (Brocket Hall)	**MARGARET HOO** m① Nicholas, s. of John Brocket m② Edmund Bardolf of Harpenden (her 2nd cousin)

> **THOMAS HOO** of St Paul's Walden and Kimpton. Acquired the manor of Hockinghanger from Lewis Lord Mordaunt in 1596. Died 1615, aged 70. m. Helen (or Eleanor) died 1618, d. of William Perient of Digswell (see Perient tree).

> **WILLIAM HOO** of Kimpton, Sheriff of Herts 1629, d.1636, m. Susan Sturman of St Paul's Walden

> **THOMAS HOO** 1612-50, m. Mary, d. of Sir Francis Bickley of Hackney.

THOMAS HOO osp 1642	**SUSAN HOO** inherited St Paul's Walden and Kimpton (page 2 ↓)

Hoo. Quarterly sable and argent.

TREVOR, Viscount Hampden. *Party sinister bendwise ermine and erminees a lion or.*

The Descent of the Manors of Kimpton
with reference to the Hoo, de Vere, Knighton, and Brand families

THE KNIGHTON FAMILY AND THE MANORS OF PARKBURY AND LEGGATS

The manors of Parkbury and Leggats passed from William de Say to John Fray, then to the Sulyard family of Suffolk. In 1579 they were acquired by John Knighton of Bayford and his son George. (see Knighton tree). They passed from George to his grandson, Sir Knighton Ferrers, from whom they went to Knighton's daughter Katherine Ferrers ('The Wicked Lady') and her husband Symon, Viscount Fanshawe, who sold them in 1665 to Sir Jonathan Keate. The three, now combined, manors of Hockinghanger, Parkbury and Leggats thereafter descended with the manor of St Paul's Walden.

SUSAN HOO, b. 1639. Inherited St Paul's Walden and Kimpton., m. Sir Jonathan Keate, who was Sheriff of London in 1677, Member of Parliament 1690, and died 1700 aged 67. He acquired manors of Parkbury and Leggats from the Ferrers family in 1665, thus uniting all the manors of Kimpton.

SIR GILBERT HOO-KEATE, 1661-1735. Sold Kimpton and St Paul's Walden in 1732 to Margaret Brand of Westminster, widow of Thomas Brand of Turvey.	**JONATHAN HOO-KEATE**	**SIR WILLIAM HOO-KEATE**, Vicar of Kimpton and Rector of Digswell

KEATE. *Argent three cats passant sable.*

MARGARET BRAND
Widow of Thomas Brand of Westminster and Turvey (*1), bought the combined manors of Kimpton and St Paul's Walden in 1732 from Sir Gilbert Hoo-Keate

BRAND, Viscount Hampden. *Azure two crossed swords argent with their hilts or between three scallops or.*

THOMAS BRAND
Inherited Kimpton and St Paul's Walden and also acquired the manors of Great and Little Bradley in Suffolk (*2), m. 1771, Gertrude, d. of Henry Roper, Lord Teynham of Kent, who, on the death of her brother, Charles Trevor Roper, 18th Lord Dacre, in 1794, became Lady Dacre in her own right. She was a relative of Alice Roper who married George Hyde of Throcking in 1520, and of William Roper, the son-in-law of Sir Thomas More. (see Roper tree)

THOMAS BRAND 20th Lord Dacre Died without issue in 1851, his brother inherited.	**HENRY OTWAY BRAND**, 21st Lord Dacre, died 1853 Took the name of Trevor. Inherited the estates from his brother Thomas in 1851. m. Pyne, d. of the Hon. and very Rev'd Dean Crosbie, and sister of Lord Brandon

THOMAS CROSBIE WILLIAM TREVOR, 22nd Lord Dacre, m. Susan Sophia, d. of Charles Compton, 1st Lord Chesham. He took the name of Trevor only. osp 1890. His brother inherited.	**HENRY BOUVERIE WILLIAM BRAND**, 23rd Lord Dacre, MP for Lewes 1852-68 and for Cambridge 1868-84. Speaker of the House of Commons 1872-84. Created Viscount Hampden in 1884.

HENRY ROBERT BRAND, 2nd Viscount Hampden, MP for Herts and later for Stroud.
m①, 1864, Victoria Alexandrina Leopoldine Van de Weyer, d. of the Belgian Minister of State
m②, 1868, Susan Henrietta, d. of Lord George Cavendish

DACRE, Lord Dacre. *Gules three scallops argent.*

(***1**) The Brands lived in the mansion which is now Turvey Abbey

(***2**) In the 19th century the Brand family still had connections with the manors of Bradley which had been connected ever since the 13th century with various ancestors of the Harmer family, including Peche, Peverell, Gedding, Notbeame, Aspall, de la Pole, Caldebeck, Underhill, Knighton, Hunt, Harvey and Soame.

The Lytton (or Litton) Family
of Knebworth

SIR ROBERT LYTTON of Litton in Derbyshire, Under-Treasurer of the Exchequer and Keeper of the Great Wardrobe to Henry VII and member of the Privy Council, knighted by Henry VIII when he became Duke of York, died 1504. Bought Knebworth from the Barre family about 1488. m. Agnes, daughter of John Hotoft (*1).

WILLIAM LYTTON, Governor of the castle at Boulogne and Sheriff of Hertfordshire in 1510, d.1517, m. Audrey, d. and heir of Sir Philip Booth of Shrublands in Suffolk.

THOMAS LYTTON

LYTTON of Knebworth. *Ermine a chief indented azure with three crowns or therein.*

SIR ROBERT LYTTON created Knight of the Bath in 1547 at the Coronation of Edward VI, d. without male issue and his brother Rowland inherited.

ROWLAND LYTTON m. Ann, d. of George Carlton of Brightwell, Oxfordshire, d.1582

HELEN LYTTON m. Sir John Brocket of Brocket Hall. He was MP and High Sheriff for Hertfordshire in 1581 (see Brocket tree).

SIR ROWLAND LYTTON, d.1616, Lord Lieutenant of Hertfordshire, conducted the Forces of Hertfordshire at Tilbury 1588, High Sheriff 1594, MP for Hertford 1597, knighted 1603. m① Anne, d. of Oliver Lord St John of Bletsoe (see St John tree). m② Margaret Tate

ANNE LYTTON m. Sir William Webb.

JUDITH LYTTON, m① Sir George Smyth of Annables (*2), m② Sir Thomas Barrington

SIR WILLIAM LYTTON, MP for Hertford 1628 and 1641, d.1660 m. Ann, d. of Stephen Slaney of Norton, Salop.

MARY LYTTON, m. Edward Pulter.

SIR ROWLAND LYTTON 1614-74, MP for Hertford 1672 — m① Judith d.1659, d. of Sir Humphrey Edwards. — m② Rebecca, d. of Thomas Chapman. She was cousin of Rebecca Piggot and niece of the poet George Chapman

MARGARET LYTTON m① Thomas Hillersden of Elstow, Beds, m② Thomas Hewitt of Ampthill, Beds

ANNE LYTTON ----- **MARY LYTTON**

DOROTHY LYTTON ----- **ELIZABETH LYTTON** m. John Scroggs of Aldbury

SIR WILLIAM LYTTON, died without issue 1705. He was the last male descendant

JUDITH LYTTON, d.1662, eldest daughter, m. Sir Nicholas Strode. When Sir William Lytton died in 1705 her grandson, Lytton Strode Lytton, inherited the estate (*3).

REBECCA LYTTON m. Lord Falkland

Knebworth House, Hertfordshire about 1824

(***1**) There were family connections with the Barres through the Hotofts. Sir John Barre (d.1482) was married to Indonea Hotoft, the sister of Agnes, (see Barre tree).

(***2**) Annables, sometimes known as Kinsbourne Hall, was later the home of the Luke family and then the Bissels and the Roberts, relations of Mary Hare who married William Harmer in 1883

(***3**) He died without issue in 1710 and one of the other descendants took the name of Lytton and inherited the estate, which came down to the Bulwer Lyttons in the 19th century.

The Mannock Family
of Gifford's Hall, Stoke-by-Nayland, Suffolk

PHILIP MANNOCK acquired the manor in 1428. The family had resided in the area since the time of Edward III. They came originally from Denmark and flourished under the Danish kings

JOHN MANNOCK died 1476, m. ... d. of Sir William Waldegrave of Borley. (see Waldegrave tree)

GEORGE MANNOCK died 1541, m. Katherine, d. of Sir Thomas Waldegrave. (related to the Brownes of Abbess Roding)

WILLIAM MANNOCK d. 1558
m. Audrey, d. of John Alington and sister of Sir Gyles Alington of Horseheath, Cambridge (who m. Margaret Spencer of Althorpe) and of Mary Alington (who m. Robert Newport of Pelham) (see Spencer and Soame trees)

ELIZABETH MANNOCK

m① Robert Dacres of Cheshunt (great-grandfather of Elizabeth Dacres who m. Richard Hale of Tewin)

m② Thomas Denny of Cheshunt related to Thomas Roper (Viscount Baltinglass) and the Nevill family (Lord Abergavenny)

FRANCIS MANNOCK
———
THOMAS MANNOCK

FRANCIS MANNOCK 1523-90
Memorial in N aisle of chancel in Stoke-by-Nayland church

m① Mary, d. of William Fitch of Canfield, Essex. (see Nedham tree)

m② Ann Siscelton, widow, d. of ... Wentworth (d. 1620). There were four children of this marriage: John; Elizabeth (m. to Nicholas Bedingfield); Frances (m. to Giles Green) and Bridget (m. to Thomas Sulyard of Wetherden)

GILES MANNOCK
———
WILLIAM MANNOCK

A DAUGHTER m. ... Cornwall of Essex.
———
A DAUGHTER m. ... St Clere of Essex

WILLIAM MANNOCK, eldest son and heir. In 1596 Queen Elizabeth took away two thirds of his estates because of recusancy. Pardoned by James I in 1603 and estates returned, but taken away again in 1612. m. Audrey, d. of Ferdinand Parys of Linton, Cambs. Memorial stone in Stoke-by-Nayland church.

MARGARET MANNOCK
m. Thomas Crawley of Maldon, Essex.

MARY MANNOCK
———
ANN MANNOCK
m. Thomas Gaudy Everard of Linsted in Suffolk

ELINOR MANNOCK
m. Richard Martin of Long Melford. (Effigy in Melford church)

SIR FRANCIS MANNOCK, d. 20 Nov 1634 aged 49, m.1608, Dorothy, d. of William Sanders of Welford, Northants. Sir Francis was created Baronet by Charles I in 1627. Dorothy died 1632 aged 42, after the birth of her daughter Ann. Both Dorothy and Francis were recusants and most of their estates were sequestered. There is a memorial to Francis in the N wall of church at Stoke-by-Nayland, and a brass to Dorothy Sanders on the floor of the N chapel.

WILLIAM MANNOCK
b. 1611, eldest son and heir, died young.

JOHN MANNOCK

SIR FRANCIS MANNOCK, 2nd baronet, d. 1687, m. Mary, d. of Sir George Heneage of Hainton, Lincs (who provided for the younger members of the Mannock family left penniless by the sequestration).

KATHERINE MANNOCK
m. John, s. of Edward Newport of Brent Pelham

ANN MANNOCK
b.1632

SIR WILLIAM MANNOCK, 3rd baronet

SIR FRANCIS MANNOCK, 4th baronet

SIR WILLIAM MANNOCK
5th baronet

SIR FRANCIS MANNOCK
7th baronet, d. 1778

SIR THOMAS MANNOCK 8th baronet, d. 1781, m.1780, Anastasia Browne (2nd wife) descendant of 1st Viscount Montague (see Browne of Sussex tree)

SIR GEORGE MANNOCK, 9th baronet, killed 3rd June 1787 by the overturning of the Dover coach (*1).

SIR ANTHONY MANNOCK, 6th baronet, d. 1776. His three uncles succeeded in turn to the title.

(*1) When Sir George died in the Dover coach accident in 1787, leaving no issue, the baronetcy expired. The manor went to William Comyns who took the name Mannock and died in 1819. It then went to his kinsman (through a Strickland marriage) Patrick Power, who again took the name of Mannock by royal licence in 1830. The mansion house of Giffords Hall remains, the oldest part, built by Peter Gifford, dating back to the time of Henry III. The main part is Tudor, built by the Mannock family (picture on page 80). Nearby are the ruins of an old chapel built by Richard Constable in 1216 and endowed by his son William. Since this is 'Constable country' this is almost certainly the family of John Constable the painter. The Mannock family were related by marriage to the Chapmans of Hitchin (George Chapman the Elizabethan poet).

The Mordaunt Family of Turvey and Drayton Park
with connections in Suffolk, Essex and Hertfordshire (Kimpton)

The manor of Mordaunts in Turvey was held by the Mordaunt family from the early 13th century.

EUSTACE MORDAUNT named in 1225 in an assize of Morte d'ancestor

WILLIAM MORDAUNT succeeded and his son WILLIAM held the manor in 1278

ROBERT MORDAUNT inherited the manor before 1346

EDMUND MORDAUNT, d. 1372. The Sunday before the feast of St Simon and St Jude he was seized with homicidal mania, killed his wife Ellen and drowned himself in a pool at Turvey.

ROBERT MORDAUNT. United the two manors of Mordaunt and Ardres. Died before 1397

ROBERT MORDAUNT, a supporter of the house of York in the Wars of the Roses. Died 1448, having considerably impoverished the estate to support the Yorkist army.

WILLIAM MORDAUNT and his wife were 'frugal and provident' and the family became prosperous again.

MORDAUNT. *Argent a chevron between three stars sable.*

MAUD (or Elizabeth) MORDAUNT m. Sir Weston Browne of Abbess Roding (Browne tree ⬇)

SIR JOHN MORDAUNT succeeded about 1475. He was wounded when fighting on the Lancastrian side in the battle at Barnet. Made King's Sergeant in 1495 and is said to have been instrumental in arranging the marriage between Margaret Tudor and James IV of Scotland in 1503. He was Speaker of the House of Commons 1487. Died 1504

JOHN LORD MORDAUNT, created baron in 1533. He accompanied Henry VIII to the Field of the Cloth of Gold. He received Anne Boleyn at the Tower when she came to be crowned and took part in her trial three years later. He lived at Drayton in Northamptonshire and used Turvey Park as a Dower House. Died 1561

JOHN 2ND LORD MORDAUNT. Lived at Thorndon, West Horndon, near Ingatestone Hall. Died 1571. A supporter of Queen Mary who made him a Privy Counsellor. Inherited part of the manor at Kimpton in Hertfordshire by his marriage to Elizabeth, d. of Henry de Vere and sister of Ann and Audrey de Vere who were both married into the Browne family. John was a friend and kinsman of the Petres of Ingatestone Hall and made a gift of an ox at the wedding of Catherine Tyrrell (see chapter 3). Lady Mordaunt sent presents for the christening of Master John Petre in 1549 (*1).

GEORGE MORDAUNT (3rd son) His daughter Katherine married Robert Barnardiston of Northill. (see Barnardiston tree)

LEWIS LORD MORDAUNT of Northill, Bedfordshire, d.1601. A judge who took part (unwillingly) in the trial of Mary Queen of Scots and also of Thomas Duke of Norfolk. Sold the manor of Kimpton to Thomas Hoo of St Paul's Walden. He m. Jane Nedham of Wymondley Priory (see Nedham tree)

HENRY 4TH LORD MORDAUNT. A Roman Catholic. Was sent to the Tower under suspicion of being involved in the Gunpowder Plot (1605). Released after long imprisonment. Died 1608 and in his will he states that his conscience is clear, and that he had no knowledge of the Gunpowder Treason (*2). When Sir Henry died his widow lived on at Turvey. The government took away her eldest son so that he should be brought up as a Protestant, but Lady Turvey remained a determined Roman Catholic. From 1625-31 she even had resident in her house at Turvey the Vicar Apostolic who travelled round the county in a coach with four horses, accompanied by 9 or 10 priests (*3). The jurisdiction of the Vicar Apostolic extended over Roman Catholics in the whole of England and also in the American plantations

JOHN MORDAUNT. made Earl of Peterborough in 1628 but took the Parliamentarian side in the early part of the Civil War. Died 1642

HENRY MORDAUNT 2nd Earl of Peterborough, was a Royalist (unlike his father). Wounded at Newbury and several times imprisoned. His estates sequestered in 1648 and recovered in 1655 at a cost of £5,106 - 15s. At the Restoration he was made a member of the Privy Council, and conducted negotiations for the marriage of the then Duke of York (later James II) and Mary of Modena. Became a Roman Catholic and was impeached for High Treason, but later released. Created Earl of Monmouth in 1689. He died at an advanced age in 1697 without male issue. His only daughter Mary died unmarried in 1705.

⬇

CHARLES MORDAUNT 3rd Earl of Peterborough, d.1735, nephew of the 2nd Earl, General in the Spanish War of Succession.

⬇

CHARLES MORDAUNT 4th Earl of Peterborough, grandson of the 3rd Earl. Died 1774

CHARLES MORDAUNT 5th (and last) Earl of Peterborough. In 1786 he sold the property, including Turvey Abbey, to Claude Higgins, Sheriff of London for that year. The estates remained in the Higgins family until the 19th century (*4).

The Mordaunt Family of Turvey and Drayton Park
with connections in Suffolk, Essex and Hertfordshire (Kimpton)

(*1) For the christening of Master John Petre at Ingatestone Hall in 1549, Lady Mordaunt of Thorndon (previously Elizabeth de Vere) sent: 'a guinea fowl, a mallard, a woodcock, two teals, a basket of wafers and other cakes'. Her husband, John Lord Mordaunt, often came to play backgammon with Sir William Petre at Ingatestone Hall.

(*2) See Family Connections with the Gunpowder Plot on page 153/4.

(*3) Lady Mordaunt's house at Turvey, about 1644, is described by Joyce Godber. It had three parlours, one of them wainscotted, the drawing room, where the chairs were of Turkey-work, the red room and the gallery and 14 bedchambers - her own containing a white wrought bed.

(*4) Until the 17th century the Mordaunt estate at Turvey was known as Mordaunts Manor. Another manor belonging to the Dudleys (later Earls of Leicester) was generally known as Turvey Manor and the two were united in 1660 by the Mordaunts who were related to the Brownes and Knightons of Little Bradley in Suffolk, and to the de Vere family of Kimpton in Hertfordshire. Another branch at Northill married into the Barnardiston family. The Oakley branch married into the Booth family of Shrublands in Suffolk and the Snagges of Marston Morteyne. The house now known as Turvey Abbey was occupied by another Roman Catholic family - the Brands, who were kinsmen of the de Veres and Brands of Kimpton.

TURVEY ABBEY.

The Mordaunt Family of Oakley

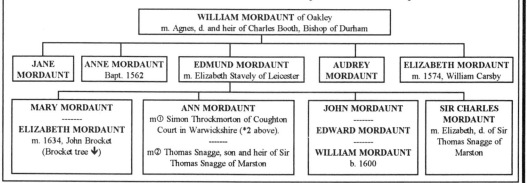

WILLIAM MORDAUNT of Oakley
m. Agnes, d. and heir of Charles Booth, Bishop of Durham

JANE MORDAUNT	ANNE MORDAUNT Bapt. 1562	EDMUND MORDAUNT m. Elizabeth Stavely of Leicester	AUDREY MORDAUNT	ELIZABETH MORDAUNT m. 1574, William Carsby

MARY MORDAUNT

ELIZABETH MORDAUNT
m. 1634, John Brocket
(Brocket tree ↓)

ANN MORDAUNT
m① Simon Throckmorton of Coughton Court in Warwickshire (*2 above).
----
m② Thomas Snagge, son and heir of Sir Thomas Snagge of Marston

JOHN MORDAUNT

EDWARD MORDAUNT

WILLIAM MORDAUNT
b. 1600

SIR CHARLES MORDAUNT
m. Elizabeth, d. of Sir Thomas Snagge of Marston

- 191 -

Sir Thomas More
of More Hall or Gobions at North Mimms, Hertfordshire

SIR JOHN MORE
d. 1526. Studied at Lincoln's Inn and became one of the Justices of the King's Bench. m. ... Hancombe of Bedfordshire. He held the manor of Gobions (sometimes called More Hall) at North Mimms, Hertfordshire.

SIR THOMAS MORE 1478-1535
Born at Milk Street in London in 1478 and went to the Free School there. He was later educated at the home of Cardinal Moreton, Archbishop of Canterbury, and finally at Oxford. He married Jane, d. of John Colte of Newhall, Essex (a relative of the Coltes of Coltes Hall, Cavendish in Suffolk and also of the Hunts and Knightons). He was made Speaker of the House of Commons in 1523 and Lord Chancellor in 1529. He resigned in 1532 and was imprisoned the following year. Finally, in 1535 he was executed for refusing to take the Oath of Supremacy.

JOHN MORE
only son and heir.
m. Ann, d. of Edward Cressacre of Baronburgh in Yorkshire. When his father was executed all the family property was taken away, but was returned after the death of Queen Elizabeth

MARGARET MORE
the 'beloved daughter' and 'a woman of singular wit, great wisdom, rare piety and extraordinary learning'. She was married in 1525 to William Roper of Well Hall, Eltham, Kent (the brother of Alice Roper an ancestor of the Harmer family).
(see Roper and Hyde trees)

ELIZABETH MORE
m. Sir John Darcy, s. of Robert Darcy and Elizabeth Wentworth.
(see Darcy tree)
———
CECILY MORE
m. Giles Heron

THOMAS MORE
osp
———
AUGUSTINE MORE
osp

THOMAS MORE
the younger. 1532-1606.
b. at Chelsea
m. Margaret Scrope, d. of John, second son of Henry Lord Scrope

BARTHOLOMEW MORE
died young
———
EDWARD MORE

MARGARET MORE
———
ELIZABETH MORE

CECILY MORE

CRESSACRE MORE
1572-1649
m. Elizabeth, d. of Thomas Gage, a relative of Sir John Gage of Sussex (see Darcy tree) who m. Penelope Darcy of Hengrave Hall

HELEN MORE
———
BRIDGET MORE

THOMAS MORE
m. Mary, d. of Sir Basil Brooke.
He bought or inherited his great-grandfather's estates in Hertfordshire. He had one son, Basil More, who m. Ann, d. of Sir William Humble.

SIR THOMAS MORE probably spent much of his early life at Gobions, his country estate in Hertfordshire, but later lived mainly at Chelsea, where some of his younger children were born. His 'Utopia' is thought to have been written at Gobions. It was illustrated by his friend Hans Holbein, who also painted several portraits of Thomas More.

There was a large family portrait by Hans Holbein, probably commissioned by his son-in-law William (the brother of Alice Roper), which hung in the Great Hall at the Roper family home in Eltham, Kent. The original painting was lost when the home was sold in the 18th century but several variant copies still exist.

In the Frick Collection in New York there is a Holbein portrait of Thomas More, which seems to have been painted from the original sketch which he did for the family group. (There is a note about this painting on the Roper tree.) The Mores had several links with the family, through the Ropers, Scroops, Darcys, Brookes, and the Colte family of Coltes Hall in Cavendish, Suffolk.

The Nedham Family
of Wymondley Priory, Hertfordshire

JOHN NEDHAM of Nedham Grange in the High Peak of the County of Derby

CHRISTOPHER NEDHAM

JAMES NEDHAM, Surveyor to the King. Bought Marden in Tewin and the Priory at Little Wymondley about 1536. Fought for the King [Henry VIII] in France where he died in 1545 and was buried at Boulogne. (Memorial plaque in Little Wymondley church). He married Alice, d. of ... Merry (or Goodyer) of Hatfield.

JOHN NEDHAM, b. about 1523, d. 1591. m① Ann Coppin of Canterbury | m② Jane Weldish of Cranbrooke, Kent.

MARY NEDHAM	COPPIN NEDHAM	GEORGE NEDHAM	SIR JOHN NEDHAM	THOMAS (OR JAMES) NEDHAM	JANE NEDHAM	JULIANA NEDHAM	BRIDGET NEDHAM
m. John Parker of Radwell (d.1595). Died with her infant son in 1574 (Memorial in Radwell church)	b. 1559 ——— ANN NEDHAM m. Thomas Pole of London	1557-1626 m. Margaret, (d. 1609), d. of Sir Henry Style of Kent	1565-1618 m. Elizabeth, d. of Sir Edward Watson. She later m. Sir Edward Tyrrell	m. Elizabeth, sister of Beckingham Butler of Tewin Bury	m. Lewis Mordaunt of Northill, Beds (see Mordaunt tree)	m. William Warren (alias Bygrave) (Warren tree) ↓)	m. Benjamin Piggot of Gravenhurst. (Piggot tree) ↓

JAMES NEDHAM, died in infancy 1603
———
JOHN NEDHAM of Welwyn, b.1594, m. Ann, d. of Matthew Denton of Barton, Beds.

EUSTACE NEDHAM d.1658
m① Anne, d. of Luke Norton of Offley | m② 1626, Frances, d. of Edward Wingate of Lockleys and his wife Mary Taverner of Hexton. (see Wingate and Taverner trees)

JOANNA NEDHAM d.1666 m. Francis Taverner of Hexton (brother of Eustace's mother-in-law) (↓ Taverner tree)

MARGARET NEDHAM	LETTICE NEDHAM	GEORGE NEDHAM	FRANCES NEDHAM	MARY NEDHAM
bapt. May 1619 at Wymondley Priory ——— LUKE NEDHAM b. 1620	m① William Langhorne of Bedford m② Richard Shoard, Vicar of Shephall and Rector of Stevenage, d. 1679 M.I. at Shephall	1618-69 m. Barbara, d. of Sir William Fitch of Essex. Inherited Wymondley Priory.	——— MARGARET NEDHAM ——— ANN NEDHAM	b. 1636, m. John Harmer of Weston (↓ Harmer tree)

LUKE NEDHAM	GEORGE NEDHAM	FITCH NEDHAM	MAURICE NEDHAM b. 1653	BARBARA NEDHAM
bapt. Graveley July 1641	d. 1692 m. Lydia Banks d. 1728	——— JAMES NEDHAM	——— CHARLES NEDHAM b. 1655	——— ANN NEDHAM ——— ELIZABETH NEDHAM

GEORGE NEDHAM	EUSTACE NEDHAM	BARBARA NEDHAM b.1673	ELIZABETH NEDHAM 1683-1753	MARGARET NEDHAM
1672-1726 m. Barbara Gregory of Nottingham. Died with no male heir	1675-1708 ——— BANKS NEDHAM b. 1676, d. in infancy	——— MARY NEDHAM b. 1678 ——— LETTICE NEDHAM b. 1681	m. Simon Degge (Memorial in Graveley Church) (*1)	b. 1686

SUSAN NEDHAM	BARBARA NEDHAM	MARTHA NEDHAM
b. 1702 (*2)	b. 1704, m. John Sherwin of Nottingham	1706-73, m. Thomas Browne, Garter King of Arms 1701-80, lived at Wymondley Priory and later Camfield Place, Essendon (*3). (Memorial in Essendon church)

(*1) **Memorials in Graveley Church.** To Simon Degge and his wife Elizabeth Nedham, and to the Revd Francis Nedham (nephew to the late Sir Henry Penrice of Offley Place) 40 years Rector of the parish. Also his wife Sarah who died in 1770 aged 66.

(*2) Susan, Barbara and Martha Nedham were the joint heirs of George Nedham. In 1731 they sold Wymondley Priory to Samuel Vanderplank, from whom it descended through his daughter Anna (who married Gilbert Joddrell) to their daughter Anna, wife of Christopher Clitheroe of Essendon. He sold it in 1806 to Samuel Heathcote of Shephallbury, a descendant of the Nodes familiy (see Nodes tree). Samuel Heathcote also bought Wymondley Bury and became Lord of the Manor of Wymondley.

(*3) Camfield Place is now the home of the novelist Dame Barbara Cartland.

The Newport Family
of Brent Pelham, Furneaux Pelham and Stocking Pelham

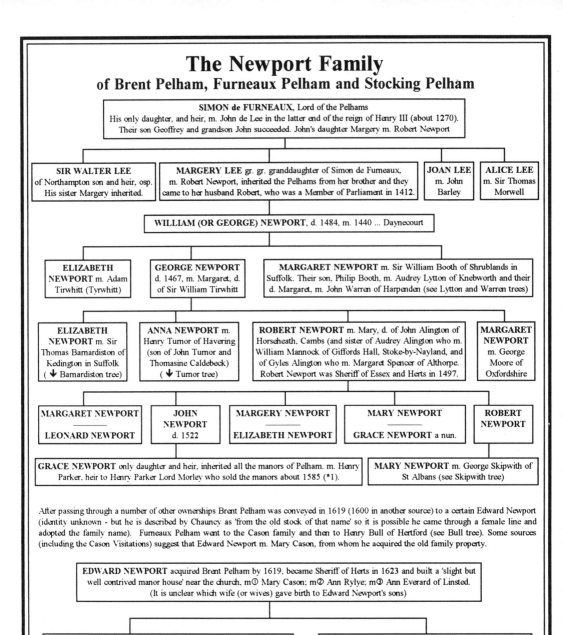

SIMON de FURNEAUX, Lord of the Pelhams
His only daughter, and heir, m. John de Lee in the latter end of the reign of Henry III (about 1270). Their son Geoffrey and grandson John succeeded. John's daughter Margery m. Robert Newport

SIR WALTER LEE of Northampton son and heir, osp. His sister Margery inherited.	**MARGERY LEE** gr. gr. granddaughter of Simon de Furneaux, m. Robert Newport, inherited the Pelhams from her brother and they came to her husband Robert, who was a Member of Parliament in 1412.	**JOAN LEE** m. John Barley	**ALICE LEE** m. Sir Thomas Morwell

WILLIAM (OR GEORGE) NEWPORT, d. 1484, m. 1440 ... Daynecourt

ELIZABETH NEWPORT m. Adam Tirwhitt (Tyrwhitt)	**GEORGE NEWPORT** d. 1467, m. Margaret, d. of Sir William Tirwhitt	**MARGARET NEWPORT** m. Sir William Booth of Shrublands in Suffolk. Their son, Philip Booth, m. Audrey Lytton of Knebworth and their d. Margaret, m. John Warren of Harpenden (see Lytton and Warren trees)

ELIZABETH NEWPORT m. Sir Thomas Barnardiston of Kedington in Suffolk (↓ Barnardiston tree)	**ANNA NEWPORT** m. Henry Turnor of Havering (son of John Turnor and Thomasine Caldebeck) (↓ Turnor tree)	**ROBERT NEWPORT** m. Mary, d. of John Alington of Horseheath, Cambs (and sister of Audrey Alington who m. William Mannock of Giffords Hall, Stoke-by-Nayland, and of Gyles Alington who m. Margaret Spencer of Althorpe. Robert Newport was Sheriff of Essex and Herts in 1497.	**MARGARET NEWPORT** m. George Moore of Oxfordshire

MARGARET NEWPORT ———— **LEONARD NEWPORT**	**JOHN NEWPORT** d. 1522	**MARGERY NEWPORT** ———— **ELIZABETH NEWPORT**	**MARY NEWPORT** ———— **GRACE NEWPORT** a nun.	**ROBERT NEWPORT**

GRACE NEWPORT only daughter and heir, inherited all the manors of Pelham. m. Henry Parker, heir to Henry Parker Lord Morley who sold the manors about 1585 (*1).	**MARY NEWPORT** m. George Skipwith of St Albans (see Skipwith tree)

After passing through a number of other ownerships Brent Pelham was conveyed in 1619 (1600 in another source) to a certain Edward Newport (identity unknown - but he is described by Chauncy as 'from the old stock of that name' so it is possible he came through a female line and adopted the family name). Furneaux Pelham went to the Cason family and then to Henry Bull of Hertford (see Bull tree). Some sources (including the Cason Visitations) suggest that Edward Newport m. Mary Cason, from whom he acquired the old family property.

EDWARD NEWPORT acquired Brent Pelham by 1619, became Sheriff of Herts in 1623 and built a 'slight but well contrived manor house' near the church. m① Mary Cason; m② Ann Rylye; m③ Ann Everard of Linsted. (It is unclear which wife (or wives) gave birth to Edward Newport's sons)

JOHN NEWPORT (*2) m①. about 1660, Katherine, d. of Sir Francis Mannock of Giffords Hall. m②. Mary, d. of Thomas Sulyard of Grundisburgh in Suffolk. John and Mary had 13 children, but they did not inherit the manor, which went to John's brother William.	**WILLIAM NEWPORT** m. ... d. of Mr Slaughter, Clerk [in Holy Orders], inherited Brent Pelham from his brother John and sold it to Richard Meade, whose son sold it to the Cason family of Astonbury (see Cason tree).

(***1**) Henry Lord Morley was the father of William Lord Monteagle and Morley who received the famous 'Monteagle letter' giving warning of the Gunpowder Plot (see Petre tree and also notes on the Gunpowder Plot).

(***2**) Chauncy writes about this John Newport: 'Anno 10 Car. I [1635] he manifested his loyalty to that King, in the time of the Rebellion, when his majesty was exposed to excessive Distresses, for then he engaged himself with Horse and Arms on behalf of his Majesty, and continued in the Wars until his Army was totally dissipated; during which time, his House was plundered, all his Goods and Cattel taken away, his Mother, Brothers and Sisters turned out of their House, exposed to great Want; and his Estate was sequestered, until King Charles II was restored to his Crown, then he returned to his own, and married Katharine one of the daughters of Sir Francis Mannock, of Giffords Hall, in the Parish of Stoke-Neyland, in the County of Suffolk'

The Nodes Family
of Shephallbury

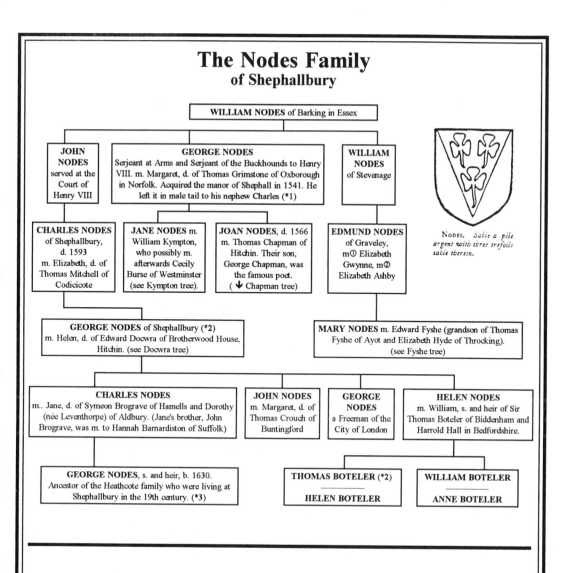

WILLIAM NODES of Barking in Essex

JOHN NODES served at the Court of Henry VIII

GEORGE NODES Serjeant at Arms and Serjeant of the Buckhounds to Henry VIII. m. Margaret, d. of Thomas Grimstone of Oxborough in Norfolk. Acquired the manor of Shephall in 1541. He left it in male tail to his nephew Charles (*1)

WILLIAM NODES of Stevenage

Nodes, Sable a pile argent with three trefoils sable therein.

CHARLES NODES of Shephallbury, d. 1593 m. Elizabeth, d. of Thomas Mitchell of Codicicote

JANE NODES m. William Kympton, who possibly m. afterwards Cecily Burse of Westminster (see Kympton tree).

JOAN NODES, d. 1566 m. Thomas Chapman of Hitchin. Their son, George Chapman, was the famous poet. (↓ Chapman tree)

EDMUND NODES of Graveley, m① Elizabeth Gwynne, m② Elizabeth Ashby

GEORGE NODES of Shephallbury (*2) m. Helen, d. of Edward Docwra of Brotherwood House, Hitchin. (see Docwra tree)

MARY NODES m. Edward Fyshe (grandson of Thomas Fyshe of Ayot and Elizabeth Hyde of Throcking). (see Fyshe tree)

CHARLES NODES m.. Jane, d. of Symeon Brograve of Hamells and Dorothy (née Leventhorpe) of Aldbury. (Jane's brother, John Brograve, was m. to Hannah Barnardiston of Suffolk)

JOHN NODES m. Margaret, d. of Thomas Crouch of Buntingford

GEORGE NODES a Freeman of the City of London

HELEN NODES m. William, s. and heir of Sir Thomas Boteler of Biddenham and Harrold Hall in Bedfordshire.

GEORGE NODES, s. and heir, b. 1630. Ancestor of the Heathcote family who were living at Shephallbury in the 19th century. (*3)

THOMAS BOTELER (*2)
———
HELEN BOTELER

WILLIAM BOTELER
———
ANNE BOTELER

(*1) George Nodes left the manor of Shephallbury in 'male tail' to his heirs, and since he had only daughters it went to his nephew Charles. Later the two sons-in-law, William Kympton and Thomas Chapman, claimed a right to the property, but did not succeed, and when Charles died it passed to his son George. Jane Kympton, the elder daughter, inherited a messuage called Copidhall, originally part of the manor, but Joan Chapman seems to have inherited nothing.

(*2) Joyce Godber refers to this George Nodes in her 'History of Bedfordshire'. Speaking of the sadness of families divided by the Civil War (1642-49) she writes 'George Nodes of Hertfordshire in 1642 was glad to see his Boteler grandchildren; "I am old and crazy [ill] and I doubt whether I shall see them again. We think the times more dangerous now than ever they were - I pray God amend them".' The Boteler grandchildren would have been Thomas, William, Helen and Ann, the children of Helen and William Boteler who lived at Harrold Hall in Bedfordshire.

(*3) The Nodes family were still at Shephallbury in the 18th century. The accounts of Thomas Green, a music teacher and instrument tuner, show that he was visiting Shephallbury several times a year between 1752 and 1764 to tune a harp, a spinet, and a harpsichord for Mrs Nodes. In the 19th century Shephallbury was owned by the Heathcote family, who were direct descendants of George Nodes through the female line, having presumably inherited in spite of the 'male tail'. The old manor house was replaced in 1865 by a new Gothic style building adjoining the site of the original house. In 1806 the Heathcotes bought the Manor of Wymondley, which included the Priory and Wymondley Bury. In 1609 this property had belonged to Thomas Piggot and his wife Elizabeth Chapman, who was a granddaughter of George Nodes of Shephallbury. Thus, although they may not have realised it, the Heathcotes were acquiring a property which had been in their family 250 years earlier.

The Perient Family (tree A)
of Digswell

JOHN PERIENT (*1) born in Gascoigne, came to England with Edward the Black Prince. Standard bearer to Richard II, Henry IV and Henry V and Master of the Horse to the Queen., m. Joan (d. 23 April 1415), d. of Sir John Risain. (Brass in Digswell church)

JOHN PERIENT Lord of Digswell, Master of the Horse to Richard II, d. 1432. Acquired the manor of Lockleys and the manor of Gobions at Stapleford near Ware (*2). There is a memorial to this John, and to his son John, in Welwyn Church. m. Joan, d. of Thomas Mansfield

WALTER PERIENT of Great Munden

JOHN PERIENT 1417-42, Lord of Digswell, died sp. Gravestone below rails in chancel of Digswell church

EDMUND PERIENT d. 1473 m. Ann, d. of Thomas Vernon. Succeeded his brother as Lord of Digswell and Lockleys and Gobions

THOMAS PERIENT b. 1443, m. Mary Brocket, d. of ... Brocket of Wheathampstead. Sheriff of Essex and Herts 1498

THOMAS PERIENT d. 1539, Sheriff of Herts and Essex in 1536, m. Alice, d. of Edward Brocket of Brocket Hall (see Brocket tree).

SIR JOHN PERIENT of Hatfield, Auditor of the Courts of Wards and Liveries, m. ... d. of Sir William Tendringe and had 2 daughters: Joyce, m. William Barley of Aldbury, and Gertrude, m. ... Gill.

GEORGE PERIENT d. 1532 m. Agnes, d. of Thomas Sporne of Lavenham, Suffolk. (↓ Perient tree B)

THOMAS PERIENT 1497-1545, m. Ann, d. of Richard Drewell and sister of Sir Humphrey Drewell (who m. Katherine Perient - see Perient tree B). Thomas divided Lockleys between his daughters Dorothy and Ann. He also inherited Gobions from his father in 'male tail' (*3), and Quickswood from his wife.

WILLIAM PERIENT of Ayot Mountfitchet, d.1580, m. Elizabeth (d.1582), d. of George Hyde of Throcking, relict of Thomas Fyshe and sister of Lucy Hyde who m. Edmund Kympton. (see Hyde tree)

JOHN PERIENT m. Elizabeth Hopton
————
ALICE PERIENT m. Richard, s. of John Bowles of Wallington and his wife Ann Devenish of Weston. (see Hyde tree)

DOROTHY PERIENT b. 1527, m. George Burgoyne who inherited Quickswood
————
ANN PERIENT b. 1529, m. Anthony Carleton. She left a house and land for the poor of Welwyn (*4)

ELIZABETH PERIENT b.1531, m. ... Ibgrave
————
MARY PERIENT eldest d. and heir, 1525-51. m① Affabel Rowlett (d. 1546) of St Albans (see Skipwith tree), m② George Horsey (Sheriff of Herts in 1572), who later m. Ann Sadlier (see Docwra tree).

SIR GEORGE PERIENT of Ayot Mountfitchet, d.1621. Sheriff of Herts 1604. Bought Digswell from Sir Ralph Horsey, his nephew, and then sold it to Richard Sidley. Inherited Gobions from his uncle Thomas.

m① at Watton, 1580, Mary (or Martha), d. of Sir John Boteler	m② Elizabeth Barnes, relict of Richard Hare (*5) & of George Rotherham of Someries Manor, Luton.

HELEN (OR ELEANOR) PERIENT m. Sir Thomas Hoo of St Pauls Walden (who d. 1613). Helen d. 1618. Both are buried in St Paul's Walden church. (see Descent of the Manor of Kimpton)

SIR RALPH HORSEY of Melcombe Horsey in Dorset. Sold the manor of Digswell to his uncle, Sir George Perient.

JASPER HORSEY m. Helen, d. of Thomas Docwra of Putteridge. (↓ Docwra tree)

HELEN HORSEY m. Thomas Docwra of Putteridge. (↓ Docwra tree)

PHILIP PERIENT, b.1583, admitted to Gray's Inn 1601

MARY PERIENT, m. Sir Nicholas Trott

ANN PERIENT 1586-1624, m. Martin Trott
————
ELIZABETH PERIENT b.1596, m. William Exelbie

(*1) An earlier John Perient, probably this John's grandfather, d. 1324 and left £200 to build a Chantry Chapel at Digswell and to provide for prayers and masses for himself, his wife and his parents. This Chantry was replaced in the 16th century by the present North Chapel in Digswell Church.

(*2) There were 2 manors called Gobions - this one in Stapleford, and another in North Mimms, once owned by Sir Thomas More. John Perient bought the Stapleford manor in 1412 from William Gobion, whose family had lived there since 1295.

(*3) Thomas's 'male tail' inheritance of Gobions meant that it could not be left to any of his 4 daughters and it went to his nephew Sir George Perient.

(*4) From Dorothy and Ann Perient the manor of Lockleys went to their uncle William, then to Jasper Horsey and the Nedhams and Wingates.

(*5) Richard Hare, Esq., married Elizabeth Barnes who later married Sir George Perient and became Dame Elizabeth Perient. She died in 1655 aged 90 years. Richard Hare was almost certainly an ancestor of Mary Hare of Thrales End and Heath Farm at Kings Walden, who married William Harmer in 1883.

The Perient Family (tree B) of Digswell

GEORGE PERIENT, d. 1532, m. Agnes, d. of Thomas Sporne of Lavenham in Suffolk. Agnes afterwards m Robert Rokewood of Lavenham

GEORGE PERIENT, 'a great hunter', d. unmarried in 1585 ———— **MARGERY PERIENT** m. Caesar Delamare (commonly called Julius Caesar) Doctor of Physick to Queen Elizabeth. (↓ Caesar tree)	**ELIZABETH PERIENT** m① Sir Humphrey Style of Beckenham (see Nedham tree) m② Nicholas Rokewood, Prothonotary to the Court of Common Pleas. m③ Thomas Townsend of Norfolk	**KATHERINE PERIENT** m① Sir Humphrey Drewell m② John Bacon of Troston, Suffolk m③ John Spring of Norfolk ———— **HENRY PERIENT** m. Joan Foster of Great Birch, Essex	**MARY PERIENT** m① 1550, William Clopton of Kentwell Hall, Suffolk m② George Barnardiston of Northill, Beds, who died 1575. (Barnardiston and Clopton trees ↓)

THOMAS PERIENT of Colchester, d.1612, admitted to Grays Inn 1581, m. Ann, d. of John Browne of Wickham Hall, Essex, sister of Sir Anthony Browne and niece of Weston Browne of Abbess Roding. (see Browne of Essex tree)	**MARY PERIENT**, m. Sir Edward Burton of Bourne in Sussex

SIR THOMAS PERIENT b.1592, Knighted at Theobalds 1615, admitted to Grays Inn 1618. m① Ann, d. of Sir Roger Aston, Keeper of the Great Wardrobe. m② Mary, d. of John Pennington of Chigwell	**MARY PERIENT**, m. John, 4th s. of Sir Stephen Soame of Brickendon, Herts, and of Little Bradley in Suffolk. (see Soame tree) ———— **HUMPHREY PERIENT**, admitted to Grays Inn 1615, m. Mary, d. of Sir Roger Aston, and sister of Ann who m. Sir Thomas Perient.	**EDWARD PERIENT** ———— **ANN PERIENT** m. John Taylor ———— **JANE PERIENT**	**HENRY PERIENT** ———— **BARBARA PERIENT** m① John Hollet m② Humphrey Sander, of the King's Bench, s. of Valentine Sander of Chiswick

The Pulter Family of Wymondley and Cottered

EDWARD PULTER of Wymondley Magna, m. Julian, only daughter and heir of Edmund Cave of London, (who later married Sir Thomas Cotton of Peckham in Kent).

EDWARD PULTER, Sheriff of Herts 1586, commanded the militia at Tilbury when the Spaniards attempted to invade (*1), JP and Deputy Lieutenant of Herts, m. Mary, d. of Sir Rowland Lytton and Margaret Tate (who was probably the daughter of Sir John Tate, Lord Mayor of London in 1514). (see Lytton tree)	**ALICE PULTER**, m. Sir Henry Boteler of Hatfield Woodhall (son of Sir John Boteler and Grizzel Roche who were the ancestors of the Botelers of Queenhoo Hall in Tewin). (↓ Boteler tree)

LITTON PULTER d.1608 (before his father), buried in Cottered Church, m. Penelope, d. of Sir Arthur Capell of Hadham Hall. (see Capell tree)	**JOHN PULTER** osp ———— **THOMAS PULTER** ———— **WILLIAM PULTER** ———— **SHIMUELL PULTER**	**EDWARD PULTER** of Bradfield ------- **ELEANOR PULTER** m. Thomas Morrison of Cassiobury	**MARY PULTER** m. Sir John Fyshe of Southill, Beds (Fyshe tree ↓) ———— **ROWLAND PULTER**	**ANN PULTER** m. Tyndall Perte ------- **MARGARET PULTER** m. Ralph Wilson

ARTHUR PULTER, d. 1689, Sheriff of Herts 1641, inherited the estate from his grandfather, m. Lady Hester Ley, d. of James Earl of Marlborough	**JOHN PULTER** ------- **HENRY PULTER**	**MARGARET PULTER** m. Richard Newman, Rector of Datchworth	**ALICE PULTER** m① George Skipwith of St Albans (see Skipwith tree), m② Gregory Warren of St Peter's, St Albans and had two children, Gregory and Bridget. (Warren Tree ↓)

JOHN PULTER eldest son and heir, d. before his father.	**ARTHUR PULTER** ------- **EDWARD PULTER** ------- **WILLIAM PULTER**	**CHARLES PULTER** ------- **JOHN PULTER**	**MARGARET PULTER** m. John Forester	**PENELOPE PULTER** m. Sir Thomas Longueville	**ANN PULTER** m. Thomas Fairclough (see Fairclough tree)	**ELIZABETH PULTER** unmarried	**MARY PULTER** m. William Capell of Stanton in Suffolk

JAMES FORESTER the only living descendant at the time of his grandfather's death, m. Martha, d. of Sir Henry Chauncy, and had one son, Pulter Forester, who was Lord of the Manor of Wymondley about 1700.

(***1**) For 22 years Edward Pulter served as unpaid captain of the N and E Herts foot soldiers. On his memorial in Cottered Church is the inscription ' ... he held divers worshipful offices both civil and martial wherein he was careful to do well.'

The Petre (Petter or Peter) Family
of Ingatestone Hall in Essex

JOHN PETRE of Tor Brian in Devonshire, m. Joane ...

JOHN PETRE m. Alice, d. of John Collinge of Woodland in Devon

SIR WILLIAM PETRE, 1505-72,
Deputy to Thomas Cromwell and later Chancellor and Principal Secretary to Queen Mary. He was a Doctor of Laws from Oxford, and tutor to George Boleyn (brother of Anne Boleyn). Built Ingatestone Hall in 1540-45.

m① Gertrude ... who died 1541. She was previously m. to John Tyrrell of Warley, a distant cousin of John Tyrrell of Heron Hall who was the first husband of Sir William Petre's second wife.

m②, in 1542, Anne Tyrrell, widow, b. 1509, d. of William Browne of Abbess Roding (who was Lord Mayor of London in 1507 and again in 1513/14). Anne had previously been married to John Tyrrell of Heron Hall, East Horndon. (*1) (see Browne tree and Tyrrell tree)

DOROTHY PETRE b.1535, m. 1555, Nicholas Wadham. They founded Wadham College, Oxford.

ELIZABETH PETRE m. John, s. of William Gostwick, of Willington, Beds, and his wife Mary Boteler of Woodhall.

SIR JOHN PETRE (*2) 1549-1613, m. 1576, Mary, d. of Sir Edwar d Waldegrave (d. 1605). Sir John was created Lord Writtle by James I in 1603. (see Waldegrave tree)

THOMASINE PETRE b. 1543, m. Lodwich Grenville of Wilcotts.

KATHERINE PETRE m. John Talbot of Grafton Manor near Bromsgrove. Their daughter Gertrude was married to Robert Wintour, one of the conspirators in the Gunpowder Plot. (*3)

SIR WILLIAM PETRE, 2nd Lord Petre of Writtle, m. Katherine, d. of Edward Somersett Earl of Worcester.

JOHN PETRE, m. Catherine, d. of William Parker, Lord Monteagle and Morley. (*4)

THOMAS PETRE of Cranham in Essex, m. Elizabeth Baskerville of Wiltshire.

SIR ROBERT PETRE 3rd Lord Petre of Writtle, d. 1638, m. 1620, Mary (b.1603), d. of Anthony-Maria Browne 2nd Viscount Montague of Sussex. (see picture on page 153) Mary died in 1684 and was buried at Ingatestone Hall. (*5)

FRANCES PETRE of Cranham, m. Elizabeth, d. of Sir John Gage, of Firle in Sussex, and his wife Penelope Darcy, of Hengrave Hall in Suffolk. (see Darcy tree and More tree)

MARY PETRE m. John Roper 3rd Lord Teynham of Kent (see Roper tree)

EDWARD PETRE

ELIZABETH PETRE

(*1) The wedding of Catherine Tyrrell, daughter of Anne and step-daughter of Sir William Petre, is described in Chapter 3.

(*2) The Christening of 'Master John' in 1549 is described in 'Tudor Food and Pastimes' (see (*1) on Mordaunt tree).

(*3) Robert Wintour and his brother Thomas were two of the 8 main conspirators in the Gunpowder Plot. They were hung, drawn and quartered on 30th January 1606.

(*4) William Parker Lord Monteagle (later Lord Monteagle and Morley) was married to Elizabeth Tresham, a first cousin of the conspirator Robert Catesby. On 26th October 1605 Lord Monteagle received an anonymous letter (now known as the 'Monteagle Letter') warning him not to attend Parliament on 5th November. The letter led to the discovery of the Gunpowder Plot. Lord Monteagle was one of those who searched the cellars under the Houses of Parliament and discovered the barrels of gunpowder.

(*5) The Petres were closely connected with both the Brownes of Abbess Roding, who were close friends and neighbours, and the Brownes Lords Montague, of Sussex, who were connected with the family by this marriage and by other 'network' links.

The Petre Family of Ingatestone Hall

At the time of the dissolution of the monasteries Sir William Petre was one of the King's Visitors and Chief Deputy to Thomas Cromwell. He travelled all over the country, obtaining the surrender of a large number of Abbeys and Priories. We are told that, unlike many of the royal agents, 'Petre emerged with no stain and even earned a few econiums on his leniency and honesty in this arduous task'. The nuns at Barking Abbey were very happy with the terms he offered them, and he was able to buy one of their most important properties, the manor of Gyng Abbess or Abbess Hall, afterwards known as Ingatestone Hall. (This is not to be confused with the Abbess Hall which was an alternative name for Abbess Roding, the home of the Browne family).

It is emphasised that Petre paid the full market price for the property (£849 12s. 6d to be paid over 4 years). The Abbess of Barking and thirty nuns assembled on 14th November 1539 to hand the deed of surrender to Dr Petre. Among them were ladies from many of the leading families in Suffolk and Essex, including the Mordaunts, Tyrrells, Wentworths, Drurys, Sulyards and Kempes, who all appear on the family pedigrees. All were very happy with their annuities, Abbess Barley's being £133 13s. 4d.

Sir William Petre was married first to Gertrude, daughter of Sir John Tyrrell of Warley Hall in Essex, and secondly to Anne Tyrrell, the widow of another John Tyrrell, a distant cousin of Sir William's first wife. Anne was the daughter of William Browne of Abbess Roding, (who died in 1514 during his second term as Lord Mayor of London, when Anne was only 4 years old). It was Catherine Tyrrell, the daughter of Anne's first marriage, whose wedding feast is described in 'Tudor Food and Pastimes' by F G Emmison, from which extracts are quoted in Chapter 3.

Sir Anthony Browne who appears on the Browne pedigree is mentioned as one of the guests at Catherine Tyrrell's wedding. We are told that three oxen were given for the wedding feast, one by Sir John Mordaunt, one by Sir Harry Tyrrell, and one by Sir Anthony Browne. (The Petres were also connected with the Brownes Lords Montague of Cowdray in Sussex, but there seems to be no obvious link between the Brownes of Sussex and the Brownes of Essex).

Sir Richard Rich, later Richard Lord Rich, who was related to the Piggots of Gravenhurst and the St Johns of Bletsoe, was a frequent visitor to Ingatestone Hall. He lived at Leigh's Priory in Essex (another property which previously belonged to Barking Abbey). Lord Rich later founded Felsted School on his estate.

William Byrd, the Court musician and composer, spent as much time as possible on his manor at Stondon, which was not far from Ingatestone Hall, and Sir William Petre and his son John were his very good friends and patrons.

Another frequent visitor to Ingatestone Hall was Lady Darcy. She was the wife of Thomas Lord Darcy, who owned St Osyth's Priory. He was a Privy Counsellor, and was treated with great respect when he visited Ingatestone Hall. Lady Darcy was previously Elizabeth de Vere, daughter of John Earl of Oxford (known as 'ye little Earl of Oxford'). The grandson of Lord and Lady Darcy (another Thomas Lord Darcy), became Earl Rivers and married Mary Kitson of Hengrave Hall. Their descendants (through the 2nd marriage of their daughter and heir Penelope), were the Gage family, who held Hengrave for nine generations, until the late 19th century. Sir John Petre's grandson Francis Petre married Elizabeth, daughter of Sir John Gage.

Ingatestone Hall, Essex
Reproduced by courtesy of the Essex Record Office

The Piggot Family
of Wheathampstead, Cardington, Houghton and Renhold

After the Norman Conquest the largest barony in the area was that of Hugh de Beauchamp of Bedford Castle. He held land in Beds, Herts and Bucks. There was a younger branch of the Beauchamp family at Eaton Socon who founded Bushmead Priory. They were probably the ancestors of the Greys of Wrest Park and of Margaret Beauchamp of Bletsoe. (see St John tree)

HUGH DE BEAUCHAMP, living 1066, was probably already married to Matilda Tallebosc at the time of the Conquest

MILES DE BEAUCHAMP, son or grandson of Hugh

BEATRICE DE BEAUCHAMP

PAYNE DE BEAUCHAMP, m.1144, Rose Mandeville who founded Chicksands Priory about 1150

SIMON DE BEAUCHAMP, founded Newnham Priory in 1166, Sheriff of Beds and Bucks 1198

WILLIAM DE BEAUCHAMP, grandson of Simon, held Astwick in 1261, and Renhold (which was divided into 3 manors).

BEAUCHAMP, Lord St. Amand. *Gules a fesse between six martlets or with a border argent.*

JOHN DE BEAUCHAMP, last male heir, killed 1265 in the Battle of Evesham. The family estate was divided among his 3 sisters

BEATRICE DE BEAUCHAMP, ancestor of the Latimers and the Nevills, inherited the largest of the 3 manors of Renhold, also inherited Astwick and Cardington.

MAUD DE BEAUCHAMP, ancestor of the Mowbray family (Earls of Nottingham and Dukes of Norfolk), inherited the smallest of the manors of Renhold.

ELA DE BEAUCHAMP, inherited (finally) all 3 manors of Renhold, m. Baldwin Lord Wake of Stapleford, Wheathampstead, Gobions and Blakemore.

ELIZABETH WAKE, inherited part of the manor of Renhold, m. John de Hoo and the manor became known as Hoobury (Howbury) Hall

JOAN WAKE, m. John (or Michael) Piggot of Wheathampstead (d.1318), inherited Houghton from the Piggot family and Howbury from Elizabeth Wake (*1)

IDA WAKE

BALDWIN PIGGOT named after his grandfather, predeceased his father. (*2)

JOHN PIGGOT, in 1318 inherited from his grandfather, Wheathampstead, Houghton and Howbury in Renhold, about 1360 exchanged Howbury for Cardington (which was previously owned by his kinsmen the Nevills and the Latimers.

WAKE. *Or two bars gules with three roundels gules in the chief.*

MARGARET PIGGOT, Abbess of Elstow in 1409.

SIR BALDWIN PIGGOT of Cardington, Member of Parliament for Bedford 1389-1401, probably an ancestor or kinsman of Sir Randolf Piggot (who appears in Piggot tree B).

DOROTHY PIGGOT, m. c.1586, James Gascoigne. The Gascoigne family acquired Cardington through this marriage.

DOROTHY GASCOIGNE, m. Sir Gerard Harvey of Thurleigh (see Harvey tree).

ELIZABETH GASCOIGNE, m. Sir George Blundell

(*1) The Piggot family held estates in Renhold throughout the 14th century, and the Piggot arms can still be seen carved on the tower of Renhold Church.

(*2) Two main branches of the family have been identified in Hertfordshire and Bedfordshire. The first descends from the Piggots of Wheathampstead. Baldwin Piggot of Wheathampstead was the grandson of Baldwin Lord Wake who was the grandson of Baldwin de Clare who owned vast estates in Herts and Beds. He was a kinsman of Gilbert de Clare Earl of Pembroke who died in 1148. This branch of the Piggot family was also descended from the Beauchamps, barons of Bedford.

The second branch comes down through the Peverells, who also held estates from the Earls of Pembroke, and who were related to the Harmer family through the de la Poles, and also through the Caldebecks and Underhills of Little Bradley in Suffolk. The earliest Piggot on this tree, Sir Randolf Piggot, was probably a close relative (perhaps even a son) of Sir Baldwin Piggot on the other tree.

Both branches of the family held land at Astwick, and both had connections with the Enderby family.

The Piggot Family
of Wallington, Kingswoodbury, Edworth, Astwick, Stratton and Holme, and Gravenhurst

ALICE DE LANGTON, m. Edmund Peverell. Alice was sister and heir of Walter de Langton who was Bishop of Lincoln and Coventry and chief advisor to Edward I. Walter held Edworth from the Earls of Pembroke in 1307, he died in 1321 (*1).

MARGARET PEVERELL m. William de la Pole

JOHN PEVERELL, osp, m. Isabella ...

KATHERINE DE LA POLE m. John Bullok of Sharnbrook. Inherited Edworth

SIR JOHN DE LA POLE, m. Joan, d. of John 3rd Lord Cobham (↓ Brooke tree)

ROBERT BULLOK, m.1419

ELIZABETH BULLOK, m. William Furtho of Furtho

JOHN ENDERBY of Astwick and Kingswoodbury, d.1457

m① ALICE FURTHO who inherited Edworth

m② Maud ... , who was probably related to the Piggots. When she died in 1471 her part of the Enderby estates went to Richard Piggot

RICHARD ENDERBY, inherited Edworth, d.1487

JOHN ENDERBY, inherited Edworth, d.1509

PIGGOT. *Argent three picks sable.*

ENDERBY. *Argent three bars dancetty sable with a pale ermine in the chief.*

SIR RANDOLPH PIGGOT, probably a kinsman of Sir Baldwin Piggot of Cardington, who appears on the previous Piggot tree.

GEOFFREY PIGGOT

SIR RANDOLPH PIGGOT m. Anne Miniot

GEOFFREY PIGGOT, m. Margaret Plompton

RICHARD PIGGOT, m. Alice Finnet, acquired Kingswoodbury and Astwick in 1471 from Foljambes and **Enderbys**

ROBERT PIGGOT m. Margaret Gifford

THOMAS PIGGOT, Sergeant-at-Law to Henry VIII, m. Agnes Forster, acquired Tottemhoe Manor 1518, d.1521

FRANCIS PIGGOT of Gravenhurst, High Sheriff of Beds 1527 and 1548

m① ELEANOR ENDERBY. The marriage brought Edworth into the Piggot estates

m② Margery St John (*2), widow of Henry Grey Earl of Kent, d. of Sir John St John of Bletsoe (see St John tree)

WILLIAM PIGGOT of Tottemhoe, 1497-1575

SIR THOMAS PIGGOT of Edworth and Stratton & Holme, High Sheriff of Beds 1552, 1557 and 1571, d.1581. Bought Wymondley Bury for his son John in 1544 (*3)

m① Ann, d. of Richard Lord Rich who was Chancellor of England and a friend of the Petres of Ingatestone Hall

m② Elizabeth Thynne of Erith

BENJAMIN PIGGOT of Gravenhurst, 1551-1606 (*4), m③ Bridget Nedham (d.1617) of Wymondley Priory. Their d. Judith m.1617, Symon Hale of Clifton (see Hale tree)

ROBERT PIGGOT, inherited Tottemhoe, d.1587

MICHAEL PIGGOT (Disinherited)

JOHN PIGGOT, b.1524, m.1544 Margaret Grainger, lived at Wymondley Bury

LEWIS PIGGOT inherited Edworth in 1581 and sold it in 1588 (*1).

THOMAS PIGGOT of Tewin Water, 1540-1610, m.1571, Elizabeth, d. of Thomas Chapman of Hitchin, inherited Wymondley Bury in 1609 from his nephew Maurice.

FRANCIS PIGGOT sold Tottemhoe in 1595

MAURICE PIGGOT, d.1609, inherited Wymondley Bury from his grandfather Thomas in 1581.

REBECCA PIGGOT, 1577-1637, m.1596 Henry Bull of Hertford (↓ Bull tree)

ELIZABETH PIGGOT, b.1583, m. Beckingham Butler of Tewin Bury (↓ Butler tree)

(*1) The descent of the manor of Edworth can be traced in a direct line from 1307 to 1896, and its history from 1307 to 1588 is shown on this tree. In 1588 Lewis Piggot sold it to Sir Edmund Anderson, Chief Justice of the Kings Bench. It then went to John Spurling, whose widow Ann sold it in 1614 for £3,000 to John and Richard Hale. It decended in the Hale family through William (d.1634), Robert, William, and Paggen (d.1754). It then went to his cousin William and his grandson Charles Cholmondley Hale. He died in 1896 and Edworth was sold to John Inns.

(*2) Margery St John who married Francis Piggot was the widow of Henry Grey Earl of Kent and the mother of his sons Reginald, Henry and Charles who later succeeded to the title. Thus Benjamin Piggot was a half-brother of the Earls of Kent and closely connected with them for several generations. His mother Margery St John was the sister of Oliver St John who was Lord Chancellor to Queen Elizabeth. The Free School at Biggleswade or Holme was set up by Francis Piggot in 1557 and received a bequest from Benjamin Piggot's will in 1606.

(*3) Although he bought Wymondley Bury Sir Thomas Piggot was never Lord of the Manor. This title was held continuously by the Argenteins and Alingtons for 600 years (see Descent of the Argenteins and Alingtons)

(*4) Benjamin Piggot was married three times, 1st to Mary Astry of Harlington, 2nd to Anne Wiseman of Essex, and 3rd to Bridget Nedham.

The Poley Family
of Boxted, Badley and Stowmarket in Suffolk, with roots in Cottered, Herts

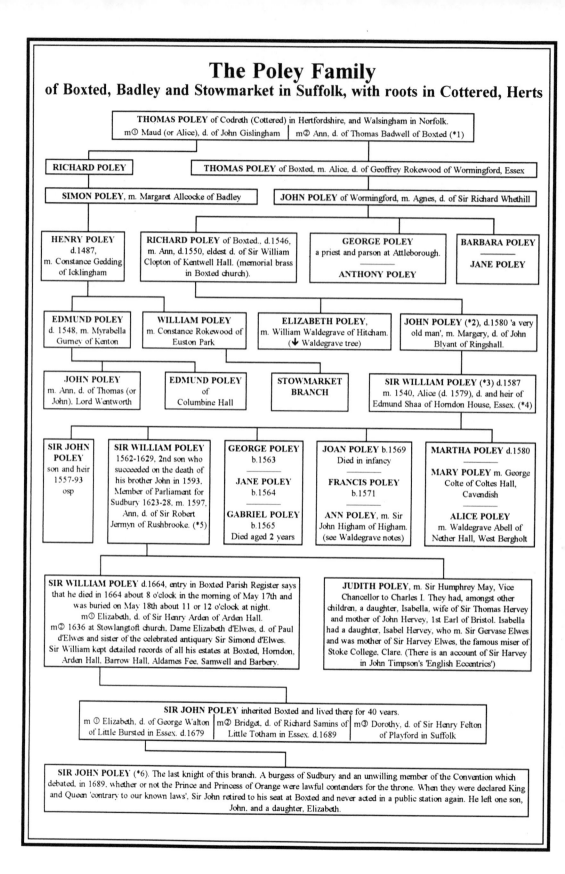

THOMAS POLEY of Codreth (Cottered) in Hertfordshire, and Walsingham in Norfolk.
m① Maud (or Alice), d. of John Gislingham | m② Ann, d. of Thomas Badwell of Boxted (*1)

RICHARD POLEY

THOMAS POLEY of Boxted, m. Alice, d. of Geoffrey Rokewood of Wormingford, Essex

SIMON POLEY, m. Margaret Allcocke of Badley

JOHN POLEY of Wormingford, m. Agnes, d. of Sir Richard Whethill

HENRY POLEY
d.1487,
m. Constance Gedding
of Icklingham

RICHARD POLEY of Boxted., d.1546,
m. Ann, d.1550, eldest d. of Sir William
Clopton of Kentwell Hall. (memorial brass
in Boxted church).

GEORGE POLEY
a priest and parson at Attleborough.

ANTHONY POLEY

BARBARA POLEY

JANE POLEY

EDMUND POLEY
d. 1548, m. Myrabella
Gurney of Kenton

WILLIAM POLEY
m. Constance Rokewood of
Euston Park

ELIZABETH POLEY,
m. William Waldegrave of Hitcham.
(↓ Waldegrave tree)

JOHN POLEY (*2), d.1580 'a very
old man', m. Margery, d. of John
Blyant of Ringshall.

JOHN POLEY
m. Ann, d. of Thomas (or
John). Lord Wentworth

EDMUND POLEY
of
Columbine Hall

STOWMARKET
BRANCH

SIR WILLIAM POLEY (*3) d.1587
m. 1540, Alice (d. 1579), d. and heir of
Edmund Shaa of Horndon House, Essex. (*4)

SIR JOHN
POLEY
son and heir
1557-93
osp

SIR WILLIAM POLEY
1562-1629, 2nd son who
succeeded on the death of
his brother John in 1593.
Member of Parliament for
Sudbury 1623-28, m. 1597,
Ann, d. of Sir Robert
Jermyn of Rushbrooke. (*5)

GEORGE POLEY
b.1563
—
JANE POLEY
b.1564
—
GABRIEL POLEY
b.1565
Died aged 2 years

JOAN POLEY b.1569
Died in infancy
—
FRANCIS POLEY
b.1571
—
ANN POLEY, m. Sir
John Higham of Higham.
(see Waldegrave notes)

MARTHA POLEY d.1580
—
MARY POLEY m. George
Colte of Coltes Hall,
Cavendish
—
ALICE POLEY
m. Waldegrave Abell of
Nether Hall, West Bergholt

SIR WILLIAM POLEY d.1664, entry in Boxted Parish Register says
that he died in 1664 about 8 o'clock in the morning of May 17th and
was buried on May 18th about 11 or 12 o'clock at night.
m① Elizabeth, d. of Sir Henry Arden of Arden Hall.
m② 1636 at Stowlangtoft church, Dame Elizabeth d'Elwes, d. of Paul
d'Elwes and sister of the celebrated antiquary Sir Simond d'Elwes.
Sir William kept detailed records of all his estates at Boxted, Horndon,
Arden Hall, Barrow Hall, Aldames Fee, Samwell and Barbery.

JUDITH POLEY, m. Sir Humphrey May, Vice
Chancellor to Charles I. They had, amongst other
children, a daughter, Isabella, wife of Sir Thomas Hervey
and mother of John Hervey, 1st Earl of Bristol. Isabella
had a daughter, Isabel Hervey, who m. Sir Gervase Elwes
and was mother of Sir Harvey Elwes, the famous miser of
Stoke College, Clare. (There is an account of Sir Harvey
in John Timpson's 'English Eccentrics')

SIR JOHN POLEY inherited Boxted and lived there for 40 years.
m ① Elizabeth, d. of George Walton
of Little Bursted in Essex. d.1679 | m② Bridget, d. of Richard Samins of
Little Totham in Essex. d.1689 | m③ Dorothy, d. of Sir Henry Felton
of Playford in Suffolk

SIR JOHN POLEY (*6). The last knight of this branch. A burgess of Sudbury and an unwilling member of the Convention which
debated, in 1689, whether or not the Prince and Princess of Orange were lawful contenders for the throne. When they were declared King
and Queen 'contrary to our known laws', Sir John retired to his seat at Boxted and never acted in a public station again. He left one son,
John, and a daughter, Elizabeth.

The Poley Family
of Boxted, Badley and Stowmarket in Suffolk, with roots in Cottered, Herts

(*1) Ann's great-grandfather was William Harvey, whose family held the manor of Boxted and also of Ickworth in the 13th century. It appears that the male line died out and the Harveys of Thurleigh acquired Ickworth in the 15th century, by a marriage with Jane Drury.

(*2) In 1561, John, now an old man, handed over Boxted to his son William, reserving for his own use only 'the parlour at the end of the hall with the chamber within the said parlour, stabling for two horses in the stable at the end of the barn, liberty to fish in the moat, river and other waters ... and liberty to be in walks, orchards and other gardens at all times meet and convenient'

(*3) After he inherited the estate in 1561 William built a mansion house, Boxted Hall. He died in 1587 and was buried in the church at Boxted, where an effigy remains.

(*4) Edmund Shaa's father, Sir John Shaa, was Lord Mayor of London in 1501, and his grandfather, Edmund Shaa was Lord Mayor in 1482.

(*5) Sir Robert Jermyn was grandfather to Henry, Earl of St Albans KG, and his sister, Susan Jermyn, was the wife of Sir William Hervey of Ickworth and grandmother to John Hervey, 1st Earl of Bristol.

(*6) A Thomas Poley of Boxted (possibly a brother of John) had a daughter, Elizabeth 1681-1761, who married Robert Weller 1676-1751. They had a son, George Weller, born in 1710, who took the name of Poley. The Weller Poley family still owned Boxted in the 19th century.

The Poleys of Bedfordshire and Hertfordshire were a branch of the same family and held the manors of Clothall, and Astwick. Richard Sheldon held land at Astwick from 1487 until his death in 1495. His son Richard held court at Astwick from 1497 until he died without issue some time after 1513, when it passed to his sister Prudence and her husband John Poley. In 1539 they sold Astwick and Clothall to Edmund Kympton. These manors had previously belonged to the Piggot family who were kinsmen of the Sheldons and Poleys.

Boxted Hall near Bury St Edmunds, Suffolk

The Roper Family (A)
of Well Hall Eltham and Lynsted Court near Teynham, Kent

WILLIAM ROPER (or Rosper or de Rubra Spatha)
A great benefactor to St Martin's Priory, Dover, in the reign of Henry III

JOHN ROPER of St Dunstan's and Patrixbourne, Canterbury.
In 1377 he lent £40 to Richard II to help furnish a fleet against the French and the Scots

EDWIN ROPER of Canterbury. He also held manors in Gloucestershire, Nottinghamshire and Derbyshire

ADAM ROPER

THOMAS ROPER. m. ... d. of Thomas Apuldore

EDMUND ROPER. Prior of Bilsington in Romney Marsh

m① Beatrix, d. of Sir Thomas Lewkenor **RALPH ROPER** m② ... d. of Thomas Kempe of Wye in Kent

EDMUND ROPER of St Dunstan's, Canterbury.
An eminent man under Henry IV and Henry V. Justice of the Peace for Kent. Died 1434 and buried at St Dunstan's.

JOHN ROPER
osp 1401

AGNES ROPER
m. Walter Culpepper of Bedgebury (kinsman of Sir William Culpepper who m. Ellen Spencer)

EDMUND ROPER

JOHN ROPER of Swacliffe (or Swacline). Surveyor of the Customs of the Cinque Ports under Henry VII. d. 1488.
m. Margery, d. and heir of John Tattersall (who inherited the manors of Easeborne and Well Hall with other estates in Woolwich and the neighbouring area)

THOMAS ROPER. m. Alice, d. of William Tooke of Essendon, Herts (see Tooke tree)

JOHN ROPER of Well Hall and St Dunstan's, Canterbury, Sheriff of Kent 1521, Attorney General and Prothonotary of the King's Bench. d. 1524, and buried in the Roper vault at St Dunstan's. m. Jane, d. of Sir John Fineux, Chief Justice of England

MARY ROPER
m. John Boys of Nonington, Kent

SIR WILLIAM ROPER 1496-1577
MP for Rochester and later for Canterbury. Prothonotary of the King's Bench. Sheriff of Kent 1553. m. 1525, Margaret, d. of Sir Thomas More, Lord Chancellor of England. Margaret was 'a woman most learned in the Greek and Latin tongues'. She is buried with her husband at St Dunstans at Canterbury, where their memorial remains.

ALICE ROPER, b.1499
m. 1520, George Hyde of Throcking in Hertfordshire. She was an ancestor of the Kymptons and the Harmers.
(↓ Hyde tree)

ELIZA ROPER
m. George Vaux and was later known as The Dowager of Harrowden (Northants) (see notes on Gunpowder Plot)

CHRISTOPHER ROPER
inherited Lynsted Court near Teynham. Ancestor of the Lords of Teynham and of Trevor Roper, Lord Dacre and the Brands of Kimpton Hoo. m. Elizabeth, d. of ... Blore of Rainham.
(↓ B)

SIR THOMAS ROPER. Prothonotary of the King's Bench.
m. Lucy, d. of Sir Anthony Browne of Cowdray House in Sussex and sister of Anthony Browne, First Lord Montague (see Browne of Sussex tree). Sir Anthony Browne was a distant cousin of Sir Anthony Browne of Abbess Roding in Essex. In the next generation we find a link with the Brownes of Essex.

SIR WILLIAM ROPER of Well Hall and St Dunstan's, Canterbury. m. Katherine, d. of Sir Humphrey Browne of Ridley Hall in Essex Justice of the Court of Common Pleas. (see Browne of Essex tree)

ANTHONY ROPER of Well Hall

m① Maria, d. of William Gerarde of Trent in Somerset

m② Dorothy, d. of Thomas Holte of Ashton in Warwickshire

m③ ... d. of Sir Henry Compton of Sussex (a younger brother of William Compton, 1st Earl of Northampton)

MARGARET (OR MARY) ROPER

ANTHONY ROPER

ELIZABETH ROPER

EDWARD ROPER, b. about 1640, sole heir. m. Catherine, d. of James Butler of Sussex

ELIZABETH ROPER. m. Edward Henshaw of Hampshire. He inherited all the Roper estates at Well Hall and St Dunstan's, Canterbury. He died in 1726 and their only daughter inherited. She sold all the property in 1733.

The Roper Family (B)
of Lynsted Park in Kent, Barons of Teynham
Showing links with the manor of Kimpton in Hertfordshire

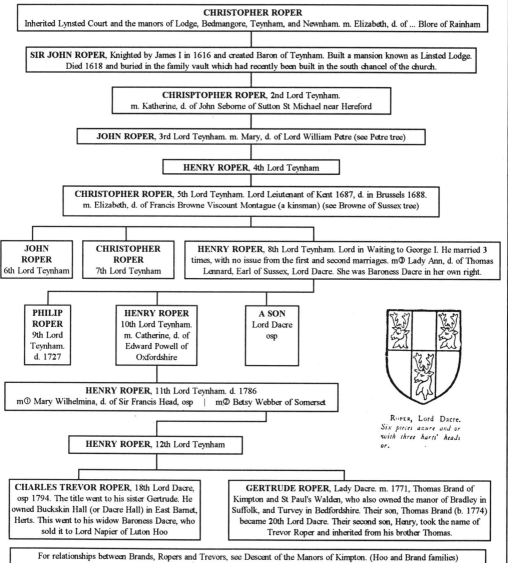

CHRISTOPHER ROPER
Inherited Lynsted Court and the manors of Lodge, Bedmangore, Teynham, and Newnham. m. Elizabeth, d. of ... Blore of Rainham

SIR JOHN ROPER, Knighted by James I in 1616 and created Baron of Teynham. Built a mansion known as Linsted Lodge.
Died 1618 and buried in the family vault which had recently been built in the south chancel of the church.

CHRISPTOPHER ROPER, 2nd Lord Teynham.
m. Katherine, d. of John Seborne of Sutton St Michael near Hereford

JOHN ROPER, 3rd Lord Teynham. m. Mary, d. of Lord William Petre (see Petre tree)

HENRY ROPER, 4th Lord Teynham

CHRISTOPHER ROPER, 5th Lord Teynham. Lord Leiutenant of Kent 1687, d. in Brussels 1688.
m. Elizabeth, d. of Francis Browne Viscount Montague (a kinsman) (see Browne of Sussex tree)

JOHN ROPER
6th Lord Teynham

CHRISTOPHER ROPER
7th Lord Teynham

HENRY ROPER, 8th Lord Teynham. Lord in Waiting to George I. He married 3 times, with no issue from the first and second marriages. m③ Lady Ann, d. of Thomas Lennard, Earl of Sussex, Lord Dacre. She was Baroness Dacre in her own right.

PHILIP ROPER
9th Lord Teynham.
d. 1727

HENRY ROPER
10th Lord Teynham.
m. Catherine, d. of Edward Powell of Oxfordshire

A SON
Lord Dacre
osp

HENRY ROPER, 11th Lord Teynham. d. 1786
m① Mary Wilhelmina, d. of Sir Francis Head, osp | m② Betsy Webber of Somerset

Roper, Lord Dacre.
Six pieces azure and or with three harts' heads or.

HENRY ROPER, 12th Lord Teynham

CHARLES TREVOR ROPER, 18th Lord Dacre, osp 1794. The title went to his sister Gertrude. He owned Buckskin Hall (or Dacre Hall) in East Barnet, Herts. This went to his widow Baroness Dacre, who sold it to Lord Napier of Luton Hoo

GERTRUDE ROPER, Lady Dacre. m. 1771, Thomas Brand of Kimpton and St Paul's Walden, who also owned the manor of Bradley in Suffolk, and Turvey in Bedfordshire. Their son, Thomas Brand (b. 1774) became 20th Lord Dacre. Their second son, Henry, took the name of Trevor Roper and inherited from his brother Thomas.

For relationships between Brands, Ropers and Trevors, see Descent of the Manors of Kimpton. (Hoo and Brand families)

In the 17th century Ruth, d. of Thomas Roper Viscount Baltinglass, m. Sir Edward Denny of Norwich. The Denny family were related to the Mannocks, Nevills (Lords Abergavenny), James Earl of Carlisle (who m. Margaret, d. of Francis Earl of Bedford), the Gates, Astrys and Foresters, all of whom are connected with the family. In the 16th century the Dennys bought Cheshunt Nunnery and sold it to the Dewhursts (see Butler tree).

In 1707 the manor of Bromham, in Bedfordshire, was purchased by Sir Thomas Trevor. It had previously been owned by the Boteler, Mowbray, Wake and Nevill families. Sir Thomas Trevor, Baron Trevor of Bromham, and later the Rt Hon Thomas Hampden Trevor, Viscount Hampden, was an eminent lawyer and Chief Baron of the Exchequer. He was descended from Sir Richard Trevor, a military officer who was knighted in the field by Queen Elizabeth. He died in 1730 and was buried in Bromham Church, where there is a monument to his memory.

Descent of the Ropers of Well Hall, Eltham, Kent

In the 17th century the Ropers held twenty extensive manors in Kent. These came to the family through the Chichele and Apulderfeld ancestors. The Ropers came from the parish of St Dunstan's and Patrixbourne in Canterbury, and Alice Roper's grandfather John inherited Well Hall about 1450. Alice was baptized at Eltham in 1499, and married there to George Hyde of Throcking in 1520. Her Fineux and Apulderfeld ancestors held the manors of Teynham, Linsted Lodge (now known as Lynsted Park), Bedmangore, Lodge and Newnham.

SIR WILLIAM APULDERFELD, 1422-83, lived in the reign of Henry VI and Edward IV. His sister Anne married Robert Kempe of Cavendish in Suffolk and Spain's Hall, Finchingfield. (Monument in Finchingfield Church)	**WILLIAM CHICHELE**, younger brother of Henry Chichele who became Archbishop of Canterbury in 1414. Held Well Hall before 1400.
	JOHN CHICHELE, Citizen and Chamberlain of London. m. Margery, d. of Sir Thomas Knollys
ELIZABETH APULDERFELD, only daughter and heir. m. Sir John Fineux, Chief Justice of the King's Bench, who died 1525.	**AGNES CHICHELE**, m. John Tattersall
	MARGERY TATTERSALL, m. John Roper of Swacliffe (d.1488)

JANE FINEUX m. **JOHN ROPER** Attorney General, d.1524

ALICE ROPER, b. at Well Hall, 1499. m. 1520. George Hyde of Throcking. (⬇ Kympton and Harmer trees)

Well Hall, Eltham

The mansion house at Well Hall, Eltham, which had been the home of the Roper family and their ancestors (Foliot, Chichele, Knollys and Tattersall) for 400 years, was pulled down by the new owners in 1733 (the Tudor barn is said to have survived) and replaced by a handsome farmhouse. This house has also disappeared, but the area still retains the name of Well Hall.

In the great hall of the original mansion hung a painting by Hans Holbein, showing Sir Thomas More and his family. It was described by Edward Hasted (a Kent historian, writing about 1790) as ' a most valuable painting of Sir Thomas More, Lord Chancellor, and his family, in all about twelve figures, all drawn with great strength and beauty, and so large as to take up almost the whole end of the hall. It was valued at one thousand pounds and remained here from the time it was painted till the year 1731 when Sir Roland Wynne removed it from the house'. The original painting, executed in tempera on linen or canvas, disappeared in the 18th century, possibly destroyed by fire, but the preliminary pen and ink drawing still survives. Holbein also painted several later versions of the picture in oils.

The More Family Group - pen and ink sketch by Hans Holbein. Inscribed overall by Holbein and Nicolaus Kratzer. Reproduced by permission of Oeffentliche Kunstsammlung Basel, Kupferstichkabinett.

The St John Family
of Bletsoe

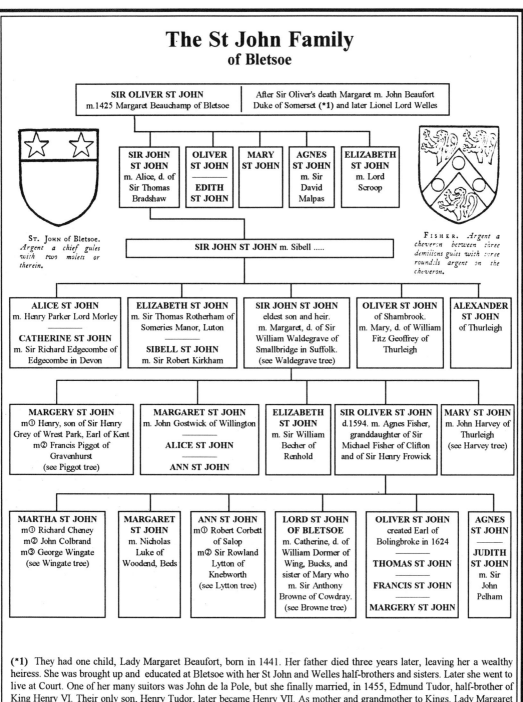

SIR OLIVER ST JOHN m.1425 Margaret Beauchamp of Bletsoe	After Sir Oliver's death Margaret m. John Beaufort Duke of Somerset (*1) and later Lionel Lord Welles

St. John of Bletsoe. *Argent a chief gules with two molets or therein.*

FISHER. *Argent a cheveron between three demilions gules with three roundels argent on the cheveron.*

SIR JOHN ST JOHN m. Alice, d. of Sir Thomas Bradshaw	OLIVER ST JOHN ——— EDITH ST JOHN	MARY ST JOHN	AGNES ST JOHN m. Sir David Malpas	ELIZABETH ST JOHN m. Lord Scroop

SIR JOHN ST JOHN m. Sibell .....

ALICE ST JOHN m. Henry Parker Lord Morley ——— CATHERINE ST JOHN m. Sir Richard Edgecombe of Edgecombe in Devon	ELIZABETH ST JOHN m. Sir Thomas Rotherham of Someries Manor, Luton ——— SIBELL ST JOHN m. Sir Robert Kirkham	SIR JOHN ST JOHN eldest son and heir. m. Margaret, d. of Sir William Waldegrave of Smallbridge in Suffolk. (see Waldegrave tree)	OLIVER ST JOHN of Sharnbrook. m. Mary, d. of William Fitz Geoffrey of Thurleigh	ALEXANDER ST JOHN of Thurleigh

MARGERY ST JOHN m① Henry, son of Sir Henry Grey of Wrest Park, Earl of Kent m② Francis Piggot of Gravenhurst (see Piggot tree)	MARGARET ST JOHN m. John Gostwick of Willington ——— ALICE ST JOHN ——— ANN ST JOHN	ELIZABETH ST JOHN m. Sir William Becher of Renhold	SIR OLIVER ST JOHN d.1594. m. Agnes Fisher, granddaughter of Sir Michael Fisher of Clifton and of Sir Henry Frowick	MARY ST JOHN m. John Harvey of Thurleigh (see Harvey tree)

MARTHA ST JOHN m① Richard Cheney m② John Colbrand m③ George Wingate (see Wingate tree)	MARGARET ST JOHN m. Nicholas Luke of Woodend, Beds	ANN ST JOHN m① Robert Corbett of Salop m② Sir Rowland Lytton of Knebworth (see Lytton tree)	LORD ST JOHN OF BLETSOE m. Catherine, d. of William Dormer of Wing, Bucks, and sister of Mary who m. Sir Anthony Browne of Cowdray. (see Browne tree)	OLIVER ST JOHN created Earl of Bolingbroke in 1624 ——— THOMAS ST JOHN ——— FRANCIS ST JOHN ——— MARGERY ST JOHN	AGNES ST JOHN ——— JUDITH ST JOHN m. Sir John Pelham

(*1) They had one child, Lady Margaret Beaufort, born in 1441. Her father died three years later, leaving her a wealthy heiress. She was brought up and educated at Bletsoe with her St John and Welles half-brothers and sisters. Later she went to live at Court. One of her many suitors was John de la Pole, but she finally married, in 1455, Edmund Tudor, half-brother of King Henry VI. Their only son, Henry Tudor, later became Henry VII. As mother and grandmother to Kings, Lady Margaret Beaufort became a very powerful lady in the country. Her half-brother's son, Sir John St John, later became her Chamberlain. Oliver St John, the grandson of this John, was educated at Court with Lady Margaret's grandson, Prince Henry, later Henry VIII, who spent long periods at Bletsoe Castle with his St John cousins. Oliver St John later became guardian to the two princesses Mary and Elizabeth (later Queen Mary and Queen Elizabeth) and was Chamberlain to Elizabeth when she became Queen. Lady Margaret Beaufort founded two of the Cambridge Colleges - Christ's College in 1505 and St John's College in 1508. She died in 1509.

The Skipwith Family
of St Albans

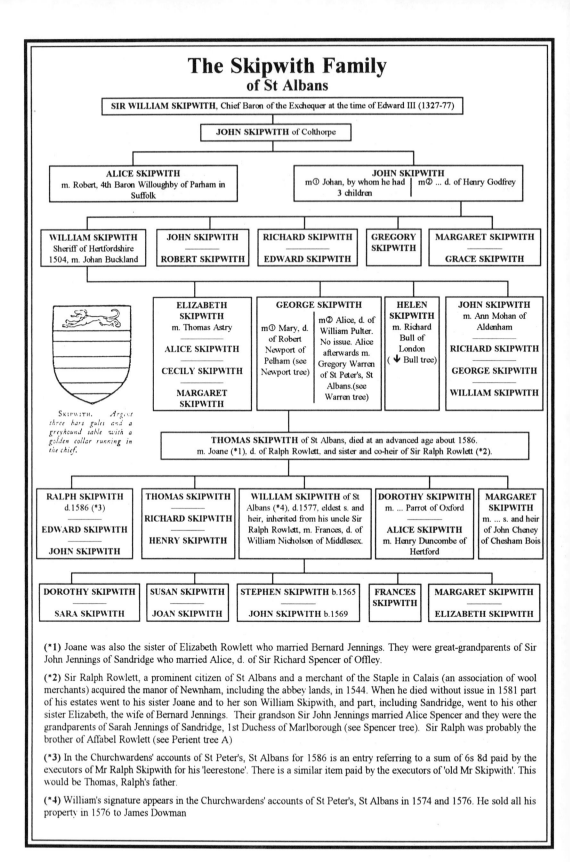

SIR WILLIAM SKIPWITH, Chief Baron of the Exchequer at the time of Edward III (1327-77)

JOHN SKIPWITH of Colthorpe

ALICE SKIPWITH
m. Robert, 4th Baron Willoughby of Parham in Suffolk

JOHN SKIPWITH
m① Johan, by whom he had 3 children | m② ... d. of Henry Godfrey

WILLIAM SKIPWITH
Sheriff of Hertfordshire 1504, m. Johan Buckland

JOHN SKIPWITH
————
ROBERT SKIPWITH

RICHARD SKIPWITH
————
EDWARD SKIPWITH

GREGORY SKIPWITH

MARGARET SKIPWITH
————
GRACE SKIPWITH

Skipwith. *Argent three bars gules and a greyhound sable with a golden collar running in the chief.*

ELIZABETH SKIPWITH
m. Thomas Astry
————
ALICE SKIPWITH
————
CECILY SKIPWITH
————
MARGARET SKIPWITH

GEORGE SKIPWITH
m① Mary, d. of Robert Newport of Pelham (see Newport tree) | m② Alice, d. of William Pulter. No issue. Alice afterwards m. Gregory Warren of St Peter's, St Albans.(see Warren tree)

HELEN SKIPWITH
m. Richard Bull of London
(↓ Bull tree)

JOHN SKIPWITH
m. Ann Mohan of Aldenham
————
RICHARD SKIPWITH
————
GEORGE SKIPWITH
————
WILLIAM SKIPWITH

THOMAS SKIPWITH of St Albans, died at an advanced age about 1586.
m. Joane (*1), d. of Ralph Rowlett, and sister and co-heir of Sir Ralph Rowlett (*2).

RALPH SKIPWITH
d.1586 (*3)
————
EDWARD SKIPWITH
————
JOHN SKIPWITH

THOMAS SKIPWITH
————
RICHARD SKIPWITH
————
HENRY SKIPWITH

WILLIAM SKIPWITH of St Albans (*4), d.1577, eldest s. and heir, inherited from his uncle Sir Ralph Rowlett, m. Frances, d. of William Nicholson of Middlesex.

DOROTHY SKIPWITH
m. ... Parrot of Oxford
————
ALICE SKIPWITH
m. Henry Duncombe of Hertford

MARGARET SKIPWITH
m. ... s. and heir of John Cheney of Chesham Bois

DOROTHY SKIPWITH
————
SARA SKIPWITH

SUSAN SKIPWITH
————
JOAN SKIPWITH

STEPHEN SKIPWITH b.1565
————
JOHN SKIPWITH b.1569

FRANCES SKIPWITH

MARGARET SKIPWITH
————
ELIZABETH SKIPWITH

(***1**) Joane was also the sister of Elizabeth Rowlett who married Bernard Jennings. They were great-grandparents of Sir John Jennings of Sandridge who married Alice, d. of Sir Richard Spencer of Offley.

(***2**) Sir Ralph Rowlett, a prominent citizen of St Albans and a merchant of the Staple in Calais (an association of wool merchants) acquired the manor of Newnham, including the abbey lands, in 1544. When he died without issue in 1581 part of his estates went to his sister Joane and to her son William Skipwith, and part, including Sandridge, went to his other sister Elizabeth, the wife of Bernard Jennings. Their grandson Sir John Jennings married Alice Spencer and they were the grandparents of Sarah Jennings of Sandridge, 1st Duchess of Marlborough (see Spencer tree). Sir Ralph was probably the brother of Affabel Rowlett (see Perient tree A)

(***3**) In the Churchwardens' accounts of St Peter's, St Albans for 1586 is an entry referring to a sum of 6s 8d paid by the executors of Mr Ralph Skipwith for his 'leerestone'. There is a similar item paid by the executors of 'old Mr Skipwith'. This would be Thomas, Ralph's father.

(***4**) William's signature appears in the Churchwardens' accounts of St Peter's, St Albans in 1574 and 1576. He sold all his property in 1576 to James Dowman

The Spencer Family
of Offley, Herts and Althorpe, Northants

SPENCER, Earl Spencer. *Argent quartered with gules fretty or over all a bend sable with three scallops argent thereon.*

SIR JOHN SPENCER of Wormleighton. m. Isabel, d. of Walter Graunt	

SIR WILLIAM SPENCER of Althorpe, m.1510, Susan, d. of Sir Richard Knightley of Fawsley

SIR JOHN SPENCER of Althorpe m. Catherine Kitson of Hengrave Hall in Suffolk

SIR JOHN SPENCER m. Mary, d. of Sir Robert Catlin, Lord Chief Justice. Sir Robert was married to Ann, d. of Thomas Bowles of Wallington and Ann Hyde of Throcking. (see Hyde tree)	SIR WILLIAM SPENCER m. Margaret, d. of Sir Francis Bowyer. Margaret's sister Elizabeth married Sir John Anderson. (see Anderson tree)	SIR RICHARD SPENCER m. Helen, d. of Sir John Brocket of Brocket Hall (see Brocket tree)	MARGARET SPENCER m. Sir Gyles Alington of Horseheath, Cambs (*1)	ELIZABETH SPENCER m. Sir George Cary Lord Hunsdon. (see Cary tree)

ROBERT SPENCER created Baron of Wormleighton in 1604, m. Margaret, d. of Sir Francis Willington	SIR JOHN SPENCER created Baron in 1626 m.① Mary (or Sarah), d. of Sir John Anderson and Elizabeth Bowyer, m.② ... d. of Sir Thomas Rotherham	BROCKET SPENCER created Baron in 1642, m. Susan, d. of Nicholas Cary ———— ELIZABETH (or Ann) SPENCER, m. Sir John Boteler of Watton, Woodhall. (↓ Boteler tree)	ALICE SPENCER m. Sir John Jennings of Sandrich (Sandridge), Knight of the Bath. They were the grandparents of Sarah, 1st Duchess of Marlborough (*2).	ELLEN SPENCER m. Sir William Culpepper of Alesford in Kent. (Kinsman of Walter Culpepper who m. Agnes Roper - see Roper tree)

JOHN SPENCER eldest son, died in France	MARGARET SPENCER m. Sir Richard Anderson of Pendley (d.1632) who was brother of Mary who m. Sir John Spencer above. Sir Richard's mother was Elizabeth Bowyer, sister of Sir William Spencer's wife Margaret. (see Anderson tree) (*3)	SIR WILLIAM SPENCER Knight of the Bath, Baron of Wormleighton, m. Lady Penelope, d. of Henry Wriothsley, Earl of Southampton	RICHARD SPENCER m. .... daughter of Edward Sandys ——— SIR EDWARD SPENCER m. ... daughter of John Goldsmith of Wilby in Suffolk	

SANDYS. *Or a fesse dancetty between three crosslets fitchy gules.*

(*1) Sir Gyles was the brother of Audrey Alington who m. William Mannock and of Mary Alington who m. Robert Newport. Giles Alington, the son of Gyles Alington and Margaret Spencer, m. Ursula Drury of Hawstead (brass in Hawstead Church).

(*2) Sir John Jennings and Alice Spencer had a son Richard who was the father of Sarah Jennings of Sandridge 1st Duchess of Marlborough (6x great-grandmother of Sir Winston Churchill). The Jennings were related to the Bull family through the Skipwiths and the Rowletts.

(*3) The Spencers and Andersons were intricately connected. Sir William Spencer married Margaret Bowyer and his great-niece, Margaret Spencer, married Richard Anderson, the son of Margaret Bowyer's sister Elizabeth Bowyer. Richard Anderson's sister, Mary Anderson, married his wife's uncle, Sir John Spencer

The Spencer Family of Cople in Bedfordshire

THOMAS SPENCER of Cople, m. Anne, d. of Robert Bulkley of Burgate in Southampton

ROBERT SPENCER, m. Rhose, d. of ... Cockaine of Cockaine Hatley	ANNE SPENCER, m. John Fairclough of Weston, Herts (Fairclough Tree ↓)

MARGARET SPENCER, m. Thomas Cary of Chilton, Devon	NICHOLAS SPENCER m. Mary, d. of Thomas Elmes of Lylford, Northants

ALICE SPENCER, m. Gaius, son and heir of Rowland Squire	NICHOLAS SPENCER, m. Mary, d. of Sir Edward Gostwick of Willington, Beds.	ROBERT SPENCER ------- MARY SPENCER	CHRISTIAN SPENCER ------- RHOSE SPENCER

WILLIAM SPENCER, b. 1632	NICHOLAS SPENCER, b. 1634

The Soame Family
of Little Bradley in Suffolk, and Throcking and Aspenden in Hertfordshire
(showing links with the Alington family of Horseheath in Cambridgeshire)

SIR WILLIAM ALINGTON of Horseheath, killed in the battle of Bosworth 1485 (*1), m. Elizabeth Wentworth

SIR GYLES ALINGTON m. Margaret Spencer of Althorpe (↓ Spencer tree)

MARY ALINGTON m. Robert Newport (↓ Newport tree)

AUDREY ALINGTON m. William Mannock of Giffords Hall (Mannock tree ↓)

SOAME, baronet.
Gules a cheveron between three mallets or.

ROBERT ALINGTON of Horseheath, Cambs

SIR GILES ALINGTON 1500-86, Lord of the Manor of Wymondley, m. Ursula Drury (*2).

THOMAS SOAME of Beetley, Norfolk, d. 16 April 1569, m.23 December 1558, Ann, d. of Thomas Knighton of Little Bradley, (widow of Richard le Hunt of Hunts Hall who died 1540 - see Hunt tree). They had 14 children.

ELIZABETH ALINGTON m. **THOMAS SOAME** of Little Bradley. Thomas lived 1543-1606. There is a brass in Little Bradley Church showing Thomas and Elizabeth with five sons and two daughters

SIR STEPHEN SOAME of Brickendon Herts and Beetley in Norfolk. 1544-1619, Lord Mayor of London 1598, Patron of St Andrew's Church, Hertford (where he would have known the Bull family), buried at Little Thurlow, Suffolk (next to Little Bradley), m. Anne (d.1622), d. of William Stone of Segenhoe in Bedfordshire. (*3)

ROBERT SOAME, osp 1589, Doctor of Divinity, Master of Peterhouse, Cambridge.

BARTHOLOMEW SOAME of London, silkman. m. Katherine, d. of Thomas Banks. She later m. Sir Thomas Barnardiston of Keddington, Suffolk. (Barnardiston tree ↓)

SIR WILLIAM SOAME, d.1655, Sheriff of Suffolk in 1632, followed Thomas Knighton as patron of St Andrew's, Hertford, m. Bridget, d. of Benedict Barnham, Alderman of London.

SIR STEPHEN SOAME of Haydon, Essex, d.1639, m.1619, at Sotterley, Elizabeth (b.1598), d. of Thomas Plater of Sotterley

SIR THOMAS SOAME of Throcking, d.1670, Sheriff of London 1635, MP for the City of London 1640, m.1620, Joan, d. of William Freeman of Aspenden, buried at Throcking. Memorial in Throcking Church (*4).

JOHN SOAME of Burnham, Norfolk. m. Mary, d. of Thomas Perient (see Perient tree)

MERCY SOAME, m. Sir Calthorpe Parker

ANNE SOAME m. Sir John Wentworth

JANE SOAME m. Sir Nathanial Barnardiston (see Barnardiston tree)

JUDITH SOAME m. Sir Francis Anderson of Stratton and Edworth, Beds (Anderson tree ↓)

SIR PETER SOAME 1633-97, m. 1656, Susannah, d. of Ralph Freeman of Aspenden (who was probably the brother of Joan who married Peter's uncle Thomas. Susannah would be the sister of Elizabeth who married Robert Elwes in 1684).

JOHN SOAME osp

STEPHEN SOAME osp

ANNE SOAME m. Sir Gabriel How

JANE SOAME m. Sir John Hoskyns

MARY SOAME m. Edward Fettiplace

WILLIAM SOAME

STEPHEN SOAME

EDMUND SOAME

All died young and are buried at Throcking

SAMUEL SOAME bapt at Throcking 1636, osp.1714, buried at Little Thurlow, Suffolk.

MARY SOAME m. Abraham Clark of London

ELIZABETH SOAME m. John Garneys of Boyland Hall, Norfolk

ANNE SOAME d.1679, buried at Kelveden, Essex, m. Sir Thomas Abdy (d.1685) of Felix Hall, Essex.

SIR PETER SOAME, d.1709, m. Jane, d. and heir of George Shute of Stockwell. They had one son, Peter (osp) and three daughters

The Soame Family
of Little Bradley in Suffolk, and Throcking and Aspenden in Hertfordshire
(showing links with the Alington family of Horseheath in Cambridgeshire)

(*1) In 1427 the Alingtons had inherited the Lordship of Wymondley from the Argenteins when Elizabeth, sole heir of John Argentein, married William Alington (grandfather of this William). With the manor they also inherited the office of Cup-bearer to the King, which had been granted to the Argenteins in the 12th century. The Lords of the Manor of Wymondley are still officially Cup-bearers to the monarch. It is unlikely that the Alingtons ever lived at Wymondley, preferring their mansion house at Horseheath (see Descent of the Argenteins and Alingtons).

(*2) In St Leonard's Church Bengeo there is a chalice and patten inscribed 'An Fanshawe 1626-27'. She was the daughter of Sir Giles Alington of Horseheath 1572-1638 and the granddaughter of Sir Giles Alington and Ursula Drury. The silver was probably presented on the occasion of her marriage to Sir Thomas Fanshawe of Ware, who later married the widow of Knighton Ferrers (see Knighton tree).

(*3) Ann Stone, wife of Sir Stephen Soame, was the daughter of William Stone of Segenhoe in Bedfordshire. He was married to Massy Grey, whose family had held the manor of Segenhoe and other land in the area since the 12th century, when Rugemont Castle (situated near Brogborough) was a stronghold of the Grey family. They also held Wrest Park and the Pelhams. Sir Stephen Soame's mother, Ann Knighton of Little Bradley, had previously been married to Richard Hunt, and they had a daughter Alice Hunt (Stephen's half-sister). Alice Hunt, who first married John Daye the printer, afterwards married William Stone, who was the nephew of her half-brother Stephen's wife Ann. Their memorial brass, shown on page 184, is in Little Bradley Church in Suffolk.

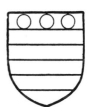

GREY OF WREST.
*Barry argent and azure
with three roundels gules
in the chief.*

The chart below may help to clarify this very involved relationship.

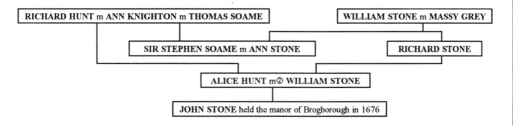

There were two other links with the Stone family. William Stone's wife Massy Grey was first cousin to Elizabeth Waldegrave of Suffolk, and Ann Stone's great-niece Dorothy married Thomas Docwra of Lilley (see (*3) on the Docwra tree).

(*4) In 1684 William Freeman's granddaughter Elizabeth Freeman married Robert Elwes and it was probably through this connection that Throcking passed from the Soames to the Elwes family. Their son Robert Elwes married Martha, daughter of Richard Cary and they had a son, Cary Elwes.

The Taverner Family
of Norfolk and Hexton in Hertfordshire

RALPH LE TAVERNER had land in North Elmham in Norfolk about the beginning of the reign of Edward I (1272)

WARREN LE TAVERNER inherited in 1300

SIR NICHOLAS LE TAVERNER

WILLIAM LE TAVERNER of Dunwich and Sibton Abbey in Suffolk, about 1317

JOHN TAVERNER m. Cecile Gelham

HENRY TAVERNER Councillor at Law in the reign of Henry V and Henry VI. He had land at North Elmham. d.1467

JOHN TAVERNER A soldier in the battle of Agincourt

WILLIAM TAVERNER Freeman of London. d.1454

TAVERNER. Argent a bend indented sable with a roundel gules in the cantle.

NICHOLAS TAVERNER d.1492 m. Margaret, d. of Thomas Dethick of Wrongey in Norfolk

HENRY TAVERNER

THOMAS TAVERNER

JOHN TAVERNER d.1545, buried in Brisley Church
m① Alice, d. and heir of Robert Silvester of Brisley, Norfolk | m② Ann Crow (or Crane) of Bilney in Norfolk. (*1)

ROBERT TAVERNER A Canon in the monastery of Walsingham

RICHARD TAVERNER of Oxford, d.1575. Clarke of the signet to Henry VIII. JP and High Sheriff of Oxfordshire.
m① Margaret, d. of Walter Lambert and Margaret Guildford (*2) | m② Mary, d. of Sir John Harecourt of Stanton Harecourt, Oxon (*3)

ROGER TAVERNER of Upminster. Surveyor General of the King's Woods on this side of the Trent. His son John (who married into the Wentworth family) took over as Surveyor of the King's Woods.

ROBERT TAVERNER of Lamborn, Essex. Surveyor of the King's Woods beyond the Trent. m. ... d. of Charles Newcomen of Sallowby in Lincolnshire. Had 2 sons: Robert and Thomas (a London merchant)

SILVESTER TAVERNER of Marston in Bedfordshire. Father of Silvester, Thomas, John, and Richard, and grandfather of Henry Taverner, a sea captain.

RICHARD TAVERNER m. ... Heyton of Surrey

JANE TAVERNER m. Thomas Waynman of Witney Park

JOHN TAVERNER a Divine

MARTHA TAVERNER m. George Calfield of Gray's Inn

EDMOND TAVERNER, JP of Soundess, Oxfordshire. m. Lucy Hales

PETER TAVERNER of Hexton, d.1601. m. Frances, d. of Thomas Docwra of Putteridge, Herts. (There is a monument to Peter and Frances in Hexton Chucrh) (see Docwra tree)

MARGARET TAVERNER Wife of ... Freer of Water Eaton., and mother of Sir Edward Freer

FRANCIS TAVERNER of Hexton, JP. m. Joanna, d. of George Nedham of Wymondley Priory, Herts. (*4)

JOHN TAVERNER, one of the Professors of Gresham College, and Rector of Stoke Newington. d.1638. (*5)

MARY (OR MARGARET) TAVERNER m. Edward Wingate of Welwyn, Justice of the Peace for Hertford. (Wingate tree ↓)

RICHARD TAVERNER m. Martha, d. of Matthew Bedell, Alderman of London 1636

FRANCES WINGATE m.1626, Eustace Nedham. (*6) (↓ Nedham & Harmer trees)

(*1) John and Ann had 3 children: James, Thomas, and Margaret. James's daughter, Frances, m. Sir William Denny of Gray's Inn, Recorder of the City of Norwich. (see Denny notes on Roper tree B)

(*2) Walter Lambert was the son of Sir Oliver Lambert. Margaret Guildford was the daughter of Sir John Guildford of Crowhurst, Surrey.

(*3) Richard Taverner and his 2nd wife. Mary, had a son, Harecourt Taverner, and a daughter, Penelope.

(*4) The Taverners and Nedhams were closely related. Mary Taverner was the mother-in-law of Eustace Nedham, and Mary's brother Francis was married to Eustace's sister Joanna. There were also close links with the Docwra and Wingate families.

(*5) This is the John Taverner who was mentioned in Thomas Docwra's will (see Docwra tree). Thomas was John's grandfather and left John all his books. urging him to concentrate on his studies. John evidently fulfilled his grandfather's expectations and became a professor at Gresham College (see Docwra tree & notes).

(*6) Eustace was brother of Joanna Nedham who m. Francis Taverner (uncle of Frances Wingate).

The Tooke Family
of Popes (or Holbeaches) Manor at Hatfield and Essendon, Herts

JOHN TOQUE (or TOOKE) of Westcliffe, Kent, m. Joyce Hoo, the sister of Lord Hoo

THOMAS TOOKE of Westcliff, Kent

RALPH TOOKE of Dover, m. Jane, d. of Roger Haute of Kent

WILLIAM TOOKE, m. ...

WALTER TOOKE, m. Mary Stanhope

ALICE TOOKE, m. Thomas Roper of Eltham, Kent (cousin of Alice Roper, who m. George Hyde of Throcking, and of William Roper, who m. Margaret, the daughter of Sir Thomas More)

RALPH TOOKE of Goddingston, Kent. m. Alice, d. of William Meggs of Canterbury.

WILLIAM TOOKE, 1508-1588, eldest son and heir, of Popes in Hatfield, Herts. Auditor of the Court of Wards and Liveries in 1548. m. Alice, d. of Robert Barley of Bibesworth, Herts. They were buried in the church at Essendon (marble monument on the north side of the altar).

WILLIAM TOOKE	WALTER TOOKE	NICHOLAS TOOKE	JASPER TOOKE	DOROTHY TOOKE
of Hertford, Lord of the Manor of Essendon, died 12 Feb 1611, m. Mary, d. of Nicholas Tichborne of Royden, Essex. (died 1623)	of Popes, d. 1609. Auditor of the Court of Wards and Liveries 1588 m.① Jane, d. of Richard Goldstone and widow of ... Thrale m.② Angelett, d. of William Woodliff of London	of Essendon Parsonage, m. Alice, d. of Thomas Hickman and sister of Margery Hickman who m. Gilbert Warren of Colney (see Warren tree).	of Stanstead, m. Anne, d. of Henry Rows of Rygate, Surrey ——— 5 more sons	m. Nicholas Bashe of St Margaret's, Stanstead ——— 2 more daughters

WILLIAM TOOKE	JAMES TOOKE	RALPH TOOKE,	THOMAS TOOKE	ALICE TOOKE	ANN TOOKE
Lord of the Manor of Essendon, m. Judith, d. of William Hastings	of St Albans, d. 1655, m. Dorothy, d. of John Gray of London. James and Dorothy died within 7 days of each other in November 1655 (memorial south side of chancel in Essendon church)	1558-1635 (M.I. under the altar in Essendon church), eldest son, m. Jane Bysh of Surrey. ——— **JOHN TOOKE** of Wormley, Auditor of the Court of Wards and Liveries, osp	of Wormley d.1638, youngest son, Auditor of the Court of Wards and Liveries, m. Judith Trott of Colney Hatch. Sold Popes in 1664 to Stephen Ewer and Joshua Lomax	**ANGELETT TOOKE** m. William Dighton of Lincolnshire ——— **RICHARD TOOKE** ——— **GEORGE TOOKE** ——— **TRISTRAM TOOKE**	m. Philip Jennings of Sandridge (relative of Sarah Jennings, wife of John Churchill, 1st Duke of Marlborough - see notes on Spencer and Skipwith trees)

MARIE TOOKE	20 CHILDREN	JOHN TOOKE	THOMAS TOOKE
m. Henry Darnell of Bird's Place (previously known as Essendonbury)	including Ann Tooke, b. 1633, who m. Thomas Harmer at St Albans Abbey 1656 (see Harmer tree)	m. daughter of Sir Thomas Dacres of Cheshunt and sister of Elizabeth Dacres who m. Richard Hale of Tewin (see Hale tree).	**ANGELETT TOOKE**

TOOKE. *Party cheveronwise sable and argent three griffons' heads razed and countercoloured.*

The Turnor Family
of Haverhill and Little Wratting in Suffolk

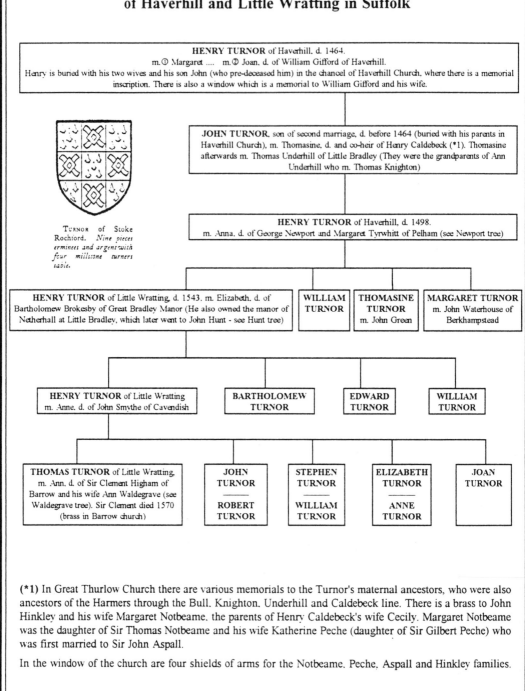

HENRY TURNOR of Haverhill, d. 1464.
m. ① Margaret .... m. ② Joan, d. of William Gifford of Haverhill.
Henry is buried with his two wives and his son John (who pre-deceased him) in the chancel of Haverhill Church, where there is a memorial inscription. There is also a window which is a memorial to William Gifford and his wife.

JOHN TURNOR, son of second marriage, d. before 1464 (buried with his parents in Haverhill Church), m. Thomasine, d. and co-heir of Henry Caldebeck (*1). Thomasine afterwards m. Thomas Underhill of Little Bradley (They were the grandparents of Ann Underhill who m. Thomas Knighton)

TURNOR of Stoke Rochford. *Nine pieces erminees and argent with four millstone turners table.*

HENRY TURNOR of Haverhill, d. 1498.
m. Anna, d. of George Newport and Margaret Tyrwhitt of Pelham (see Newport tree)

HENRY TURNOR of Little Wratting, d. 1543, m. Elizabeth, d. of Bartholomew Brokesby of Great Bradley Manor (He also owned the manor of Netherhall at Little Bradley, which later went to John Hunt - see Hunt tree)

WILLIAM TURNOR

THOMASINE TURNOR m. John Green

MARGARET TURNOR m. John Waterhouse of Berkhampstead

HENRY TURNOR of Little Wratting m. Anne, d. of John Smythe of Cavendish

BARTHOLOMEW TURNOR

EDWARD TURNOR

WILLIAM TURNOR

THOMAS TURNOR of Little Wratting, m. Ann, d. of Sir Clement Higham of Barrow and his wife Ann Waldegrave (see Waldegrave tree). Sir Clement died 1570 (brass in Barrow church)

JOHN TURNOR

ROBERT TURNOR

STEPHEN TURNOR

WILLIAM TURNOR

ELIZABETH TURNOR

ANNE TURNOR

JOAN TURNOR

(*1) In Great Thurlow Church there are various memorials to the Turnor's maternal ancestors, who were also ancestors of the Harmers through the Bull, Knighton, Underhill and Caldebeck line. There is a brass to John Hinkley and his wife Margaret Notbeame, the parents of Henry Caldebeck's wife Cecily. Margaret Notbeame was the daughter of Sir Thomas Notbeame and his wife Katherine Peche (daughter of Sir Gilbert Peche) who was first married to Sir John Aspall.

In the window of the church are four shields of arms for the Notbeame, Peche, Aspall and Hinkley families.

The Tyrrell Family
of Heron Hall at East Horndon in Essex and Gipping Hall near Stowmarket, Suffolk

SIR JOHN TYRRELL of Heron Hall, Essex, m. Ann Coggeshall (d. 1422)

SIR WILLIAM TYRRELL, m. Eleanor, d. of Sir Robert Darcy (and sister of Sir Robert, Margaret and John below)

SIR THOMAS TYRRELL

WILLIAM TYRRELL of Heron Hall, m. Margaret, d. of Sir Robert Darcy of Maldon (see Darcy tree). It is probable that the so-called Abbot's Tomb in Stowmarket Church, with effigies (formerly in brass) of a lady in mitre head-dress, with 5 sons and 8 daughters, is for this Margaret.

ANN TYRRELL m. John Darcy

ELIZABETH TYRRELL m. Sir Robert, s. of Sir Robert Darcy

TYRRELL. *Argent two cheverons azure and a border engrailed gules.*

SIR JAMES TYRRELL of Gipping Hall, d.1502, Master of the Horse to Richard III. Stated by some authorities to have been responsible for the murder of the Princes in the Tower. Beheaded for treason in May 1502, accused of communicating with the de la Poles. m. Ann, d. of Sir John Arundell of Lanherne, Cornwall.

JOHN TYRRELL whose d. Alice m. George Brooke (↓ Brooke tree)

SIR THOMAS TYRRELL Knighted in 1487. A friend of the Browne family of Abbess Roding

DOROTHY TYRRELL m. John Boteler of Hatfield, Woodhall (↓ Boteler tree)

7 MORE DAUGH-TERS

2 MORE SONS

SIR THOMAS TYRRELL of Gipping, d.1551. Attainted of treason with his father and imprisoned in 1502, pardoned 1504, estates restored 1507, Knighted 1513, Master of the Horse 1520

m① Margaret, d. of Christopher, Lord Willoughby of Parham

m② Joan

JAMES TYRRELL of Columbine Hall near Stowmarket, m. Anne, d. of Sir John Hotoft of Columbine Hall

ANNE TYRRELL m. Sir Richard Wentworth

JOHN TYRRELL betrothed as a child to Anne, 4-year-old d. of William Browne of Abbess Roding (Lord Mayor of London, who died 1514). John and Anne were married before 1521 - when Anne would have been 12 years old. John died without a male heir in 1540 and Anne m.1542, Sir William Petre of Ingatestone Hall.

SIR JOHN TYRRELL of Gipping, d. 1574. Attended Mary Tudor at Kenninghall July 1553, knighted Oct 1553, m. Elizabeth, d. of Sir John Mundy (Lord Mayor of London 1522)

ANN TYRRELL d.1576 and buried at Cotton 14 May 1576 m.1529 Sir John Clere of Ormesby in Norfolk. (In Sir Thomas Tyrrell's will there are scathing remarks about his son-in-law)

ANNE TYRRELL m.1548

CATHERINE TYRRELL m.1552 Richard, s. of Sir John Baker (Privy Councillor) (Her marriage feast is described in Chapter 3)

JOHN TYRRELL osp 1590

m① 1556 Ann, (d.1558), d. of Sir John Sulyard of Wetherden, Suffolk.

m② 1565 Mary, d. of Sir William Drury of Hawstead, Suffolk. Mary was the widow of Sir Richard Corbett of Assington. Their d. Mary m. her cousin George Waldegrave (*1). (see Waldegrave tree)

THOMAS TYRRELL d.1606, inherited Gipping and Wetherden from his brother, m. Mary, d. of John Gray of Gosfield. Effigy in Stowmarket church erected by his sister Margaret

EDMUND TYRRELL m.1571, Prudence, d. of Martin Frense of Dickleburgh, Norfolk

MARGARET TYRRELL (*2) m. twice, her 2nd husband was Edward English

OTHER ISSUE: Charles Tyrrell, George Tyrrell, James Tyrrell, Vincent Tyrrell, Anne Tyrrell, Joan Tyrrell, Alice Tyrrell.

(***1**) Below is a chart showing the Drury/Corbett/Waldegrave/Alington relationship:

SIR ROBERT DRURY of Hawstead, Speaker of the House of Commons, buried in an armorial altar tomb in St Mary's Church, Bury St Edmunds, married Ann Calthorpe of Norfolk

SIR WILLIAM DRURY, d.1557, member of Queen Mary's Privy Council, m② Elizabeth Sotehill

ANN DRURY, m. George Waldegrave of Smallbridge

URSULA DRURY, d.1552, m. Giles, s. of Sir Gyles Alington and Margaret Spencer

MARY DRURY, m① Sir Richard Corbett, m② John Tyrrell

MARY CORBETT m. **GEORGE WALDEGRAVE**

In Hawstead Church in Suffolk there is a brass to Sir William Drury (d.1557) on a chest tomb on the south side of the nave. There is also a brass in the floor of the chancel to his sister Ursula (Alington) who d.1522. Sir William Drury appears in the Mannock tree and in the note on the Spencer tree.

(***2**) There is an effigy of Margaret in Stowmarket Church showing her kneeling, facing her brother Thomas and his wife, Mary, with their 6 sons and 4 daughters. Margaret herself had no children. She left £100 to provide an annuity for the relief of the poor of Stowmarket.

The Waldegrave Family (A)
of Smallbridge and Bures in Suffolk, and Borley in Essex

SIR RICHARD WALDEGRAVE, of Smallbridge, Suffolk. d. 1406. m. Joan, d. of ... Silvester of Bures.

SIR RICHARD WALDEGRAVE, d. 1434, m. Jane, d. and heir of Sir Thomas Mountchancy.

SIR WILLIAM WALDEGRAVE
m. Joan, d. of William Dorward of Barking, Essex

AGNES WALDEGRAVE, m. William Hunt of Hunts Hall in Ashen
(↓ Hunt tree)

RICHARD WALDEGRAVE,
d. 1440 sp, m. Alice ... d. 1479

DAUGHTER, m. John Mannock of Giffords Hall, Stoke-by-Nayland

SIR THOMAS WALDEGRAVE, m. Elizabeth, d. of Sir John Fray (She later m. Sir William Saye)

EDWARD WALDEGRAVE
d. 1561, in the Tower, at an advanced age, m. Elizabeth, d. of John Cheney of Lynde (↓ B)

RICHARD WALDEGRAVE
—
JANE WALDEGRAVE
m. Sir Edmund Arundell. osp

ANN WALDEGRAVE
m. ... Fabion
—
KATHERINE WALDEGRAVE,
m. George Mannock of Giffords Hall, Stoke by Nayland. (↓ Mannock tree)

SIR WILLIAM WALDEGRAVE
d. 1526, m. Margaret, d. of Sir Henry Wentworth and sister of Sir Roger Wentworth of Codham

ANTHONY WALDEGRAVE
m. Elizabeth, d. and heir of Ralph Grey of Burnt Pelham, Herts, and Wrest Park, Beds. Anthony was one of the Barons of the Exchequer. They had 2 sons, William and Thomas (who m. Elizabeth, d. of Robert Gurdon of Assington, Suffolk)

GEORGE WALDEGRAVE
of Smallbridge, d. 1528. (*1) m. Anne, d. of Sir Robert Drury of Hawstead, Speaker of the House of Commons, who is buried in an armorial altar tomb in St Mary's, Bury St Edmunds. Anne later m. Sir Thomas Jermyn of Rushbrooke. She d. 1572. There is a memorial brass in Debden Church to Lady Anne Jermyn. The Drury family memorials are at Hawstead. (*2)

WILLIAM WALDEGRAVE
—
EDMUND WALDEGRAVE
—
MARY WALDEGRAVE
m. John, Lord Marney
—
MARGARET WALDEGRAVE
m. John Lord St John of Bletsoe, Beds (see St John tree)
—
A DAUGHTER m. Robert Drury

JANE WALDEGRAVE
a nun in The Minories, London
—
DOROTHY WALDEGRAVE
m. Sir John Spring of Lavenham
—
BRIDGETT WALDEGRAVE
m. Sir John Findenne
—
ANN WALDEGRAVE
m. ... Barley of Hertfordshire

EDWARD WALDEGRAVE
of Lawford Hall, 1514-1584, m. Joan, d. of George Ackworth of Lawford and widow of William Bulmer. Edward and his future wife Joan were confined in the Tower during the trial of Queen Katherine Howard for witholding information. Joan d. 1590 aged 84.

GEORGE WALDEGRAVE of Hitcham, d.1551, m. Mary, d. of Richard Corbett of Assington. George lived at Witherton Manor at Hitcham, Suffolk. Mary d. 1562 (wall monument in Hitcham Church). George and Mary were cousins, their mothers were Ann and Mary Drury (see Tyrrell tree).

ANN WALDEGRAVE
m① Henry Bures (or Bewers) of Acton
m② Sir Clement Higham (*3) (see Turnor and Poley trees)
—
PHYLLIS WALDEGRAVE
m. Thomas Higham (brother of Sir Clement)

SIR WILLIAM WALDEGRAVE
m. Julian, d. of Sir John Rainsford. Sir William died in Calais in 1554 and was buried there in St Marie's Church
(↓ C)

EDWARD WALDEGRAVE
m① Elizabeth, d. of Bartholomew Averell
m② Sarah, d. of John Higham of Giffords Hall, Wickhambrook (*4).

MARGERY WALDEGRAVE
m. William Clopton of Bretton in Essex

RICHARD WALDEGRAVE,
m. Margaret Knighton of Barnardiston Manor.
(↓ Caldebeck tree)

WILLIAM WALDEGRAVE
of Hitcham, Suffolk m. Elizabeth, d. of Richard Poley of Boxted. (see Poley tree)

ANN WALDEGRAVE
m. Drew, s. of Sir Drew Drury

JEMIMA WALDEGRAVE
unmarried

WILLIAM WALDEGRAVE
osp

THOMASINE WALDEGRAVE
m① William Kempe of Cavendish
m② Harsenett, Bishop of Chichester

SIR GEORGE WALDEGRAVE of Hitcham. m. May, d. of John Moore of Ipswich

ELIZABETH WALDEGRAVE
m. William Appleton of Kettlebaston

(*1) George Waldegrave was buried at Sudbury, although he requested to be buried at Bures with his father. His widow Anne m. Sir Thomas Jermyn of Rushbrooke Hall. They had 2 sons, John and Thomas. John married Mary, daughter of Lionel Tollemache of Helmingham Hall and they had 12 children.

(*2) The Drury family memorials in Hawstead Church include a set of brasses on a chest tomb to Anne's brother, Sir William Drury, and also a memorial to Anne's sister, Ursula Drury, who married Giles Alington. The Drury mansion in London gave its name to Drury Lane. The heiress, Joan Drury, who married Thomas Harvey of Thurleigh and founded the Harvey family of Ickworth Hall was also a member of this family.

(*3) Sir John Higham, the son of Sir Clement Higham and Ann Waldegrave, was married to Ann Poley, and their daughter Ann Higham was married to Thomas Turnor. There are brasses to Sir Clement Higham and his family in Barrow Church. (see Poley and Turnor trees).

(*4) There are two manor houses known as Gifford's Hall, both originally built by the Gifford family. The Stoke-by-Nayland mansion was later the home of the Mannocks, and Wickhambrook was the home of the Higham family.

The Waldegrave Family (B)

EDWARD WALDEGRAVE, d. 1561 in the Tower, at an advanced age, m. Elizabeth, d. of John Cheney of Lynde.

ELIZABETH WALDEGRAVE m. Thomas Eden, Clarke of the Star Chamber	JOHN WALDEGRAVE of Borley, Essex, d.1514, m. Laura, d. of Sir John Rochester	MARGERY WALDEGRAVE m. Robert Rye of Preston

ROBERT WALDEGRAVE ———— JOHN WALDEGRAVE ———— THOMAS WALDEGRAVE	SIR EDWARD WALDEGRAVE Lord of the Manor of Borley in Essex (*1), Chancellor of the Duchy (1553-58) and Privy Councillor to Queen Mary. m. Frances, d. of Sir Edward Nevill	MARY WALDEGRAVE m. ... Abell of Coggeshall ———— ANNE WALDEGRAVE

CHRISTOPHER (OR CHARLES) WALDEGRAVE m. Jeromina, d. of Sir Henry Jernagen of Costessy in Norfolk	NICHOLAS WALDEGRAVE of Borley m. Katherine, d. of Weston Browne of Abbess Roding (↓ Browne tree)	MARY WALDEGRAVE m. Lord John Petre of Writtle. (see Chapter 3) (↓ Petre tree)

EDWARD WALDEGRAVE m. ... d. of Sir Thomas Lovell of Harlinge	FRANCIS WALDEGRAVE m. Richard, Earl of Portland, Lord Treasurer of England.	PHILIP WALDEGRAVE Lord of the Manor of Borley m① ... d. of Richard White of Hutton / m② Margaret, d. of John Eve of Essex	ANN WALDEGRAVE ———— DOROTHY WALDEGRAVE ———— BARBARA WALDEGRAVE ———— JEMIMA WALDEGRAVE	CHARLES WALDEGRAVE ———— NICHOLAS WALDEGRAVE ———— MAGDALAN WALDEGRAVE m. John Whitbread of Writtle Essex

JOHN WALDEGRAVE, b.1615	WILLIAM WALDEGRAVE	FRANCES WALDEGRAVE	MARY WALDEGRAVE

(*1) In the 1930's Borley Rectory, once the home of members of the Waldegrave family, gained the reputation of being the most haunted house in England. It was investigated by a number of eminent people, including the philosopher C E M Joad. The ghost, a nun, is claimed to have been strangled there on 17th May 1667. In 1939 the Rectory was mysteriously destroyed by fire, said to have been started by an oil lamp knocked over by an unknown hand. In 1943 the bones of a young woman were found buried 3 feet beneath the cellar floor.

The Waldegrave Family (C)

SIR WILLIAM WALDEGRAVE
m. Julian, d. of Sir John Rainsford. Sir William died at Calais in 1554 and was buried there at St Marie's Church

MARGERY WALDEGRAVE m. John Wiseman of Canfield in Essex	A DAUGHTER	SIR WILLIAM WALDEGRAVE of Smallbridge, near Bures in Essex m① Elizabeth Mildmay, d. 1581, sister to Thomas Mildmay of Moulsham in Essex. / m② Grissel, d. of William Lord Paget and widow of Sir Thomas Rivett	MARY WALDEGRAVE m. Sir Walter Mildmay	AGNES WALDEGRAVE m. William le Hunt of Ashen (Hunt, Bull & Knighton trees ↓)

ELIZABETH WALDEGRAVE m. Sir Thomas Beckingham of Essex	SIR WILLIAM WALDEGRAVE d. 1613 m① Judith, d. of Sir Robert Jermyn / m② Jennemache, d. of Sir Nicholas Bacon of Redgrave	MARY WALDEGRAVE m. Sir Thomas Clopton of Kentwell Hall	FIVE MORE SONS ———— TWO MORE DAUGHTERS

ELIZABETH WALDEGRAVE m. Sir Charles Gawdey	WILLIAM WALDEGRAVE of Smallbridge, m. Frances, d. of Thomas Athlow, Sergeant at Law	JENNEMACHE WALDEGRAVE	PHILIPPA WALDEGRAVE m. Gyles Barnardiston (see Barnardiston tree)	SIR WILLIAM CLOPTON (see Clopton tree)

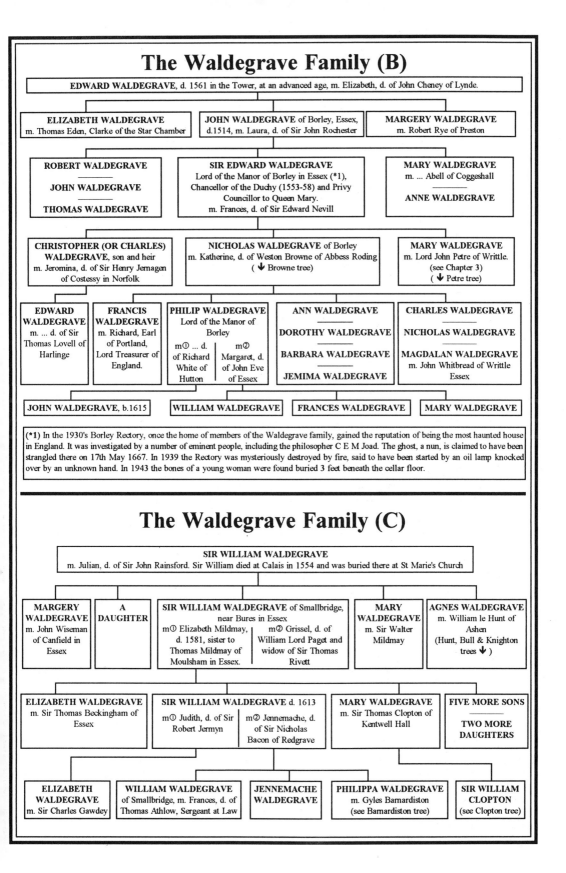

The Warren Family
of Hertfordshire

SIR JOHN WARREN of Pointon in Cheshire

LAURENCE WARREN
of Pointon, d. 1556, m. Joan ... .
Bought the manor of Bygrave in 1550

JOHN WARREN (5th son)
m. Margaret, d. of Sir William Booth of Shrublands in Suffolk
and Mary Newport of Brent Pelham. (See Newport tree)

LAURENCE WARREN
A younger son

WILLIAM WARREN, alias Bygrave, d. 1589
m. Juliana, d. of John Nedham of Wymondley Priory

HENRY WARREN m. Alice, d. of
Thomas Snagge of Letchworth

JOHN WARREN
of Harrow
m. .... Edlin

WILLIAM WARREN of Ashwell, b.1584,
m. Elizabeth Hammond, sold Bygrave in
1613 in order to pay his debts

GREGORY WARREN of St Peter's St Albans, m. Alice, d.
of William Pulter and widow of George Skipworth of St
Albans. (see Skipwith and Pulter trees)

GILBERT WARREN of
Aldenham, m.
Martha, d. of John
Long, Alderman
of London

WILLIAM WARREN
m. 1638, Ann
Skegg of
Baldock

EDWARD WARREN,
alias Waller of Ashwell
and Simonds Inn

m① Margaret Gray	m② Margaret, d. of Richard Glascock

GREGORY WARREN
of Harpenden, m. Joan, d.
of Jeremy Thornton of
Greenford. (The Thornton
family later owned Marden
in the 19th century)

BRIDGET WARREN
m. .... Field of Ascot.
Probably the parents of
Edmund Field who sold
Marden to Richard
Warren in 1672.

GILBERT WARREN of Colney, m.
Margery, d. of Thomas Hickman Lord of
the Manor of Bushey and sister of Alice
Hickman who m. Nicholas Tooke of
Essendon Parsonage.

JOHN WARREN
b. 1639.
m. Elizabeth
....

EDWARD WARREN
(alias Waller)

RICHARD WARREN
m. Elizabeth ... ,
acquired Marden from his
4th cousin Edmund Field
in 1692

EDMUND FIELD
MP for Hertford
1671-76, related to
the Lamb family.

ANN WARREN b. 1676, m. 1698. John Harmer of
Weston who was previously m. to Mary Nedham (*1).
(Harmer Tree ↓)

DR RICHARD WARREN MA LLD,
Rector of South Warnborough in Hampshire,
m. Catherine, d. of Sir Anthony Vincent of Stoke in Surrey

RICHARD WARREN 1686-1768
m. 1728, Mary Collet, 1703-33, d. of Joseph Collet of Hertford Castle (*2)

ARTHUR WARREN m. Mary ... ,
sold Marden in 1785. Mary d. 1787

COLLET WARREN,
died young

WARREN. *Checky or
and azure a quarter
gules with a lion argent
therein.*

**ARTHUR
WARREN**
d. 1762 aged 9
years, buried at
Hertingfordbury

**LOUISA
WARREN**
d. 1762 aged 2
years, buried at
Hertingfordbury

**FRANCES MARIA
WARREN**
d. 1762 aged 3
years, buried at
Hertingfordbury

COLET. *Sable a cheveron between three hinds
tripping argent with three
rings argent on the cheveron.*

(*1) John's first wife, Mary Nedham, was second cousin twice removed to his second wife Ann Warren. Mary's great-aunt, Juliana Nedham, was
Ann's great-great-grandmother.
The Skegg family, ancestors of Ann Warren, are frequently mentioned in the histories of Hertfordshire. Queenhoo Hall at Tewin was said to have
been built by Edmund Skegg in 1550. He was Lord of the Manor of Brantfield (Bramfield) and in 1567 he acquired Panshanger, which later went
to Gervase Elwes (who also acquired the manor of Throcking) and then to the Cowper family.

(*2) Joseph Collet (or Colet) of Hertford Castle, whose daughter Mary married Richard Warren, was a descendant of the Colet family of
Barkway. Sir Henry Colet of Barkway was Lord Mayor of London in 1495 and his son John Colet was the famous Dean of St Pauls who, in
1505, re-founded St Paul's School.

The Wingate Family
of Sharpenhoe, Harlington and Lockleys Manor at Welwyn

EDMUND WINGATE of Sharpenhoe, Bedfordshire. Died 1559
m① Elizabeth, d. (or sister) of Ralph Astry of Wood End, Bedfordshire (*1) | m② Mary, d. of William Belfield of Studham

---

GEORGE WINGATE of Harlington, Biscot and Lewsey;
Justice of the Peace for Bedford.

| m① Ann Belfield of Studham | m② Ann, d. of William Wiseman of Canfield Hall in Essex (*1) | m③ Martha, d. of Oliver Lord St John of Bletsoe |

ROGER WINGATE
of Bourne End in Bedfordshire
m. Jane, d. of Henry Birch of Sundon

THOMAS WINGATE
m. the daughter of William Lockley of Welwyn

MARY WINGATE
m. William Whitbread of Gravenhurst

EDWARD WINGATE
of Lockleys Manor, acquired Lockleys in 1624 from the Perient and Horsey families, m. Margaret, d. of Peter Taverner of Hexton and his wife Frances Docwra of Putteridge (see Taverner tree)(*2)

ROBERT WINGATE
1574-1603, m. Amy, d. of Roger Warre of Hestercombe in Somerset.

ROGER WINGATE
m. Dorothy Bedell of Catworth (probably sister of Martha Bedell who married Richard Taverner)

EDWARD WINGATE of Grays Inn, 1594-1656. m. (at Harlington) Elizabeth Button of Wootton, lived at Ampthill, a noted mathematician, went to France to teach the young princess Henrietta Maria (later queen of Charles I). In 1654 his name appears in the Ampthill registers attesting marriages as a Justice of the Peace.

EDWARD WINGATE
of Lockleys, m. Mary, d. of Ralph Alway of Cannons, Herts, d. 8 August 1685 age 79 years (tomb in Welwyn Church). Left 5 sons and 7 daughters.

FRANCES WINGATE
m. Eustace Nedham of Wymondley Priory.
(↓ Nedham tree)

JOAN WINGATE
m. John Boteler, son and heir of William, younger son of old Sir John Boteler of Woodhall.

JOHN WINGATE,
b. 1601, Justice of the Peace, m. Alice, d. of Francis Smallman of Kinersley, Hereford.

GEORGE WINGATE
of the Middle Temple

MARY NEDHAM
b. 1636 at Wymondley Priory, m. John Harmer of Weston. (Harmer Tree ↓)

FRANCIS WINGATE of Biscot, 1628-75, m. Lettice, d. of Dr. Pierce. Francis was Justice of the Peace for Bedford and tried to persuade John Bunyan to give up his preaching because he was loth to send him to prison. He argued that John Bunyan could not possibly interpret the Scriptures since he knew no Greek,

GEORGE WINGATE of Lewsey, d.1670, m. Elizabeth Pierce (sister of Lettice who married his brother Francis)

POMFRETT TREE.
In 1592 John Harmer married Ann Pomfrett of Baldock, d. of Thomas Pomfrett of Baldock - almost certainly part of this family.

THOMAS POMFRETT Rector of Luton 1660-1705 ... m. Catherine ...

JOHN POMFRETT, baptised at Luton under the name Thomas Pomfrett on 12 March 1667. Died aged 35 in 1702. m. 1692 Elizabeth Wingate

JOHN POMFRETT, 'Rouge Croix', d.1751

SIR FRANCIS WINGATE
d. 1691, m. Ann, d. of Arthur, Earl of Anglesey

GEORGE WINGATE
b. 1655. m. Katherine, d. of John Griffith

ELIZABETH WINGATE
m. 1692 (at Luton) John Pomfrett, poet and Rector of Maulden

ARTHUR WINGATE
Sold Biscot in 1718 to John Crawley of Stockwood Park. (Related to the Hare family)

MARY WINGATE
m. George Snagge of Maulden

WINGATE of Lockleys. *Sable a bend ermine cotised or between six martlets or.*

(***1**) The Wiseman Family of Canfield Hall and the Astry family of Wood End have several other connections with the family. Both Mary, d. of Ralph Astry, and Ann, d. of Thomas Wiseman were married to Benjamin Piggot of Gravenhurst.

(***2**) In 1627 there seems to have been great interest in a certain walnut tree belonging to Mr Penn of Scissevernes Manor in Codicote. Edward Wingate of Lockleys and Jasper Docwra of Hallwoods made the following declarations:
'Edward Wingate, Esq. one of the Justices of the Peace for this County, did certifie under his Hand, Anno 1627, that there was a great Walnut Tree, grew on Scissevernes Greene, in this Parish, which was of that great extent that the Branches thereof cover'd 76 Poles of Ground: it fell with Age, and the weight of the Boughs cleft the Body of the Tree in the Middle to the Ground. Mr Penn (who was Lord of the Manor) sold so much of it to a Gunstock-maker of London as he would carry thither for ten pounds which he paid, and sawed out in Planks of two inches thick, and half as much as filled nineteen Carts and Waggons. Mr Penn had thirty Loads more which the Man left with the roots and branches; with the end of one root he wainscoted a fair Room, made a Portall and many Chairs and Stools of the remainder; and Mr Penn averred to my self and others, that he had divers times been offered fifty pounds for this Tree.'
'Jasper Docwra born in Hallwoods in Codicote, doth averre that in the year 1622 he measured the circumference of Mr Penns Walnut Tree, he being then 15. years old, and it was eight of his Fathomes of both arms in compasse round the Body.'

Appendix B

Extracts from the Archives and from the histories of Chauncy, Clutterbuck and Cussons

[Note: Names in Appendix B have not been included in the index]

A trewe and p[er]fect Inventory of all and singular the
goodes and chattelles of John [?] late of [?]
in the countie of [?] deceased [?]
[?] made and prysed the [?] daie of Novem[ber]
16[?] by those whose names are here under written
and in man[n]er and forme followinge viz.

In p[ri]mis

Item p[ri]mis one Table with a frame and two [?]
joyned stooles .... xxviijs

Item one Cubbard apon [?] one little table two
[?] and one forme [?] .... xxxvoj

Item two Spites two [?] [?] two
Andirons and [?] of iron a paire of bellowes [?]
[?] two paire of pothokes
two [?] with other small implementes

In the p[ar]ler next the hall

Item one bedsteed a bed a paire of [?]
a paire of [?] a liverie table a joyned [?]
a chayre a brasse pott and a [?] .... xlvs

Item a table with a frame a forme a benche board
and three stooles and a [?] a chaire and one
iron panne one window [?] and fower
other [?] .... xls

In the loft over the hall

Item one bed one bedsteed a coverlett a mattris
a paire of [?] a bolster two pillowes
two blankettes and [?] .... viijs

Item a liverie table viij [?] two [?]
fyve boxes a livery table [?] .... lijs

Item one table with a frame one forme a benche
and bence board two [?] three stooles xxvij s iiijd

Item fower silver spones .... xxiiijs

Item three paire of sheetes .... vs

Item [?] paire of [?] twelve [?]
[?] and other [?] .... iijs oj

Item fyve dossen of [?] napkins vj table
[?] three [?] .... vs

Item x [?] .... vj s iiijd

Item all his weareinge apparell .... vs

Transcript of the inventory of John of Baldock 1613

A true and pfect Inventory of all and singuler the
goodes and chattelles of John Harmer late of Baldock
in the Countie of Hertford and dioces of Lincolne
deceased, made and praysed the xxiiii th daie of November
1613 by those whose names ar hereunder written
and in manner and forme followinge vizt

In the Hall

Imprimis one table with a frame and sixe joyned stoles	xxviii s
Item one cubbard a pott shelfe one little table twoo chaires and one benchboarde	xxxv s
Item twoo spites twoo painted cloathes twoo Andirons and -- of Iron a paire of bellowes Certaine -- twoo paire of potthookes twoo Cushines with othere small implementes	xx s

In the plor nexte the hall

Item one beedsteed a bede a paire of curtaines a paire of valence a -- table a pott shelfe a chayre a brasse pott and a truncke	x £
Item a table with a frame a forme a benchboard and three stooles and a wicker chaire a warme inge panne one window cushine and fower othere cushines	xl s

In the lofte over the hall

Item one bede and bedsteed a coverlett a materice a paire of curtaines a boulster twoo pillowes twoo blanketes and valence	viii £
Item a -- table viii cushines two chaires fyve boxes a -- table cloth	lii s
Item one table with a frame one forme a bench and benchboard twoo Coffers three stooles	xxxiii s iiii d
Item fower silver spones	xxiiii s
Item thirtie paire of sheetes	x £
Item nine paire of pillowbeares fower -- cloathes and othere childbeed lynen	iii £ x s ii d
Item fyve dossen of table napkins xi table cloathes three drinkinge cloathes	v £
Item ix --	vi s viii d
Item all his weareinge apparell	v £

In the lofte over the parlor

Item one fetherbed and joyned bedsted
covorlett and other furniture _____ v s

Item one other bedd and a trundle bedd
with their furniture one Chest and
a certayne pounder of flex _____ } vl s

In the lofte over the gate house

Item a presse two coffers a cradle a litle
table a spinell of woole and other
implementes _____ } xx s

In the lofte over the kitchen

Item one bedd with other implementes — xx s

In the Celler

Item three barrells ferkins and
fimnells and other implementes _____ } xx s

In the kitchen

Item the brasse and .... two parles
two ..... panns a .... a payre of andirons
a ...... and other smale thynges _____ } iij s

Item one brasse ... . to his daughter .... ..

In the Brewe house

Item one leade or copper to brew in
and the brewinge vessells with
other smale thynges _____ } iiij s

In the yard

Item fower hogges one horse one ....
of .... and ...... latter ...... _____ } v s

Item the woode and .... in the yard — iiij s

Item all the corne and grayne
both thresshed and unthresshed _____ } xxxvj s

Item agayne a ...... and .... — xx s

Item two Cartes _____ iiij s

Item graine sowen in the feilde and
.... acres of tilth lande _____ } xx s

Dettes oweinge to the deceased
Item .... _____ iij s viij d
Item .... _____ xx s iiij d

- 224 -

In the lofte over the plor

Item one fethere beed one Ionned beedsteed Coverlett and othere furniture	v £

Item one othere beede and a truckle bede
with there furniture one cushine and eyght poundes of F --

xl s

In the lofte over the gate house

Item a cheste two chaires a cradle a litle
table one pcell of woole and othere
implementes

xxx s

In the lofte over the kitchin

Item one beede with othere implementes

xxx s

In the seller

Item three barrells ix firkins and
-- and othere implementes

xxv s

In the kitchin

Item -- pewter dishes and candel

--

Item -- brasse and driping panns tow pailes
twoo fryinge panns a table a paire of Andiorns
a forme and othere smale thinges

iii £

Item one brasse pot given to his daughter Annis

x s

In the Brewe house

Item one leade or copper to brewe in
and the brewinge velselles with
othere smale thinges

iiii £

In the yard

Item fower hogges one horse one pcell
of haye and a pcell of lathes

x £

Item the woode and strawe in the yard

iii £

Item all the corne and graine
boath threshed and unthreshed

lxxxvi £ x s

Item a -- a screne and a bushell

xx s

Item twoo carfes

iiii £

Item graine -- in the feilde and
three acres of tilth lande

xx £

Debts owing to the deceased

Item Michall Foster

iii £ xii s

Item Nicholas Phipp

xv s iiii d

The inventory ends with the names of the 'praysers': Robert Yardley; --; Thomas -- and James Slone. Finally we have 'Sum totalis ccv £ x s vi d' [£205 10s 6d]

The final page of John Harmer's will dated 14th September 1711.

Item I give and bequeath unto my daughter Jillis Harmer the some of on hundred pounds
of good and lawfull money to be paid to her at her age of one and twenty yeares, Item I
give and bequeath unto my Son Edward Harmer the some of one Shilling to be paid to him
with in owne yeare after my decease, Item I give and bequeath unto my brother Edward Harmer
the some of forty Shillinge to be paid with in owne yeare after my decease, Item I give unto my
Son John Harmer and to his heires for ever, all that my wood ground lyeing and being in
west on called or knowne by the name of Suberg wood containeing by estimation foure acres,
be the same or lesse, and one closse of pasture ground,
called or knowne by the name of Duttads lyeing and being in Westen above said
neare the dile fist theire containeing by estimation two acures be the same more
or lesse I give unto my said Son John Harmer, and to his heires for ever, Item I give and
bequeath unto my daughter Burbery Stanton the some of five pounds of lawfull money
to be paid at four shillings by the yeare untill that sume is paid Item all the rest of my good
Chattels and personall estate whatsoed I doe give & bequeath unto the said Anne
Harmer my wife whoe I doe hereby make & appoint Sole Executrix of this my
Will and I doe hereby revoake & unto vide all former Wills whatsoed by me made
In witnes whereof I have hereunto set my hand & Seale the foureteenth Day of
September Anno Dni 1711 And in the tenth yeare of Queene Anne over Great
Britain

John Harmer

Signed sealed & published by the
Testator in the presence of us whoe
subscribed our hand as witnesses to
the signeing sealeing & publishing of
the same in the presence of the
Testator on the Day of the date
hereof

Jo: Alston

the marke of
Thomas Harroway the younger
the marke of
William Bauer

Septimo die January 1711
Anna Harmer Executrix introiit
de bene et fideliter Administrando
jurata fuit apud Yardley cordam me
Robt: Struth Sur:

- 226 -

Hertf. ff.ᵒ Weston June the 10:ᵗʰ

Anassment made then for the Raising the Sum of 119–10: Granted to his Majesty by a Land Tax for the Service of the Year, 1732

	£	s	d
Robt. Heysham, Esqr	21	03	00
Madam Hales Estate	10	05	00
Edmond field Esqr	02	00	00
The Lady Dimsdalls Estate	04	10	00
Mr Read	00	15	00
William Underwoods Estate	09	15	00
Capt. Hadocks Estate	03	02	00
John Izard	03	14	00
Abell Clinton	02	00	00
Edward Greene	05	10	00
Thomas Kiddall	01	03	00
Mr ffletcher	03	12	00
John Harmer	01	04	00
William Honour	01	12	00
Joseph Crouch	02	15	00
John Harris	00	08	00
George Humberston	00	02	00
Hannah Eilott	00	02	00
William Lucas	00	02	00
Thomas Humberstone	00	01	00
George Wilsher	00	06	00
William Wilsher	00	01	00
Andrew Shambrock	00	01	00
Daniell Chapman	00	04	00
Mrs Woolfe	00	03	00
Elisha Beene	00	15	00

A page from Frederick Harmer's copy book - Aston School 1871

Drowsiness Malicious Admission Concession

Uncovered Conversant Peninsula Ignominy

Uncovered Conversant Peninsula Ignominy

Warehouse Adolescence Hesitation Sustained

Warehouse Adolescence Hesitation Sustained

Be patient in adversity 521

Remission Champions Serviceable Undaunted

Remission Champions Serviceable Undaunted

Attenuated Convincing Fulminate Bootmakers

Attenuated Convincing Fulminate Bootmakers

Childishness Theatrical Handicraft Wholesome

Childishness Theatrical Handicraft Wholesome

Do not attempt impossibilities

Do not attempt impossibilities

Do not attempt impossibilities

Frederick Harmer Aston School October 24th 1871

The book was found recently under the floor-boards at the old family home in Aston.

- 228 -

Regis EDW. I.

A.R.	
26	ROBERT de Hoo and John de Aygnell
28	Roger de Patemer and Robert de Welkey
30	Ralph de Monchensi and John Aygnell.

Regis EDW. II.

1	John de Aygnell and Gerard de Braybrock
2	Ralph de Monte Caniso and John de Aygnell
4	Robert de Roos and Walrand de Rochford
6	Philip de Peletot and Ralph de Braden
7	John de Somery and Ralph Baynard
8	Walrand de Rocheford and Geoffery de la Lee
12	Geoffery de la Lee and John de la Hay
15	Richard de Pyrs and John de la Hay
16	The Names cannot be read.
20	Geoffery de la Lee and Ralph de Monchensi.

Regis EDW. III.

1	Geoffery de Brockholes and Geoffery de la Lee
2	John de Mareschall and Henry Dosevill
2	Simon Flambord and Geoffery de la Lee
4	Rich. de Monte Caniso and Walter de Asklakely
4	Philip Peletot and Ralph de Monchensi
5	Richard de Monte Caniso and Geoffery de la Hay
6	Richard de Perers and Thomas de la Hay
7	Richard de Monte Caniso and Ralph de Keleshall
10	John de Walkefare and Henry Atte Hall
11	Philip Peletot and John Mallour
12	Philip de Aylesby and John Aygnell
12	Philip de Perers and John de la Lee
14	Richard de Monte Caniso and Geoffery de la Lee
17	Richard de Perers and Ralph de Monte Caniso
18	Richard de Perers and Ralph de Munchensi
20	William de Purcere and John Mayheu
21	Stephen de Bassingbourne and Philip Peletot
22	John de Bassingbourne and Philip Peletot
26	Roger de Louth { No more than one Knight
27	John de Lodewyke { apiece in these two Writs.
31	John de Lodewyke and Edward Kindale
33	Ralph de Monte Caniso and John Aygnell
34	Gilbert de Ellesfeld and Thomas de Godesfeld
36	Gilbert de Ellesfeld and Guy de Boys
37	Gilbert de Ellesfeld and Thomas Fitling
38	Thomas de Fitlin and John Foxcote
39	William de Wotton and Luke Vineter
42	Edward Fitz Symond and Thomas de Futling
43	Nicholas Golofre and John de Hinxworth
46	Thomas de Fitling and Thomas de Bassingbourne
47	Thomas de Bassingbourne and William Baud
50	William Attelee and John Westwycombe.

Regis RICH. II.

2	Robert Turk and John Onenyld
3	Walter Attelee and John Henxteworth
5	Walter Attelee and Thomas Morwell
6	Robert de Louth and John Westwycombe
7	Robert de Louth and John Westwycombe
7	Edward de Bensted and Edmund Attebrooke
8	John Turk and John Westwycombe
9	Walter Atteley and John Thornbery
10	Walter Atteley and Thomas Atteley
13	Walter Atteley and John Thornbery
15	John Thornbery and John Northbery
18	Thomas Morewell and John Ruggewyne
20	Edward Bensted and John Ruggewyne.

Regis HEN. IV.

| 1 | Edward Bensted and John Lodewyke |
| 12 | Thomas Berry and Robert Newport. |

Regis HEN. V.

1	John Hotoft and John Leventhorpe
2	John Hotoft and William Fleete
3	John de Leventhorpe and John Hotoft
5	Philip Thornbery and John Hotoft
7	Thomas Barre and William Parker
8	John Barley and John Fray
9	Philip Thornbery and John Kirkby.

Regis HEN. VI.

1	John Leventhorpe and John Hotoft
2	John Barley, Esq. and William Fleete
3	Robert Leventhorpe, Esq. and John Kirkby
6	John Terrell, Esq. and William Newport
7	John Barley, Esq. and John Kirkby
13	Thomas Brocket and Nicholas Morley
20	John Troutbek and Nicholas Morley
25	John Troutbek and Peter Paul
27	Thomas Chivall and Bartholomew Halley, Esq.
28	Sir Robert Wingfeild and Sir Henry Barley, Kts.
29	Sir William Oldhall, Kt. and Philip Boteler, Esq.
33	John Say and John Clay.

Regis EDW. IV.

| 6 | Sir John Day and Sir Thomas Leventhorpe, Knights |
| 12 | John Sturgeon and John Forster. |

Regis EDW. VI.

A.R.	
1	Anthony Denny and Ralph Rowlet, Esquires
6	Ralph Sadler and John Cock, Esquires.

Reginæ MAR.

A.R.	
1	Sir John Boteler and Sir John Brocket, Knights
2	Nath.

Regis P. et M.

| 2,3 | William Brocket and John Cobbys, Esquires |
| 4,5 | John . . . . |

Reginæ ELIZ.

1	Thomas Parrie and Sir Ralph Sadleir
14	Sir Ralph Sadleir and John Brocket, Esq.
26	Sir Ralph Sadleir and Henry Cock, Esq.
28	Sir Ralph Sadleir, one of the Privy Council ; and Henry Cock, Esq.
34	Robert Cecil, Principal Secretary of State ; and Henry Cary, Esq.
39	Robert Cecil, Secretary of State ; and Rowland Lytton, Esq.

Regis JAC. I.

| 1 | Henry Cary and Rowland Lytton, Esquires |
| 21 | Sir Charles Moryson, Kt. and Bar. and William Lytton, Esq. |

Regis CAR. I.

1	Sir John Boteler, Kt. and Bart. and John Boteler, Esq.
3	Sir William Lytton and Sir Thomas Dacres, Knights
15	
16	Sir William Lytton, Kt. and Arthur Capel, Esq.

Regis CAR. II.

12	Rowland Lytton and H. Cæsar, Conventioners
13	Thomas Lord Viscount Fanshaw, and Sir Richard Franklin, Bart.
	Same Parliament.
	Sir Henry Cæsar, Kt. in the Place of Thos. Lord Fanshaw, deceased
	Same Parliament.
29	James Lord Viscount Cranbourne, Heir Apparent to William Earl of Salisbury, in the Place of Sir Henry Cæsar, Kt. deceased
	Same Parliament.
30	William Hale, Esq. in the Place of James Lord Viscount Cranbourne, removed to the House of Lords upon the Decease of William Earl of Salisbury
30	Sir Charles Cæsar, Kt. and Sir Jonathan Keate, Bart.
31	William Hale and Silas Titus, Esquires.

Regis JAC. II.

| 1 | Ralph Freeman and Thomas Halsey, Esquires. |

Regis W. et Reginæ M.

| 1 | Sir Thos. Pope Blount, Bart. and Sir Chas. Cæsar, Kt. for a Convention |
| 2 | Sir Thomas Pope Blount, Bart. and Ralph Freeman, Esq. |

Regis WILL. III.

| 7 | Sir Thomas Pope Blount, Bart. and Thomas Halsey, Esq. |

Chauncy's list of Sheriffs of Hertfordshire and Essex 1155-1332.

From the last Year of King *Stephen* to this present Year; collected from the Pipe-Rolls in the Court of Exchequer.

HEN. II.

A.Chr.	A.R.	
1155	1	Richard Basset and Alberic de Veere
1156	2	Richard de Luci, continued two years
1158	4	Maurice de Tiretie, continued six years
1164	10	Tuelle de Bovilla
1165	11	Nicholas the Dean, continued four years
1169	15	Nicholas the Clerk
1170	16	Robert de Mancell, continued twelve years
1182	28	Oto the Son of William, continued nine years to the third of Richard I.

RICH. I.

A.Chr.	A.R.	
1191	3	Geoffery the Son of Peter
1192	4	Geoffery the Son of Peter and Richard Heriet
1193	5	Geoffery the Son of Peter
1194	6	Geoffery the Son of Peter and Simon Puteshall
1195	7	William de Longo Campo, Chancellor
1196	8	William Pointell
1197	9	Hugh de Nevil, continued four years to the third of King John

JOHN.

A.Chr.	A.R.	
1201	3	Richard de Montfitchet, continued three years
1204	6	Hugh de Nevil
1205	7	Matthew Mancell, continued four years
1209	11	Earl Alberic, continued five years
1214	16	Matthew Mancell
1215	17	Robert Mancell, Brother and Heir of Matthew.

HEN. III.

A.Chr.	A.R.	
1216	1	Robert Mancell, Brother and Heir to Matthew
1217	2	William Mareschal, continued two years
1219	4	Walter de Verdon, continued two years
1221	6	Stephen de Segne, continued two years
1223	8	Richard de Argenton
1224	9	William de Cultwarden, as Custos, continued four years
1228	13	William de Coleworth, as Custos, continued four years
1232	17	Robert de Waltham, for the first half year
		William de Holewell, for the other half
1233	18	William de Holewell
1234	19	William de Coleworth, as Custos, continued two years
1236	21	Peter de Thany of *Hunsdon*, as Custos, continued two years
1238	23	Peter de Thany, as Custos, the first half year
		Richard de Grey, as Custos, the next quarter of the year
		Bertram Cryoll of *Albury*, near *Barkhamsted*, as Custos, the last quarter of the year
1239	24	Bertram de Cryoll
1240	25	John de Watton
1241	26	John de Watton for the first half year, and
		Richard de Monfitchet of *Aiot Parva*, for the last half year
1242	27	Richard Monfitchet, continued for three years
1245	30	Richard Monfitchet for the first half year, and
		William the Son of Reynald for the last half year
1246	31	William the Son of Reynald, continued four years
1250	35	Richard de Whitland the first half year, and
		Henry de Helegeton the last half year
1251	36	Henry de Helegeton, continued three years
1254	39	Ralph de Ardene, continued two years
1256	41	Thomas Rameden the first half year, and
		Robert Delval, the last half year
1257	42	Hubert de Monte Campo of *Chevesfeld*, continued two years
1259	44	Richard de Thany of *Hunsdon*, continued two years

A.Chr.	A.R.	
1261	46	Matthias de la Mar and William de la Mar, contd. two years
1263	48	Matthias de la Mar and Will. de la Mar for the first half year
		John Bocking, as Custos, the last half year
1264	49	Nicholas de Espigornel, as Custos
1265	50	Richard de Suchirch, continued two years
1267	52	Richard de Suchirch, the first quarter of the year
		Richard de Herlaw, for the other three quarters of the year
1268	53	John de Canimill, the first three quarters of the year, and
		Walter de Essex, the last quarter of the year
1269	54	Walter de Blunmill
1270	55	Walter de Essex, contd. four years to the third of Edward I.

EDW. I.

A.Chr.	A.R.	
1274	3	Thomas de Sandwic
1275	4	Lawrence de Scaccario, continued three years
1278	7	William de Sto. Claro
1279	8	Reginald de Ginge, continued five years
1284	13	Reginald de Ginge, for the three first quarters of the year, and
		William de Lamburn for the last quarter of the year
1285	14	William Lamburn the first half year, and
		Hugh de Blund for the last half year
1286	15	Hugh de Blund
1287	16	Hugh de Blund for the first half year, and
		Ralph Boxted the last half year
1288	17	Ralph de Boxted, continued two years
1290	19	Henry Grapinel
1291	20	Henry Grapinel the first half year, and
		John Carvonel the last half year
1292	21	William le Gross, continued two years
1294	23	William de Sutton, continued three years
1297	26	Simon de Bradenham, continued two years
1299	28	John de Lee, continued two years
1301	30	William de Harpeden
1302	31	John de Wenegrave
1303	32	John de Bassingbourn
1304	33	John de la Lee
1305	34	John de la Lee for the first half year, and
		John de Bassingbourn for the last half year
1306	35	John de Harpesfend

EDW. II.

A.Chr.	A.R.	
1307	1	Walter le Baud
1308	2	Alan de Goldyngham, continued two years
1310	4	Geoffery de la Lee, for the first half year and
		John de la Lee, for the last half year
1311	5	John de la Lee
1312	6	John Aygnell of *Pentlai*
1313	7	John Ward of Hoo
1314	8	Richard Perers, continued four years
1318	12	John de Doure for the first half year, and
		Ralph Gifford for the last half year
1319	13	Ralph de Gifford
1320	14	John de Doure
1321	15	Nicholas Engain of *Hunsdon*
1322	16	Thomas Gobyn, continued two years
1324	18	Richard de Perers, continued three years to 2nd Edwd. III.

EDW. III.

A.Chr.	A.R.	
1327	2	William Baud of *Coringham*
1328	3	Richard de Perers, continued two years
1330	5	John de Wanton of *Wallington*
1331	6	John de Wanton for the first half year, and
		John de Hay for the last half year
1332	7	John de la Hay for the first half year, and
		Adam Bloy for the last half year

Chauncy's list of Sheriffs of Hertfordshire and Essex 1333-1462

A. Chr.	A. R.	
1333	8	Adam Bloy for the first half year, and
		William Baud for the last half year
1334	9	John de Cogeshale, continued six years
1340	15	William Atemore
1341	16	Richard de Monte Caniso for the first half year, and
		Henry Garnet for the last half year
1342	17	Henry Garnet
1343	18	John de Cogeshale, continued four years
1347	22	John de Cogeshale for the first half year, and
		Peter de Boxted for the last half year
1348	23	William Bret for the first half year, and
		Humphrey de Walden for the last half year
1349	24	Peter de Boxted
1350	25	Thomas Lacy
1351	26	John de Cogeshale, continued for three years
1354	29	Hugh Fitz Simon
1355	30	William de Enefield
1356	31	Thomas de Chabham, continued two years
1358	33	Roger de Louth, continued two years
1360	34	Hugh Blount
1361	36	William de Lyre
1362	37	Guy de Boys
1363	38	Thomas Futling
1364	39	John Jernoun
1365	40	Thomas de Helpeston
1366	41	John Oliver of *Sandon*
1367	42	John Oliver for the first half year, and
		John Shardelow for the last half year
1368	43	John Henxteworth
1369	44	John Henxteworth from the Feast of St. Michael, 44th Edw.
		III. until the 22nd of January following
		Roger Keterich from the 22nd of Jan. to the Feast of St. Michael
1370	45	Thomas de Bassingbourn
1371	46	William Baud of *Little Hadham*
1372	47	John de Bampton
1373	48	John Filiol
1374	49	Edward Fitz Symond: of *Hatfield*
1375	50	John Battaile
1376	51	Robert Fitz William.

RICH. II.

A. Chr.	A. R.	
1377	1	Robert Goldington of *Hunsdon*
1378	2	John Fitz Symonds
1379	3	Edward Bensted
1380	4	John Sewale
1381	5	Walter Godmaston
1382	6	Geoffery de Dersham
1383	7	Thomas Battaile
1384	8	John Walton
1385	9	Geoffery Brockhole
1386	10	John Rygewin, continued two years
1388	12	Henry English
1389	13	Walter Attelec
1390	14	Geoffery Michale
1391	15	Sir William Cogeshale, Kt.
1392	16	Adam Frances
1393	17	Thomas Cogeshale
1394	18	Thomas Sampkin
1395	19	William Bateman, continued three years
1398	22	Robert Turke.

HEN. IV.

A. Chr.	A. R.	
1399	1	Edward Bensted
1400	2	John Howard
1401	3	William Marney

A. Chr.	A. R.	
1402	4	Helming Leget
1403	5	Sir Thomas Swinbourn, Kt.
1404	6	William Cogeshale
1405	7	Gerard Braybrook
1406	8	Helming Leget, continued two years
1408	10	William Loveney
1409	11	John Walden
1410	12	Thomas Aston
1411	13	Sir William Cogeshale, Kt.

HEN. V.

A. Chr.	A. R.	
1412	1	Philip Englefield
1413	2	John Tyrell
1414	3	Sir John Howard, Kt.
1415	4	Sir Thomas Barre, Kt.
1416	5	Lewis Johan
1417	6	Reginald Malyns
1418	7	Sir John Howard, Kt.
1419	8	Robert Darcy of *Danbury*, in *Essex*
1420	9	Lewis Johan, continued two years.

HEN. VI.

A. Chr.	A. R.	
1422	1	John Tyrell
1423	2	Sir Maurice Brewyn of *South Ockington*, Kt.
1424	3	John Barley of *Albury*
1425	4	John Doreward of *Bocking*
1426	5	Conand Aske
1427	6	Thomas Tyrell of *Heron*
1428	7	John Hotoft of *Knebworth*
1429	8	Nicholas Rickhull
1430	9	Henry Langley of *Rickling*
1431	10	Sir Nic. Thorley, Kt.
1432	11	John Durward
1433	12	Robert Whytingham of *Pendley*
1434	13	Geoffery Rockyll
1435	14	Sir Maurice Brewyn, Kt.
1436	15	Edward Tyrell
1437	16	Richard Alrede
1438	17	Robert Whytingham
1439	18	Richard Witherton
1440	19	Thomas Tyrell
1441	20	Ralph Asteley
1442	21	Nicholas Morley of *Hollingbury*
1443	22	John Hende
1444	23	Thomas Tyrell of *Heron*
1445	24	Thomas Pigot
1446	25	Thomas Baud of *Hadham-hall*
1447	26	John Hende the younger
1448	27	George Langham
1449	28	Geoffery Rockbill
1450	29	Philip Boteler of *Watton*
1451	30	Thomas Barrington
1452	31	John Godmanston
1453	32	Sir Thomas Cobham, Kt.
1454	33	Humphry Bohun
1455	34	Ralph Bothe, Esq.
1456	35	John Hende the younger
1457	36	Lewis John, Esq.
1458	37	Robert Darcy of *Danbury*, Esq.
1459	38	Thomas Tyrell of *Heron*.

EDW. IV.

A. Chr.	A. R.	
1460	1	Thomas Juce
1461	2	Thomas Langley, Esq. continued two years

A. Chr.	A. R.	
1463	4	Sir John Clay, Kt.
1464	5	Roger Ree, Esq.
1465	6	Sir Lawrence Reynford, Kt.
1466	7	Henry Barley, Esq.
1467	8	Sir William Pirton, Kt.
1468	9	Walter Writell, Esq.
1469	10	Ralph Baud, Esq. of *Hadham-hall*
1470	11	Walter Writell, Esq.
1471	12	Sir Roger Ree, Kt.
1472	13	Alured Cornburgh, Esq.
1473	14	John Sturgeon, Esq. of *Hitchin*
1474	15	Richard Hance, Esq.
1475	16	Henry Langley, Esq.
1476	17	William Green, Esq.
1477	18	Alured Cornburgh
1478	19	John Wode
1479	20	John Sturgeon of *Hitchin*
1480	21	Thomas Tyrell of *Heron*
1481	22	John Fortescue, Esq. of *Hatfield*.

EDW. V. *and* RICH. III.

1483	1	William Say of *Broxborne*, from the Feast of St. Michael, 22 Edw. IV. to the 9th Day of *April* following 23 *Regni sui*, on which Day the same King died; and from the 9th Day of *April* to 25th *June*, in *Anno* 1 Edw. V. and from 26th Day of *June*, 1 Rich. III. to the Feast of St. Michael
1484	1	Sir William Say, Kt. of *Broxborne*
1485	2	John Sturgeon of *Hitchin*
1486	3	Sir Robert Percy, Kt. from the Feast of St. Michael, 2 Rich. III. to 22nd *Aug.* then next following, on which Day that King died.

HEN. VII.

1486	1	Sir John Fortescue, Kt. of *Hatfield*
1487	2	Henry Marney, Esq.
1488	3	Sir William Pyrton, Kt.
1489	4	Henry Tey, Esq.
1490	5	John Boteler, Esq. of *Watton*
1491	6	Robert Turvervile, Esq.
1492	7	John Berfeild, Esq.
1493	8	Henry Marney, Esq.
1494	9	Sir Richard Fitz Lewis, Kt. of *Thornton*
1495	10	Robert Plomer
1496	11	William Pulter of *Hitchin*
1497	12	Robert Newport, Esq. of *Pelham*
1498	13	Thomas Peryent, Esq. of *Digeswell*
1499	14	Sir John Verney, Kt. of *Pendley*
1500	15	Sir Roger Wentworth, Kt.
1501	16	Sir Henry Tey, Kt.
1502	17	William Pyrton, Esq.
1503	18	Humphry Tyrell, Esq. of *Heron*
1504	19	William Skipwith, Esq. of *St. Albans*, continued two years
1506	21	Roger Darcy, Esq.
1507	22	John Brocket, Esq. of *Hatfield*, continued two years
1509	24	Humphry Tyrell, Esq. of *Heron*.

HEN. VIII.

1510	1	John Leventhorpe, Esq. of *Shingle-hall*
1511	2	William Lytton, Esq. of *Knebworth*
1512	3	Anthony Darcy, Esq. of *Danbury*
1513	4	Edward Tyrell, Esq. of *Heron*
1514	5	John Seyntclere, Esq.
1515	6	William Fitz Williams, Esq.
1516	7	Sir John Veere, Kt.
1517	8	Thomas Bonham, Esq.

A. Chr.	A. R.	
1518	9	Sir Thomas Tyrell, Kt. of *Heron*
1519	10	Sir John Cutts, Kt.
1520	11	Sir John Veere, Kt.
1521	12	Thomas Bonham, Esq.
1522	13	Sir Thomas Tey, Kt.
1523	14	John Christmass, Esq.
1524	15	Henry Barley, Esq.
1525	16	Sir John Veere, Kt.
1526	17	Thomas Leventhorpe, Esq. of *Shingle-hall*
1527	18	Thomas Bonham, Esq.
1528	19	Edward Tyrell, Esq. of *Heron*
1529	20	Sir Gyles Capell, Kt. of *Hadham*
1530	21	John Bollys, Esq. of *Wallington*
1531	22	John Brocket, Esq. of *Hatfield*
1532	23	John Smyth, Esq.
1533	24	Sir Philip Boteler, Kt. of *Watton*
1534	25	Sir Brian Took, Kt. of *Hatfield*
1535	26	Sir William West, Kt.
1536	27	Thomas Peryent the elder, Esq. of *Digeswell*
1537	28	Sir Henry Parker, Kt.
1538	29	Sir John Raynsford, Kt.
1539	30	John Smyth, Esq.
1540	31	Sir Philip Boteler, Kt. of *Watton*
1541	32	Sir John Mordant, Kt.
1542	33	Ralph Rowlet, Esq. of *St. Albans*
1543	34	John Bowles of *Wallington*, for the first half year, and John Sewster, Esq. for the second half year
1544	35	John Wentworth, Esq.
1545	36	Anthony Cook, Esq.
1546	37	Robert Lytton, Esq. *of Knebworth*
1547	38	John Coningsby, Esq. of *North-Mims*.

EDW. VI.

1547	1	Edward Brocket, Esq. of *Hatfield*
1548	2	John Cock, Esq. of *Brokesborne*
1549	3	Sir John Gates, Kt. of *Cheshunt*
1550	4	Sir George Norton, Kt.
1551	5	Sir Henry Tyrell, Kt. of *Heron*
1552	6	Sir Thomas Pope, Kt. of *Tittenhanger*.

MARY.

1553	1	Sir John Wentworth, Kt.

PHIL. and MARY.

1554	2	Edward Brocket, Esq. of *Hatfield*
1555	3	William Harris, Esq.
1556	4	Sir John Boteler, Kt. of *Watton*
1557	5	Sir Thomas Pope, Kt. of *Tittenhanger*
1558	6	Thomas Mildmay, Esq.

ELIZ.

1559	1	Ralph Rowlet, Esq. of *St. Albans*
1560	2	Edward Capell, Esq. of *Hadham*
1561	3	Sir Thomas Goldyng, Kt.
1562	4	Thomas Barrington, Esq.
1563	5	Henry Fortescue, Esq.
1564	6	William Aloffe, Esq.
1565	7	Robert Chester, Esq. of *Royston*
1566	8	John Brocket, Esq. of *Hatfield*.

Anno 9. Eliz. this County was sever'd from the County of **Essex**, and found **Sheriffs** by themselves.

1567	9	Sir George Penruddock, Kt.
1568	10	Rowland Lytton, Esq. of *Knebworth*

E 2

Chauncy's list of Sheriffs of Hertfordshire 1569-1686

A.Chr.	A.R.	
1569	11	Henry Coningsby, Esq. of *North-Mims*
1570	12	William Doddes, Esq.
1571	13	Edward Baesh, Esq. of *Stansted*
1572	14	George Horsey, Esq. of *Digenswell*
1573	15	Thomas Leventhorpe, Esq. of *Shingle-hall*
1574	16	Henry Cock, Esq. of *Brokesborne*
1575	17	John Gill, Esq. of *Widiall*
1576	18	Thomas Bowles, Esq. of *Wallington*
1577	19	Edmund Verney, Esq. of *Pendley*
1578	20	Philip Boteler, Esq. of *Watton*
1579	21	Charles Morison, Esq. of *Caishobury*
1580	22	Thomas Docwra, Esq. of *Putteridge*
1581	23	Sir John Brocket, Kt. of *Hatfield*
1582	24	Henry Coningsby, Esq. of *North-Mims*
1583	25	Francis Heydon, Esq. of *Watford*
1584	26	Edward Baesh, Esq. of *Stansted*
1585	27	Henry Capell, Esq. of *Hadham*
1586	28	Edward Pulter, Esq. of *Bradfield*
1587	29	Thomas Leventhorpe, Esq. from the Feast of St. Michael, 29 Eliz. to the 8th of *June* following : Thomas Sadler, Esq. from the 8th of *June* to Michaelmas following
1588	30	Sir John Cutts, Kt.
1589	31	Edmund Verney, Esq. of *Pendley*
1590	32	Walter Mildmay, Esq. of *Pishobury*
1591	33	Thomas Hanchet, Esq.
1592	34	Arthur Capell, Esq. of *Hadham*
1593	35	John Leventhorpe, Esq. of *Shingle-hall*
1594	36	Rowland Lytton, Esq. of *Knebworth*
1595	37	Thomas Sadler, Esq. of *Standon*
1596	38	Ralph Coningsby, Esq. of *North-Mims*
1597	39	Richard Spencer, Esq. of *Offley*
1598	40	Thomas Pope Blount, Esq. of *Tittenhanger*
1599	41	Robert Chester, Esq. of *Royston*
1600	42	Thomas Hanchet, Esq.
1601	43	Thomas Bowles, Esq. of *Wallington*
1602	44	Sir Edward Denny, Kt. of *Waltham Abby*

JAM. I.

A.Chr.	A.R.	
1603	1	Sir Henry Boteler, Kt. of *Hatfield*
1604	2	Sir George Peryent, Kt. of *Digenswell*
1605	3	Thomas Docwra, Esq. of *Putteridge*
1606	4	Sir Leonard Hide, Kt. of *Throcking*
1607	5	Sir John Leventhorpe, Kt. of *Shingle-hall*
1608	6	Nicholas Trot, Esq. of *Quickswood*
1609	7	Ralph Sadler, Esq. of *Standon*
1610	8	Sir Richard Anderson. Kt. of *Pendley*
1611	9	Sir Robert Boteler, Kt. of *Watton*
1612	10	John Wild Esq.
1613	11	William Franklyn, Esq.
1614	12	Sir Thomas Dacres, Kt. and Thomas Dacres, Esq. of *Cheshunt*
1615	13	Sir Goddard Pemberton, Kt. and Lewis Pemberton, Esq. of *St. Albans*
1616	14	Thomas Newce, Esq. of *Hadham*
1617	15	Edward Brisco, Esq. of *Aldenham*
1618	16	Thomas Read, Esq. of *Hatfield*
1619	17	Sir Nicholas Hide, Kt. of *North-Mims*
1620	18	Roger Pemberton, Esq. of *St. Albans*
1621	19	William Hale, Esq. of *Kings-Walden*
1622	20	Edward Newport. Esq. of *Pelham*
1623	21	Sir Clement Scudamore, Kt. of *North-Mims*
1624	22	Richard Sidley, Esq. of *Digenswell*.

CAR. I.

A.Chr.	A.R.	
1625	1	Sir William Lytton, Kt. of *Knebworth*
1626	2	John Jenings, Esq. of *St. Albans*

A.Chr.	A.R.	
1627	3	Sir Thomas Hide, Bart. of *North-Mims*
1628	4	Edward Gardiner, Esq. of *Thunderidge*
1629	5	William Hoo, Esq. of *Pauls Walden*
1630	6	Sir John Boteler, Knight of the Bath, of *Watton*
1631	7	Richard Hale, Esq. of *Kings-Walden*
1632	8	Henry Coghill, Esq. of *Aldenham*
1633	9	William Plomer, Esq. of *Radwell*
1634	10	William Priestley. Esq. of *Esingdon*
1635	11	William Leman, Esq. of *North-hall*
1636	12	Ralph Freeman, Esq. of *Aspeden*
1637	13	Thomas Coningsby. Esq. of *North-Mims*
1638	14	Thomas Hewyt, Esq. of *Pishobury*
1639	15	John Gore, Esq. of *Gilston*
1640	16	Richard Cole, Esq.
1641	17	Arthur Pulter, Esq. of *Braudfeild*
1642	18	*No Sheriff because of the Wars*
1643	19	Sir John Garrard, Baronet, of *Lammer*
1644	20	Sir John Garrard, Baronet
1645	21	Sir John Garrard, Baronet and Sir Robert Jocelin, Kt. of *Hide-hall*
1646	22	Charles Nodes, Esq. of *Sheephale*
1647	23	Rowland Hale, Esq. of *Kings-Walden*
1648	24	Francis Flyer, Esq. of *Pelham*

CAR. II.

A.Chr.	A.R.	
1649	1	Toby Combe, Esq. of *Hemel Hempsted*
1650	2	John Rowley, Esq. of *Berkway*
1651	3	Thomas Keightley, Esq. of *Hertingford*
1652	4	John Fotberley, Esq. of *Rickmeresworth*
1653	5	Humphry Shalcross, Esq. of *Digenswell*
1654	6	Sir John Gore, Kt. of *Sacomb*
1655	7	Sir John Read, Knight and Baronet, of *Hatfield*
1656	8	Edward Gardiner, Esq. of *Thunderidge*
1657	9	John Berisford, Esq. of *Rickmeresworth*
1658	10	Sir John Whitwrong, Kt. of *Harpeden*
1659	11	Robert Dycer, Esq. of *Braughing*
1660	12	Sir Thomas Hewyt, Kt. of *Pishobury*
1661	13	Sir Henry Blount, Kt. of *Tittenhanger*
1662	14	Sir Rowland Lytton, Kt. of *Knebworth*
1663	15	Sir John Hale, Kt. of *Stagenhoe*
1664	16	Sir Thomas Brograve, Bart. of *Hamels*
1665	17	Sir Jonathan Keate, Bart. of *Pauls Walden*
1666	18	Edward Chester Esq. of *Berkway*
1667	19	John Ellis, Esq. of *St. Julians*
1668	20	Israel Mayho, Esq. of *Beyford*
1669	21	Sir Thomas Bide, Kt. of *Ware*
1670	22	Henry Baldwin, Esq. of *Aldenham*
1671	23	Samuel Reeve, Esq. of *Aston*
1672	24	Thomas Priestley, Esq. of *Esendon*
1673	25	Henry Coghill, Esq. of *Aldenham*
1674	26	Joshua Lomax, Esq. of *St. Albans*
1675	27	Edward Chester, Esq. of *Royston*
1676	28	Sir William Leman, Bart. of *North-hall*
1677	29	Sir Robert Jocelin, Bart. of *Hide-hall*
1678	30	Sir William Lytton, Kt. of *Knebworth*
1679	31	Thomas Halsey, Esq. of *Great Gadesden*
1680	32	Sir John Boteler, Kt. of *Watton*
1681	33	Sir Nicholas Miller, Kt. of *Sandon*
1682	34	James Willymot, Esq. of *Kelshall*
1683	35	Sir Thomas Field, Kt. of *Stansted*
1684	36	James Goulston, Esp. of *Widiall*

JAM. II.

A.Chr.	A.R.	
1685	1	Joseph Edmonds, Esq. of *Clothall*
1686	2	Francis Flyer, Esq. of *Pelham*

Clutterbuck's list of gentlemen required to pay towards the defence of the Kingdom, 1588.

The NAMES of the NOBILITY, GENTRY, and others, of the County of HERTFORD, who contributed to the defence of this Country at the time of the SPANISH INVASION, in 1588.

Marcii.	£.		£.
George Knighton, Armiger tercio die Marcii	25	Robert Wolley, gen. eodem - - 50	
Raphe Ratcliffe, Gen. eodem - - - 25		John Andrew, sen. 24 die Marcii - - 25	
Elizabeth Chufie, vidua quarto die Marcii - 25		John Binge, gen. 29 die Marcii - - 25	
William Beswicke, Gen. eodem. - - 25		William Ewer, eodem - - - 25	
William Sherwood, sexto die Marcii - - 25		Thomas Ewer, eodem - - - 25	
Edward Briscoe, jun. 10 die Marcii - - 25		Thomas Gardiner, eodem - - - 25	
Marie Browne, vidua eodem - - - 25		Thomas Ansell, 31 daie of Marche - 25	
Thomas Parsons, Gen. eodem - - - 25		April.	
John Gibbe, Gen. eodem - - - 25		Thomas Dermer, quinto die Aprilis - 25	
Jane Bashe, vidua eodem - - - 25		Foulke Onslowe, armiger, sexto die Aprilis 50	
Thomas Turner, yeoman eodem - - 25		William Crawley, eodem - - - 25	
John Tarborowe, Armiger eodem - - 25		John Hurste, eodem - - - 25	
Henrie Sadler, Armiger eodem - - 50		Henrie Foster, 13 die Aprilis - - 25	
Edward Fitz-John, 11 die Marcii - - 25		William Samme, eodem - - - 25	
Edward Bigge, Yeoman, eodem - - 25		George Grave, 14 die Aprilis - - 25	
William Grubbe, 12 die Marcii - - 25		Robert Garnett, 16 die Aprilis - - 25	
Thomas Northe, Gen. 13 die Marcii - - 25		Jo. Sutton, gen. 18 die Aprilis - - 25	
Roberte Hide, Armiger, eodem - - 50		Edward Briscoe, 28 die Aprilis - - 25	
John Clerke, eodem die - - - 25		John Rooley, 29 die Aprilis - - 25	
Clement Manestyc, 14 die Marcii - - 25		Maye.	
Henrie Mayne, 15 die Marcii - - 50		William Muffett, Gen. secundo die Maii - 25	
Robert Barber, 17 die Marcii - - 25		Edward Newport, Armiger, eodem - 50	
William Halsey, eodem die - - - 25		Andrew Gray, Armiger, tercio die Maii - 25	
John Mitchell, sen. 18 die Marcii - 25		George Chasey, Gen. eodem - - 25	
Charles Nodes, Gen. eodem - - 25		Richard Canfeild, sexto die Maii - - 25	
Michaell Meade, Gen. eodem - - 50		Richard Smithe, Armiger, 10 die Maii - 50	
George Clarke, eodem - - - 25		William Godfrey, alias Cowper, Gen. eodem 25	
William Clerk, eodem - - - 25		Rowland Bafford, Gen. 26 die Maii - 25	
Thomas Harmer, eodem - - 25		William Mayne, eodem - - - 25	
George Graveley, gen. 19 die Marcii - 25		Stephen Nobbes, 28 die Maii - - 25	
Thomas Chapman, eodem - - - 25		William Preston, Gen. 30 die Maii - 25	
Henrie Spurlinge, yeoman, 20 die Marcii - 25		John Okston, sen. eodem - - 25	
Symonde Warren, 22 die Marcii - - 25		Julye.	
George Feild, 23 die Marcii - - 25		George Kimpton, Gen. 15 die Julii - 25	
Robert Spencer, armiger, eodem - - 25		John Kent, 29 die Julii - - - 25	

From a quarto Pamphlet printed for Messrs. Leigh and Sotheby, London, 1798.

Cussons list of gentlemen required to pay towards the defence of the Kingdom, 1590.

THE following inhabitants of this County were assessed at the sum of twenty pounds each towards a subsidy for the defence of the country in the year 1590. The list is preserved in the Record Office among the State Papers. (*Domestic Series, Elizab.* vol. 236, ff. 48, 48b.)

Ralph Gape of St. Albans
Robert Fynche of Redbourne
Thomas Byscoe of Aldenham, sen.
John Warener of Radlet
Ralph Heydon of Sarrett gent
Henry Baldwyn of Watford
John Redwood of Parke Street in Watford
William Wedon of Oxley hamlett
Richard Cubbage of Watford
Francis Palmer of Rickmansworth gent
George Baldwyn of the same
William Ethroppe of Wyndrich
William Cole of Parkwarde gent
Thomas Thrale of Sandrich
Thomas Penne of Cuddicott gent
Thomas Hoo of Paleswalden gent
Lady Elizabeth Paulett of Ridge, vid.*
John Halsey of Chipping Barnett
Arthur Hewett of Northall gent
David Hollyland of the same
John Bysouth of Corner Hall
Thomas Goold of Bovingdon
Thomas Welles of the Howe
John Emes of Gaddesden pva
Thomas Waterhose of Barkampstede Peter gent
William Palmer of Wiggington gent
William Lake of Mylsterne
George Pace of Harpden
John Christian of Whethamsteed
John Brockett of the same
Henry Hickeman of Bushey
Thomas Barnard of Shenley

Leonard Fysh of Hatfeild gent
Edward Smyth of the same
John Kitchen of Tatteridge
George Peryent of Ayett pva gent
William Sell of Munden magna
John Bigge of Knebworth
La: Julian Cotten of Wimley magna vid †
John Nedeham of Wimley pva Esqʳ †
Edward Lacon of Willien gent
Thomas Whittamore of Hitchen
John Campe of Ware
Richard Colly of the same gent
Thomas Mylles of Thundrich
John Hemming of Standon
Richard Fysher of the same
Richard Greene of Braughing gent
Andrew Calton of Starforde
George Marshall of Sabsforde (Sawbridgeworth)
Alexander Chauncey of the same
John Gardiner Docter of the lawe
Robert Hemming of Benioy (Bengeo)
William Kimpton
John Harmer of Rusden
John Goodman of Clottall
John Haynes of Haddam magna gent
Phillip Allington of Burnt Pelham Esqʳ
Francys Delawood of Hormeade Magna gent
Thomas Brande of Hormeade pva gent
Thomas Chambers of Barkeway gent
John Crouche of Layston gent
Saunder Hammond of Buckland gent

The Clergy who were called upon to contribute were Marke Stubbyns of Whethamsteed, and Robert Abbott of Hatfeild Bushop, £20 each ; and Theophilus Aelmer of Greate Hadham, and William Chapman of Therfield, £30 each. (*Ib.* fol. 28.)

* Assessed at fifty pounds. † Assessed at forty pounds.

Cussons list of gentlemen called upon to lend money to Charles I in 1625

The following is a list of those Hertfordshire gentlemen who, in the year 1625, were called upon to lend money to King Charles I. This forced loan was productive of widespread discontent among the people of England, and many, to avoid the unjust tax, fled to the American Colonies. The places given in the margin are those to which the persons were summoned. The original document, from which this is taken, was presented by the Right Honourable Sir John Newport, Bart., Comptroller-General of the Exchequer, to the British Museum, where it is still preserved.

THE COUNTY OF HERTFORD.

Watford

	li.	s.	d.
Sr Cha. Morison knt & Barronett	40	0	0
The Lady Altham	20	0	0
Nich. Hampson Esqre	20	0	0
Tho. Hampson Esqre	10	0	0
Henry Ewer Esqre	10	0	0
Geo. Skidmore	10	0	0
Xtofer (Christopher) Goodfellowe	10	0	0
Henry Baldwin	10	0	0
Richard Bellamie	10	0	0
Robert Crofte	10	0	0
Tho. Ewer De Lea	20	0	0

Rickmansworth

	li.	s.	d.
John Colt	10	0	0
Hugh Plott	10	0	0
Tho. Wentworth Esqre	10	0	0
Geo. Lane	10	0	0
Ralphe Day	10	0	0

Aldenham

	li.	s.	d.
Edward Briscoe Esqre	20	0	0
Henry Coghill	10	0	0
Roger Marsh	10	0	0
Edward Smith sen	10	0	0
Tho. Warnor	10	0	0
Edward . . . . . oc	10	0	0

Abbotte Langley

	li.	s.	d.
Sir Robert Brooke knt	20	0	0
Tho. Child	10	0	0
John Nicoll of Elfrey	10	0	0
Andrew Marsh of Ridge	10	0	0

Sleape and Smaleford

	li.	s.	d.
John Robotham Esqre	10	0	0
John Cox Esqre	10	0	0
Edward Jrubb	10	0	0

St. Albons

	li.	s.	d.
Roger Pemerton	20	0	0
William Pennyman Esqre	20	0	0
Robert Skelton	10	0	0

	li.	s.	d.
Nich. Humfries	10	0	0
John Jennings Esqre	15	0	0
William Preston Esqre	20	0	0
Fra. Taverner of Hexton	10	0	0
William Edwards of Northawe	10	0	0
William Barnett of the same	10	0	0
Henry Staplford of Paules Walden	10	0	0
Henry Chantley of the same	10	0	0
Geo. Sturmore of the same	10	0	0
Robert Kentish of Wandridge	10	0	0
Tho. Michell of Coddicott	10	0	0
Tho. Kingsley of Sarrette	10	0	0
Sir Robert Brooke knt	20	0	0

Sandridge

	li.	s.	d.
William Epalbie	10	0	0
Hugh Smith	10	0	0
William Thaell	10	0	0
Tho. Adams	10	0	0
Geo. Node of Sheppall	20	0	0
Martin Fountaine of Rodberne	10	0	0
Tho. Hide Barronett	40	0	0
Sr Rich. Anderson knt	20	0	0
Anthony Belfield of Studham	10	0	0
Robt. Broomefield of Northmime	10	0	0
Edmond Faldoe of the same	10	0	0
John Grubb of the same	10	0	0

Bushy

	li.	s.	d.
Ralph Wilbraham Esqre	10	0	0
Geo. Blackwell	10	0	0
Geo. Hickman	10	0	0
Silus Tito	10	0	0
William Ewer	10	0	0

Shenley

	li.	s.	d.
John Marsh	10	0	0
Rich. Coale	10	0	0
Abell Ewer	10	0	0
Tho. Ewer	10	0	0

Hempsteede

	li.	s.	d.
Joseph Marston	10	0	0

Cussons list of gentlemen called upon to lend money to Charles I in 1625

	li.	s.	d.		li.	s.	d.
John Besouth	10	0	0	Mr. Thursden	10	0	0
Nich. Howe	10	0	0	Dr. Atkins	20	0	0
William Howe	10	0	0	Mr. Chapman of Wormley	20	0	0
Xtofer Besouth	10	0	0	Tho. Palmer of Hoddesden	10	0	0
Rich. Avery	10	0	0	William Thorne of the same	10	0	0
Rinald Horne of Kensworth	10	0	0				
William Barbor of the same	10	0	0	**Hertford**			
Will. Lake of Wilkeston	10	0	0	Henry Bull	10	0	0
Henry Reeve of the same	10	0	0	John Finch	10	0	0
Will. Palmer of Wiggenton	10	0	0	Anne Feild widow	10	0	0
Fra. Wathered of Barkamsteede	10	0	0	Rich. Willis Esq	10	0	0
Edward Bagshawe of the same	10	0	0	Edward North of Tewing	10	0	0
Rich. Dagnell of Tring	10	0	0	John Baily of Hartingfordbury	40	0	0
				Mr. Prisley of Essenden Esqre	20	0	0
North Church				Sr Edward Bashe knt	20	0	0
Timothie Dabney	10	0	0	Mr. Bower of Stansted Abbotte	10	0	0
Mr. Norbery	10	0	0				
William Elden	10	0	0	**Ware**			
William Willett	10	0	0	Tho. Fanshawe Esqre	20	0	0
William Godyard of Long Marston	10	0	0	Humfrey Packer	10	0	0
Tho. Welle of the Howe	10	0	0	Humfrey Spencer	10	0	0
				Robert Price	10	0	0
Bovingdon				Steven Lamas	10	0	0
Abiezar Hay	10	0	0	Oliver Harvie	10	0	0
Mrs. Maine	10	0	0	George Bromley	10	0	0
Henry Maine	10	0	0	Tho. Meade	10	0	0
John Gould	10	0	0	Nich. Meade	10	0	0
Joseph Prince of Flamden	10	0	0	Edward Gardiner Esqre	20	0	0
Rich. Grover of the same	10	0	0	Raphe Sadler of Standon Esqre	25	0	0
Dan. Cotton of Gasden pva	10	0	0	Mr. Baylie of the same Esqre	13	6	8
Robert Eames of the same	10	0	0	John Mordant of Starford	13	6	8
Nathan Cotton of Harpinden	10	0	0	Robert Duke of Sabrigworth	10	0	0
Sr Tho. Reade knt.	50	0	0	Symon Brograve of Broaghing	20	0	0
Edward Bowine of Hatfield	10	0	0	Samuel Hemings of Bengeo	10	0	0
				William Newce Esqre	10	0	0
Tottridge				Jasp Garnett	10	0	0
John Sturton	10	0	0	The Lady Anne Barmeston	10	0	0
John Terry	10	0	0	Daniell Cattell of Alburie	10	0	0
Samuell Willmore	10	0	0	Sr Tho. Cecill knt	20	0	0
Tho. Nicholle	10	0	0	John Rowley of Pelhã Brent	20	0	0
John Marsh	10	0	0	Robert Young of Meesden	10	0	0
Allen Snoe	10	0	0	Tho. Bownest of Hormead pva	10	0	0
John Hamond of Parton	15	0	0				
Tho. Ancell of Icleford	10	0	0	**Barkway**			
John Woodley of the same	10	0	0	Sr Robert Chester knt	20	0	0
				Mrs. Baker widow	10	0	0
Chesthunt				Mr. Cutte Esqre	15	0	0
Robert Dewhurst Esqre	13	6	8	John Rowley	20	0	0
William Robinson Esqre	10	0	0	Edward Ratcliffe Esqre	10	0	0
Rich. Walcote	10	0	0	Will. Row of Barley Esqre	30	0	0
Mr. Langhorne	10	0	0	Sr Stephen Somes knt	20	0	0

LIST OF FREEHOLDERS RESIDENT IN THE COUNTY OF HERTFORD IN THE YEAR 1561.

HUNDRED OF HITCHIN.

Hycchyn	John Andrewe		John Wells
	Edward Hurst		Thomas Welshe
	John Trustram		Valentine Hurst
	William Coker		Edward Cooper
	William Brokett		John Ford
	John Hycchynson	Offley	John Sheperd
	William Awdley		John Monk
	John Graveley		Robert Ivery
	Thomas Graveley		Thomas Carter
	Thomas Chapman	Lylley	Thomas Dockwray, armiger
	Peter Harmer		Richard Helder *als.* Spicer
	Edward Sebrok		George Feld
	William Maynard		John Feld
	Simon Warren	Kympton	Richard Barley, armiger
	Roger Lyell		John Allwey, Gen
	John Parker		Thomas Feld
	John Hynd		William Hynd
	James Chamber	Preston	John Hurst
	Walter Gyn		William Conysby
Ickleford	Thomas Aunsell	Purton	John Hemynge, Gen
	William Hartrell		Richard Copcott, Gen
Walden Regis	John Sybley		John Hammond

HUNDRED OF BRAUGHING.

Brawghinge	Thomas Hanchet Ar	Ware	Thomas Claxson
	William Wale		John Harvy, sen
	Bartholomew Browk		William Harvy
	William Watts		John Haggard
Westmyll	William Hamond gen		William Claple
	Roger Hamond		Christopher Dyxson
	Robert Aunsell		William Grener
	John Lyncoln		Henry How
Stondon	Richard Sadlier, Miles		John Myles
	Richard Fysher		Thomas Watts
	Robert Bedle		John Thyrkell
	Thomas Crowche	Hunsdon	Thomas Ward
	Thomas Mannyng		Thomas Tunbridge
	John Grene		John Elyott
	John Bussey	Estwyck	Anthony Tunbridge
	Thomas Brett		Thomas Cramphorn
	William Godfrey	Gelson	Henry Chancy ar
	Thomas Kyrby		John Howe
Thundridge	Robert Crowche	Sapsford	Edward Brokett, Generosus
	Thomas Reynold		Edward Lenthropp, Generosus

Cussons list of Freeholders resident in the County of Hertford in 1561

HUNDRED OF BRAUGHING, Continued.

	John Thurgood	Thomas Boyer
	Thomas Goodaye	William Abbatt
	Thomas Jonson	Thomas Crabb
	George Machen	John Bayford
Stonsted	John Grave	Richard Smyth als. Clerk
	Robert Grave	Nicholas Mardon
Stortford	Epī Edward Wylley	John Jarvyll

HUNDRED OF HERTFORD.

Amwell	Thomas Androw		Christopher Thurgood
	John Archer	Twynge	Edward North
Broxborn	George Penruddock, Armiᵍ		John Palmer
	William Garnett	Bengeo	Robert West
	Thomas Bole		William Shurbrok
	John Carver	Esdon	William Tucke arᵈ
	Thomas Michell	Bayford	John Knyton arᵈ
	Thomas Fuller	Hertingford-Bury	George Myn, generosus
	John Boran	Hertford	Thomas Burghley
	John Sarynge		Giles Plummer
Wormley	John Purfrey (Purvey) Arᵈ		William Hall
Cheshunt	George Dakars genᵈ		Robert Heath
	William Clerke		William Fynche
	Thomas Fuller		Christopher Bull genᵈ
	John Fletcher		William Lawrence
	Robert Hockerell		Christopher Marston
	Robert Loen		

HUNDRED OF DACORUM.

Trynge	Thomas Blache, genᵈ	Hempsted	Henry Mayn
	Thomas Hyde		Richard Bucmaster
	Henry Allen		Thomas Byrchmore
	Thomas Allen		Roger Smyth
	William Wyggington		Roger Turner
	William Lark		John Henson
	William Grave		Thomas Axtell
Albery	John Hudnall	Langley Rege	Thomas Woodchall
Gaddesden	Richard Cooms Arᵈ		John Feld
Northchurch	Thomas Axtell	Busshey	Robert Blacwell
	William Axtell		Walter Wyth
	William Wyllett		Henry Hycman
	George Parker	Shenley	Christopher Palmer genᵈ
	William Cock		Thomas Harvy genᵈ
Barkhᵃmsted	Marie Thomas Benger, Miles		John Barnett
	John Hawsey	Northmyms	William Dods armᵈ
	James Wethered		John Elwyn
	Richard Blunt		George Grubb
	Michael Clerk		John Thomson
	John Whytley		Thomas Roberts
	Robert Grubb	Kensworth	John Horn

HUNDRED OF DACORUM, Continued.

	Richard Payshe		John Bemont
	Thomas Abberit		William Besoworth
Cadington	George Ferers, Ar)	Colsell	John Saunders, Ar)
	Richard Marshe		William Redinge
	Peter Austen	Bovington	Thomas Goold
	Walter Byrchmore		Richard Goold
	Thomas Bray		Thomas Edmonds
	John Bexford	Flandon	John Prynce
Hardinge	Edward Bardolph, gen)		Thomas Pucrsfat (?)
	Thomas Smyth arm		Henry Lovett
	Thomas Johnson	Gadesden Magna	Thomas Wells
	Michael Cutt		William Hawsey (Halsey)
Whethamsted	John Brokett, Ar)		John Wells
	Nicholas Brokett gen)		Thomas Hawsey
	Thomas North	Flamstede	John Grygge
	Nicholas Sybley		Leonard Fults
	William Clerk		Bartholomew Sawyer
Studham	John Belfeld gen)		

HUNDRED OF ODSEY.

Yardley	Thomas Shotbolt gen)	Rede	Richard Turner
	John Austen		Thomas Turner
	Thomas Shodbolt ar)	Reyston	Robert Chester, Mil.
	Edward Sheppard		John Dyxon
	Thomas Cooper *als* Wheler		John Snell, Jun)
Sandon	Robert Newport gen)		John Westley
	Leonard More		Thomas Mott
	Thomas Lyncoln		Robert Palmer
	Matthew Edwards	Aswell	John Barley, Jun)
	Simon Harvy		Thomas Ward
Tharfeld	Edward Game		William Bellamye
	William Fordam		John Sewster, gen)
	William Wood		Robert Poyneard
	Henry Gynne		John Lechworth
	Ralph Luck	Wallington	Thomas Boles, Ar)
Rushden	William Goodman	Radwell	William Plumer
Kelshull	Michael Willmott		William Stokefeld
	John Fordam	Cottered	Edward Capell, Miles
	John Frost		

HUNDRED OF EDWINSTREE.

Barley	John Chapman	Mesenden	Andrew King
	Thomas Barnes		Wryght
Barkway	William Stern Gen)	Bucland and Wyddyall	George Gyll, ar)
	Thomas Chambers		John Marshe, gen)
	Payne	Hormede Magna	Francis Wood, gen)
Aspeden	William Snowe		Thomas Brond
	Parker	Hormede Pva	Thomas Bolnes (Bonest)
Anstey	Robert Gyn	Hadham Magna	George Haynes
	Allen	Hadham Pva	William Myles

HUNDRED OF EDWINSTREE, CONTINUED.

STOCKINGE PELHᴬM John Growt
Robert Boyer
ALBURY   Richard Ode, *als* Hoye
BUNTINGFORD Henry Brograve
Thomas Wheler
John Edderyche

Richard Grene
Thomas Dan
William Newnam
Thomas Brown
Thomas Batford
Robert Ayer

HUNDRED OF BROADWATER.

HATFELD   Thomas Style
John Rykemont
Thomas Porter
MUNDEN PARVA Richard Kyrby
Thomas Chery
MUNDEN MAGNA Simon Sell
Richard Browne
BALDOCK   Leonard Benet
John Glandfeld *als* Newell
Anthony Fage
Clement Gonell
Richard Collopp
James Pratt
James Rochford
Peter Bamferd
Thomas Pomfret
Christopher Croft
AYOT LAURENCE Nicholas Brystoo Ar͡)
AYOT MONFYCHET William Peryen gen͡)
DYYGONSWELL George Horsey Ar͡)
KNEBWORTH Roland Lytton Ar͡)
LETCHWORTH Thomas Snagge
WATTON   John Butler, Miles
Edward Twynyhe Ar͡)
John Feld
John Halfhyde
BENYNGTON John Chapman
William Clerk

John Hubberd
William Harvy
ASTON   William Chapman
John Kent
WELWYN   Thomas Wylshere
John Gyll
Henry Baff
John Clark
STEVENAGE Edward Nodde Gen͡)
John Clark
Henry Gyn
Thomas Porter
Edward Wilsher
WALKHORN Edward Wilson
Robert Kympton
George Clerk
WYMBLEY Edward Pulter Ar͡)
John Neadhm̄ Ar͡)
Thomas Maynd̄
WESTON   Thomas Harmar
John Yardley
John Isod
Richard Knyght
GRAVELEY cū CHISFELD William Kympton
Thomas Graveley
Thomas Barington Ar͡)
ALMSHO cū TATTRYGE John Snowe
Richard Snowe

Lansd. MS. 5 Plut. LXXIII. D. ff. 48-52.

Index of Persons

Index of Persons

Index of Persons

Index of Persons

Index of Persons

Index of Persons

Underwood 15, 115, 173
Vanderplank 93, 193
Vanlore 157
Vaux 154, 204
Vaughan 185
Van de Weyer 187
Vavasour 144
Verney 23
Vernon 196
Villiers 22, 142, 146
Vincent 98, 218
Wadham 150, 198
Wake 68, 69, 200, 205
Walcott 170
Waldegrave 144, 150, 151, 158, 171
   184, 189, 198, 202, 207, 211, 214
   215, 216, 217
Walker 176, 178, 179
Wallace 146
Waller 96, 97, 100, 147, 218
Walsingham 144, 152, 165
Walter 185
Walton 202
Warburton 143, 171
Warde 160
Warre 219
Warren 1, 54, 56, 57, 62, 63, 88, 89
   91, 94, Ch.14, 106, 109, 144, 147
   158, 176, 178, 193, 194, 197, 208
   213, 218
Waterford 174
Waterhouse 214
Wateville 46
Watson 176, 193
Watts 106, 178
Weatherley 82
Webb 152, 188
Webber 205
Weldish 193
Weller 203
Weller-Poley 203
Welles 7, 107, 207
Wentworth 143, 160, 165, 172, 189
   192, 199, 202, 210, 212, 215, 216
Whethill 166, 202
Whettall 96
Whitbread 69, 217, 219
White 185, 217
Wicked Lady 48, 185, 187
Wilkinson 172
Williams 180
Williamson 175

Willington 209
Willoughby 144, 208, 215
Wilson 16, 30, 77, 129, 174, 197
Wilshere 143
Wiltshire 181
Wingate 91, 93, 101, 146, 171, 178
   180, 193, 196, 207, 212, 219
Wingfield 167, 168, 181
Wintour 154, 198
Wiseman 71, 148, 149, 160, 201
   217, 219
Withypoole 148
Wood 177
Wood de Gosmore 99
Woodlift 213
Wrattinge 75, 76
Wright 21, 157, 176, 177
Wriothsley (Wrothsley) 152, 209
Writtle, Lord 198
Wroth 56
Wyatt 150, 160
Wycherley 102
Wynche 144
Wynne 206

Index of Places

Index of Places

Index of Places

Index of Places

Index of Places